The Cult of Saints
in Late Antiquity and the
Early Middle Ages

The Cult of Saints
in Late Antiquity and the
Early Middle Ages

Essays on the Contribution of Peter Brown

Edited by
James Howard-Johnston
and
Paul Antony Hayward

OXFORD
UNIVERSITY PRESS

OXFORD

Great Clarendon Street, Oxford OX2 6DP

Oxford University Press is a department of the University of Oxford
It furthers the University's objective of excellence in research, scholarship,
and education by publishing worldwide in

Oxford New York

Auckland Bangkok Buenos Aires Cape Town Chennai
Dar es Salaam Delhi Hong Kong Istanbul Karachi Kolkata
Kuala Lumpur Madrid Melbourne Mexico City Mumbai Nairobi
São Paulo Shanghai Singapore Taipei Tokyo Toronto

with an associated company in Berlin

Oxford is a registered trade mark of Oxford University Press
in the UK and in certain other countries

Published in the United States
by Oxford University Press Inc., New York

© James Howard-Johnston and Paul Antony Hayward 1999

The moral rights of the author have been asserted

Database right Oxford University Press (maker)

First published 1999

First published in paperback 2002

All rights reserved. No part of this publication may be reproduced,
stored in a retrieval system, or transmitted, in any form or by any means,
without the prior permission in writing of Oxford University Press,
or as expressly permitted by law, or under terms agreed with the appropriate
reprographics rights organization. Enquiries concerning reproduction
outside the scope of the above should be sent to the Rights Department,
Oxford University Press, at the address above

You must not circulate this book in any other binding or cover
and you must impose this same condition on any acquirer

British Library Cataloguing in Publication Data

Data available

Library of Congress Cataloging in Publication Data

The cult of saints in late antiquity and the Middle Ages: essays on
the contribution of Peter Brown / edited by James Howard-Johnston
and Paul Antony Howard
p, cm.
Includes bibliographical references and index.
1. Christian saints—Cult—History of doctrines—Early church,
ca. 30–600. 2. Christian saints—Cult—History of doctrines—Middle
Ages, 600–1500. 3. Muslim saints—Cult—History of doctrines.
4. Brown, Peter Robert Lamont. I. Hayward, Paul Antony.
II. Howard-Johnston, J. D.
Bt970.C85 1999 235'.2'0902—dc21 99–21466
ISBN 0-19-925354-4

1 3 5 7 9 10 8 6 4 2

Typeset by Hope Services (Abingdon) Ltd.
Printed in Great Britain
on acid-free paper by
Biddles Ltd.,
Guildford & King's Lynn

CONTENTS

ABBREVIATIONS

'A Parting of Ways' 'Eastern and Western Christendom in Late Antiquity: A Parting of the Ways', in D. Baker (ed.), *The Orthodox Churches and the West*, SCH 13 (Oxford, 1976), 1–24; repr. in *SH*, 166–95

AS *Authority and the Sacred: Aspects of the Christianisation of the Roman World*, The Tanner Lectures 1993 (Cambridge, 1995)

BS *The Body and Society: Men, Women, and Sexual Renunciation in Early Christianity* (London, 1989)

CS *The Cult of the Saints: Its Rise and Function in Latin Christianity*, The Haskell Lectures 1978 (Chicago, 1981)

'Exemplar' 'The Saint as Exemplar in Late Antiquity', *Representations*, 2 (1983), 1–25. Not to be confused with the abbreviated versions of this paper which appear under the same title in R. C. Trexler (ed.), *Persons in Groups: Social Behaviour as Identity Formation in Medieval and Renaissance Europe*, Medieval and Renaissance Texts and Studies 36 (Binghamton, NY, 1985), 183–94, and in J. S. Hawley (ed.), *Saints and Virtues* (Berkeley and Los Angeles, 1987), 3–14

'Holy Man' 'The Rise and Function of the Holy Man in Late Antiquity', *JRS* 61 (1971), 80–101; repr. in *SH* 103–52

MLA *The Making of Late Antiquity*, Carl Newell Jackson Lectures 1976 (Cambridge, Mass., 1978)

PP *Power and Persuasion in Late Antiquity: Towards a Christian Empire*, The Curti Lectures 1988 (Madison, Wisc., 1992)

RSoc.	*Religion and Society in the Age of St. Augustine* (London, 1977)
RSS	*Relics and Social Status in the Age of Gregory of Tours*, The Stenton Lecture 1976 (Reading, 1977); repr. in *SH* 222–50
RWC	*The Rise of Western Christendom* (Oxford, 1996)
SH	*Society and the Holy in Late Antiquity* (London, 1982)
'Syria'	'Town, Village and Holy Man: The Case of Syria', in D. M. Pippidi (ed.), *Assimilation et résistance à la culture gréco-romaine dans le monde ancien* (Bucharest, 1976), 213–20; repr. in *SH* 153–65
WLA	*The World of Late Antiquity* (London, 1971)

OTHER WORKS CITED

AASS	*Acta Sanctorum*, ed. J. Bolland *et al.* (Antwerp, 1643–)
AB	*Analecta Bollandiana* (Brussels, 1882–)
Asceticism	V. L. Wimbush and R. Valantasis (eds.), *Asceticism* (New York and Oxford, 1995)
Bede, HE	Bede, *Historia ecclesiastica gentis Anglorum*, ed. B. Colgrave and R. A. B. Mynors, OMT (Oxford, 1969; rev. edn., 1991)
BHG	F. Halkin (ed.), *Bibliotheca Hagiographica Graeca*, SHag. 8a, 3 vols., 3rd. edn. (Brussels, 1957)
BHL	*Bibliotheca Hagiographica Latina*, SHag. 6, 2 vols. (Brussels, 1898–9), with H. Fros (ed.), *Novum Supplementum*, SHag. 70 (Brussels, 1986)
BSOAS	*Bulletin of the School of Oriental and African Studies* (London, 1938–)
Byzantine Saint	S. Hackel (ed.), *The Byzantine Saint: University of Birmingham Fourteenth Symposium of Byzantine Studies*, Studies Supplementary to *Sobornost* 5 (London, 1981)

CCSG	*Corpus Christianorum Series Graeca* (Turnhout, 1977–)
CCSL	*Corpus Christianorum Series Latina* (Turnhout, 1953–)
CSEL	*Corpus Scriptorum Ecclesiasticorum Latinorum* (Vienna, 1860–)
CStud.	Cistercian Studies Series (Kalamazoo, Mich., 1969–)
EI¹	M. Th. Houtsma *et al.* (eds.), *The Encyclopaedia of Islam*, 1st edn., 4 vols. (Leiden, 1913–34)
EI²	H. A. R. Gibb *et al.* (eds.), *The Encyclopaedia of Islam*, 2nd edn. (Leiden and London, 1960–)
HLEUL	Harvard Library of Early Ukrainian Literature: English Translations Series (Cambridge, Mass., 1989–)
JECS	*Journal of Early Christian Studies* (Baltimore, MD, 1993–)
JRS	*Journal of Roman Studies* (London, 1911–)
JSAI	*Jerusalem Studies in Arabic and Islam* (Jerusalem, 1979–)
Markus, *End*	R. A. Markus, *The End of Ancient Christianity* (Cambridge, 1990)
MGH	*Monumenta Germaniae Historica*

	Epp.	Epistolae (Berlin, 1887–)
	Epp. Sel.	Epistolae Selectae in usum scholarum, 5 vols. (Hanover, 1887–91)
	SS rer. Germ.	Scriptores rerum Germanicarum in usum scholarum separatim editi, 63 vols. (Hanover, 1871–1987)
	SS rer. Merov.	Scriptores rerum Merovingicarum, 7 vols. (Hanover and Leipzig, 1885–1951)
	SS	Scriptores, 30 vols. (Hanover and Leipzig, 1826–1934)

OMT	Oxford Medieval Texts (Oxford, 1950–)
PG	*Patrologiae cursus completus: series graeca*, ed. J.-P. Migne, 161 vols. (Paris, 1857–66)

PL	*Patrologiae cursus completus: series latina*, ed. J.-P. Migne, 221 vols. (Paris, 1844–64)
PO	Patrologia Orientalis (Paris, 1907–)
SC	Sources Chrétiennes (Paris, 1942–)
SCH	Studies in Church History (Oxford, 1964–)
SHag.	Subsidia Hagiographica (Brussels, 1886–)
Theodoret, *HR*	Theodoret of Cyrrhus, *Historia Religiosa*, ed. P. Canivet and A. Leroy-Molinghen, *Théodoret de Cyr: Histoire des Moines de Syrie*, SC 234 and 257 (1977–9)
VAnt.	Athanasius of Alexandria, *Vita S. Antonii* (*BHG* 140), ed. G. J. M. Bartelink, *Athanase d'Alexandrie, Vie d'Antoine*, SC 400 (1994), 124–376

I

Introduction

JAMES HOWARD-JOHNSTON

THERE has been an unprecedented acceleration in the pace of research across almost the full range of the humanities in the second half of the twentieth century. It was the inevitable consequence of the expansion of the academic profession as universities proliferated and grew in size. Knowledge has grown hugely, all manner of new techniques and approaches have been developed, and there has been an immeasurable improvement in understanding of economic, social, and cultural processes and of their interplay in different material environments across different historical epochs.

Nowhere has the advance been more dramatic or more exciting to participants and a wide lay audience than in one subculture (late antique studies) of a subculture (historical studies) of the humanities. Many subtle, imaginative and scholarly intelligences have contributed to a rapid extension and deepening of knowledge, but none can match the inspiration given by Peter Brown or the energizing force which his teaching and writing have imparted to research in the field. Some day a biographer will tease out some of the experiences, exterior and interior, which helped shape his character and ideas. Starting with his birth and upbringing in Dublin, the future biographer will cast an eye over the years of formal education at Aravon School in Co. Wicklow, Shrewsbury School (a nursery of original and maverick spirits), and New College, Oxford, before homing in on a period of relative seclusion in All Souls (years preoccupied academically with the close scrutiny of Augustine's inner life and thought), and his subsequent emergence into the mainstream of academic life in 1966. Thenceforth we have no need of privileged insight to track his movements or to trace the evolution of his ideas. The three great displacements of his life are plain to see—from Oxford to London University, from England to America, and from Berkeley to Princeton—and successive publications have exposed his thinking to public view. The delicate task falling to the future biographer will be to define the impact of these very different cultural and institutional milieux on the thought of the Master and his impact on them.

It was in 1966 that Peter Brown first began to lecture regularly. Initially he turned to international relations in the Eastern Mediterranean on the eve of the rise of Islam. There was a diffident, halting quality to the presentation, but before long the words were flowing more easily, occasional pauses for the formation of a troublesome syllable adding suspense and tautening attention. Then he set about extending his audience's field of vision, bringing intellectual, religious, social, and economic history to the fore. Iran (though not Babylonia) and Islam slipped into the shadows, leaving the late Roman Empire, especially its eastern half, under scrutiny. The social order in town and country in an era of change and the tensions engendered by change were central topics. But this relatively humdrum history of man's material existence was placed in a larger, framing context of intellectual and cultural history. With a sharp, penetrating vision, which seemed to verge on clairvoyance, he trained his audience's eyes on the half-articulated ideas and nexuses of ideas which shaped much of the behaviour of individuals and groups in late antiquity. Thought-worlds, only glimpsable fleetingly and partially, became the very stuff of history. Nothing could be understood properly without attending to this cultural context, a hierarchical cosmic order with the earth at its base forming an arena of unceasing conflict between the holy and the demonic. We looked back at the era of Christianization with the eyes of young Constables, able now to see the ever-varying cloud-formations of the overarching thought-world.

Into this material and immaterial world, conjured up by the words and images of the Master, strode the figure of the half-human, dispassionate, at times autocratic holy man. In an era in which paradoxically, despite the Incarnation, the divine had receded out of direct reach of mankind, points of contact with it, channels of communication were urgently sought. None was more potent or played a more important role than the holy man who re-entered the secular world. Years of withdrawal, renunciation and solitary ascetic training had given him mastery over the demons within him (the passions) and those attacking him from without. Invested with supernatural power and a daunting presence, the holy man could be called upon to salve troubled consciences, to give spiritual advice, to offer up efficacious prayers (much more likely to be heard than those of his petitioners, because of his standing in the court of heaven), to treat or advise on the treatment of physical and mental ailments, to avert natural disasters, to foresee the future, and to ease social tensions. It was this last, social function with which Peter Brown was primarily concerned. The holy man was the supreme fixer, whom only the arrogant, foolish or possessed would dare oppose openly, given the supernatural firepower which he could call down. He dealt with all manner of individual grievances, but caught the attention of contemporaries above all when his clients were persons of high status or whole groups—say villagers at odds with each other or with the authorities—and he was called upon to offer advice, to mediate, to arbitrate, or to provide protection. He joined the urban and military patrons as a social force to be reckoned with.

Much else was said. Relics and icons made appearances as other *loci* of the holy on earth. Processes initiated in late antiquity continued into the early Middle Ages, shrines of saints being brought under the control of bishops as they proliferated in the West, the legitimacy of icons and their veneration being challenged by the united forces of Church and State in Byzantium. . . . All too much now slips the mind, thirty years later. One memory, though, remains as vivid as ever—of the smallish Hovenden Room in All Souls, where Peter Brown lectured. It must have had some magical force for him. Certainly he would not move from it. By the late 1960s, when the word had spread, the room would be full at the start of term, and, with each passing week, more and more listeners would crowd in, to be entranced by the substance of the lectures and their bewitching, image-studded language. Each week, we would emerged dazed into a normal, daylit world and would strive to isolate and fix the central, solid points of the argument in our minds. By the end of each term, the Hovenden Room was a ghastly black hole, packed with humanity, hot and humid, providing each of us with a genuine experience of self-mortification.

The World of Late Antiquity (1971) distils something but by no means all of what we heard over those years. Other themes—the holy man as social force in the Eastern Mediterranean, the relic-based cult of saints in the West, the forces at work in the Iconoclast controversy, the divergence between Orthodox and Latin Christendom (explained largely in terms of the different pattern in the way the holy spurted into normal life)—were dealt with initially in discrete articles, later collected together in *Society and the Holy in Late Antiquity* (1982). Of course, this was but the second phase— after the years devoted to Augustine—of an immensely distin- guished academic career. All too soon the small world of Oxford was to be left behind. New preoccupations were to come to the fore in the Master's mind, which are deftly summarized by Averil Cameron: first a narrowing and intensifying of focus as he delved into ethical formation in the era of Christianization, concentrating on one key aspect of individual ascetic renunciation and the rumi- nations which it provoked in the new Christian intelligentsia; then a second opening out to encompass the larger, enveloping process of cultural change in late antiquity, regulated by social élites and given real purchase in the localities by holy men.

A single article, 'The Rise and Function of the Holy Man in Late Antiquity', first published in the *Journal of Roman Studies* in 1971, has been selected as the focal point of this volume of essays. Seldom has a single scholarly piece provoked so much thought or engen- dered so enthralling and long-lasting a debate. Much has been mod- ified since it was first published, not least by Peter Brown himself in his subsequent work. Some major revisions have been suggested by others. The learned discussion has been exciting to watch but hard to follow in detail, so subtle have been its turns, both inside and outside the mind of the Master. A clear summary and cool critique of the key issues at stake is presented by Philip Rousseau. A num- ber of key issues are identified by Paul Hayward, who sketches something of the intellectual background to Peter Brown's work, particularly as it applies to the early medieval West. But there has been no demurring from Peter Brown's basic contention that the holy man, alive and dead, was a key point of intersection between spiritual, wider cultural, social, and political forces. His presence is a phenomenon which historians must acknowledge and explore if they are to understand the world of late antiquity and its medieval cultural progeny in Latin Christendom, Eastern Europe, Byzantium and the Near East.

Five of the contributors (the two editors, Paul Fouracre, Chase Robinson, and Philip Rousseau) delivered drafts of their papers to the After Rome Seminar at Oxford in summer 1996. The theme of holy men and saints was chosen, to mark the twenty-fifth anniver- sary of the publication of the article. Two others (Averil Cameron and Josef Meri) were in regular attendance. Additional papers were then solicited to round out the volume from three other graduates of Oxford (Richard Price, Claudia Rapp, and Ian Wood), and—to focus on a key development in the cult of saints in the Orthodox world—from the solitary non-Oxonian, Paul Hollingsworth. Among the contributors, six of us are former pupils of Peter Brown (five at Oxford, and one, Paul Hollingsworth, at Berkeley). All of us, though, can testify to the vivifying influence of his ideas. This volume will, we hope, demonstrate the vitality that he imparted to the study, in his former university, of a formative transitional period in West Eurasian history.

There is nothing definitive about this volume. The chief aim has been to follow Peter Brown's example and to keep the screen wide. So medieval Russia and Islam have been brought in as well as the more familiar worlds of the late antique Mediterranean and its direct, sub-Roman descendants in Western Europe and Byzantium. There has been no attempt to orchestrate the contributions, and thereby to offer a coherent set of propositions. Collective scholarly enterprises which set out with such ambitions all too easily fail to accomplish them. The editorial hand has been applied as lightly as possible, our main aim being to encourage contributors to elucidate what Peter Brown has written, to react to it, and to set off on their own lines of thought. We hope that the variety and fizz of the resulting volume will compensate for the inevitable holes in its coverage, and that the different concerns and approaches evident in the papers will provoke rather than bemuse.

––––––––––––

There is a crucial difference between the title of Peter Brown's article (*holy men* are under scrutiny) and that of this collection of essays (on the cult of *saints*). The meanings of the two words and the distinction between them need to be established clearly. The following may be suggested as working definitions, against which to set those offered explicitly or implicitly by individual contributors: a holy man or holy woman was a person of noted piety and discernment, whose prayers were reckoned to be particularly efficacious and who gained the respect of those who encountered him or her; a saint was either a martyr who died for his or her faith, or a holy man or woman singled out for posthumous commemoration and veneration, or someone with more dubious credentials. While only a small minority of acknowledged holy persons achieved posthumous sanctity, certain powerful figures, usually churchmen, who were deeply implicated in the sometimes murky politics of their times, might be invested after their deaths with sanctity by their partisans (the cases of Wilfrid, Praejectus, Bishop of Clermont, and Leudegar, Bishop of Autun, are noted by Paul Hayward and Paul Fouracre). The concept of sanctity is somewhat stretched to accommodate this third category, even more so in the case of saints manufactured to promote a cause or to serve a vested interest (for instance that of certain Constantinopolitan convents striving to rehabilitate themselves after the end of Iconoclasm).[1] It is the processes involved in the transformation of a selected minority of holy men and women and of some more worldly leaders into saints which preoccupy most of the contributors. Several conditions had to be satisfied for a holy man or woman to gain lasting recognition as a saint, although not necessarily all of them in all cases: the existence and qualities of a holy man or woman had to be known to more than a handful of contemporaries; he or she should have stood out from his or her peers, say by the exercise of religious authority or by notable feats, above all the working of miracles; a cult should have developed more or less spontaneously, focused initially on his or her tomb; high status and connections in high places were an asset;[2] but most important of all was the composition of a written record of his or her life and deeds, which might then propagate and perpetuate his or her reputation. In the case of a political leader, whose ascetic feats were modest, sanctity could only be achieved through the energetic campaigning of a powerful sponsoring institution (an episcopal see or a monastery) and an active group of partisans, and it required the production of a carefully composed hagiographical biography.

It is upon three factors, the formation of hagiographical texts, their role in promoting cults, and the social forces which stood to gain from their promotion, that attention is concentrated. Saints'

---

[1] See M.-F. Auzépy, 'De Philarète, de sa famille, et de certains monastères de Constantinople', in C. Jolivet-Lévy, M. Kaplan, and J.-P. Sodini (eds.), Les saints et leur sanctuaire à Byzance: textes, images et monuments, Byzantina Sorbonensia, 11 (1993), 117–35, for the manufacture of new cults to overlay the embarrassing pasts of two Constantinopolitan convents, which had benefited greatly from Iconoclastic endowments.

[2] Cf. I. Ševčenko, Observations on the Study of Byzantine Hagiography in the Last Half-Century (Toronto, 1995), 10, 16–17.

Lives are viewed as created artefacts, shaped by general and local hagiographical traditions which had their own internal literary dynamics. Stereotyping (of the origin, virtuous achievements, miracles and manner of death of a saint) may all too often extrude particular circumstances and idiosyncratic character traits from a Life, and thus confine vision to conventional themes which transcend time and place. Doubt may also be cast on the faithfulness of less stereotyped, more detailed saints' Lives (a category to which many Middle Byzantine texts belong) to the lived realities of the individuals who are their subjects. Much, it is implied, could be transmuted and, in extreme cases, invented. Behind the veil of the texts vested interests of several sorts (royal, aristocratic, episcopal, monastic) are discerned at work, striving to legitimize or to enhance their power, to solidify or to increase their wealth, by sponsoring new cults or by establishing close associations with those already well entrenched. Hagiographical records of the lives and posthumous feats of saints were, it is contended, reshaped to serve such interests, especially in the early medieval West where inherited administrative institutions were increasingly corroded and the powerful turned to the supernatural and to religious institutions to buttress their positions. Thus saints' Lives are presented as active agents in the interaction between competing social and political forces, as well as more or less efficient transmitters of information about notable holy men and women (and certain other leaders) for the edification of future generations.

The first proposition, with its emphasis on literary construction in hagiographical texts, is the most contentious and demands some editorial comment. The second (their function of promoting cults) seems self-evident, while the third, bringing to the fore the social and political forces involved in the cult of saints, is persuasively argued and merely needs to be supplemented with some Byzantine examples. First, though, the reader should be given a guided tour of the volume.

The task of elucidating Peter Brown's thinking is undertaken mainly by Averil Cameron who places his work on holy men in the wider context of his exploration of late antique culture and of the process of Christianization, and by Philip Rousseau who subjects the specific theses of the 'Holy Man' article to close examination.

Theirs is no mean feat. For the mundane reader can all too easily find that the Master's ideas, agitated and full of motion as they are, expressed in prose which shimmers with images and evocative phrases, squirm and slither from their grasp. Both also broach the issue of literary construction in hagiographical texts, viewing them as pieces of written discourse shaped by the prescriptions of classical rhetoric (Cameron) and targeted at an educated urban readership which liked to be transported in imagination into an exaggeratedly alien rural world (Rousseau). Averil Cameron also opens up several avenues of investigation—into asceticism, which, she stresses, was as much a process of mental as physical discipline, into literary representation of the individual and of private life in late antiquity, and into the similarities and differences between holy men of East and West as we move into the early Middle Ages. On this last point she may raise false hopes in readers of this volume. For while the holy man who achieved sanctity in the early medieval West features in four essays, his Byzantine counterpart is conspicuous for his absence, apart from two entirely fictional characters discussed by Paul Magdalino. Something will be said later in this introduction to plug this gaping hole.[3]

In spite of the distortion introduced by hagiographers, Philip Rousseau strives to peer at real holy men in action in late antiquity. For him, their chief function was educational, to orchestrate and inform an intra-communal debate founded on the careful exegesis of Scripture. Claudia Rapp also seeks out real holy men beyond hagiographical texts, eavesdropping on such fragments of dialogue between spiritual fathers and their clientele as have survived congealed in their letters. She identifies intercession as the core function of the living holy man (as it was of the few who were posthumously sanctified). His correspondents assumed that his sustained quest for spiritual perfection assured him special favour in heaven and that his prayers on their behalf (for their spiritual or material well-being) would be more efficacious than their own and might sometimes result in miracles. His ascetic conduct invited admiration and attracted devotees, who formed inner and outer prayer circles centring on him.

Paul Magdalino then whisks us east and forward through time to Byzantium in the tenth century. He concedes that hagiographi-

---

[3] A masterly survey is easily accessible: C. Mango, 'Saints', in G. Cavallo (ed.), *The Byzantines* (Chicago, 1997), 255–80.

cal texts refract reality but views the literary representation of the saint, however faithful or unfaithful to the living holy man, as part of the process of development of a cult, which should be studied as a whole. His concern, though, is not with the small band of living holy men of the period who gained recognition as saints nor with the formation of their cults, but with hagiography as a vehicle for religious commentary and criticism. He examines two fictional Lives, those of Andrew the Fool and Basil the Younger, which have an evangelical purpose and which carry rich charges of esoteric knowledge. Many connections are detected between the two texts, a single patron responsible for their production is identified, and they are contrasted with an example of a conventional saint's Life, that of a miracle-working holy man, Luke the Stylite.

At this point attention shifts to transalpine Europe in the early Middle Ages. The role of saints' Lives in promoting cults and associated vested interests forms the subject of the next three essays. Paul Hayward views hagiographical texts as forensic pieces of writing, which both served sectional interests (those which stood to gain from the promotion of a type of cult or a specific cult) and were intended to shape the ambient thought-world of society at large. He homes in on the writings of Gregory of Tours in the second half of the sixth century. Gregory, he argues, left in shadow various manifestations of the holy in contemporary Gaul (including the living, solitary, ascetic) in order to focus attention on posthumous cults centred upon relics, live with supernatural power, of dead saints, which were housed within a church subject to episcopal or abbatial control. There was, he stresses, a significant element of propaganda in Gregory's works. He was promoting a style of cult which would in turn enhance episcopal authority in general and his own in particular. From this particular example of active agency in a set of hagiographical texts, Hayward turns to consider the intellectual processes involved in the development and refinement of the cult of saints in general over the *longue durée*. He detects both logical and lateral reasoning at work, as Christian thinkers strove to accommodate anomalous phenomena, such as the Massacre of the Innocents, within their explanatory framework—the notion of martyrdom being extended to embrace the innocent young in the cited case.

Paul Fouracre also begins by questioning whether the cult of saints was already as pervasive and as regulated in the sixth century as Gregory's works would seem to imply. He places the full articulation of the cult of saints in the Frankish world some two centuries later. He distinguishes two stages in its evolution and identifies the social forces at work at each stage. First came a pro-liferation of relic-shrines in the seventh century, which, he argues, was driven by vested aristocratic interests that had been forced to turn to supernatural agencies to strengthen their position in a highly competitive and fluid world. Then, in the second half of the eighth century, royal authority was imposed on religious institu-tions and on cults of saints, by replacing aristocratic with episcopal patronage. Thenceforth the power of the saints, concentrated in their relics, would feed that of earthly monarchs rather than a mul-tiplicity of local leaders. It was thus only in the Carolingian period and as part of a general reordering of secular and religious struc-tures that sanctity was boxed, labelled, distributed and dispensed by bishops who were themselves to be subjected to effective royal control.

Ian Wood continues the theme of the influences at work shaping hagiographical production in the northern world, but confines him-self to one category of text, Lives of missionaries proselytizing on the northern and eastern fringes of the Frankish world, from Boniface in the middle of the eighth century to Bruno of·Querfurt around the year 1000. He stresses the narrative delay between the living and the writing of a Life, which made it possible, in several but not all cases, for vested interests to rework history. Such vested interests might be rival monastic foundations putting their own spin on their common founder's career or episcopal sees asserting juridical rights. In some cases, though, it was the private ruminations of a hagio-grapher, himself engaged like his subject in missionary work, which intruded into the text, giving it an almost confessional air but, at the same time, allowing the distant modern observer to glimpse the inner worlds of some missionaries. The original impulse behind the development of a new category of missionary hagiography came, he suggests, from Bede, and led to the creation of competing local hagiographical traditions. He identifies several chains of closely con-nected texts, written by authors who were reacting to preceding works. There was interplay both within and between these separate chains of texts.

The last four essays take us deep into the Middle Ages and well away from the main Mediterranean arena of classical and late antique history. They provide illuminating parallels and contrasts to the phenomena analysed in the preceding contributions. Paul Hollingsworth traces the development of the most important indigenous cult in newly Christianized Russia, that of the Princes Boris and Gleb, murdered by their half-brother Sviatopolk, in an ultimately vain bid to monopolize power after the death of their mutual father Volodimer in 1015. Acknowledging that the chief impresarios were literate churchmen, Hollingsworth insists that the cult only took firm root in the Kievan heartland of Russia by 1072, because there was a ready audience to hand in an era of rapid, unsettling, conflict-ridden change, both political and religious. The hagiographical narrative which was constructed around the deaths of the princes transformed them, like the Innocents slaughtered on Herod's orders, into martyrs, and conveyed a forceful moral message, advocating harmonious coexistence in place of violent competition for power between different branches of the royal family. It was fashioned as an ideological instrument which might aid the efforts, principally of churchmen, to moderate internecine conflict and to encourage inter-princely co-operation in the face of the menacing nomads of the steppes.

Hagiographical tradition over the *longue durée* is to the fore in Richard Price's essay. He, like Ian Wood, is concerned with the holy man as missionary. He picks out two themes—the direct attack by the holy man on the abodes of demons (pagan cult-sites) and other confrontations in which the holy man is on the defensive and undergoes an ordeal of some sort—and shows how they recur in the hagiographical representation of missions in vastly different contexts. He contends that close scholarly scrutiny reveals a solid substratum of historically sound material in several of the texts in which these and other narrative motifs occur, even those as artfully composed as Sulpicius' *Life of St Martin* (set in fourth-century Gaul) and Epiphany Premudry's *Life of St Stephen of Perm* (at work on the north-east margin of Russia in the fourteenth century). This may be accounted for partly by a tendency for similar circumstances to evoke similar responses from individuals guided by the same religious principles, and partly by conscious imitation of the practices of earlier missionaries, as reported or misreported in their Lives. For in this sphere as in many others, life imitated art. Hagiography influenced the behaviour of its latter-day readers. Other examples, unconnected with the missionary field, spring to mind: Anastasius the renegade Zoroastrian cavalryman (d. 628) who feasted on the acts of the early Christian martyrs during his years of secluded existence in the monastery of St Anastasius in Jerusalem and then left to court arrest by the Persian authorities in Caesarea in the hope (which he realized) of achieving martyrdom himself;[4] Stephen of Muret (d. 1125) who is likely to have modelled, at least in part, the austere Order of Grandmont which he founded in the Limousin on what he read in the lives of late antique saints;[5] and Neophytos, a modestly educated Cypriot who, in the twelfth century, was inspired to emulate the feats of earlier hermits by wide hagiographical reading.[6]

Holy men and saints' shrines also became familiar features of the medieval Islamic world but only after a hiatus of more than two centuries. Chase Robinson sets the scene, noting the difficulties which a many-layered historical tradition, suffused by hindsight and later preoccupations, places in the way of clear observation of the Prophet's life and the development of institutions and ideas after his death. He does not view Muhammad as an Arab counterpart of the interventionist Christian holy man, 'called upon to cure the *malaise* of an "emergent" society' in which the old tribal ethos was loosening its hold and social tensions were growing.[7] It is rather Muhammad himself who was the principal destabilizing factor, who threw his society 'into massive imbalance, creating a religious vortex into which the backward Arab pagans of Arabia and the Fertile Crescent tumbled . . .' Muhammad is portrayed as the Prophet he was, the medium through which raw revelation came direct from the awesome, a-human divinity governing all things. It is the powerful charge carried by the message together with the legislative capacity of the messenger which created an organized community of believers and galvanized it into sustained warlike action to propagate the new faith. It should be noted that Muhammad insistently denied that he possessed the miracle-working power

---

[4] *Acta M. Anastasii Persae* (*BHG* 84), ed. B. Flusin, *Saint Anastase le Perse et l'histoire de la Palestine au début du VIIe siècle*, 2 vols. (Paris, 1992), i, *Les textes*, 41–91.

[5] M. Dunn, 'Eastern Influence on Western Monasticism in the Eleventh and Twelfth Centuries', *Byzantinische Forschungen*, 13 (1988), 245–59.

[6] C. Galatariotou, *The Making of a Saint: The Life, Times and Sanctification of Neophytos the Recluse* (Cambridge, 1991), 19–39, 75–94.

[7] *WLA*, 191.

which was a key identifying characteristic of the Christian holy man.[8]

Revelation and *jihad* were therefore the chief energizing elements of the new faith, elements which were gradually brought under control as new institutions were developed and the faith was systematized. This was achieved in the first two centuries of Islam, Caliphs subordinating *jihad* to the larger interests of the State and the educated priesthood of '*ulama*' generating and codifying a fixed prophetic *sunna* (paradigm) based upon a delimited set of authoritative texts. Josef Meri now takes over and shows how holy men stepped into the Islamic world in the course of the ninth century, although it had no place for intermediaries between man and Allah, let alone any possessed of supernatural power, and although the concerted efforts of the '*ulama*' had put a cap on revelation. As in the Eastern Mediterranean of late antiquity they took various forms, including a toned down version of the late antique urban mendicant (the *salos* or holy fool) who courted the scorn or disregard of society as an aid in his private struggle against pride in his religious feats.[9] Far more influential, though, were the Sufi mystics, who first came to the fore in Khurasan in the ninth century and, by their claim to receive divine revelations, challenged the religious authority of the '*ulama*'. Eventually, they were accommodated within traditional Islam, their revelations acknowledged as inspirations but accorded lower status than the single great burst of communication from Allah to man which had passed through the Prophet.

In due course some Sufi mystics mutated into saints and were venerated at shrines where they were buried. They joined Old Testament prophets and members of the Prophet's family who had long been revered in Islam. By the eleventh century the cult of saints was taking firm root throughout Islam,[10] and provoked strong opposition from traditionalist theologians. Josef Meri shows how hard it was to square visits to the tombs of saints (*ziyara*) and their veneration (implying as it did that they were latter-day intermediaries possessing effective powers of intercession) with the austere monotheism of Islam. Ultimately an uneasy compromise was reached. The existence of saints with *baraka* ('blessing') was acknowledged, and their numbers grew as noted religious scholars

---

[8] M. Rodinson, *Mohammed* (Harmondsworth, 1973), 130.
[9] F. de Jong, H. Algar, and C. H. Imber, 'Malamatiyya', in *EI²*, vi, 223–8.
[10] Cf. *CS*, 10.

and secular leaders were included as well as mystics. Care was taken to define a correct etiquette for visits to their tombs. These definitions, several of which are quoted by Josef Meri, cast a revealing light on the ritual practices which developed at medieval Muslim shrines. Islamic writers reveal much more about such practices than their Christian counterparts, precisely because the whole phenomenon of pilgrimage to saints' shrines was contentious. There remained differences of opinion about the precise boundary between licit and illicit practice, but a general consensus emerged on the attitude to be adopted (contrition brought on by meditation on death and the awesome power of Allah) and the actions to be performed (praying for the saint as well as through the saint) on visits to the tombs of saints.

The impetus behind the cult of saints, the human need for identifiable, accessible, and efficacious sources of reassurance and help, can be shown to have had a delayed but profound effect on Islam. A different corps of saints, chiefly members of the Prophet's family, mystics, and scholars, emerged into a different thought-world and their cult evolved in distinctive ways. Nonetheless, in its fundamentals, the cult of saints in Islam resembled that manifest in different parts of Christendom in late antiquity and the early Middle Ages. Even now, at the end of the second millennium, shrines are visited and venerated throughout Islam, with considerable flouting of the recommended *ziyara* etiquette, as I have seen for myself. Families feast on lambs which they have sacrificed at the shrine of Seyit Battah Gazi in western Turkey. They place their children on the elongated sarcophagus of the giant hero of *jihad* who is buried there, lift off the turban at one end and hold it over their heads— to transmit to them some of the power concentrated in the tomb. Far away in prosperous north Tehran, businessmen call in routinely, on their way home from work with bulging briefcases, at a shrine, pray at the tomb, kiss the jamb of the doorway, and slip off into the crowd, while in the baking heat of Khuzistan, at Susa, an imperial city now shrunk to a small town, devotees press every part of their body to the grill surrounding the tomb of the prophet Daniel and mutter fervent prayers.

The principal themes of this volume are, however, those signalled at the start of this survey and commentary on the eleven essays which it contains—namely, (1) the processes involved in the construction of hagiographical texts, (2), the contribution of such texts to the creation and advertisement of saints' cults, and (3) the vested interests served by such cults and the texts which promoted them. While there is no need to add to the arguments of individual contributors on the latter two points, the first demands further, closer scrutiny. Hagiographers have been seen at work, reshaping, embellishing, doctoring, and manufacturing material about their subjects for a range of ulterior purposes. Literary conventions (in particular, the themes and structure recommended for *encomia* by writers on rhetoric), narrative motifs and moralizing *topoi* recycled from earlier Lives, the personal concerns and artistic skill of the hagiographer, the expectations of his readership (for entertainment as well as moral uplift)[11] may severally and together have acted as a powerful transforming influence when the raw materials of hagiography, the perceptions and memories of those who knew or encountered the holy man, were being gathered and shaped into written form. Beside these literary influences and constraints, account must also be taken of the effect of vested interests, whether institutional, family, or (in late antiquity, when rival parties in the Church competed with every weapon to hand) confessional, on the version of events retailed by a hagiographer. Hagiography may thus open a door into an interior space (the mind and cultural furniture of the individual author) but may provide at most a highly refracted and limited vista of a larger, outer, world inhabited by living holy men and women. Not that we should be dismayed if it were only those interior spaces which could be examined closely. For there are a very large number of them on display in the corpus of extant hagiographical texts, and, in aggregate, they provide us with many different views into the thought-world of hagiographers, at different stages of its evolution, a thought-world which surely reached out to envelop their readers and their subjects.

No one would deny that written records of events are inevitably partial in both senses of the word (the perceptions and memory of the observer being both selective and coloured by personal interests) and that further shaping takes place when what is remembered is expressed in writing (conventions of form and style, as well as individual taste, exerting a powerful influence). Nor would anyone deny

[11] Cf. Ševčenko, *Observations*, 17.

that texts are active agents as well as conveyors of information. In the case of hagiography, acts of many sorts can be performed, beside the basic one of commemorating a holy person: the Life of a saint may advance or protect a vested interest; it may defend or enhance a reputation; it may edify a small or large intended audience; it may convey propaganda designed to stiffen the resolve of Christians in difficult times;[12] or the hagiographer may choose to reflect openly on live issues, thereby introducing a personal, almost confessional element into his text. It is a moot point, however, whether these various factors—selective memory, literary constraint, ulterior purpose, to which should be added the eye of faith, ready to construe the unusual as miraculous and to credit it to the saint—transmute the life and works of the holy person commemorated to such an extent that they inhibit the normal operations of critical literary and historical inquiry. Is it no longer possible to distinguish a core of authentic material from the moralizing and embellishing accretions expected of hagiographers? Have the omissions and emphases which serve to enhance the reputation of saints been rendered undetectable? Does the conceptual framework of late antique and early medieval hagiography so obscure our vision of the phenomena which are interpreted as miracles as to prevent us from discerning other, mundane causes?

Even a hasty scan of a selection of saints' Lives, which have been subjected recently to close examination, gives a firm and encouraging answer to these questions and enables us to shy away from a stance of extreme scepticism. Not that there is a dearth of fanciful hagiography. To the two examples adduced by Paul Magdalino may be added a multitude from late antiquity: only the bare outlines of the career of Sergius, a well-connected army officer martyred in the persecution of 311–13, can be recovered from the *passio* composed in the middle of the fifth century to advertise his recently constructed intramural shrine at Rusafa;[13] the same is true of the carefully filleted Life, laced with legendary matter, written some time after his death to rehabilitate Epiphanius, Bishop of Constantia on Cyprus 367–403, who had been too ready to plunge into contro-

---

[12] Cf. Ševčenko, *Observations*, 15–16.

[13] *Passio antiquior SS. Sergii et Bacchi* (*BHG* 1624), ed. I. van den Gheyn, *AB* 14 (1895), 375–95; discussion by E. K. Fowden, *The Barbarian Plain: Saint Sergius between Rome and Iran* (Berkeley, 1999).

versy and tangle with leading figures in the Church;[14] even a comparatively nondescript religious leader, such as John, Chalcedonian Patriarch of Alexandria (610-19), who seems to have been a good administrator, organizing, among other things, an aid programme for Christians in Palestine after the sack of Jerusalem in 614, could be thoroughly restyled and transformed into the Almsgiver through the wholesale transfer to him of the charitable activity of one of his sixth-century predecessors;[15] and, to give a final, Byzantine example, the chronicler Theophanes, a high-born and assuredly well-educated abbot, could be stripped of his learning and presented as a simple, suffering monk whose purity of heart endowed him with knowledge.[16] The crucial point, though, is that, in these and many other cases of more or less thorough reworking of real lives, it is possible, with the aid of a modicum of independent evidence, to separate the historical from the legendary.

It is not, however, to Lives such as these that historians turn in the main for information about individual saints, about the social order in specific localities or about the evolving, fluctuating Christian thought-world of hagiographers and their subjects. Many examples can be cited among hagiographical texts emanating from the East Roman empire and its Byzantine successor-state of works densely packed with precise information about named individuals, specific places, urban and rural, and events narrated in considerable and lifelike detail. They may be topped and tailed with edifying passages praising the saint, but they appear to be closely engaged with realities. Often judgement as to whether to trust appearances must rely on accumulation of circumstantial detail, verisimilitude, and

[14] *Vita S. Epiphanii* (BHG 596-9), ed. D. Petau, PG 41, cols. 24-113; discussion by C. Rapp, 'Epiphanius of Salamis: the Church Father as Saint', in 'The Sweet Land of Cyprus'; *Papers Given at the Twenty-Fifth Jubilee Spring Symposium of Byzantine Studies, Birmingham, March 1991* (Nicosia, 1993), 169-87.

[15] Leontius Neapolitanus episcopus, *Vita S. Ioannis eleemosynarii* (BHG 886), ed. A. J. Festugière, *Vie de Syméon le Fou et Vie de Jean de Chypre* (Paris, 1974), 343-409; discussion by C. Mango, 'A Byzantine Hagiographer at Work: Leontios of Neapolis', in I. Hutter (ed.), *Byzanz und der Westen: Studien zur Kunst des europäischen Mittelalters*, Sitzungsberichte der Österreichischen Akademie der Wissenschaften, phil.-hist. Klasse 432 (Vienna, 1984), 25-41.

[16] Theodorus Studites, *Laudatio S. Theophanis* (BHG 1792b), ed. S. Efthymiadis, AB 111 (1993), 268-84. C. Mango and R. Scott, *The Chronicle of Theophanes the Confessor: Byzantine and Near Eastern History AD 284-813* (Oxford, 1997), xliii-lxiii, are ready to accept the hagiographical portrayal of Theophanes as ill-educated and, in his last years, incapacitated by a wasting disease of the kidneys; consequently they doubt whether he contributed much to the chronicle which bears his name.

compatibility with what is independently known (mainly about structures and high politics), but external controls are available, especially for late antiquity, thanks to a wealth of extant sources, and they can be used to test the quality of a wide range of texts.

Take the well-told story of Theodotus of Ancyra, like Sergius, a victim of the 311-13 persecution. A careful comparison of the detailed information given in the text—about the Christian community to which Theodotus belonged (identifiable as Montanist), about the identity and policy of the governor of Galatia Prima, about the spring festival of Cybele and Attis, about localities in the territory of Ancyra and the saint's shrine—with independent evidence (topographical, archaeological, epigraphic, and literary) has convinced Stephen Mitchell of its authenticity.[17] Such external controls are available in greater abundance for testing the worth of the Life of a metropolitan saint such as Daniel the Stylite (d. 493), who was consulted by Emperors and the court. The meticulous investigation carried out by Robin Lane Fox leads him to conclude that the hagiographer was well-informed but discreet, skating over some matters, applying a strong spin to others but also displaying a firm grasp of events which are carefully retailed in their correct historical order.[18] The accuracy of the Lives of two early seventh-century saints, the Galatian Theodore of Sykeon (d. 613) and Anastasius the Persian (martyred early in 628), can be documented in similar ways. There is a 'punctilious precision' in the hagiographer's description of Theodore's activity and its main Galatian setting which leads Stephen Mitchell to prize the insight which it gives into the lived realities of local Anatolian life and the ambient thought-world above all other sources, literary, archaeological, and documentary.[19] Bernard Flusin has an equally high regard for the Life of Anastasius, which he has dissected with delicate thoroughness

[17] Nilus, *Passio M. Theodoti* (BHG 1782), ed. P. Franchi de' Cavalieri, *Studi e testi*, 6 (Rome, 1901), 61–84; discussion by S. Mitchell, 'The Life of Saint Theodotus of Ancyra', *Anatolian Studies*, 32 (1982), 93–113.

[18] *Vita S. Danielis stylitae* (BHG 489), ed. H. Delehaye, *Les saints stylites*, SHag. 14 (Brussels, 1923), 1–94; discussion by R. Lane Fox, 'The *Life of Daniel*', in M. J. Edwards and S. Swain (eds.), *Portraits: Biographical Representation in the Greek and Latin Literature of the Roman Empire* (Oxford, 1997), 175–225.

[19] Georgius, *Vita S. Theodori Syceota* (BHG 1748), ed. A.-J. Festugière, *Vie de Théodore de Sykéôn*, SHag. 48 (Brussels, 1970), i, 1–161; discussion by S. Mitchell, *Anatolia: Land, Men, and Gods in Asia Minor*, ii, *The Rise of the Church* (Oxford, 1993), 122–50.

and tested against overlapping testimony culled from a full range of reliable sources.[20]

The response of Byzantinists has been similar. As long as a text is forthcoming with information, they are reasonably confident that they can distinguish between the spurious or the massaged and the authentic. Marie-France Auzépy has the surest of touches as she scrutinizes the hagiographical record of Byzantine Iconoclasm, which is pervaded by self-serving hindsight. But even in retrospective accounts of periods of intense controversy, a great deal of authentic material is conveyed—as, for example, in the *Life of St Stephen the Younger*, a victim of Constantine V's crack-down on political and religious dissidence in 765–7.[21] The balance between heavy interpretation and fairly accurate reporting varies, of course, from text to text, but Rosemary Morris, who extends the survey of Byzantine hagiography into the twelfth century, has no hesitation in treating the Lives which she exploits as valuable historical sources.[22]

The deep methodological doubt raised by several contributors to this volume may be allayed by considerations such as these. The Lives of saints, if handled with care, may yield a great deal of information of the sort garnered and reinterpreted by Peter Brown in his pathfinding article. For many of the small minority of holy men, who, being endowed for whatever reason with written Lives, were classified as saints, do come into reasonably clear historical view and can be placed in social as well as spiritual settings. There may also have been less tampering with the record of holy men's dealings with the rich and powerful, less laundering of the secular patronage which benefited their foundations than Peter Brown has been ready to concede recently.[23] For, whether resources were plentiful as in the late antique Mediterranean or straitened as in Byzantium,[24] it is likely that the chief generator of endowments and donations was not fund-raising by holy men and their careful cultivation of the highly placed but rather the laity's faith, their

---

[20] *Acta M. Anastasii Persae*: discussion by Flusin, *Saint Anastase*, ii, *Commentaire* (Paris, 1992).

[21] Stephanus diaconus, *Vita S. Stephani iunioris confessoris* (*BHG* 1666), ed. M.-F. Auzépy, *La Vie d'Étienne le Jeune par Étienne le Diacre* (Aldershot, 1997), 87–177.

[22] R. Morris, *Monks and Laymen in Byzantium 843–1118* (Cambridge, 1995), 64–89.

[23] *AS*, 62–4; cf. Mango, 'Saints', 279.

[24] M. Whittow, *The Making of Orthodox Byzantium 600–1025* (London, 1996), 59–66, 89–95.

striving for salvation.[25] Confirmation, for the Byzantine period, is to hand in documentary sources, in particular in the legislative efforts of tenth-century emperors to limit grants of land to monasteries.[26]

We have returned to the territory explored by Peter Brown in his original article on the holy man, the territory where the spiritual life intersects with the secular. This *is* susceptible to traditional historical inquiry as long as the chief sources of information, hagiographical texts, are handled with discriminating care. It *is* possible to observe holy men in retreat and in action, and to make historical generalizations of the sort offered by Peter Brown.

Important qualifications have been made to the theses propounded in the article since it was published. Attention has been paid to the large, anonymous majority of holy men who strove to sustain their secluded, ascetic striving for spiritual purity and enlightenment for a whole lifetime, creating what Peter Brown calls 'an impalpable chain of intercession', in which 'human prayer to the one God, offered up by the continent, replaced the natural, cosmic hierarchy that had been thought to link the exuberant earth, through ethereal ministering spirits, to the gods who dwelt among the stars'.[27] It was perhaps more often the importunate demands of the laity for spiritual guidance, for blessing, for hope in adversity and illness, above all for effective intercession,[28] which drew a small minority back into the secular world rather than evangelical commitment on the part of holy men themselves. Holy men who did re-engage with the laity were primarily concerned with satisfying these needs. The social functions of mediation, arbitration, and protection were normally the prerogative of the secular clergy, some of whom constituted an important subcategory of saints in late antiquity. But there is no denying that the freelance activities of holy men acting as sometimes flamboyant supernumeraries could be extraordinarily effective in crises and could catch the imagination of contemporaries.[29]

---

[25] M. Kaplan, *Les hommes et la terre à Byzance du VIe au XIe siècle: propriété et exploitation du sol* (Paris, 1992), 294–302; Morris, *Monks and Laymen*, 120–42.

[26] N. Svoronos, *Les novelles des empereurs macédoniens concernant la terre et les stratiotes* (Athens, 1994), 151–61, 190–217.

[27] *BS*, 437.   [28] *AS*, 60–2.

[29] M. Whitby, 'Maro the Dendrite: An Anti-Social Holy Man?', in M. Whitby, P. Hardie, and M. Whitby (eds.), *Homo Viator: Classical Essays for John Bramble* (Bristol, 1987), 309–17; Lane Fox, 'The *Life of Daniel*', 210–25.

Saints, the holy men and women from whom most of them were drawn, and the generality of monks remained a vital and influential force in the spiritual life of Latin Christendom throughout the Middle Ages. The same was true of Byzantium, although there soon developed distinctive patterns to the manifestation of the holy there. Much changed when the Eastern Roman Empire was dismembered in the seventh century. The provincial city shrank and lost its central place in economic, social, political, and intellectual life. The rump-state which was Byzantium was increasingly geared for war. All available resources, spiritual as well as material, were called on to ensure the survival of a beleaguered Christian people.[30] This was the first great change to affect the monastic world in Byzantium's dark age. Monks at all stages of ascetic renunciation and spiritual ascent, living communally or as hermits, were expected to pray for their fellow-Christians and the State which defended them. Their prayers would be more efficacious if made *en masse* and orchestrated.[31] The second great change enhanced the seclusion of those who had withdrawn from the secular world. Monasteries tended to cluster in relatively remote and rugged country. Holy mountains emerged as the nodal points of Byzantine spiritual life.[32] This concentration and distancing of the monastery from the lay world reinforced its gravitational field and enhanced its resistance to the steady pull exerted by the faith and needs of the laity.

Nonetheless there was no undue regimentation of monastic life and the basic rhythm of withdrawal and re-entry (if only into the small society of a monastery) was not impaired. Those monks eager to subject their bodies to severe discipline and to purify their souls in a staged ascent towards the ultimate goal of union with God, who would eventually merit the accolade of holy men, followed ascetic trajectories of their own choosing, which were only monitored and regulated by their spiritual fathers at the initial stage. When, after many years of striving, they achieved a new equilibrium on a higher spiritual plane, they differed markedly from each other. There was no erasure of identity, no convergence of functions performed.

Even the hastiest of glances at eight real contemporaries of the fabricated holy men discussed by Paul Magdalino uncovers great

[30] Whittow, *Making of Orthodox Byzantium*, 89–95, 113–26, 165–93.
[31] Morris, *Monks and Laymen*, 107–109; Auzépy, *Vie d'Étienne*, 36–9.
[32] Morris, *Monks and Laymen*, 31–51.

variety—and this was well before the urban mendicant reappeared as a familiar figure (in the twelfth century).[33] All were re-engaged to differing degrees in the secular world. The engagement was greatest in the case of those who held high office in the Church, above all in the case of the most notable of them, Euthymius, Patriarch from 907 to 912, who sanctioned the fourth marriage of the Emperor Leo VI and split the Church but who is portrayed as an independent, plain-speaking ascetic, drawn out into high affairs of State by the Emperor, his spiritual son.[34] The great mystic, Symeon the New Theologian, whose writings, especially his poetry, enable us to enter the consciousness of the ascetic, could not detach himself completely, especially during his controversial period as Abbot of the monastery of St Mamas in the metropolitan area.[35] Michael Maleinos and his protégé Athanasios, founder of the Lavra on Mount Athos, were involuntarily co-opted as spiritual advisers to the Phokas family at the apogee of its power.[36] Despite the deliberate vagueness and selectivity of his Life, Luke the Stylite can be seen acting as miracle-working guru to the official classes of Constantinople from his column near Chalcedon for over forty years.[37] To the west, in provincial Greece, two other active holy men come into view—Nikon the Metanoeite, a peripatetic evangelist, who founded his own monastery in Sparta, and Luke the Younger, a solitary contemplative, noted for his clairvoyance and love of animals, who strove hard but failed to avoid entanglement in the world.[38] Finally, in western Asia Minor, on one of its premier holy mountains, Paul of Latros's ascetic practices (together with something of his own mental experiences) and his earnest but vain

[33] P. Magdalino, 'The Byzantine Holy Man in the Twelfth Century', in *Byzantine Saint*, 51–66.

[34] *Vita Euthymii patriarchae Constantinopolitani* (*BHG* 651), ed. P. Karlin-Hayter, *Bibliothèque de Byzantion*, 3 (Brussels, 1970), 3–147.

[35] Niketas Stethatos, *Vita S. Symeonis novi theologi* (*BHG* 1692), ed. I. Hausherr and G. Horn, *Un grand mystique byzantin: Vie de Syméon le Nouveau Théologien (949–1022) par Nicétas Stéthatos*, Orientalia Christiana 12/45 (1928), 1–228; Morris, *Monks and Laymen*, 95–100; G. Collins, 'Simeon the New Theologian: An Ascetical Theology for Middle-Byzantine Monks', in *Asceticism*, 343–56.

[36] Theophanes, *Vita S. Michaelis Maleini* (*BHG* 1295), ed. L. Petit, *Revue de l'Orient chrétien*, 7 (1902), 549–68; *Vitae duae antiquae S. Athanasii athonitae* (*BHG* 187, 188), ed. J. Noret, *CCSG* 9 (1982), 3–124, 127–213.

[37] *Vita S. Lucae stylitae* (*BHG* 2239), ed. Delehaye, *Saints stylites*, 195–237.

[38] *Vita S. Niconis* (*BHG* 1366, 1367), ed. D. F. Sullivan, *The Life of Saint Nikon* (Brookline, Mass., 1987), 26–270; *Vita S. Lucae iunioris* (*BHG* 994), ed. C. L. and W. R. Connor, *The Life and Miracles of St Luke* (Brookline, Mass., 1994), 2–142.

attempt to keep his distance from his fellow men are reported in the most graphic of these Lives (which includes a brief description of the saint's appearance).[39]

There was great diversity of character, ascetic practice, and activity in that small percentage of Byzantine holy men who were commemorated as saints, as this sample from the tenth century demonstrates. Nonetheless there was a common basic rhythm to their lives, which accords with that identified by Peter Brown in late antiquity. The regular internal migration of men and women to monasteries and convents, and the ferocious ascetic thrusts of the most determined among them into inner deserts of their devising, were followed by the re-engagement of all too many of them with society, within and beyond their monasteries. This reciprocating movement remained an important, dynamic element in the spiritual life of Byzantium and of the Orthodox world subject to its cultural influence. It replicated, but usually in a less dramatic way, the rhythm identified by Peter Brown in the lives of holy men in late antiquity, and served as an essential, revitalizing religious force, a Christian analogue of the annual *hajj* in Islam.

POSTSCRIPT

As Paul Hayward and I were applying the finishing editorial touches to this book, the Fall 1998 fascicle of volume 6 of the *Journal of Early Christian Studies* appeared on the shelves of the Bodleian Library in Oxford. It publishes eight papers delivered at a four-day conference held in Berkeley, in March 1997, to mark the quarter-centenary of the 'Holy Man' article. These are prefaced with an introduction outlining the central theme of the conference and its published proceedings, and with a memoir by Peter Brown highlighting three intellectual preoccupations which had a profound influence on the article in its gestation in the late 1960s. The central theme is identical to the first theme of this book—namely, the interplay between hagiographical representation and social reality, and, within hagiography, between author and audience. The conclusions tally in the main with ours, although they are sometimes couched in more modish language and more space is allocated to

---

[39] *Vita S. Pauli iunioris in monte Latro (BHG 1474)*, ed. H. Delehaye, *AB* 11 (1892), 19-74, 136-81.

exploring methodological issues. But there are two fundamental differences: our book is far broader in geographical and temporal scope than the Californian conference publication, which confines its scrutiny to late antiquity and, within it, mainly to the Eastern Mediterranean. Although we lacked the physical presence of Peter Brown (which may have inhibited as well as enriched discussion at Berkeley), and could only observe the evolution of his thought and the influences upon it from the outside, we only passed over one of the three intellectual enthusiasms detailed by him, a concern with dynamic interaction within small groups which was enhanced, as he acknowledges with remarkable candour, by his personal involvement in Kleinian analysis from 1968 to 1974. I was aware of this, but I confined myself to the briefest and most allusive of hints (in the second paragraph of this introduction). For it was not proper for a distant observer to pass on information received nearly thirty years ago from a friend who, it so chanced, often travelled up and down between Oxford and London on the same train and in the same compartment as the Master on the way to and from his analyst.

PART I

The cult of saints in Peter Brown

2

On defining the holy man

AVERIL CAMERON

IT falls to few of us to write an article that justifies the epithet 'seminal', but Peter Brown's 'Rise and Function of the Holy Man' was certainly that. Appearing in 1971, the year after *The World of Late Antiquity*, it represented a major change of direction from *Augustine of Hippo* (1967), the importance of which is evident for Peter Brown himself as well as for his readers. *The World of Late Antiquity* moved away from the close textual analysis and the psychological interpretation which are the marks of the book on Augustine towards a broader sweep, even if still in the same chronological period. Its horizons were vast, its energy enviable. Brown was staking out a new field. With the article on the holy man he could be seen stepping more confidently into the territory of social anthropology, using a wide range of 'data' to construct a social definition, not of a saint, but of the 'holy man' in late antiquity as a typically interstitial figure exercising a patronage role based on the symbolic capital of his perceived authority. Such figures were presented— mainly on the basis of Eastern, and especially Syrian, sources—as rural patrons, able to mediate between town and country, and between the powerful and the poor. There was to be more to say.[1]

Rightly avoiding the term 'saint', for in this early period there were no formal processes of sanctification, and no official bestowal of sainthood, Peter Brown was drawn to explore instead what was meant by the more amorphous and more spiritual concept of 'the holy'. This resulted in a group of articles published together in *Society and the Holy in Late Antiquity* (1982), a book very different from his first collection, *Religion and Society in the Age of St Augustine* (1972). The latter consists of studies for the most part closely

[1] As Brown well knew: the first footnote of 'Holy Man' speaks of 'problems worth following through for many years to come'. This paper partly draws on material presented to a seminar at the University of Oslo; I should like to thank Hugo Montgomery and Halvor Moxnes in particular for their hospitality on that occasion.

associated with the work on Augustine, which give little hint of
what was to come, except perhaps in the matter of literary style. In
contrast *Society and the Holy*, no longer published in London by
Faber and Faber but by the University of California Press at
Berkeley, marked both a personal and an intellectual break with the
past. Like the earlier collection, it contains reviews and pieces on
the history of scholarship, but it also contains the article on the holy
man and associated papers such as that on 'Town, Village and Holy
Man: the Case of Syria'.[2] 'Relics and Social Status in the Age of
Gregory of Tours'[3] was in turn related to *The Cult of the Saints*, published in 1981, and continued the socio-anthropological approach
announced by the original 'Holy Man' paper. There is also a concern about the relation of the Eastern and Western Mediterranean,
reflective of the fact that *The Cult of the Saints* largely deals with the
West.[4] But Brown's Inaugural Lecture at Royal Holloway College,
London, of 1977, and his remarks on icons in *Society and the Holy*,
written in collaboration with Sabine MacCormack,[5] seem to point
away from the functional and towards a more 'spiritual view' of
religious history.

The model proposed in 'The Rise and Function of the Holy Man'
was immediately influential, as can be seen from the number of references to it in the edited proceedings of the Fourteenth Symposium
of Byzantine Studies at Birmingham, whose subject was the cult of
saints in Byzantium.[6] Scholars soon pointed out that holy men
operated in urban as well as rural contexts, that there were pagan
holy men too,[7] and that the Brownian definition did not exhaust
the possible ways of understanding the phenomenon. Nevertheless,
the model was so powerfully expressed that it set a pattern which
many followed. Meanwhile Brown himself had become interested in
asceticism. Stimulated by meeting Michel Foucault who was giving
seminars at Berkeley, Brown was drawn into the Parisian world of
Paul Veyne and the Collège de France, and entered a phase which

---

    [2] 'Syria'.   [3] *RSS*.   [4] See Brown, 'A Parting of Ways' (1976).
    [5] 'Learning and Imagination' and 'Artifices of Eternity', in *SH*, 3–21 and 207–21.
But 'A Dark Age Crisis: Aspects of the Iconoclastic Controversy', 251–301, which
first appeared in the *English Historical Review* in 1973, retains the functionalist
approach; it is interesting to compare it with the chapter on Byzantine Iconoclasm
in *RWC* (1996).
    [6] *Byzantine Saint* (1981).
    [7] G. Fowden, 'The Pagan Holy Man in Late Antique Society', *Journal of Hellenic
Studies*, 102 (1982), 33–59.

resulted in his contribution to volume I of the *History of Private Life*, edited by Veyne (1985),[8] and in the publication in 1988 of his book *The Body and Society in Late Antiquity*, which again came out in Britain under the aegis of Faber and Faber.

The Body and Society ranges in a confident sweep from the first century to the fifth, ending in the West with Augustine and, in words taken from Jacques le Goff, with 'the definitive "rout of the body" that marked the end of the ancient world and the beginning of the middle ages'.[9] It addresses one of the most characteristic marks of Christian holiness in late antiquity (though Christians did not have a monopoly on it), namely sexual abstinence, which frequently went together with other kinds of renunciation of bodily pleasure and comfort. *The Body and Society* constitutes a bravura display of empathy with the abundant source material; yet the index does not have entries either for holy man or even for monks and monasticism. If we now turn back to 'The Rise and Function of the Holy Man', we shall find that asceticism is taken for granted,[10] but that sexual abstinence is not discussed as such and that the emphasis is rather on social power, and moreover, that this is a kind of power that is based on 'achieved status'.[11] Brown is interested already, as he continued to be, in 'ascetic stars';[12] their asceticism is 'histrionic',[13] their power 'supernatural' and 'palpable'.[14] But his interest at this point lies not in asking 'why?', but 'what did it do?', or 'what was it for?' In *The Body and Society* he gives us an abundance of material relevant to the former question, but remains sparing with answers to the latter. Sexuality was a natural topic for one so steeped in the thought of Augustine, but in *The Body and Society* Brown veers away from proposing or revising the kind of social model offered in the 'Holy Man' article. The canvas is now bigger: high society as well as rural economies, the West as well as the East, the educated as well as the general populace. While the book's theme is closely connected to the definition of holiness or sainthood, Brown is now looking for something much more general—religious change itself, perhaps, or the interplay of the intellectual and the

---

[8] 'Antiquité tardive' in P. Veyne (ed.), *De l'empire romain à l'an mil*, vol. 1 of P. Ariès and G. Duby (eds.), *Histoire de la vie privée* (Paris, 1985), 226–99 (Eng. tr., Cambridge, Mass., 1986).

[9] *BS*, 441.

[10] 'Holy Man', 114, 131.   [11] Ibid., 138.   [12] Ibid., 109.

[13] Ibid., 131.   [14] Ibid., 121.

popular in Christianization. The opening section focuses on topics
familiar from Paul Veyne—the deportment of Roman upper-class
males, the bourgeoisification of Roman upper-class marriage in the
age of Plutarch and Musonius Rufus—and the book as a whole
deals with literary sources as much as with social history.

Three other books by Brown, all arising from lecture series—*The
Making of Late Antiquity* (1978), *Power and Persuasion in Late
Antiquity: Towards a Christian Empire* (1992), and *Authority and the
Sacred. Aspects of the Christianization of the Roman World* (1995)—
carry forward similar themes, though in differing ways. In the first,
changes in the role of the Roman aristocracy between the high
Empire and late antiquity provide an explanatory device for social
and religious change. In the other two, while we still encounter the
ascetic stars in all their exoticism, there is an increasing emphasis
on the evolution of a Christian *paideia* which could replace the classical model, even if it partly did so by absorbing it. *Paideia* had
already emerged as a powerful theme as early as the 1983 essay
'The Saint as Exemplar', where it is linked with an emphasis on the
saint as the imitator of Christ,[15] in an article in which Brown's
anthropological mentors are Edward Shils and Clifford Geertz rather
than Mary Douglas and E. E. Evans-Pritchard. Brown is already
conscious of the need to revise his earlier model, referring to his
1971 article as having been painted 'in more *grisaille* tones'.[16] The
rural patrons of 'Holy Man' had already by 1983, as he admitted,
yielded up the centre of the stage, based as they were on 'a specific
tradition of anthropological work available to me at that time'.[17] It
nevertheless took time for this strand to develop in Brown's work.
When it did, having located holy men in 'The Saint as Exemplar' in
what he recognized as 'a thoroughly unsystematic evolution',[18] he
was to present them in *Power and Persuasion* and *Authority and the
Sacred* in the context of an altogether more kaleidoscopic and certainly more comprehensive picture of late antiquity than that originally depicted in the 'Holy Man'.[19]

[15] See 'Exemplar', 1, 7 ff.

[16] Ibid., 10–11; cf. ibid., 12: 'if that tradition did have a limitation . . . it was the
tendency to isolate the holy man yet further from the world of shared values in
which he operated as an exemplar.' At p. 14, Brown depicts his shift as a shift from
'a largely British tradition of social anthropology to a largely American tradition of
cultural anthropology'.

[17] Ibid.   [18] Ibid., 15.

[19] This is also true of Brown's most recent book, *RWC* (1996).

Peter Brown has always been highly aware of his own development as a historian, and several of his later writings serve almost
as commentaries on the 'Holy Man', which, as he himself points
out, sprang from a relatively early stage in his remarkable trajectory, when he was still unaware of some of the influences which
later lay strongest upon him.[20] The sources on which 'Holy Man'
was mainly based are listed in the first footnote of the article, and
consist entirely of what we generally call saints' lives, with the addition of some compendia—the *Apophthegmata Patrum*, the *Lausiac
History*, and Theodoret's *Historia Religiosa*. The first page of the article refers to traditional scholarship in this field, and proposes no
challenge in terms of method: 'The intention of this paper is to
follow well-known paths of scholarship on all these topics.'[21] Brown
did not offer a new interpretation so much as a new means of
exploitation of the rich vein of material offered by hagiography. In
The Body and Society, too, the focus is always on the subjects and
their doings and thought—the proper stuff of history, some might
think—rather than on the articulation of the texts which describe
them.

Brown is a historian through and through. He wants to understand how things came about as they did; so when in *Power and
Persuasion* the theme of *paideia* again becomes important to him, it
is in the context of the social power enjoyed by the educated élites
of late antiquity, whose members displayed their standing like their
predecessors of the high Empire by adopting particular models of
decorum and deportment.[22] The emphasis in *Power and Persuasion*
is again on social mechanisms, though the functionalism of 'Holy
Man' has been dispersed or at least tempered by a more glittering
surface and a wider cast of characters. Chapter 4, the last chapter
of the book, is titled 'Towards a Christian Empire'. As in *The Body
and Society*, the story ends with the move into the fifth century, and
the emphasis here is less on the rural than on the gradual absorp-
tion of the old élites into a more generally Christian society. Shared
paideia, not excluding the habits of mind and behaviour that went
with it, becomes a key to the process.

Even now I suspect that Brown has not yet given us his complete
view of the process of Christianization in late antiquity. With
Authority and the Sacred, he returned to themes expressed in *Power*

---

[20] See 'Exemplar', 10–15, and, for example, 11 with n. 57.
[21] 'Holy Man', 105.   [22] *PP*, ch. 2 '*Paideia* and Power'.

and Persuasion by arguing again against an excessive emphasis on violence and intolerance (even if based on contemporary sources) and too black-and-white a view of the process of Christianization. Contemporaries had their own reasons for presenting the age in terms of 'conflict' between Christians and others, and it has suited modern scholars to follow them. But 'beyond the vivid flashes of pagan indignation and Christian self-justification that light up for us the incidents of violence which occurred in the late fourth and early fifth centuries, it is possible to detect a solid fog-bank of tacit disapproval'.[23] After all, power was at stake, and the élites would make sure that if change came it was properly controlled: 'all over the Mediterranean world, profound religious changes, heavy with potential for violence, were channelled into the more predictable, but no less overbearing "gentle violence" of a stable social order.'[24]

In this history of social power, the role of élites was crucial. But so, it turns out, was the holy man. Chapter 3 of *Authority and the Sacred* returns consciously to the theme of Brown's original article: 'I am far less certain than I once was—now over twenty years ago—when I first wrote on "The Rise and Function of the Holy Man", as to how exactly to fit the holy man into the wider picture of the religious world of late antiquity.'[25] Brown goes on to explain that the view expressed in the original article was too limited, too much influenced, perhaps, by the 'vivid' (a word used twice on this page as well as in the passage quoted above) '*Lives* of individual holy men, usually written by their disciples, after their death'. A thicker context is needed, in the Geertzian sense. The scope is broader now; for example, it embraces holy women, and spreads over the whole geography of the Mediterranean. Then Brown returns to the Lives; it is these texts which for their own purposes presented the holy man in a patronage role, in what Brown now terms 'a carefully censored language of "clean" patronage'.[26] The role of hagiography was, it now seems to him, 'to bring order to a supernatural world shot through with acute ambiguity, characterized by uncertainty as to the meaning of so many manifestations of the holy, and as a result, inhabited by religious entrepreneurs of all faiths'.[27] It is a recognition of the gap between the narratives and 'what really may have happened', the latter now more elusive than ever. The holy man is still interstitial,[28] but he has now become less

---

[23] *AS*, 50.   [24] Ibid., 53.   [25] Ibid., 59.   [26] Ibid., 64.
[27] Ibid., 68.   [28] Ibid., 70.

a patron than a facilitator,[29] and his territory less that of social difference between town and country than that of the imaginative landscape of the spirit. Ambiguous himself, he is well placed to channel the uncertainties of others. He has also become less powerful. 'In times of acute crisis, Christian explanatory systems collapsed like a house of cards . . .' The influence of Christian holy persons was extremely limited, 'in what had remained, to an overwhelming extent, a supernatural "subsistence economy", accustomed to handling life's doubts and cares according to more old-fashioned and low-key methods'.[30]

Read in conjunction with Brown's earlier writings, not least 'Holy Man', the last pages of *Authority and the Sacred* are extremely interesting. Brown is less sure now about Christianization itself: indeed, mankind had lapsed into 'a perpetual twilight', almost reminiscent of the superstitious world evoked by Ramsay MacMullen.[31] The confident narratives of Christian hagiography were far from telling the whole story of late antique religion (p. 75). Nevertheless, it is now a new imaginative model of the world that is in point, and holy men were even more likely to be effective in facilitating the acquisition of this for other people than in fulfilling the role of social patron assigned to them in Brown's original article (p. 78). They are now seen as easing the passage to the uncertain world of the future, in which prayers were a real necessity, and whose start is placed here, as in *The Body and Society*, at some time in the fifth century.

I have dwelt so far on the afterlife of the 'Holy Man' in Brown's own work, which is fascinating enough. Since the 'Holy Man', we can perhaps say that the horizon has expanded for him and the material come to seem more complex, the answers less sure. Only a history of late antiquity on a large scale would give us Brown's final balancing of the factors given differing amounts of emphasis in his various writings. *The Rise of Western Christendom* is not on that scale; its sweep is wider still, but the effect of that, together with the book's brevity, is to add even more to the mix. Now, however, I want to turn to an aspect of the afterlife of the 'Holy Man' which Peter Brown himself has not directly explored, though indeed *Authority and the Sacred* shows him to have become increasingly aware of the traps laid by the ancient narratives.

[29] Ibid., 64. [30] Ibid., 72.
[31] Ibid., 71; cf. e.g. R. MacMullen, *Christianity and Paganism in the Fourth to Eighth Centuries* (New Haven, Conn., 1997), ch. 3.

Brown's original article proposed a model for understanding the role of the holy man. But it was a model for our understanding of the phenomena. It did not address the extent to which the phenomena themselves (recorded in the Lives and other stories of holy men) are models constructed by the writers. Brown did not try to analyse or define what constitutes a holy man, or, to put it differently, how a holy man is constructed in the sources. Still less did he address the question of how much the holy man and the ascetic have in common: are all ascetics holy, for example? Is asceticism a necessary qualification for holiness? How do the narratives differentiate between the two concepts? Yet since 1971 these questions have intrigued those who have written on the subject as much as the social issues surrounding the late antique holy man. I would like to focus on three particularly prominent themes: first, the nature of asceticism itself, second, *mimesis*, in the sense in which ascetics and holy men are themselves models, and third, the Lives of holy men and their relation to biography in general in the period.

First, then, asceticism. This has attracted the attentions of many recent scholars, including some from disciplines quite other than that of the history of late antiquity or early Christianity. One can point first to the two collections edited by Vincent Wimbush in 1990 and 1996, which give a very good introduction to the many different types of asceticism, and their cross-cultural implications.[32] Geoffrey Harpham's *The Ascetic Imperative in Culture and Criticism* (1987) and Edith Wyschogrod's *Saints and Postmodernism* (1990) broaden the topic into realms of aesthetics, morals, and literary criticism. In thinking about asceticism, it seems to me that we are confronted with a tangle of problems which may or may not be connected, and that we need to start if possible by separating out some of the strands. Asceticism (*askesis*, discipline) can perhaps best be defined as a term used of a specific set of attitudes and practices. These involve the choice of discipline as a way to virtue, purity, and enlightenment. Such a cast of mind became more and more important in Christian antiquity. Since it mainly involved individuals, it affected their own lives and the role models they offered to others; it also affected how they were depicted in literature (and later, in art). It is clearly closely related to the monastic movement and to

---

[32] V. L. Wimbush (ed.), *Ascetic Behavior in Greco-Roman Antiquity* (Minneapolis, 1990), and *Asceticism*. Two special issues of the journal *Semeia* (vols. 57 and 58, both 1992) also contain some interesting contributions.

types of monasticism, although as Peter Brown shows in *The Body and Society* asceticism was well established before monasticism began. But asceticism is not only Christian. It may also spring from a Platonic separation of soul and body and it is inherent in classical Greek thought, for instance in Pythagorean precepts. It also features in pagan lives of holy men in the Christian period—thus the writings of Porphyry, his *Lives* of Plotinus and Pythagoras, his *Letter to Marcella* and others.[33] We might therefore suspect that asceticism's roots are essentially Platonizing, and that its appearance among early Christians is connected with a Hellenizing tendency. This however is altogether too simple, for early Christians had other models too, the Qumran community and the Essenes among them. Asceticism also seems to be a fundamental religious phenomenon, shared by other religions and cultures, including Hinduism and Buddhism, as some of the papers in the Wimbush and Valantasis collection indicate.

The first and fundamental question, then, is that posed in *The Body and Society*: in what specific ways did early Christians relate to this basic religious phenomenon, and why did they take it up with such profound consequences? Brown's book confines itself to sexual renunciation, without considering in detail its relation to other forms of asceticism, although the wider phenomenon has occupied other scholars including those who have contributed to the recent and large literature on the body.[34] The comparison between pagan and Christian ascetics and holy men has also been a major theme. Interestingly, the social explanation offered by Brown's 'Holy Man' is not to the fore here; rather, the comparison is on the literary or

[33] See *BS*, 180 f.; see also *Iamblichus: On the Pythagorean Life*, tr. G. Clark, Translated Texts for Historians, Greek ser. 8 (Liverpool, 1989); J. Dillon, 'Rejecting the body, refining the body: some remarks on the development of Platonist asceticism', in *Asceticism*, 80–7.

[34] Recent examples: G. Clark, ' "The Bright Frontier of Friendship": Augustine and the Christian Body as Frontier', in R. W. Mathisen and H. S. Sivan (eds.), *Shifting Frontiers in Late Antiquity* (Aldershot, 1996), 217–29; A. Rousselle, 'Body Politics in Ancient Rome', in P. Pantel (ed.), *A History of Women in the West I: From Ancient Goddesses to Christian Saints* (Cambridge, Mass., 1992), 296–337; P. Cox Miller, ' "The Blazing Body": Ascetic Desire in Jerome's Letter to Eustochium', *JECS* 1 (1993), 21–45; idem, 'Desert Asceticism and "the Body from Nowhere" ', ibid., 2 (1994), 137–53; C. Walker Bynum, *The Resurrection of the Body in Western Christianity, 200–1336* (New York, 1995); D. Montserrat (ed.), *Changing Bodies, Changing Meanings. Studies on the Human Body in Antiquity* (London, 1998). Note also the recent conference entitled *After the Body*, which was organized by Elaine Graham and Kate Cooper, at the University of Manchester.

ideological level. Of course, Peter Brown himself is well aware of, for example, philosophical or Manichaean asceticism,[35] but these cases serve to vary the already dense texture of his writing rather than to contextualize Christian practice. I would suggest in contrast that exploring the connection between the broader issues of asceticism and the concept of the Christian holy man is one of the more necessary desiderata suggested by the reception of the original article. It is also desirable to carry further Brown's exploration of the likenesses and differences between East and West, and the varieties of holy men in the later Byzantine East, for although Brown is indeed sensitive to Byzantium, he did not take this particular topic further in that direction, any more than did Robert Markus in *The End of Ancient Christianity* (1990).

The effect of the influence exerted by Foucault and other theorists during these years is an interesting question.[36] Certainly sexuality and abstinence have become major topics. So has the body, both as symbol and as reality. Equally, one can point to questions of personhood and the development of the concept of the individual.[37] It would have to be admitted, I think, that during the past generation the socio-anthropological approach of the 'Holy Man' has yielded in the work of very many scholars of religion in late antiquity to a more structural and literary analysis; social power is seen to rest, as indeed Peter Brown himself sees in *Authority and the Sacred*, on a wider nexus than functionalism itself would allow. But Brown himself has avoided the deconstructive turn even in its milder forms.

As we have seen, *Authority and the Sacred* questions whether the Lives of holy men, the 'ascetic stars', do in fact present us with the neutral historical data which they appear to convey. Without devaluing the essential editorial and critical work of traditional scholars of hagiography such as the Bollandists, whom Peter Brown

---

[35] For the latter, see *BS*, 197 ff.

[36] Some connections between Foucault and Brown are explored in Averil Cameron, 'Redrawing the Map: Early Christian Territory after Foucault', *JRS* 76 (1986), 266–71. The most relevant volume of Foucault's *History of Sexuality*, tr. R. Hurley, 3 vols. (New York, 1978–86), is *Le souci de soi*, which first appeared in 1984, since when there has developed a large literature by Foucault's admirers and detractors, on which see the introduction to S. Goldhill, *Foucault's Virginity: Ancient Erotic Fiction and the History of Sexuality* (Cambridge, 1995).

[37] Cf. G. Misch, *A History of Autobiography in Antiquity*, tr. E. W. Dickes, 2 vols. (London, 1950).

praises at the beginning of his 'Holy Man' article, one of the most noticeable developments in this generation's scholarship has been directed to this very issue, and to the narratological and literary-critical analysis of the various types of the hagiographic genres.

Here I will pick out only two of the issues. First, following Peter Brown's remarks in *Authority and the Sacred*, the extent to which the Lives which are recorded in the early Christian period are themselves model lives, portrayals of heroic individuals who are carefully presented to others for their imitation.[38] This is spectacularly the case with Antony as reported in the *Life of Antony*, and of the Emperor Constantine in Eusebius's *Life of Constantine*.[39] It is true of the Gospel narratives; and it is equally true of the lives of sages and holy men which may or may not be the prototypes for Christian saints' lives, for example the Life of Apollonius of Tyana by Philostratus, which Eusebius knew well, and the Lives of Plotinus and Pythagoras by Porphyry.[40] Equally, it applies to earlier texts such as the apocryphal Acts of the Apostles, for instance the narrative of Thecla in the Acts of Paul and Thecla, and the related pseudo-Clementine *Recognitiones*.[41] Those who heard or read these texts read them in this way themselves. The holy man is indeed an exemplar, to use Peter Brown's own term, not only in his actions but also for the mind and the imagination of others through the stories that grew up about him. He needs an audience; doing good by stealth was not enough in itself, and many hagiographic tales turn precisely on recognition and revelation. The writing of a Life recognizes this explicitly by making his deeds known to the world, and to posterity.

[38] On this, see Averil Cameron, *Christianity and the Rhetoric of Empire: The Development of Christian Discourse*, Sather Classical Lectures 55 (Berkeley and Los Angeles, 1991), chs. 2 and 3; Brown's emphasis on imitation in 'Exemplar' focuses rather on the holy man's *repraesentatio Christi*.

[39] See Averil Cameron, 'Form and Meaning: the *Vita Constantini* and the *Vita Antonii*', in P. Rousseau and T. Hägg (eds.), *Greek Biography and Panegyrics in Late Antiquity* (forthcoming).

[40] On the general topic, and on specific examples, see M. J. Edwards and S. Swain (eds.), *Portraits: Biographical Representation in the Greek and Latin Literature of the Roman Empire* (Oxford, 1997).

[41] See, for example, Cameron, *Rhetoric of Empire*, ch. 3; J. Perkins, *The Suffering Self: Pain and Narrative Representation in the Early Christian Era* (London, 1995); G. Anderson, *Sage, Saint and Sophist: Holy Men and their Associates in the Early Roman Empire* (London, 1994); J. R. Morgan and R. Stoneman (eds.), *Greek Fiction: The Greek Novel in Context* (London, 1994). On 'acts', see R. Mortley, *The Idea of Universal History: From Hellenistic Philosophy to Early Christian Historiography* (Lewiston, NY, 1996).

The Lives are self-consciously written: they make frequent reference to audiences, to the projected readership, to the reasons for writing. They are not works of introspection. Nor are they biographies in our present sense of the term. They tell of the great or heroic deeds of their hero, and fit them into recognizable categories. In addition, the Lives are closely related to rhetorical *encomia*, a genre in which all ancient schoolboys were well trained and which enjoyed a renewed importance in the urban culture of the empire. In origin, these Lives, including the Christian ones, are implicated in the literary history of the Second Sophistic, though it remains to be clarified exactly in what manner. They also have an intellectual and a rhetorical context: the early subjects are often 'sages' or philosophers; formal debate, in which the hero triumphs over false 'philosophers' as St Paul did over Simon Magus, is a common feature;[42] the hero may be pitted against worldly wisdom, but his skill with words prevails. All of this is apparent even in the *Life of Antony*, by common consent the first real saint's life, where Antony is described debating with 'Greek' philosophers.[43] Even the action of the Lives expresses these ideological confrontations between true and false knowledge and between town and country. Antony goes into the desert, but never loses contact altogether with the outside; his greatest gesture is to go himself to face the crowds in Alexandria, just as the great stylite saints sometimes come down from their columns in order to give advice to the powerful. The holy man talks to visitors, or gives advice by other means. He needs an audience, whether it is the audience bestowed by the texts themselves, or that encountered during the occasional public appearances which feature so often in the Lives. Finally, the Lives also have to do with accounts of martyrs, though it is too simple to suppose, as has often been thought, that they are their direct replacement. It is no surprise that Eusebius's *Ecclesiastical History*, which sets out the exemplary deaths of martyrs, also provides a proto-saint's life, the life of Origen in book 6. Early Christian martyrdom, too, demanded an audience; its hallmark was public show.[44] These

---

[42] See M. Edwards, 'Simon Magus, the bad Samaritan', in Edwards and Swain (eds.), *Portraits*, 69–91.

[43] *VAnt.*, 72–80 (pp. 320–40).

[44] On this and on the connection of martyr accounts with the literary production of second-century Asia Minor, see G. W. Bowersock, *Martyrdom and Rome* (Cambridge, 1995), esp. ch. 3; also Perkins, *The Suffering Self*, passim.

late antique Lives, then, are not modern biographies, but exemplars of virtue and heroism. There is no psychological fascination with the individual, and little attempt to delineate character. As a rule, only those aspects of the hero's private life are recounted that have a bearing on the narrative, or which fit the preconceived categories of heroicization.

These remarks lead us to my final section, and here we can return to Peter Brown. Scholars have wondered whether there was in fact a growing interest in biography in early Christianity and late antiquity, going hand in hand with a new sense of personhood and the individual. Augustine's *Confessions*, which Brown expounded so sensitively in *Augustine of Hippo*, has often been cited as an example of a real spiritual autobiography, apparently the first such to be written in antiquity. But others emphasize the ruthlessness with which Augustine concentrates on a limited range of themes, most of all his own dialogue with God, which makes the puzzling last three books explicable if seen as part of a long and continuous sequence of thought.[45] Much is left out that would have been included in a modern biography. A modern work whose author no doubt had Augustine in mind is Cardinal Newman's *Apologia* (1875), yet this is an austere work in which virtually nothing is said of Newman's personal or private life, only about his spiritual development. His many surviving letters show that it gives a very incomplete picture of Newman as a man, or even of the events of his life. The same is true of Augustine's *Confessions*.

Peter Brown lent himself to the enterprise of exploring the history of the individual in late antiquity when he agreed to take part in the French enterprise of writing about 'private life' in the early Christian and late antique periods. But problems remain, not least the looseness of the term 'private life'. Is it about the ordinary details of living, housing, domestic equipment, utensils, and so on? This is indeed part of what the contributors to the Ariès-Duby volume write about. Is it about interior consciousness? But there is little direct evidence to use here. Or was it in fact seen by the editor and participants in a more limited way, in terms of sexual attitudes?

---

[45] See G. Clark, *Augustine: The Confessions* (Cambridge, 1993), and cf. Brown, *St Augustine of Hippo* (London, 1967), 167: 'The *Confessions* are a masterpiece of strictly intellectual autobiography. Augustine communicates such a sense of intense personal involvement in the ideas he is handling, that we are made to forget that it is an exceptionally difficult book.'

Foucault himself wrote of the self in the context precisely of a history of sexuality, and so essentially did Brown, while Paul Veyne's own influential, if now somewhat controversial, paper of 1978 was focused on marriage.[46] In practice the constraints imposed on attempts to write about private feelings, emotions, or sexuality in late antiquity when so many of the texts themselves are so highly artful and self-conscious render these projects perilous from the start. Among the literary texts, collections of letters are perhaps the most promising material, except that these too are deeply conditioned by rhetorical tropes; certainly the mass of literature about the desert fathers on which Brown partly draws in the 'Holy Man' is so shot through and through with ideological, romantic, and literary themes that we must seriously question its purpose before making any attempt to use it 'straight'.[47]

It is a remarkable feature of the period that individual women should also have become the subjects of Lives. Arnaldo Momigliano's paper on the *Life of Macrina* by Gregory of Nyssa reminds us that it was something remarkable that an educated bishop from the upper class chose to write about his sister at all.[48] There were soon others, like the *Life of Melania*, and many more.[49] Gregory of Nazianzus wrote about his mother, and an autobiographical poem about himself. Perhaps most famous of all are Augustine's words about his mother, Monica, in the *Confessions*.[50] Some of these texts bear the mark of real feeling, and the phenomenon must surely be seen as connected with Christianization, and with the construction of the person. But women also featured in the pagan ascetic writings, for example, the wives and female relatives of philosophers like Porphyry's wife Marcella who form a rival topic of attention to the Christian ones, and whose stories, like theirs,

[46] 'La famille et l'amour sous le haut empire romain', *Annales*, 33 (1978), 35-63.

[47] See Averil Cameron, 'Desert Mothers: Women Ascetics in Early Christian Egypt', in E. Puttick and P. B. Clarke (eds.), *Women as Teachers and Disciples in Traditional and New Religions* (Lewiston, 1993), 11-24.

[48] 'The Life of St. Macrina by Gregory of Nyssa', in J. Ober and J. W. Eadie (eds.), *The Craft of the Ancient Historian* (Lanham, Md., 1985), 443-58.

[49] Including striking, if sometimes fictionalized, examples from among the Syrian material on which Brown drew in the 'Holy Man': cf. Theodoret, *HR* (one of Brown's texts), and S. Brock and S. A. Harvey, *Holy Women of the Syrian Orient* (Berkeley and Los Angeles, 1987). On Melania, see E. A. Clark, *The Life of Melania the Younger: Introduction, Translation and Commentary* (New York, 1984).

[50] Cf. *Augustine of Hippo*, 29: 'Few mothers can survive being presented to us exclusively in terms of what they have come to mean to their sons, much less to a son as complicated as Augustine.'

exemplify the intellectual context of this apparently 'personal' literature. Yet while some real and indeed forceful women become highly visible in late antiquity (one thinks of Olympias, the Elder and the Younger Melania, Jerome's female friends, and even the mysterious Egeria), the ground is often unsafe. Despite the fact that Palladius's *Lausiac History* has a whole section on holy women, in the *Sayings* and *Lives of the Desert Fathers*, for every female 'desert mother', like Syncletica (who is, incidentally, almost entirely a mouthpiece for philosophical sayings),[51] there are dozens of genderbound desert fathers. The reformed prostitutes and fallen women who feature in the early Byzantine texts, like Pelagia, or Mary of Egypt, are almost entirely rhetorical constructions composed of clichés of the gender discourse which is a central phenomenon in late antiquity.[52] Thecla herself, one of the major female role models for real women in late antiquity, is after all a wholly fictional character. The 'real' woman of early Christian and late antique texts is a pretty elusive creature. She is even more 'constructed' than the men.[53]

For late antiquity, at least, the focus has moved from the anthropological approach of the 'Holy Man' to the study of discourse. I myself have been intrigued by the question of whether the ascetic urge could also be seen by the historian to extend to culture and society at large.[54] This is the premise of Harpham's book, and it is assumed in important, though unexplained ways by Brown and Markus, by the latter in the argument of his book *The End of Ancient Christianity*, and by Brown in the concluding pages of *The Body and Society* and *Authority and the Sacred*. Yet it is a very large assumption. For instance, it begs the question of how far the asceticism we see in the texts of late antiquity really did operate in society at large. Might it not be primarily a textual matter, internal to writing? As I have suggested, the process of Christianization is one of Brown's

[51] The fifth-century *Vita S. Syncleticae* (*BHG* 1694) attributed to Athanasius is translated by E. A. Castelli in Wimbush (ed.), *Ascetic Behavior*, 265–311.

[52] See e.g. Averil Cameron, 'Early Christianity and the Discourse of Female Desire', in L. J. Archer, S. Fischler, and M. Wyke (eds.), *Women in Ancient Societies: An Illusion of the Night* (London, 1994), 152–68; in general, G. Clark, *Women in Late Antiquity: Pagan and Christian Lifestyles* (Oxford, 1993).

[53] E. A. Clark, 'Ideology, History and the Construction of "Woman" in Late Ancient Christianity', *JECS* 2 (1994), 155–84; K. Cooper, *The Virgin and the Bride: Idealized Womanhood in Late Antiquity* (Cambridge, Mass., 1996).

[54] Averil Cameron, 'Ascetic Closure and the End of Antiquity', in *Asceticism*, 147–61.

main themes. Yet determining the markers of Christianization in late antiquity is a very difficult matter. Much of the disagreement between those who have written about it recently is not a real disagreement at all;[55] it arises from the fact that the scholars in question are using different markers, different diagnostic tools. This is as true for judgements on the fourth century as it is for later periods. According to Brown and Markus, asceticism brought a kind of 'closing-in' of society, a narrowing of possibilities, a shrinkage of horizons. This closure is identified with a Christian society, but in the relevant passages, both write primarily of the West.[56] This is something to remember.

In my own paper, as in the last chapter of my book,[57] I was interested in arguing for the steady development of a Christian authoritarian discourse—rule-bound—and I saw asceticism and its rhetorical expression as contributing towards that. In the paper I was interested in applying this to Byzantium, both because I was dissatisfied with Brown and Markus's failure to deal with the Eastern Empire, or rather, with the assumption on Brown's part that everything had already 'closed in', and because I was also thinking about the question of heresy and heresiology in the early Byzantine period, for Byzantium is certainly marked in various stages of its history by a strong sense of defending orthodoxy against 'heresy'.

There is a danger in these arguments. It is that of going along unwittingly with the stereotype of Byzantium as an unchanging, theocratic, and 'closed' society. That is a view against which I have argued, and which has been challenged by other scholars, though it is still very persistent.[58] But I still believe that Byzantinists, like scholars of early Christianity and late antiquity, should be trying to understand discourse, the rhetorical strategies which combine to produce sets of ideas and practice, which in turn determine the nature of culture. This is the element which I find most wanting in

---

[55] For example, R. MacMullen, 'What Difference did Christianity Make?', *Historia*, 35 (1986), 322–43, starts from a completely different idea of what constitutes Christianity than, say, T. D. Barnes, 'Statistics and the Conversion of the Roman Aristocracy', *JRS* 85 (1995), 135–47.

[56] See Markus, *End*, ch. 14, 'Within Sight of the End'; cf. ibid., 225, referring to 'epistemological excision'.

[57] *Rhetoric of Empire*, ch. 6.

[58] Averil Cameron, *The Use and Abuse of Byzantium*, Inaugural Lecture, King's College London, 1992; A. Kazhdan and G. Constable, *People and Power in Byzantium: An Introduction to Modern Byzantine Studies* (Washington, DC, 1982).

the otherwise enormously stimulating work of Peter Brown. Recently I have been trying to use the insights from sociology of knowledge to understand the otherwise very difficult subject of the Byzantine Dark Ages, a period from which (contrary to common views) there is a very large amount of surviving literature, even if it is true that it is a type of literature which is usually written off as theological, and stereotyped theology at that. But that is quite another story. Meanwhile what is relevant now is to try to understand to what extent the apparent focus on the person in the early Christian period is actually a matter of texts, and why they lead in such a direction. I would like to suggest that some of the contributions to the collections edited by Vincent Wimbush, and to the two *Semeia* volumes, make this point very clearly.

A final question, then: in what way should we now approach the issue of the holy man? As religious history, as social anthropology, or as a literary project? Are they incompatible? But if not, can they actually be separated, and *should* they be?

3

Ascetics as mediators and as teachers

PHILIP ROUSSEAU

PETER Brown's 'Holy Man' has proved a remarkably durable piece of work. It is still referred to constantly, most often as a whole, as the exposition of an argument or theory: his particular judgements receive less direct attention. The significance of the article is twofold. It set a debate in train: it stood at or near the beginning of a new approach to the history of religion (new also, at the time, to Brown himself). It has subsequently taken on a life of its own: for a long process of intervening criticism has brought it now into the hands of a third generation of readers.

I do not intend to subject the essay to piecemeal scrutiny. I have already commented elsewhere on Brown's use of Theodoret of Cyrrhus (d. c. 466).[1] Theodoret was a bishop, intent upon defending his own authority and that of his episcopal colleagues. There are (in Brown's sense of the word) very few 'patrons' in his *Historia religiosa*. Brown used the term 'patron' in order to identify the holy man's 'function'. He argued that anyone's chance of becoming what he called a 'hinge-man'[2] depended on the extent to which other people in the district had either withdrawn from or been displaced from a patronal role. That withdrawal or displacement, which does seem to have occurred, reflected broader social and political developments that Brown, here at least, was prepared to take for granted.[3] His own use of the term 'patronage' was extended

---

[1] P. Rousseau, 'Eccentrics and Coenobites in the Late Roman East', in Lynda Garland (ed.), *Conformity and Non-Conformity in Byzantium = Byzantinische Forschungen*, 24 (Amsterdam, 1997), 35–50.

[2] 'Holy Man', 118.

[3] For the inexorable drift of the élite, in the East especially, away from local pre-occupation and into the service of the empire, see, in addition to other essays in the collection, P. Heather, 'New Men for New Constantines? Creating an Imperial Élite in the Eastern Mediterranean', in P. Magdalino (ed.), *New Constantines: The Rhythm of Imperial Renewal in Byzantium, 4th–13th Centuries* (Aldershot, 1994), 11–33. Brown made comments on the issue in 'Syria'.

to include any arbiter, any 'strangers' or outsiders, the healing of divisions, the calming of anxieties, the settling of large-scale political disputes. But he did not always provide an explicit account of either the distinctions or the connections involved.

Difficulty is caused also by the way in which Brown associated different areas of the Mediterranean—suggesting without further inquiry that 'holy man' was a universal type. One needs to take note of both the differences and the similarities between, say, Syria and Egypt—geographical, to start with.[4] If we look at a wide body of evidence—the literature connected with the Egyptian pioneer Pachomius (d. 346), the *Apophthegmata patrum* or 'sayings' of the desert fathers, the writings of Jerome in the fourth and early fifth centuries, and of John of Ephesus and Cyril of Scythopolis in the sixth—we find that those regarded as holy men in Egypt, for example, often lived in populous communities, close to village life; some Syrian devotees, on the other hand, could be footloose and remote. If one wished to argue that 'patrons' were normally of the latter sort—'strangers' in Brown's sense—then one would need to demonstrate that ascetics who lived in monasteries, for example, failed to exercise that function. It seems, rather, that holy men interacted with society in both provinces, but differently—a possibility that Brown did not explore with vigour. His distinction between being 'antithetical' and being 'marginal' to village life is not sharp enough to be helpful. Once he begins to make even broader comparisons, some odd contrasts emerge—as, for example, between the Eastern and Western Empires: 'In western Europe, the circle of spiritual power was drawn from a single *locus*. The clergy stood unchallenged, under the awesome shadows of the long-dead heroes of the faith.'[5] Such a judgement fails before a close reading of Gregory of Tours or of Gregory the Great's *Dialogues*. Even when we recognize that both men were bishops, it is clear that they faced too many challengers for comfort.[6]

These are important difficulties; but more fundamental problems are caused by the way Brown handled texts generally. He criticized

---

[4] 'Distinctive in Syria; but . . . not exclusively Syrian' ('Holy Man', 129) is less than thorough. In the later 'Syria', local evidence is still very loosely associated with developments in Egypt and in the Eastern Mediterranean generally.

[5] 'Holy Man', 139. Here we see later work anticipated: *RSS*, *CS*, and *PP*.

[6] I defend these judgements at greater length in my 'Monasticism', in Averil Cameron, B. Ward-Perkins, and M. Whitby (eds.), *The Cambridge Ancient History*, 14 (Cambridge, forthcoming), ch. 26.

historians who 'tended to stress the spectacular occasions on which
the holy man intervened to lighten the lot of the humble and
oppressed';[7] but that was in some ways what he himself proceeded
to do. Not only did he assume, generally, that the holy man had a
'function' (which, from an anthropological point of view, is a prob-
lematically loaded word), but he asserted that behind the 'spectacular occasions', the 'dramatic interventions', as he went on to call
them, there really did lie 'hard, unobtrusive (and so, for us, partly
obscure) work among those who needed constant and unspectacular ministrations'.[8] If we look first and more closely at this term
'function', we observe Brown's wish 'to analyse this image as a
product of the society around the holy man'.[9] Such conjunction of
terminology makes for some complexity: the function is now an
image; the image is a product; and the product springs, as it were,
not from the holy man himself but from those around him. He is
sought out, made use of, defined in others' terms; removed from the
historian's eye by an unusually extended series of intervening ambitions and techniques. As for a declared belief in the unspectacular,
Brown quickly returned to his own more brightly-lit scene, with a
startling methodological assertion:

In studying both the most admired and the most detested figures in any
society, we can see, as seldom through other evidence, the nature of the
average man's expectations and hopes for himself . . . Just as the miracle
demonstrates a hidden, intangible nucleus of power, so the miracle story is
often no more than a pointer to the many more occasions on which the
holy man has already used his position in society. The miracle condenses
and validates a situation built up by more discreet means.[10]

Who, first of all, was the 'average man'? More problematic,
Brown's quotations from the texts appear to provide substance to
the 'occasions' he mentions, to the 'situation'. But the circumstances of the central figure may be a mirage: they themselves
appear only in the texts. We come dangerously close to saying that
a text is sufficient witness to its own background.

'Holy man' marked an important moment in Brown's own devel-
opment, as well as in ours. After his great biography *Augustine of
Hippo* (1967) and his first volume of collected essays *Religion and
Society in the Age of St Augustine* (1977), new adventures were

[7] 'Holy Man', 105.   [8] Ibid., 105-6.   [9] Ibid., 106.
[10] Ibid., 106, 121-2.

called for. Hence the combination of deep immersion and brilliant summary in *The World of Late Antiquity*, where the holy man was also prominent.[11] These new interests and emphases were marked especially by a reference to anthropology—a feature that would do much to determine the axis of Brown's research for a long time.[12]

In these later enterprises, it seems fair to say, some of the shortcomings of 'Holy Man' were allowed to persist.[13] In *The Making of Late Antiquity*, for example, the characteristic components of a work by Brown are vividly laid out—the notion of a shift in the *locus* of the holy in chapter 1 (essentially, from place to person); the holy man's role in the resolution of competitive tensions in chapter 2; the description of what was almost a new class, the 'friends of God', in chapter 3. All those elements would have been familiar to those who attended Brown's Oxford lectures in the 1960s. Chapter 4, on the heroes of Egyptian asceticism, Antony and Pachomius, was obviously intended to be an explanatory or illustrative climax to the argument of the book. Here was the new *locus* of the holy: the mediator, the resolver of disputes. The novelty of the achievement was wholly dependent, for Brown, on the way in which holy men intruded from elsewhere. This idea of the influential outsider had figured in *The World of Late Antiquity* and in Brown's treatment of the 'stranger' in 'The Holy Man'.[14] In the later work, he linked it to 'a dramatic and readily intelligible ritual of social disengagement'.[15]

Brown had begun to draw more consciously, at this point, upon the socio-anthropological notion of 'centre and periphery', familiar in the work of Clifford Geertz and others, and visibly more to the fore in 'The Saint as Exemplar in Late Antiquity'.[16] Even there, however, we still find a belief that one can embroil the holy man himself in 'the world of shared values in which he operated', and uncover in the process 'the abiding mental structures of the

---

[11] *WLA*, 96–112, quick on the heels of 'Holy Man' itself.

[12] In *MLA*, *CS*, *BS*, and now in *PP*.

[13] See my review of *BS*, 'The Development of Christianity in the Roman World: Elaine Pagels and Peter Brown', *Prudentia*, 22.2 (1990), 49–70.

[14] *WLA*, 96 ('the new people'), 101 ('the monk's act of "displacement"'); 'Holy Man', 130–1 ('the holy man was deliberately not human . . . the "stranger" *par excellence*', and 'the burden of difficult or of unpopular decisions comes to rest on the individual who is the "stranger"').

[15] *MLA*, 87.

[16] 'Exemplar', esp. 8–9, 14. The essay represents in part a desire to reassess 'Holy Man', 10–15. See also his reference, n. 90, to Raymond van Dam, 'Hagiography and History: The Life of Gregory Thaumaturgus', *Classical Antiquity*, 1 (1982), 272–308.

Mediterranean villagers'.[17] It is hard at times to understand how this proximity of the withdrawn, this usefulness of the disdained (my phrases, not Brown's) was supposed to work. Brown, in 'The Saint as Exemplar', appealed to 'unspoken bonds of admiration and love', which may or may not have been evident at the time.[18] But it might be more reliable, even if more wry, to appeal to what Averil Cameron, in a different context, has called a 'rhetoric of paradox'. Christians were using, she suggests, what one might have expected them to reject. In particular, they brought the apparent 'simplicity' of the ascetic into line with the ambitions of the literate élite.[19] A similar sensitivity to 'uncertainty', 'ambiguity', and 'paradox', in a similar cause, has inspired Robert Markus's most recent extended study of religious change in the period.[20]

Rhetoric was indeed a central device in the presentation of holiness. Whatever 'distance' from society the holy man may seem to have desired or achieved (in order to re-engage with it on different terms), that distance is located in the texts, and was desired or achieved, therefore, more by their authors, perhaps, than by their subjects. It is always dangerous to take 'reality' for granted. When we are able to discover, in cautious reading, what seem to be genuinely inadvertent records of immediate experience—not calculated, in other words, or burnished with authorial intent—we often have reason to suppose that holy men stood out less vividly against the background of the society they supposedly judged, inspired, or placated.[21] It is not just a matter of identifying the necessary balance between 'accessible exemplars' and '"removed"

---

[17] 'Exemplar', 12, 14.   [18] Ibid., 13.

[19] Averil Cameron, *Christianity and the Rhetoric of Empire: The Development of Christian Discourse*, Sather Classical Lectures 55 (Berkeley and Los Angeles, 1991), 67, 85, 87–8, 123, 139, and the bulk of ch. 5 ('The rhetoric of paradox'), 154–88. This was the 'bridge of shared values' that Brown mentioned in 'Exemplar', 13, acknowledging a debt to Cameron. Compare 'the narrow bridge . . . between town and village' in the more 'patronal' analysis of 'Syria', 158–9.

[20] *End*, ch. 3, esp. 34–6.

[21] In relation to Pachomian, and more generally Egyptian, evidence, I admit to analogous mistakes: see J. Goehring, 'Pachomius' Vision of Heresy: The Development of a Pachomian Tradition', *Muséon*, 95 (1982), 241–62; *The Letter of Ammon and Pachomian Monasticism* (Berlin, 1985); and 'The Origins of Monasticism', in H. W. Attridge and G. Hata (eds.), *Eusebius, Christianity and Judaism* (Leiden, 1992), 235–55. We revert always to the salutary account given by E. A. Judge in 'The Earliest Use of *monachos* for "Monk" (P. Coll. Youtie 77) and the Origins of Monasticism', *Jahrbuch für Antike und Christentum*, 20 (1977), 72–89.

decision-makers', as Brown put it:[22] we face again the problem of textuality itself. Having described for us, in *The Making of Late Antiquity*, 'a danger that we may draw the nets of explanation too tightly around the average inhabitant of the Roman world'—may saddle a whole society, in other words, with one writer's convention or ideal—Brown was happy to focus on 'a limited number of exceptional human agents', as if he could be sure that both the limitation and the exceptionality were more than a writer's conceit.[23]

I want to turn now to the more recent Tanner Lectures, *Authority and the Sacred*, in particular to the third one, 'Arbiters of the Holy: the Christian Holy Man in Late Antiquity'.[24] We should take seriously Brown's admission that he was rather less clear on these matters than he had felt in 1971; but old difficulties continue to interfere. We face again the problematic phrases: 'average Christian believers', and 'holy persons of this kind'. It is not clear whether such persons are thought to lie behind, or beyond, or outside the texts themselves; but, if they do, how can we gain access to them, how can we discern their features and behaviour, except on the terms dictated to us by the authors of the texts? 'Average Christian believers', we are told, would have thought of holy men in just the way that the grand old man Barsanuphius supposedly portrayed his ascetic colleagues in his correspondence. They are, as it happens, surprisingly few in number: Barsanuphius had much more to do with laity and clergymen. But the letters, like all such collections, are in any case tendentious, and subject to editorial and interpretative influence. A miracle-working holy man was, according to Brown, surrounded by 'a whole range of less clearly focussed expectations', and served as 'a validator of practices that were widespread'. 'The holy man's activities, though usually presented, in retrospect, in our sources as dramatic and utterly exceptional were, in reality, no more than a highly visible peak in a spiritual landscape that rose gently upwards from the expectations and activities of ordinary Christians in towns and villages.' It is difficult to know how we might be certain of that. In spite of the phrase 'in reality', the 'spiritual landscape' is also in the text. Indeed, Brown later admitted that it was *the function of the literature* to make things seem less complicated; 'to bring order to a supernatural world shot

---

[22] 'Exemplar', 13.   [23] *MLA*, 4, 12.
[24] For what follows, see *AS*, 58–69, 91.

through with acute ambiguity'. Texts are now behaving in the argument as holy men did in its previous stages. Where are we left, then, when we read that 'holy men themselves were frequently less tidy, in practice, in their choice of explanatory systems than were their biographers, in retrospect'? What evidence is being appealed to? What sudden critical scepticism is being embraced?

Scepticism of some sort is unavoidable. Any judgement on the 'function' of the holy man must take into account the function of the texts. Successful analysis depends on assessing the role configured, not just within the anecdote, but by the very nature of the text itself. It may be that a holy man could have a 'public *persona* as a courtier and a patron'. We may feel able to presume on an author's part some personal engagement with a set of circumstances wherein a person recognized as 'holy' had acted as 'validator' or 'facilitator' (especially 'facilitator in the transition from paganism to Christianity'); had been able to 'negotiate an honourable surrender for the gods'. We might even agree that 'a very large part of their appeal, as facilitators of religious change, lay in the fact that [holy men] were thought to be able to embrace and validate a wide range of potentially exclusive explanatory systems'.[25] Nevertheless, in addition to the uncertainty of an author's access to and use of sources, oral and otherwise, we have to accept that the role of the holy man was being promoted as much as it was recorded, without necessarily a reliable balance being achieved between the two. The difficulty is well illustrated by the ease with which, in the passage just quoted, Brown slipped from 'appeal' [to whom?] through 'thought' [by whom?] to 'explanatory' [for whom?]. Equally deceptive is the statement that holy men 'belonged to a category of persons who were assumed, *by their supplicants,* to have access to knowledge of the holy in all its manifestations'.[26] It was the author who made that assumption—such, at least, is all *we* can assume in the first instance. As Brown himself admitted, we do not know 'how exactly to fit the holy man into the wider picture of the religious world of late antiquity'[27]—in other words, how to fit the holy man *as described by the texts* into the religious world of late antiquity *as conceivable on other evidence.*

Most of our literary evidence about holy men comes from texts that were written by ascetics themselves. The implications have

---

[25] *AS*, 60, 64–5, 69, 73.   [26] Ibid., 69 (italics mine).   [27] Ibid., 59.

been assessed with great astuteness by Évelyne Patlagean[28] and Gilbert Dagron.[29] Patlagean reminded us that hagiography was an élite enterprise. Its use of 'distancing' techniques—what she called *étrangeté*—was designed to make the desert present to the city: for the readers, paradoxically, were transported from the city to the desert. Holy men were drawn in book form into the imaginations of the political class. Readers were thereby liberated ('removed' or 'disengaged', as Brown might have said), to assess in suspended tranquillity symbols and archetypes more clearly defined against a savage world they rarely visited (supposing it was indeed available in such a guise). The dramatic holiness of the 'stranger' could then be superimposed upon more mundane and more immediately accessible exemplars of devotion. Dagron, for his part, suggested that hagiography was produced in the presence of, indeed belligerently in the face of, a possibly widespread scepticism about the 'holiness' of holy men.

In this light, 'function' becomes predominantly the function of the *genre*. Let us take the particular example of miracles—certainly, in some eyes, one of the signs of sanctity. The late Roman miracles that we 'know' about occur in books; and those books, at least for the few who originally could read them, presented miracles with a special force. Augustine understood the issue well: he criticized attachment to miracle for its own sake, the credulity and fascination that could be reflected in naive wonder. When faced with a picture, a scene, a striking event—something visible, in other words—one remained, he felt, no more than a spectator: curiosity was the only available reaction. When faced with the written word, however, genuine understanding was brought into play; and the vital skill was to observe as if one were reading, to engage with the

---

[28] 'Ancienne hagiographie byzantine et histoire sociale', *Annales*, 23 (1968), 106–26; tr. J. Hodgkin, 'Ancient Byzantine Hagiography and Social History', in S. Wilson (ed.), *Saints and their cults* (Cambridge, 1983), 101–21. Brown mentioned Patlagean in 'Holy Man', n. 3, not least as one who brought us closer to 'the average man in the Eastern Empire', 104. See also nn. 11 and (in relation to her other work) 35, 51, 56, and 84.

[29] 'Le saint, le savant, l'astrologue: Étude de thèmes hagiographiques à travers quelques recueils de "Questions et réponses" des Ve–VIIe siècles', in É. Patlagean and P. Riché (eds.), *Hagiographie, Cultures et Sociétés 4e–12e Siècles*, Études Augustiniennes (Paris, 1981), 143–56. The argument is echoed in his 'L'ombre d'un doute: l'hagiographie en question, VI^E–XIE siècle', *Dumbarton Oaks Papers*, 46 (1992), 59–68, and finds felicitous analogies in V. I. J. Flint, *The Rise of Magic in Early Medieval Europe* (Princeton, NJ, 1991).

visible as with a text. Many texts demanded, of course, and their authors expected, a level of inquiry not normally directed at the merely visible. But persons reared on texts—members precisely of the élite that read saints' Lives—might, as 'readers', prove more critical of what they saw around them.[30] Whatever a supposedly charismatic figure might have said or done in the physical presence of a specific audience, any erudite observer would have sensed the limit placed on understanding. When it came to reading, however, the text created a presence of its own, within which understanding found more scope. The deeds or sayings of a holy man became available to independent and reiterated usage; and it was within that framework that holiness acquired its definition and exerted its influence. Brown appears to have accepted that emphasis in his 'Arbiters' lecture: 'The society that turned to Christian holy persons was more niggardly than our hagiographic sources might lead us, at first sight, to suppose, in lavishing credulity upon them'.[31] The evidence for belief itself is not, however, disclosed.

Much of the debate about holy men has revolved around the notion of authority; around the question of who was able to claim leadership and admiration in the late Roman world. That debate continues and, although the results have not always been either tidy or conclusive, we can ask now where further the debate might lead. I am willing, thanks not least to Brown's inspiration and guidance, to focus still on the ascetic community—not as if to suggest that all authority fell into the ascetic lap, but in the belief that ascetics became major contenders for status and influence in the later empire. *Power and Persuasion in Late Antiquity* has brought bishops as protagonists into the same arena, taking account of reactions to *The Body and Society* and reflecting Brown's engagement with the broader issue of Christianization, evident in his splendid paper, 'Dalla "plebs Romana" alla "plebs dei"'.[32] Ascetics and bishops are therefore pitted more clearly against each other; and texts were among their weapons. My own *Ascetics, Authority, and the*

---

[30] Augustine, *In Iohannis Evangelium*, xxiv. 2 (ed. A. Meyer, CCSL 36 (1954), 244–5), with specific reference to *miracula*. For comparable scepticism in Cassian, see my *Ascetics, Authority, and the Church* (Oxford, 1978), 213–4. Flint is astute in her observations, *Rise of Magic*, esp. 46–7, with emphasis on literary transmission.

[31] *AS*, 73.

[32] 'Dalla "plebs Romana" alla "plebs dei": aspetti della cristianizzazione di Roma', in P. Brown, L. C. Ruggini, and M. Mazza (eds.), *Governanti e intellettuali: popolo di Roma e popolo di Dio (I–VI secolo)* (Turin, 1982), 123–45.

Church had fumbled part-way towards that position. The book, however, was too Western, saying little, for example, about Basil or Chrysostom; and its final focus on Cassian was confusing, since I failed to explain why so apparently remote a figure could be the channel for such public influence. I assumed too readily that the impact of ascetic ideals on episcopal practice was best detected in southern Gaul, where monks from Lérins in particular captured the province's most prestigious sees.[33] My attempts to redress the balance have included, I hope, a more sophisticated caution in regard to texts,[34] but have moved me also to acknowledge a degree of integration with society that the texts themselves were sometimes inclined to disguise—an inclination now revealed with further force and clarity by the work of other scholars.[35]

Yet authority—or at least competition for authority—should remain, I think, the focus of our attention. The holy man who sought status—or at least the holy man who was aided in that enterprise by literary admirers—represented the holiness that most endured in its influence and in the detail of its definition. The struggle for leadership was, I believe, engaged in throughout the empire. We need to assess, therefore, the degree of unity in ascetic practice and theory within the Mediterranean world. It is not enough, for example, to take stylites as paradigms, since we know that they were severely limited in their geographical distribution. A less spectacular, a more transportable 'type' of ascetic has to be found, and one who could persistently threaten other types of leader. The central expression of authority within ascetic society was the relationship between masters and disciples. The ascetic was seen above all as a teacher—that was his (or occasionally her) 'function'. Ascetics did not abandon or destroy traditional society: they made their specific contribution to a wide debate—not just about authority but

---

[33] See F. Prinz, *Frühes Mönchtum im Frankenreich* (Munich, 1965), esp. 47–87; S. Pricoco, *L'Isola dei santi* (Rome, 1978); R. Mathisen, *Ecclesiastical Factionalism and Religious Controversy in Fifth-Century Gaul* (Washington, D.C., 1989); Markus, *End.* I tried to redress the balance in my 'Cassian: Monastery and World', in M. Fairburn and W. H. Oliver (eds.), *The Certainty of Doubt: Tributes to Peter Munz* (Wellington, 1996), 68–89.

[34] *Pachomius: The Making of a Community in Fourth-Century Egypt* (Berkeley, CA, 1985); *Basil of Caesarea* (Berkeley, CA, 1994).

[35] Especially that of James Goehring referred to in n. 21 above, to which add now his 'Withdrawing from the Desert: Pachomius and the Development of Village Monasticism in Upper Egypt', *Harvard Theological Review*, 89 (1996), 267–85.

about the appropriate mechanisms of social formation and about those aspects of its own past that gave Christianity its credibility in the debate.

Brown has not followed this line of thought as much as one might have expected. He wrote of 'a redistribution and a reorchestration of components that had already existed for centuries in the Mediterranean world'. But he shied away (at least in this passage, and even in *Power and Persuasion*) from making 'mechanisms of social formation' as full-blooded a component of the process as they deserve to be.[36] Recent work on ascetic women has, among other things, pinpointed the household as an enduring *milieu* within which and out of which new (Christian and feminine) social relations were allowed to develop.[37] One should inquire in tandem about the enduring *milieu* within which and out of which new (Christian and masculine) social relations were allowed to develop. I believe it was the *schola*, the world of the *paidagogos*—the other major instrument of social formation in the Roman world (distinguished, that is, from the *domus*, the household, the realm of the mother). Here was the *milieu* that the Christian ascetic wished to capture, to colonize, to redefine. One is hardly surprised at either the ambition or the success, when one observes how, even in the secular eye, rigorous morality went hand in hand with the right to teach.[38]

One has to give Brown his due. In a passage tucked away at the end of 'Holy Man', he identified a programme that still has a future, although one yet to be explored in full—'a redistribution and a reorchestration of components' with a vengeance.

There was a long-standing uncertainty about the rôle of the father in preserving the traditions of society. The society of the Empire was overtly patri-

---

[36] *MLA*, 8. For further reflections of my own, see 'Cassian: Monastery and World'; 'Christian Culture and the Swine's Husks: Jerome, Augustine, and Paulinus', in M. Vessey and W. E. Klingshirn (eds.), *The Limits of Ancient Christianity* (Ann Arbor, forthcoming); 'Orthodoxy and the Coenobite', in E. A. Livingstone (ed.), *Studia Patristica*, 30 (Leuven, forthcoming), 239–56; 'Antony as Teacher in the Greek *Life*', in T. Hägg and P. Rousseau (eds.), *Greek Biography and Panegyrics in Late Antiquity* (forthcoming). In all these enterprises, I have gained enormously from the advice and encouragement of Kate Cooper and Mark Vessey.

[37] S. Elm, *Virgins of God: The Making of Asceticism in Late Antiquity* (Oxford, 1993); and, deliberately within a broader context, K. Cooper, *The Virgin and the Bride: Idealized Womanhood in Late Antiquity* (Cambridge, Mass., 1996).

[38] *Codex Theodosianus*, ed. T. Mommsen, 2 vols. (Berlin, 1905), vi. 21. 1; xiii. 3. 5–7; and note the analogues to ascetic social structures in xiv. 9. 3.

archal. Respectable provincial families liked to regard their members as so
many avatars of the virtues of their forefathers. Yet in reality the father
remained a distant and awesome figure compared with the true educators.
It was the τροφεύς [*tropheus*] and the ῥήτωρ [*rhetor*], silently but effectively
reinforced by the mother, who passed on the values of society.   .

And he follows with his own question:

Did the definitive rise of the πνευματικὸς πατήρ [*pneumatikos pater*], coinciding as it did with a period when education alone, as opposed to family
traditions, partly decided the recruitment of the governing class of the
Roman world, represent the final sharpening of the old dilemma?[39]

Let us concentrate for the moment on the passing on of values.
In *The Making of Late Antiquity,* Brown presented the *paideia* of
these 'true educators' not only as a feature of traditional Roman
society but of early Christian society as well—espoused as far back
as Justin Martyr. What holy men did, according to Brown, was sup-
plant that inherited *paideia,* not only in its traditional but also in its
Christian form. Later Christian enthusiasts moved from a world of
instruction to a world of initiation—an initiation 'conceived of as
producing men shorn of the complexities of their earthly identity',
who would awaken 'unalloyed loyalty to a high-pitched class of
"friends of God"'.[40] Brown was thinking here of baptism, and of all
the ritual and symbol-driven incorporation that flowed from it. I
believe, however, that sober moralists like Clement of Alexandria
and Lactantius had long set in place another agenda, espousing a
lifelong *disciplina* that would remain alive and well in ascetic circles
from the time of Evagrius and Cassian onwards. It may not have
been a simple, stark alternative to the culture of initiation; but it
maintained the educative values of an older society.

Basil and Augustine, among others, made, of course, their contribution to that development. It no doubt matters that they
presided over initiation and over cult generally; that they were bishops. But the devotees whom they inspired and guided could not dis-
pense with the intense discipline of ascetic formation, any more
than they had dispensed with it themselves. When Brown embraces
more readily, in *Power and Persuasion,* the notion that Christian
leaders continued to lay claim to the role of pedagogue, it is chiefly
bishops he now thinks of. A 'wild man of the Syrian hilltops' can

[39] 'Holy Man', 149–50.   [40] *MLA*, 73–7.

be presented as an oddity, even among the new 'philosophers' that brought to *paideia* 'a heavy charge of novel meaning'.[41] Brown promises to describe jointly 'the emergent Christian culture of the bishops and the monks', marked by a 'change in "theatrical style"'.[42] But in the end the monks, even in the texts of their literate admirers, become 'a warning signal'; they 'broke the spell of *paideia*'.[43] Those 'poised to take over the high ground of Roman society'[44] were not the rough heroes of the *vitae*, but the clerical and well-born peers of those who wrote about them.

An earlier and stimulating addition to the debate, acknowledged by Brown, was Rita Lizzi's *Potere episcopale*. She shows how, while monks challenged philosophers, bishops also challenged monks—both challenges articulated in the presence of the 'people'.[45] Challenging philosophers brings to mind famous incidents in the *Life of Antony*.[46] Antony makes no apology for a claim to instruct, and in that sense meets the philosophers on equal terms. Samuel Rubenson's work on the *Letters* of Antony corroborates the impression of a self-confident *paidagogos*.[47] There are, in the Life, few signs of deference to others claiming such authority, Christian or otherwise; but not because the role itself is disdained. Antony (like Pachomius) is not only cautious in his regard for the clergy but also intent upon the protection and development of a group of disciples. He operates in a setting where several types of teacher bid for status. There is no reason why we should think of this as an isolated example of ascetic aspiration.[48]

We come close, then, to identifying our future task. Here is a story, I believe, that can be written large. We are talking about a new *kind* of teacher and a new *kind* of *paideia*. The soil has been prepared by, among others, Averil Cameron, Richard Lim, and

---

[41] *PP*, 3. [42] Ibid., 34; and see 105-6.
[43] Ibid., 72-3; and see 94. [44] Ibid., 76.

[45] R. Lizzi, *Il potere episcopale nell' oriente romano: rappresentazionne ideologica e realtà politica (IV-V sec. d. C.)* (Rome, 1987), 16-17, 21, 40, 46-7.

[46] Mentioned by Brown, *PP*, 71 and above by Averil Cameron (see her n. 43).

[47] *The Letters of St Antony: Monasticism and the Making of a Saint*, 2nd edn. (Minneapolis, 1995).

[48] See Eusebius's account of 'village teachers' in *Historia Ecclesiastica*, vii. 24. 6-9 (ed. G. Bardy, *Eusèbe de Césarée: Histoire Ecclésiastique*, vol. 2, SC 41 (1955), 203-4), and my *Pachomius*, 59, 161-2. The 'philosophers' who disputed with Antony may have been pagans, but they could equally have been Gnostic or Melitian or even marginally orthodox Christians. The issues are developed further in my 'Orthodoxy and the Coenobite' and 'Antony as Teacher'.

Robert Kaster.[49] The characteristics of the new 'formative programme', as put into effect *by ascetics,* were, first, as firm a dependence on the Bible as that of any bishop. We make too strict a
distinction, in this regard, between the catechesis of a spiritual master like Pachomius and the homily of a Basil or an Ambrose.
Second, there was, within the imparted message, a tension between
the vertical and the horizontal, between the inspirational and the
inherited, between insight and technique. This is akin, but not identical, to Brown's assessment in *The Making of Late Antiquity,* where
the ' "vertical" imagery' referred to 'closeness to a "heavenly"
source of power', while ' "horizontal" imagery' referred to the 'ritual of social disengagement' (that is, *anachoresis*).[50] More apposite
is a comparison with the Latin panegyrics, in which we find an
appeal to contact with the divine but also, horizontally, with tradition—with both the traditional content of cultural formation and
the traditional providers of it. There was, third, in the terms advocated by Rita Lizzi, a degree of opposition to the episcopate and to
the 'sacramental economy' in general (the sphere, precisely, of 'initiation'). The point is well expressed by David Brakke in his book on
Athanasius:

The conflict was between two parties: on the one hand, the episcopate,
which was centred around the practices of worship and dealt with conflicts
juridically as questions of admission to the cult; on the other hand, the
school, which was centred around the personalities of outstanding teachers and dealt with conflicts scholastically as questions of intellectual speculation and disagreement.[51]

One is led to imply also, therefore, that, just as bishops affected the
quality of asceticism by giving approved and privileged status to, for
example, veiled virgins, so they gave their own twist to *paideia,*
attempting to exclude the *scienter nescius* who recurs more and
more in ascetic literature.

The 'ignorance' of such ascetics, as is clear in the case of Antony,
has to be seen as at once an argumentative ploy and a literary con-

---

[49] Cameron, *Rhetoric of Empire*; R. Lim, *Public Disputation, Power, and Social Order
in Late Antiquity* (Berkeley, CA, 1995); R. A. Kaster, *Guardians of Language: The
Grammarian and Society in Late Antiquity* (Berkeley, CA, 1988).

[50] *MLA*, 86–7.

[51] *Athanasius and the Politics of Asceticism* (Oxford, 1995), 59. See also L. C.
Ruggini, 'Imperatori romani e uomini divini (I–VI secolo d. C)' in *Governanti e intellettuali,* 23, concerning the 'grandezza dell' uomo di dio sopra i vescovi più celebri'.

ceit. The agenda for scholars now, as for Christians then, is to distinguish adequately between the episcopal programme of homily and sacrament and the ascetic programme of wisdom, dialogue, and moral effort. Their concurrent rivalry would have been readily recognizable to any pagan. That suggests that the 'functions' were old: it was the guise, the opportunity, the emphasis that changed.[52]

[52] The longer-term context is more specifically illustrated by J. Hahn, *Der Philosoph und die Gesellschaft: Selbstverständnis, offentliches Auftreten und populäre Erwartungen in der höhen Kaiserzeit* (Stuttgart, 1989); and U. Neymeyr, *Die christlichen Lehrer im zweiten Jahrhundert: ihre Lehrtätigkeit, ihr Selbstverständnis und ihre Geschichte* (Leiden, 1989).

PART II
The cult of saints in Eastern Christendom

4

'For next to God, you are my salvation': reflections on the rise of the holy man in late antiquity

CLAUDIA RAPP

THIS article is an experiment. It aims to propose a new view of holy men in late antiquity and their literary descriptions in the sources. 'Hagiography' is not a genre, I shall propose. The predominant attention to saints' Lives and other literary works written after their death has coloured our understanding of the role of the holy man within his social context. A new explanation of the function of the holy man can be achieved by the study of non-literary documents produced during their lifetime. I will examine the letters addressed to or written by holy men in the fourth and sixth centuries which reveal them in the roles of intercessor and spiritual father of a prayer community. In conclusion, I shall argue that the relation between spiritual leaders and their followers spills over to the textual level in the preference given to specific forms of hagiographical writing.[1]

Holy men emerged from the end of the third century, in the context of the growing monastic movement in Egypt, Palestine, and Syria. Men and women searching for spiritual perfection abandoned their normal life to pursue a regimen of renunciation, asceticism, prayer, and contemplation. Their contemporary

---

[1] This article would not have been written if not for the congenial surroundings of the Institute for Advanced Study in Princeton where I had the good fortune to spend the year of 1997-8. It would not have been conceived had not Richard Mowrer directed my attention to the importance of intercessory prayer in a seminar paper entitled 'Medicus et Patronus. The Expansion of Intercessory Functions in Late Antiquity' which he subsequently presented at the First UCLA Graduate Student's Conference in Late Antiquity, 18 May 1996. And it would not appear in its present form if I had not benefited from the advice, stylistic and otherwise, of Joshua Landis. Last but not least, I am especially grateful to Peter Brown, Glen Bowersock, and Graeme Clark for their incisive comments on the first draft of this article.

admirers sought to record the deeds of these 'athletes of Christ'. In doing so, they left us a rich body of texts that employ a great variety of literary forms. Evidence for this diversity are the aphorisms of Egyptian hermits assembled in the *Sayings of the Desert Fathers*; Evagrius Ponticus' *Praktikos*, a 'how-to' guide by a prominent practitioner of the contemplative life; the anecdotes in the *Spiritual Meadow*, collected by John Moschus and Sophronius in the course of their extended visits to the holy men and women of Egypt, Palestine, and Syria; and the biographical collections of selected highlights in the life of holy men and women in Theodoret's *History of the Monks of Syria*. The most detailed texts are the full-length biographies or *Vitae* in which the hagiographer presents the sequence of events in the life of a holy man from his birth to his death, the pioneering example being the *Life of Anthony*. In contrast to the biographical descriptions of living holy men, the subject of a *Vita* is dead, his sanctity demonstrated over the complete course of his life and proved by posthumous miracles. Though all these different works are conventionally labelled 'hagiography', or subsumed under the 'genre of hagiography', it is more accurate to call them monastic literature. Most of the men and women described in these works were merely ascetics who attracted numerous admirers and followers. They often did not work miracles, the *conditio sine qua non* of sainthood.

Scholars have tended to devote most attention to saints' Lives and, as a consequence, have posited the existence of a 'genre of hagiography' despite the variety of late antique literary formats in which the various aspects of the quest of pious men and women for the holy life are related. The label misleads since it presupposes that hagiographical writing follows a specific set of rules, such as typically defined the composition of particular genres in classical and late antiquity. For example, Menander Rhetor provided a set of guidelines for the composition of panegyrical speeches which prescribed what subject material was appropriate, how it was to be arranged, and in what style it was to be presented. Aspiring rhetoricians used these rules as the stock-in-trade of their training. No such guidelines were ever formulated for writing about saints. In fact, it is the subject matter alone that defines what we call 'hagiography', and not the manner of its literary representation which could take a variety of literary forms—most prominently, the *Vita*, the *miraculum*, or, as we shall see below, the letter. In the stricter

sense, hagiography is not a 'genre'.[2] Still, it did have conventions—
such as stock phrases and oft-repeated miracle stories—that developed over time, as more and more texts were added to the corpus
of saints' Lives, each continuing and often subtly manipulating the
established tradition of hagiographical writing.

The prevailing attention to saints' Lives has skewed our understanding of the interaction between holy men and their followers.
The purpose of a saint's Life is to glorify a particular individual by
claiming his status as a saint. There is no better way to exalt the reputation of a holy man than by a lively recounting of his miracles.
Such stories affirm that the saint enjoyed a special God-given grace
already during his lifetime; also, they announce that this grace is
available to those who turn to him in prayer even after his death and
especially to those who seek him out at his shrine. The *Life of Symeon
the Stylite*, for example, relishes the description of the hundreds of
men and women, Christian and non-Christian, who flocked to the
saint's column from the four corners of the world in the hope of having their ailments healed, their poverty alleviated, or their travails
eased. Miracles and the miraculous dominate the biographies of
saints and shape our perception of the interaction between saints and
their followers, suggesting that it was the grateful adulation of their
beneficiaries that turned the holy man into a cult figure. This model
defines the miracle as primary 'commodity' which the holy man dis-
penses to others. They become his clients and their loyalty and devotion then raise his status to that of recognized sainthood. They
depend on him as a *patronus* and an arbiter. This is the model put
forward by Peter Brown in his seminal article on 'The Rise and
Function of the Holy Man in Late Antiquity'. It broke new ground by
placing this phenomenon in the context of social and economic conditions in fourth- and fifth-century Syria. For the purpose of the present argument, it is worth noting that this article relies heavily on
biographical sources, especially the *Life of Symeon the Stylite* and the
History of the Monks of Syria by Theodoret of Cyrrhus.[3]

---

[2] This much was already emphasized by M. van Uytfanghe, 'Heiligenverehrung',
in T. Klauser *et al.* (ed.), *Reallexikon für Antike und Christentum* (Stuttgart, 1950-),
xiv, 150-83, and idem, 'L'hagiographie: un "genre" chrétien ou antique tardif?', *AB*
111 (1993), 135-88.

[3] Brown, 'Holy Man'. In this article, Peter Brown also shows his awareness of
two of the sources that form the backbone of my study, the Paphnutius papyri (see
ibid., 82 n. 17) and the correspondence of Barsanuphius and John which was just
then being published (ibid., 98 n. 229).

Peter Brown has continued to revise his model of the interaction between the holy man and his followers—the mark of a true scholar. In several works since 1983, he has developed the notion of the holy man as 'exemplar': as a 'role model' whose own spiritual perfection is reflected in his exceptional personal conduct. He attracts not so much a clientele, but disciples and admirers who wish to imitate and emulate him. His role is thus comparable to that of the late antique philosopher. The formulation of this model draws heavily on additional evidence from philosophical and theological treatises.[4] Most recently, Peter Brown has introduced the concept of the 'arbiter of the holy' who combines the social role of the *patronus* with the propaedeutic role of the exemplar, but whose reach extends beyond a merely Christian following. As a mediator of the divine, he represents Christianity in its most palpable form to a local population that is still largely pagan and thus paves the way for the Christianization of the later Roman Empire. In this study, Brown made use of a vast number of historical, hagiographical, and religious sources—including the *Letters of Barsanuphius and John* which will concern us again here.[5]

I shall propose a further model, that of the holy man as intercessor. Rather than replacing the two main Brownian models of the holy man as *patronus* and exemplar, this model intersects with them. The power of the holy man as intercessor depends on the perceived efficacy of his prayer. His prayers are mostly for the general well-being of those who are in contact with him and rarely produce miraculous healings. The prayers of the holy man as intercessor are thus broader in scope than the prayers of the holy man as *patronus* which result in spectacular miracles of healing, of famine-relief or of social restoration. If a holy man's prayers are heard, this signals divine approval of his quest for spiritual perfection. His conduct invites admiration and emulation, and in this regard the model of the holy man as intercessor overlaps with that of the holy man as exemplar. Yet, the follower of the holy man as intercessor is different from the client who depends on the holy man as *patronus* or the disciple who emulates the holy man as exemplar. The saint as intercessor is at the centre of a prayer community of men and women who repay his favour by offering prayers on his behalf. The social ties within this group are conceptualized in terms of kinship—the community constituting, as it were, a 'spiritual family'.

---

[4] Brown, 'Exemplar'.   [5] Brown, *AS*, 60 ff.

This is, in a nutshell, the model I propose in the following. It is formulated by deliberately avoiding hagiographical sources, concentrating instead on the correspondence of living holy men. I will consider a number of papyrus letters from Egypt from the mid-fourth and the late sixth centuries and the extensive letter collection of the sixth-century hermits Barsanuphius and John of Gaza. Revealing the direct and largely unadulterated voice of the holy men and their correspondents, these letters provide a corrective to the literary creations of hagiographers. They remind us that the day-to-day interactions between the holy man and his followers were centred on prayer and not the more spectacular miracles that were so artfully depicted by later hagiographers.

This exclusive focus on epistolography is also instructive as an exercise in historical methodology. Different kinds of source materials produce very different impressions. The greater the range of sources employed, the more comprehensive and accurate we can hope our reconstructions of the past to be. James Goehring has advocated the study of papyri as a corrective for the ' "big bang" theory of monastic origins' generated by the literary works of late antique authors.[6] In much the same way, the letter collections provide an alternative view to the picture of the saint that is propagated in the hagiographical literature.

Paphnutius was an Egyptian in the mid-fourth century, known to us by the eight surviving letters addressed to him by such varied correspondents as the laywoman Valeria, the Prefect of Augustamnica, Ausonius, and perhaps the Patriarch Athanasius.[7] Paphnutius was linked to his correspondents through the force of prayer. Most letters

[6] G. E. Goehring, 'The Origins of Monasticism', in H. W. Attridge and G. Hata (eds.), *Eusebius, Christianity and Judaism* (Leiden, 1992), 235–55, at 235. For his advocacy of the importance of non-literary sources, see also idem, 'Through a Glass Darkly: Diverse Images of the *Apotaktikoi(ai)* of Early Egyptian Monasticism', *Semeia*, 58 (1992), 25–45.

[7] Ed. and tr. H. I. Bell, *Jews and Christians in Egypt* (London, 1924), nos. 1923–9 (pp. 100–20, and cited hereafter as 'PJews'). To this group should perhaps be added the letter by Justinus to Paphnutius, ed. A. Deissmann, *Die Septuaginta-Papyri und andere altchristliche Texte der Heidelberger Papyrus-Sammlung* (Heidelberg, 1905), no. 6 (cited hereafter as 'PHeid I (1905)'), and also reproduced in M. Naldini, *Il Cristianesimo in Egitto: Lettere private nei papiri dei secoli II–IV* (Florence, 1968), no. 41 (hereafter 'Naldini'). For Valeria, see PJews, 1926; for Ausonius, PJews, 1924, with Bell, p. 100; and for Athanasius, PJews, 1929, with Bell, pp. 115–18.

include a general and formulaic request for Paphnutius' prayers—a request common in late antique epistolography.[8] In a few letters, the correspondents volunteer their own prayers for Paphnutius' health in the hope that his longevity will be to their benefit.[9] The official Ausonius, for example, writes: 'May God preserve you in health and in prayer on our behalf, beloved father.'[10] More significant than these requests for prayer in general are those for Paphnutius' intercession on behalf of the sins of his correspondents. Ammonius writes: 'I always know that by your holy prayers I shall be saved from every temptation of the Devil and from every contrivance of men, and now I beg you to remember me in your holy prayers; for after God you are my salvation.'[11] Some correspondents request Paphnutius' prayer to obtain healing from an illness and at the same time express their faith in the efficacy of his prayers. Athanasius, who may be identical with the Patriarch of Alexandria, states: 'for the prayers which you offer are taken on high owing to your holy love, and according as you ask in your holy prayers so will our state prosper.'[12] No mention of miracles is made in the letters to Paphnutius. Prayer is the glue which binds the holy man to his followers.

The followers considered themselves tied to Paphnutius in ways that mirror kinship relations. Although they usually address him as 'father' or, more colloquially, as '*apa*', the application of kinship terms and the hierarchical relations they imply shows some variation. Pianius, for example, addresses his letter to 'my beloved brother Paphnutius', but then switches to 'Apa Paphnutius' and finally concludes by calling him 'my most desired lord'.[13] Several letters also reveal that Paphnutius seems to have nurtured an inner circle of disciples around him who were considered his 'brothers'. Pianius conveys his greetings to 'all the brethren who are with your holiness', while Heracleides declares that no 'brother' can save him from his current affliction except Paphnutius.[14]

---

[8] PJews, 1924–5, 1927, 1929. On requests for or assurances of prayer as epistolographic conventions, see H. Koskenniemi, *Studien zur Geschichte und Phraseologie des griechischen Briefes bis 400 n. Chr.* (Helsinki, 1956), 134–7 and 147–8.

[9] PJews, 1923–6, 1928–9. [10] PJews, 1924. My translation.

[11] PJews, 1923. Similarly, PJews, 1925 and PHeid I (1905), 6 = Naldini, 41.

[12] Letter by Athanasius: PJews, 1929. See also PJews, 1926, 1928.

[13] PJews, 1925. Compare the letter by Justinus, PHeid I (1905), 6 = Naldini, 41. Dorotheus of Oxyrhynchus also addresses him as 'most valued brother': PJews, 1927.

[14] Letter by Pianius: PJews, 1925; letter by Heracleides: PJews, 1928. Cf. PJews, 1923 (mention of 'our brother Didymos'), PJews, 1927, and PHeid I (1905), 6 = Naldini, 41.

Paphnutius' role as a 'father' and intercessor was based on his reputation for leading a pious lifestyle. Paphnutius' personal conduct lent particular force to his prayers which were coveted, and often reciprocated, by those who were in contact with him. Justinus probably expresses the sentiment of all of Paphnutius' 'children' when he writes: 'for we believe that your citizenship is in heaven, and therefore we regard you as our master and common patron.'[15] Valeria, who calls herself Paphnutius' 'daughter', addresses him as 'bearer of Christ' and then declares: 'I trust by your prayers to obtain healing, for by ascetics and devotees revelations are manifested.'[16] Another correspondent is confident that he can depend upon him 'by reason of your most glorious and most revered way of life, since you renounced the boasting of the world and abhorred the arrogance of the vainglorious. . . . because God in abundant measure, it seems, granted you favour to find a fitting and salutary renunciation accordant with the times'.[17] Recognized by his contemporaries for his personal conduct, sought after by his correspondents for his prayers, surrounded by men and women who formed part of his spiritual family, Paphnutius is our first example of the holy man as intercessor.

Nepheros, a monastic leader and priest in the Herakleopolite nome of Egypt, provides the second example of a holy man who occupied a position of fatherhood at the centre of a spiritual family. The Nepheros archive consists of forty-two papyri, written mostly in Greek, although some are in Coptic.[18] Sixteen of these papyri are letters to Nepheros in which, like Paphnutius, he is addressed variously as 'father', 'brother', 'lord', and 'master'. The followers of Nepheros included many pious laymen and laywomen, most prominently Paulos, the author of the first nine letters to the holy man, along with his wife Tapiam and their children. This extended 'spiritual family' attached to Nepheros formed something resembling a business association, as the many additional letters that contain references to joint economic enterprises attest. Some letters include

---

[15] PHeid I (1905), 6 = Naldini 41 (my translation). The text is uncertain. Deissmann and Naldini prefer the reading κενὸν ⟨π⟩άτρωνα assuming that the correct spelling of κενὸν is καινὸν, 'new'. In my view, the correct spelling (considered unlikely by Deissmann, p. 98) should be κοινὸν, 'common', highlighting Paphnutius' role within his group of monastics.

[16] PJews, 1926.   [17] PJews, 1927.

[18] *Das Archiv des Nepheros und verwandte Texte*, ed. B. Kramer, J. C. Shelton, and G. M. Browne (Mainz, 1987), 3—which edition is cited in what follows.

Nepheros' name alongside other addressees, while others make reference to the existence of further 'brothers'. Similar to Paphnutius, Nepheros must thus have held the position of a 'father of monks' under whose guidance a loosely connected network of monks lived individually or in groups of two or three. This clustering of smaller groups of two or more individuals represents an intermediary form of monastic arrangement (*Zwischenstufe*) that coexisted with eremiticism of the Antonian type and cenobiticism according to the Pachomian model. Jerome and Cassian inveighed against it, probably because they were suspicious of the all-important role of the spiritual father in such an association of brothers.[19]

The power of prayer figures less prominently in the Nepheros papyri than in the letters to Paphnutius. The papyri usually convey a mundane message relating to travel arrangements or the production, transport, and sale of foodstuffs and other goods.[20] They often conclude with the promise of the correspondents to pray for the holy man and his health, but this is a common greeting formula.[21] Only three letters ask Nepheros to intercede for a specific goal. The first of these relies on his prayer to alleviate an illness,[22] the second asks for his prayer for the safe return home of the writer and his children,[23] and the third requests his intercession to ensure that 'in the end we shall be restored to our home', an obscure reference either to a concrete destination or to the eternal resting place.[24] Nonetheless, Nepheros must have enjoyed a reputation as a proven worker of miracles since two of his correspondents point out the efficacy of his prayers on previous occasions.[25] But he was not always singled out for his intercessory powers. Four further letters ask not for the prayers of Nepheros alone, but also for those of the other 'brothers' around him—a reference to the members of his wider monastic 'family'.[26] The spiritual roots of Nepheros' position are not

---

[19] *Das Archiv des Nepheros und verwandte Texte*, ed. B. Kramer, J. C. Shelton, and G. M. Browne (Mainz, 1987), 3, 10 and 19–20. Jerome, *Ep.* 22.34 (ed. I. Hilberg, *CSEL* 54–56 (1910–18), i, 196–7); Cassian, *Conlationes*, xviii.4.2–3 (ed. M. Petschenig, *CSEL* 13 (1886), 509). Cf. ibid., xviii.7.1–7 (513–16). Cassian also seems to have been troubled by the business acumen of these small monastic groups.

[20] Nepheros, *Epp.* nos. 1–9, 11–12.   [21] Ibid., 1, 2, 4, 5, 7, 9, 10, 12, 13.

[22] Ibid., 1.   [23] Ibid., 4.   [24] Ibid., 10.

[25] Ibid., 1, addressed to 'Nepheros, Ophellios and the others', explains that 'your [pl.] prayers' have already once before brought healing to the author's children. *Ep.* 10 asserts: 'for I know that as long as you remember me in your prayers, the Lord God will not abandon me'.

[26] Ibid., 5, 9, 11, 12.

brought up at all, except for a fleeting reference to his being 'just' as a guarantee that his prayers will be heard by God.[27] Although the papyri of the Nepheros archive provide less insight into his spiritual and intercessory role than the letters to Paphnutius, they offer additional evidence for the existence of loosely structured communities of monastic 'brothers' and lay people under the leadership of a spiritual father who were engaged in praying on each others' behalf.

Another 'spiritual family' was centred around the hermit John. He lived during the fourth century in the region of Hermopolis. We have only three letters written to him, and one by him.[28] These letters illustrate the several roles which an *apa*, a spiritual father, was expected to perform. The first letter asks John for assistance in the mundane matter of securing a release from military duty because of the author's disability.[29] Of greatest significance in illuminating John's position of spiritual leadership is the second letter. It consists entirely of a request for John's prayers on behalf of the author and his whole household. The author calls John a 'man of God' and expresses his hope that just as John's prayers have relieved him in the past of a great burden—either an onerous labour or an illness[30]—they will continue to do so in the future.[31] He ends his letter by conveying his regards to 'all the brethren who labour with you', a reference to an inner circle of fellow monastics around John. The existence of such fellow monastics is confirmed by the third letter, written by Chairemon, which combines a request for prayer with greetings to the 'beloved [brothers] and those who love the word of my Lord God in the faith'. This letter also attests to the fluidity of kinship designations, for John is addressed as 'master', 'father', and 'brother'.[32] The fourth and very fragmentary letter is written by John and others who jointly ask a close acquaintance to intervene in a judicial proceeding.[33] This group of letters shows John in a similar position to Paphnutius and Nepheros: he is surrounded by an inner circle of monastic 'brothers' while his

[27] Ibid., I.
[28] Ed. and tr. B. R. Rees, *Papyri from Hermopolis* (London, 1964), nos. 7–10 (pp. 12–20, cited hereafter as 'PHerm.'); also reproduced in Naldini, nos. 82–5.
[29] PHerm., 7 = Naldini, 82.
[30] For the translation of τοῦ κ[α]μάτου as 'illness', see *Nepheros Archiv*, 22 n. I.
[31] PHerm., 8 = Naldini, 83.
[32] PHerm., 9 = Naldini, 84. Naldini's punctuation is followed here.
[33] PHerm., 10 = Naldini, 85.

correspondents are men of the world who depend on him, not merely for his intercession, but also for his assistance in mundane matters.

The fourth and last Egyptian example are the several hundred papyri and ostraka on limestone and pottery shards from the turn of the seventh century which were found at the monastery of Epiphanius at Thebes.[34] They document the existence of a thriving spiritual family centred around several holy men, among whom Epiphanius was the most prominent. The authors of these brief messages to Epiphanius and the other holy men usually address them as 'father' and include prayer requests of the formulaic kind. On many occasions, though, the letter-writers have more concrete concerns. They either ask the 'fathers' for help from the torment of their sins,[35] or hope to obtain more concrete benefits such as the restoration of health in sickness.[36] The men and women who approach Epiphanius and his fellows are emphatic and explicit in their belief that these men are holy and possess the power of intercession. They are convinced that the exemplary ascetic lifestyle of these holy men assures their prayers being heard by God. Acknowledging these men's privileged connection to the divine, they often praise them for having perfected all virtues[37] and address them as 'bearer of Christ'.[38] It is only through the mediation and intercession of these holy men that these letter-writers hope for access to God. The extent to which the supplicants depend on the holy men is expressed in terms such as these: 'I have set my heart upon thy fatherhood next after God'; 'I have no helper beside God and thee.'[39]

The Egyptian papyri and ostraka demonstrate the importance of holy men as intercessors and spiritual fathers of loosely-knit monastic 'families'. This pattern is further corroborated by the *Letters of Barsanuphius and John*. In this instance, the holy men are the authors, not the recipients, of the letters. Barsanuphius established himself as a hermit at Tawatha, near Gaza on the coast of Palestine, sometime during the first two decades of the sixth century. Around

---

[34] Ed. W. E. Crum and H. G. Evelyn White, *The Monastery of Epiphanius at Thebes*, pt. ii (New York, 1926; repr. 1973). For the historical context of this monastic institution, see pt. i, H. E. Winlock, *The Archaeological Material* (New York, 1926, repr. 1973).

[35] e.g. *Epp.* nos. 129, 199, and 279.   [36] Ibid., 144, 246, 250, 329, 359.

[37] Ibid., 130, 164, 184, 319, 359, 473, 483.

[38] Ibid., 133, 142, 144, 180, 261, 306, 315, 474, 515.

[39] Ibid., 192 and 271.

525, he was joined by John, known as 'the Prophet', who became his disciple and adopted the same lifestyle. They both enjoyed a reputation as holy men despite their refusal to interact face-to-face with anyone, whether monastic brothers, disciples, or visitors. Instead, they communicated through letters, which they dictated in response to the queries and requests addressed to them.[40] These letters, 850 in total, are a fascinating repository of the spiritual wisdom which they shared with monks, priests, and bishops, as well as pious laymen, philosophy professors, and military leaders. In addition, they also dispensed advice on such mundane matters as the proper way of eliminating an infestation of grasshoppers without angering one's neighbours.[41] Barsanuphius' and John's interaction with their correspondents shows how spiritual guidance, personal holiness, and the creation of ties of spiritual kinship are interconnected.[42]

Barsanuphius maintained an extensive correspondence with his disciple John of Beersheba.[43] As the older and more experienced of the two, Barsanuphius assumed the role of guide and teacher in writing forty-nine extant letters of support, encouragement, and instruction to his younger *confrère*. Their association was sealed by a significant gift. With his first letter, Barsanuphius sent his *koukoullion* to John, instructing him to keep the garment until death and not to pass it on to anyone else. This 'gift of God you are receiving from my hands', Barsanuphius explained, was to protect John

---

[40] Tr. into French by L. Regnault, Ph. Lemaire, and B. Outtier, *Barsanuphe et Jean de Gaza, Correspondance* (Solesmes, 1971). Jennifer Hevelone-Harper (Princeton University) is currently preparing her dissertation on spiritual guidance in late antique Palestine, based largely on the letters of Barsanuphius and John. I am very grateful to her for making accessible to me a copy of the complete Greek edition by Nikodemos Hagioreites, $Βίβλος$ $ψυχωφελεστάτη$ . . . $Βαρσανουφίου$ $καὶ$ $Ἰωάννου$, ed. S. Schoinas (Volos, 1960). D. J. Chitty's edition of letters 1–214, *Barsanuphius and John, Questions and Answers*, PO 31/3 (1966), has now been superseded by a new edition of letters 1–223 by F. Neyt and P. De Angelis-Noah which incorporates the revised translation of L. Regnault: *Barsanuphe et Jean de Gaza, Correspondance*, SC 426–7 (1977–8).

[41] *Ep.* 684.

[42] There is an extensive literature on spiritual guidance and 'fatherhood', of which I. Hausherr, *Spiritual Direction in the Early Christian East*, tr. A. P. Gythiel, CStud. 116 (1990), and A. Louf, 'Spiritual Fatherhood in the Literature of the Desert', in J. R. Sommerfeldt (ed.), *Abba: Guides to Wholeness and Holiness East and West*, CStud. 38 (1982), deserve special mention.

[43] He cannot be identical with John the Prophet, the author of many letters in the collection, since both are mentioned in *Epp.* 3 and 9.

against evil and temptations.[44] It served as a precious token of their bond and as a reminder of Barsanuphius' personal care for his disciple. They were linked by ties of intense friendship: Barsanuphius carried John in his heart and in his soul, their relation was marked by 'love'; they were of 'one spirit'.[45] Their association extends beyond death: their lives, Barsanuphius asserts, are joined for ever and they will be together as 'brothers' even in the life to come.[46] In their exchange of letters, both employ the kinship designations appropriate to their relative status: John addresses Barsanuphius respectfully as his 'father', while Barsanuphius acknowledges that John has joined him in the spiritual quest by calling him a 'brother'.

Barsanuphius did not shirk from the tremendous responsibility which his position as John's spiritual guide entailed. On the contrary, he was rather outspoken in affirming this role. John should regard him as a role model and, held by his hand, follow in his footsteps.[47] He regarded his letters as instruments in shaping his disciple's spiritual progress. Barsanuphius' last letter in the sequence reads like a graduation speech. He affirmed that, through his letters, he has given John a complete course of instruction, from the noviciate to perfection. John should meditate on his words as a means to his personal salvation, for they contain 'the Old and the New Testament'.[48] In other words, Barsanuphius was fully aware that he is the channel through which the divine *logos* is communicated to John.

Barsanuphius also maintained fraternal relationships with other fellow-monks, including Euthymius and Andrew. While the teacher–disciple dynamic was prevalent in Barsanuphius' relationship with John, his contact with Euthymius was dominated by affirmations of a close bond of brotherhood.[49] Barsanuphius sent his scapular as a token to Euthymius, as he had done with John.[50] The continuation of their fraternal ties after death, which Barsanuphius had promised to John in general terms, here takes much more concrete form: Euthymius expected to be buried in the same tomb as Barsanuphius. He was confident that, on the Day of Judgement, the Old Man's abundant good deeds would also be counted in his own

---

[44] *Ep.* 1. Cf. ibid., 44 and 47, for the sending of such 'gifts' as a gesture of encouragement.
[45] Ibid., 13, 16, 27-8, 36.   [46] Ibid., 6, 7.   [47] Ibid., 22, 31.
[48] Ibid., 49.   [49] Ibid., 59-71.   [50] Ibid., 71.

favour.[51] In other words, Barsanuphius' virtues make up for any deficiencies on the part of his brother Euthymius.

A further fifty-one letters of correspondence between Andrew and the two Old Men—that is, Barsanuphius and John the Prophet—highlight Barsanuphius' ability to convey the certainty of God's forgiveness of sins and his willingness to shoulder part of his brothers' sins.[52] Andrew was a complainer. Plagued by a chronic illness and irritated by the 'brother' who lived with him, he was anxious about his inability to fast, troubled by his unkind thoughts towards his companion, and concerned about these impediments to his spiritual progress. Barsanuphius sent him numerous letters of assurance, promising his prayers, invoking their spiritual unity, and expressing his desire to take Andrew to heaven with him.[53] Similar to Euthymius, who hoped to benefit from the abundance of Barsanuphius' good deeds on the Day of Judgement, Andrew could depend on the Old Man's pledge to carry half of his burden.[54] But Andrew was not to remain passive. He was expected to bear the full weight of the remaining share. Also, Barsanuphius was in the habit of concluding his letters to Andrew by asking him for his prayers. Andrew's supplications did not, however, measure up to the power of Barsanuphius' intercessory prayers. The Old Man asserted that his prayers would sustain Andrew in times of tribulation.[55] He even had the confidence to announce that, through him, Christ had assured Andrew of the complete remission of all his sins from the time of his birth to the present.[56] Barsanuphius' letters to Andrew thus confirm the existence of a small groups of monks, in this instance Andrew and his irksome 'brother', who were gathered into one large spiritual family under the paternal guidance of a holy man. These letters also underscore the crucial importance of prayer in shaping the interaction between the holy man and his followers. Barsanuphius' intercessory powers enabled him to absolve Andrew from the burdensome conscience of his sins. This ability would be of more vital importance than the working of miracles to those dedicated Christians who had embarked on the path to perfection. Elsewhere in the collection, Barsanuphius demonstrated his disregard for miracles when he berated a pious layman for broadcasting a healing miracle, while failing to mention all the other blessings

---

[51] Ibid., 60; cf. 69.
[52] Ibid., 72–123.
[53] Esp. ibid., 93, 96, 105, 113, 118.
[54] Ibid., 73.
[55] Ibid., 105, 107.
[56] Ibid., 115.

that had been bestowed on him.[57] Barsanuphius' and John's entire
correspondence with their fellow-monks is permeated by the idea
that a fraternal relationship based on mutual prayer and the bearing of each other's burdens provides a safeguard against the dangers on the path to perfection and a remedy against the punishment
that follows sin. Barsanuphius often encourages his associates by
quoting Galatians 6: 2, 'Bear one another's burdens, and in this
way you will fulfil the law of Christ', and Proverbs 18: 19, 'A
brother who is assisted by a brother is like a strong and fortified
city.'[58]

The letter collection of Barsanuphius and John reveals a pattern
of interaction between holy men and their followers. They were surrounded by an inner circle of monks who formed the core of their
spiritual family. The outer circle was constituted by laymen who
appealed to Barsanuphius and John for help and guidance in mundane and in spiritual matters, often maintaining a correspondence
that extended over several letters.[59] Their questions to the holy men
show that these men were committed to leading a life of piety and
virtue, but that they lived outside the monastic community. The differences between the two groups in their interaction with the Old
Men were minimal. Just as Barsanuphius and John were always
respectfully addressed as 'fathers' by both groups of correspondents,
they themselves did not make any distinction in their use of kinship
designations. Rather, the specific nature of their interaction at a
given moment determined whether they addressed a monk or a
layman as 'brother' or 'child'. They emphasized the fraternal bond
when they dispensed advice and encouragement, but spoke to their
'children' when they employed a sterner tone of admonishment.[60]
Both the monks and the laymen could expect to benefit from the
prayers of the Old Men. But only those in the inner circle were asked
by Barsanuphius and John to reciprocate by offering up their own
prayers. The effectiveness of intercessory prayer was believed to
increase exponentially with perfection in the monastic life.

---

[57] *Ep.* 643. Cf. ibid., 189: although holy men are capable of working miracles,
they sometimes choose not to do so.

[58] My translation of the Septuagint text.

[59] e.g. the sequence of letters beginning with *Ep.* 399.

[60] Monks addressed as 'child': ibid., 5, 24, 25, 124, 194, 209, 227, 253, 493,
497, 534, 572, 573, 605; laymen addressed as 'brother': ibid., 411, 617, 644, 655,
762, 772; laymen addressed as 'child': ibid., 662, 837, 849.

The letters of Barsanuphius and John challenge the conventional definitions of holiness. Neither Barsanuphius nor John qualify as saints by the prevailing criteria of current scholarship, just like the holy men depicted in the Egyptian papyri and ostraka. No *Vita* existed to extol their virtues and no posthumous cult developed at their tombs. All the same, their correspondence shows that they fulfilled all the functions that are commonly associated with holy men: miraculous healings, and the dispensation of advice on both mundane and spiritual matters. The monastic brothers received favours of the kind that usually characterize the cult of dead saints. They acquired 'contact relics' in the form of garments worn by Barsanuphius,[61] and Euthymius enjoyed the prospect of the privilege usually referred to as 'burial *ad sanctos*'—the much-desired grave situated in the immediate vicinity of a saint's tomb. In contrast to the cult of saints, however, the ties between the holy men Barsanuphius and John and their correspondents were not forged by miracles but by the prayers which united them in a 'spiritual family'.[62]

How an individual came to be considered a member of the 'spiritual family' of a holy man remains to be established. The 'brothers' of the holy man are fellow-monastics who have embarked on the same quest for personal perfection. They are also his 'sons', in as much as they request guidance and apprentice themselves to him. But how do lay people come to be the spiritual 'sons' and 'daughters' of a holy man? To answer this question, we must draw on the meagre evidence offered by hagiographical sources. These texts suggest that this lasting bond was usually initiated by the lay person. It entailed mutual obligations: the dispensation of advice and prayers on the 'father's' side and loyalty and continued support on the 'child's' side.

Several members of the imperial family prided themselves on being the 'sons' or 'daughters' of holy men or women. The Emperor Constantine and his sons Constantius and Constans are said to have sent a letter to St Anthony 'as a father' that was answered with a

---

[61] Ibid., 210: Barsanuphius grants the request of a 'brother' to wear his *koukoullion* and scapular for three days, then sends them back, along with his prayers.

[62] D. Konstan, *Friendship in the Classical World* (New York and Cambridge, 1997) argues that, among Christians in late antiquity, the classical language of friendship is replaced by kinship terminology. For expressions of close personal sentiments in the monastic context, see also C. White, *Christian Friendship in the Fourth Century* (Cambridge, 1992), 164–84.

letter of spiritual admonition which signalled the holy man's willingness to consider them his spiritual sons. The passage in the *Life of Anthony* concludes: 'thus he was beloved by all and all asked to have him as a father'.[63] Clearly, an individual had to take the initiative in order to enjoy the coveted privilege of being recognized by Anthony as his 'child'. Women, too, treasured such relationships of spiritual parentage. The Empress Eudoxia, for example, visited Melania the Younger during her pilgrimage to the Holy Land. She treated the holy woman 'as a truly spiritual mother' and regarded the pious virgins who lived under Melania's guidance as 'her own sisters'.[64] Similar expressions are used in a late third- or early fourth-century papyrus letter; here, a woman thanks her 'lord father' for his letter and expresses her joy and gratitude that 'such a father remembers me'—in his prayers or, maybe, in his letters?[65] A rich example is the *Life of Hypatius*, the founder of a monastic community near Constantinople in the early fifth century. He was cherished 'as a father' by visitors of all ranks, including the Emperor Theodosius II,[66] the *comes sacrarum largitionum* (finance minister),[67] an imperial chamberlain,[68] the clergy of the Church of the Holy Apostles,[69] and two lawyers.[70] People in the East and West who heard about his fame wrote to him 'as a father', anxious to receive letters and tokens of affection from him, while Hypatius in turn asked his correspondents for their prayers on his behalf.[71] These scattered passages seem to imply that, next to the spiritual 'brothers', the closest affiliation with holy men and women was enjoyed by those whom they addressed as their spiritual children. In an extended sense, though, the 'sons' and 'daughters' of a holy man included everyone who recognized his spiritual gifts by asking for

---

[63] *VAnt.*, § 81 (340–4). The foreign visitors to Anthony return home 'as if sent by a father', and after his death, all considered themselves 'orphans deprived of their father': ibid., § 88.3 (362, lines 15–17).

[64] *Vita S. Melaniae iunioris* (BHG 1241), § 58 (ed. D. Gorce, *Vie de sainte Mélanie*, SC 90 (Paris, 1962), 124–270, at 242–4). Compare also the treatment of this passage in the tenth-century paraphrase by Symeon Metaphrastes, *Vita S. Melaniae iunioris* (BHG 1242), PG 116, 753–93, at cols. 788B–C.

[65] Ed. B. P. Grenfell and A. S. Hunt, *The Oxyrhynchus Papyri*, pt. xii (London, 1916), no. 1592 = Naldini, 31.

[66] Callinicus, *Vita S. Hypatii* (BHG 760), § 37.2 (ed. G. J. M. Bartelink, *Vie d'Hypatios*, SC 177 (Paris, 1971), 62–298, at 226).

[67] Ibid., 22.19 (p. 144).   [68] Ibid., 12.12 (p. 118).

[69] Ibid., 13.4 (p. 122).   [70] Ibid., 38.1 (p. 228).

[71] Ibid., 36.7–8 (p. 226).

prayers and guidance. After a holy man's death, all the participants in his cult, indeed all people who invoked the saint in their prayers, could thus consider themselves his 'children'.[72]

To bring this argument to a close, we must define what role hagiographical texts have in the creation of a spiritual community after the holy man's death. The primary means of interaction between a spiritual father and his 'son' was the one-on-one personal encounter. Usually, the spiritual father would give words of instruction, encouragement, and admonition that struck a chord with his visitor, affirming the father's ability to recognize his listener's innermost troubles. It goes against the nature of these highly personal and situational encounters to be reproduced in writing and thus accessible to others. An interesting hybrid in this regard are the *Letters of Barsanuphius and John* since these holy men preferred to communicate solely through letters rather than personal conversation. The compiler of that letter collection was well aware of this dilemma: in his preface he encouraged his readers to be selective in their reading and to take to heart only those letters which spoke directly to them.

Oral communication between a holy man and his followers was the ideal, and letter-writing was the next best form after it. The epistolary format mimics the direct contact between the author and his correspondent. It creates intimacy through the expression of private sentiments and the communication of personal matters. The reader of a letter is drawn into the personal orbit of the author and feels as though he is being addressed as an individual.[73] This dynamic is at work even when a letter is ostensibly addressed to one person, but in fact intended for wider circulation.

It has often been noted that the fourth and fifth centuries saw an explosion of letter-writing in comparison to the classical period.[74] In

---

[72] This dynamic applies also to anyone who reads or listens to the narration of a saint's exceptional conduct. By the force of the text and through the efforts of the hagiographer the audience is drawn into the 'family' circle around the saint and transformed into admirers, disciples, and emulators. See further C. Rapp, 'Storytelling as Spiritual Communication in Early Greek Hagiography: The Use of Diegesis', *JECS* 6 (1988), 431–48.

[73] On letter-writing as a substitute for personal conversation, see K. Thraede, *Grundzüge griechisch-römischer Brieftopik*, Zetemata 48 (Munich, 1970), 157–87.

[74] See H. Leclerq, 'Lettres chrétiennes', in F. Cabrol and H. Leclercq (eds.), *Dictionnaire d'archéologie chrétienne et de liturgie*, 15 vols in 30 pts. (Paris, 1907–53),

fact, a large portion of patristic literature is written in the letter format. Ever since St Paul addressed his Epistles to the communities of
Corinth and Ephesus, letters became the medium of choice for
Christians. As a means of religious instruction, they produced a
tone of personal intimacy between the author and his public.
Reports of noteworthy events were also shared among the Christian
communities in the form of letters. This is the case with the earliest
acts of the martyrs, such as the *Martyrdom of Polycarp* and the
account of the martyrs of Lyon preserved in Eusebius' *Church
History*. The same applies to the work which conventionally stands
at the beginning of every study of the rise of the cult of saints and
the beginnings of hagiography, the *Life of Anthony*. Despite its modern title, it was not written as a biography—a literary form with its
own tradition since the classical period.[75] Rather, it is presented as
a letter, addressed by Athanasius, Archbishop of Alexandria, to the
'brothers overseas' shortly after the holy man's death in 356.[76]
Subsequent authors imitated this combination of epistolary format
and hagiographical content. The work commonly referred to as the
Life of Pachomius was in fact also composed and circulated as a letter.[77] Another example of hagiography written as a letter is the *Life
of Macrina*. Its full title is: 'Letter on the Life of St Macrina by
Gregory, Bishop of Nyssa'. Gregory begins by apologizing that his
work has expanded beyond the normal length of a letter because of
the sheer wealth of his material. He explains that his account reiterates, in written form, an earlier conversation with his addressee
about the praiseworthy life of Macrina.[78] The letter format thus
replicates the personal encounter.

viii, cols. 2683–5, and J. Schneider, 'Brief', in Klauser *et al.* (ed.), *Reallexikon*, ii, cols.
564–85.

[75] See esp. F. Leo, *Die griechisch-römische Biographie nach ihrer literarischen Form*
(Leipzig, 1901; repr. Hildesheim, 1990), and A. Momigliano, *The Development of
Greek Biography* (Cambridge, 1993).

[76] *VAnt.*, 124. The manuscripts give differing versions of the title. But the tenor
of the preface tallies with the majority of manuscripts in treating this work as a letter.

[77] *Vita S. Pachomii* (*BHG* 1396), ed. F. Halkin, *Sancti Pachomii Vitae graecae*, SHag.
19 (1932), 1–96.

[78] Gregory of Nyssa, *Vita S. Macrinae* (*BHG* 1012), § 1 (ed. P. Maraval, *Grégoire de
Nysse, Vie de Sainte Macrine*, SC 178 (Paris, 1971), 136–266, at 136–42). The manuscripts disagree on the identity of Gregory's addressee. Mention should also be made
of Jerome's eulogizing accounts of recently deceased practitioners of the holy life with
whom he was personally acquainted, which appear in the form of letters of consolation. His letter 108 on the death of Paula is ostensibly intended to offer comfort to

The hagiographer who uses the letter format pretends to enter into a conversation with his audience. He poses as someone who shares his own knowledge of the holy man directly with his readers. In this highly personalized form of communication, the author of a hagiographical epistle assumes the dual role as disciple of the saint and as spiritual guide for his audience. In this manner, the hagiographer invites his readers and listeners to become members of the saint's 'spiritual family'.

This study has, I hope, highlighted the importance of original letters in understanding the role of holy men in late antiquity. Although this evidence is textual, it is the closest thing to the oral ideal that has survived. It places the activities of holy men in their historical context. Whereas Peter Brown's masterful exploration of the hagiographical and other literary sources has produced a 'thaumatocentric' interpretation of the holy man as patron and exemplar, the evidence of the papyri, ostraka, and letters demands a 'supplicatory' model. It helps us to understand better the importance of prayer and its role in shaping early notions of brotherhood and spiritual leadership. This view of the social interaction among Christians as a spiritual family may very well point to an explanation for the unprecedented popularity of the letter-format among the Christian authors of late antiquity, who were anxious to preserve the cohesion, unity, and familial character of the Christian communities.

---

her daughter Eustochium, but in fact amounts to a detailed biography of this Roman noblewoman who had founded a convent on the Mount of Olives in Jerusalem: Jerome, *Ep.* 108 (ii, 306–51). For other examples, see ibid., nos. 23, 39, 60, 66, 77, and 127. Cf. also A. A. R. Bastiaensen, 'Jérôme hagiographe', in *Corpus Christianorum Hagiographies*, ed. G. Philippart, 5 vols. (Turnhout, 1994–), i, 102–5.

5

'What we heard in the Lives of the saints we have seen with our own eyes': the holy man as literary text in tenth-century Constantinople

PAUL MAGDALINO

THE late 1960s and early 1970s were a time of liberation movements, and Peter Brown's seminal lectures and articles caught the mood of the moment. His perception of the late-antique holy man as the device of 'a vigorous and sophisticated society' helped to liberate hagiography from more than one form of oppression: from élitist disdain for what was deemed a low-life, popular genre; from positivist quarrying for nuggets of 'hard' information; and, last but not least, from purist concerns with authenticity which had dominated the best of hagiographical scholarship. Suddenly it did not matter so much whether a text was an *Urtext* or whether a 'saint' really deserved canonization: what mattered was the role accorded to the 'holy man'. 'Saint' or 'holy man': Peter Brown was the first to exploit the unique choice of words available to writers of English. By introducing the Anglo-Saxon alternative with its tribal, pre-Christian, resonances he transformed the object of inquiry from a stained-glass image into a dynamic and transferable anthropological model. We learned to read saints' Lives with new eyes, and our reading had all the excitement of fieldwork.

But liberation from old-fashioned élitism, positivism, and purism did not bring release from the underlying problem of the construction which a hagiographical text imposes on historical and material reality. If the saint was off the hook, the *vita* and *miracula* were more than ever on the spot to reveal the secrets of their composition, under interrogation from the old, tried methods of source criticism and analysis. The one sure lesson we have learned from all our renewed reading is that saints' Lives are not straightforward documents of holy men in action. No texts could be closer to their subject than the three hagiographies of the elder St Symeon the Stylite, yet their combined effect is to mystify rather than clarify the picture of Peter Brown's holy man *par excellence*. Not only do the three eyewitness accounts have almost nothing in common, but the longest of them, the Syriac Life, exists in two parallel versions.[1] What we see is not a single living, functioning holy man but the multiple facets of his reception. If the outline of the original Stylite could thus be overlaid by a wealth of first-hand representation, it is not surprising that a greater cover-up has been discerned in the second-hand portrait of his sixth-century namesake, the paradigm of the *salos* or 'holy fool', by the seventh-century Cypriot bishop Leontios of Neapolis.[2] Like the other hagiographical work of Leontios now extant, the *Life of St John the Almsgiver*,[3] his *Life of Symeon the Fool for Christ's Sake* has a colourful urban setting that makes it irresistible to students of Byzantine urban life, and thus could not fail to attract the critical scrutiny of Cyril Mango.[4] The large chronological gap separating Leontios from the historical Symeon and the contrasting styles within Leontios' narrative led Mango to see the author as an unashamedly inventive manipulator of earlier written sources. More recently, Derek Krueger, a student of Peter Brown, has argued that the Life, while owing little to real memories, whether oral or written, of the historical Symeon and the Syrian city of Emesa where he performed his outrageous antics, is grounded in the author's experience of his own, Cypriot urban milieu and in his intention to construct a Christ-like answer to the ascetic model of the Cynic philosopher Diogenes.[5] It is doubtful whether Krueger's thesis will prevail against the more cautious explanation advanced by Vincent Déroche who, in a major study of

[1] See further R. Doran, tr., *The Lives of Simeon Stylites*, with a foreword by S. A. Harvey, CStud. 112 (1992).

[2] *Vita S. Symeonis sali confessoris* (*BHG* 1677), ed. L. Rydén, *Das Leben des heiligen Narren Symeon von Leontios von Neapolis*, Studia Graeca Upsaliensia 4 (Uppsala, 1963), 121–70, and again by A.-J. Festugière in *Vie de Syméon le Fou et Vie de Jean de Chypre* (Paris, 1974), 55–104.

[3] *Vita S. Ioannis eleemosynarii* (*BHG* 886), ed. Festugière, *Syméon et Jean*, 343–409.

[4] 'A Byzantine Hagiographer at Work: Leontios of Neapolis', in I. Hutter (ed.), *Byzanz und der Westen: Studien zur Kunst des europäischen Mittelalters*, Sitzungsberichte der Österreichischen Akademie der Wissenschaften, phil.-hist. Klasse 432 (Vienna, 1984), 25–41.

[5] *Symeon the Holy Fool: Leontius's Life and the Late Antique City* (Berkeley and Los Angeles, 1996).

Leontios which appeared at the same time, situates the author thoroughly in the tradition of late-antique asceticism and the popular theology of the seventh century, and thus makes the hypothesis of a fabrication inspired by a pagan model less convincing.[6] Yet Leontios emerges from all recent studies as a creative hagiographer, a constructor of holy men whose individual, paradoxical quirks illustrate a single didactic ideal that is crafted for a lay audience from an assembly of prefabricated commonplaces.[7]

In more ways than we ever suspected, hagiography is turning out to be too good to be true. Where does that leave the study of the holy man? We can regard the text as an impenetrable partition, more wall than window, which will never allow us to interview the historical holy person. Alternatively, we can look on the text as an integral part of the holy person's historical agency, indeed as the beginning of his or her historicity. If we adopt this perspective, we can complete the process of liberation begun by Peter Brown. It allows us to study the dynamism of the model projected by the text, even where the model behind the text eludes recovery or turns out to be fabricated; in other words, it gives historical meaning and function to those holy men who never existed in the flesh.

We do not know how Leontios' *Life of Symeon the Fool* was received by his seventh-century contemporaries, but we do know that it became a medieval Byzantine classic. Some time before the mid-tenth century, it inspired an author who calls himself Nikephoros to write another classic, the *Life of Andrew the Fool*.[8] Even more than Symeon, Andrew was the model of foolishness for Christ's sake, who represented a potent if hazardous ideal for later Orthodox ascetics.[9] Yet the most certain thing that can be said about Andrew is that he existed only in the imagination of his hagiographer. His story is set, and supposedly written, in the late fifth century, but there are many pointers to a later date, beginning with the reference to Andrew 'playing in the manner of the

---

[6] *Études sur Léontios de Néapolis*, Studia Byzantina Upsaliensia 3 (Uppsala, 1995).

[7] See also C. Ludwig, *Sonderformen byzantinischer Hagiographie und ihr literarisches Vorbild* (Frankfurt, 1997), 167–219.

[8] *Vita S. Andreae sali* (*BHG* 115z), ed. and tr. L. Rydén, *The Life of St Andrew the Fool*, 2 vols., Studia Byzantina Upsaliensia 4:1–2 (Uppsala, 1995), ii, 12–303.

[9] The most complete surveys are now Déroche, *Études sur Léontios*, 154–225, and Ludwig, *Sonderformen*, 291–348.

admirable Symeon of old', which suggests that the author lived long after Symeon, and also, probably, Leontios of Neapolis.[10]

For the study of the holy man as text, Andrew the Fool is an excellent starting point. He is a clear case of literary construction, he makes for a good read, and he embodies that paradoxical, promiscuous quality of holiness which both the Bollandists and Peter Brown saw, in their different ways, as quintessentially Eastern. He provides an interesting example of a medieval effort to recover an ancient ideal of holiness from the heroic age of saints in the fifth and sixth centuries, and to reuse it in the context of an East Roman world drastically transformed by the decline of the ancient city, the Islamic conquest of the great homelands of Eastern asceticism, and the trauma of Iconoclasm. He is also now accessible in a modern edition of his Life. The editor, Lennart Rydén, has provided not only a critical text, an English translation, and detailed notes, but also a substantial introduction which recapitulates, updates, and refines his own previous studies of the *Life of Andrew* and its context. Above all, he restates his belief that the Life was composed in the sixth decade of the tenth century, and answers the objections of Cyril Mango, who argued for the late seventh century.[11] The jury will not be able to retire until Mango has had time to reply, but as things stand, Rydén looks to have the stronger case, especially if we allow for the possibility that the text as we have it contains earlier levels of composition.[12] The tenth-century dating is based on a more straightforward interpretation of the anachronisms, and it places the Life in a more credible context—the Constantinople-centred culture of encyclopaedism, apocalypticism, and antiquarianism which characterized the age of Constantine Porphyrogenitus.[13] Against the objection that the tenth century is too late for the urban environment in which Andrew moves, it can be pointed out that this world—which is not evoked in any great detail—was the natural setting which an author, who had evidently read the *Life of Symeon the Fool* and other early Byzantine hagiography, would have used

[10] Rydén, *St Andrew*, ii, 28. See further ibid., i, 46.
[11] 'The Life of St Andrew the Fool Reconsidered', *Rivista di studi bizantini e slavi*, 2 (1982), 297-313; repr. in idem, *Byzantium and its Image* (London, 1984), no. VIII.
[12] See the review of Rydén's edition by S. Ivanov in *Byzantinoslavica*, 57 (1996), 405-6, and the fuller discussion by Ludwig, *Sonderformen*, 220-90.
[13] If the idea of successive layers of composition is adopted, the work can be seen as analogous to various 'encyclopaedic' works of the tenth century, such as the *Synaxarion*, the *Book of Ceremonies*, and the *Patria*.

in constructing a fifth-century urban saint who lived his entire ascetic life in public places. Little Byzantine literature survives from the late seventh century, probably because little was written; only certain pieces of apocalyptic writing offer a point of comparison with one section of the *Life of Andrew*. In the tenth century, on the other hand, points of comparison abound—with visionary literature, with writings on the monuments of Constantinople, with hagiographical compilations such as the *Synaxarion* and the Metaphrastic corpus, and with 'romantic' hagiographies such as the Lives of St Theoktiste of Lesbos[14] and St Eirene of Chrysobalanton.[15] Most crucially, the work shows close affinities with the *Life of Basil the Younger*, a hagiography set in the first half of the tenth century and written some time after 956.[16] The basic similarities were noted by Christina Angelidi and have been discussed more systematically by Rydén.[17] But the comparison between the two works can be taken further: in the context of their similarities, their very differences are complementary to a degree which makes it impossible to understand either text and its place in Byzantine hagiography without reference to the other.

Andrew and Basil are both introduced as adults, with none of the usual information about their parentage and childhood. Both are brought to Constantinople against their will—Andrew as a slave, Basil as a suspected spy—yet having reached the city, both live out their lives in it. They are, indeed, the most uncompromisingly urban of all medieval Byzantine holy men, for in contrast to the vast

[14] *Vita S. Theoctistae* (BHG 1723-4), ed. H. Delehaye, *AASS Novembris*, iv (Brussels, 1925), 224-33; tr. A. C. Hero in *Holy Women of Byzantium: Ten Saints' Lives in English Translation*, ed. A.-M. Talbot (Washington, DC, 1996), 95-116.

[15] *Vita S. Irenae hegumenae* (BHG 952), ed. and tr. J. O. Rosenqvist, *The Life of St Irene Abbess of Chrysobalanton*, Studia Byzantina Upsaliensia 1 (Uppsala, 1986), 1-113.

[16] *Vita S. Basilii iunioris*: there is, unfortunately, no accessible edition of the text in Moscow, Greek MS 249, which has been variously published in three fragments by S. G. Vilinskij in *Zapiski Imperatorskogo novorosijskogo universiteta* (Odessa, 1911), 283-326 and 326-46 (BHG 263 and 264b: hereafter, 'Vilinskij') and by A. N. Veselovskij in *Sbornik Otdela russkogo jazyka i slovesnosti Imperatorskoj akademii nauk*, 46 (St Petersburg, 1889), 6, suppl., 10-76 (BHG 264d: hereafter, 'Veselovskij I') and 53 (1891) 6 suppl., 3-174 (BHG 263: hereafter 'Veselovskij II').

[17] Chr. G. Angelidi, *Ὁ Βίος τοῦ Ὁσίου Βασιλείου τοῦ Νέου* (Ioannina, 1980), 98-102; L. Rydén, 'The *Life* of St. Basil the Younger and the Date of the *Life* of St. Andrew Salos', in C. Mango and O. Pritsak (ed.), *Okeanos: Essays Presented to Ihor Ševčenko on his Sixtieth Birthday*, Harvard Ukrainian Studies, 7 (Cambridge, Mass., 1983), 568-86.

majority of hagiographical heroes and heroines after Iconoclasm, neither is ordained or belongs to a monastic community.[18] In this, Andrew the Fool goes further than Symeon the Fool, who at least observes the formality of entering a monastery and then spends many years in the desert as a 'grazer' ($\beta o\sigma\kappa\acute{o}s$) acquiring the 'dispassion' ($\mathring{a}\pi\acute{a}\theta\epsilon\iota a$) necessary to undertake his evangelical mission in the town. Very little action takes place in church. Andrew lives in the streets, squares, and porticoes; Basil lives in a series of houses owned by laymen—a modest couple called John and Helen,[19] the *primmikerios* Constantine Barbaros, and the Gongylios brothers, *praipositoi* at the imperial court; he also spends a week in the Palace as the guest of the Empress Helen.[20] This means, among other things, that neither saint owns any property and both depend entirely on charity. Each saint has a special relationship with a young man—Epiphanios in the *Life of Andrew*, Gregory, also the narrator, in the *Life of Basil*—to whom he acts as spiritual mentor, and who eventually enters religion, but only after the saint's death. Here again, Andrew has more in common with Basil than with his role-model Symeon, who does not have a disciple, and whose relationship with the narrator of his story serves mainly as a device to explain how the author got his information.

However, both the *Life of Andrew* and the *Life of Basil* are pointedly didactic and convey their teaching through supernatural visions which are either experienced by the saints themselves or which they inspire in their disciples. Andrew is transported to heaven one winter's night,[21] he takes Epiphanios on a tour of hell,[22] Epiphanios beholds him in glory at the court of heaven,[23] and Andrew foretells the course of events at the end of the world;[24] Andrew and Epiphanios also have shorter excursions into or encounters with the heavenly and the demonic.[25] Basil arranges for his disciple Gregory to be granted three protracted visions. In the first, Gregory sees himself caught up in the drama of his recovery from an illness caused by an evil spell: Basil, aided by St Stephen, brains the offending demon in the shape of a monstrous mouse.[26]

---

[18] See E. Patlagean, 'Sainteté et pouvoir', in *Byzantine Saint*, 88–105, at 98–9.
[19] *Vita Basilii*, ed. Vilinskij, 289–91, 296, 299.   [20] Ibid., 302–3.
[21] *Vita Andreae*, ed. Rydén, 46–61.   [22] Ibid., 164–9.
[23] Ibid., 124–31.   [24] Ibid., 258–83.
[25] Ibid., 14–17, 20–7, 63–7, 70–3, 76–9, 104–5, 112–17, 122–5, 132–5, 142–7, 184–5, 198–9, 248–53, 255, 295–7.
[26] *Vita Basilii*, ed. Vilinskij, 322–5.

In the second vision, Gregory again visits the heavenly mansion reserved for Basil and his spiritual children; here the saint's recently deceased housekeeper, Theodora, relates her experience of the demonic toll-houses which the soul passes through on departing from the body, in order to be searched for unconfessed sins.[27] In the third and final vision, Gregory is treated to an extended preview of the Second Coming and the Last Judgement.[28] The visions and their edifying messages occupy so much space that the Lives can easily be seen as frame stories for set pieces of apocalyptic exegesis, in which the saints themselves are of secondary importance.

The difference between them is that while the *Life of Andrew* betrays its fiction as a historical novel set somewhat inconsistently in the fifth century, Basil the Younger is firmly grounded in the historical reality of the tenth, and his hagiographer gives the impression of knowing that reality at first hand. Basil personally encounters several historical figures, including the Emperor Romanos I,[29] and he predicts the outcome of three historical events: the revolt of Constantine Doukas in 913,[30] the Russian invasion of 941,[31] and the Magyar invasion of 943.[32] There is nothing concrete to cast doubt on the identity of the author with Gregory the narrator, and hence on the reality of his acquaintance with Basil, after as well as before the latter's death. For another notable difference between the Lives is that while Andrew's mortal remains are mysteriously spirited away,[33] Basil's are disputed by his followers and eventually interred in a specified church, the monastery of the Chartophylax, where they are said to operate miraculous cures.[34] May we therefore conclude that Basil really existed? On the one hand, it is hard to see what purpose could have been served by the pure invention of a recent saint whose non-existence would have been obvious to contemporaries. On the other hand, the monastery of the Chartophylax, like Basil himself, is known only from the *Life of Basil*. Where Basil's reputation is concerned, the author provides himself with two discreet 'escape clauses'. At one point he

---

[27] *Vita Basilii*, ed. Veselovskij I, 12-48. Cf. G. Every, 'Toll Gates on the Air Way', *Eastern Churches Review*, 8 (1976), 139-51.
[28] *Vita Basilii*, ed. Veselovskij II, 12-173. The account is largely based on the apocryphal *Apocalypse of St Paul*: see Angelidi, Ὁ Βίος, 110-11, 188-204.
[29] *Vita Basilii*, ed. Vilinskij, 303.
[30] Ibid., 291-6.
[31] *Vita Basilii*, ed. Veselovskij I, 65-8.
[32] Ibid., 64-5.
[33] *Vita Andreae*, ed. Rydén, 300-1.
[34] *Vita Basilii*, ed. Vilinskij, 341-2.

undermines his portrait of a famous and popular holy man by saying that Basil revealed his true charisma only to a chosen few, and
put most people off by appearing to talk nonsense and act like a
fool.[35] At the end, he detaches himself from the saint's death and
burial by saying that he missed these because of his seclusion during Lent.[36] His personal involvement with Basil ends when the saint
gives him his final blessing, promising to keep in touch through
dreams and visions.[37] He has no part in the dispute over Basil's final
resting place, and he does not even mention visiting the tomb; here
the self-appointed guardian of the cult is not the hagiographer but
a eunuch called John, who becomes a monk, dies soon afterwards,
and is buried beside the saint.[38] If Basil was the object of a posthumous cult, why does the author of his Life have nothing to do with
it?

It is also strange that Basil's name does not figure in any version
of the *Synaxarion* of Constantinople, the calendar of local commem-
orations.[39] Perhaps this was compiled too soon for Basil to be
included; however, it is a fact that he spectacularly failed to conform to the norms of tenth-century sainthood. At a time when all
male saints were monks, this saint felt under no pressure to join a
monastery, but was content to enjoy the hospitality of laymen, in
whose houses he attracted a vast clientele of spiritual children, said
to include magnates, priests, bishops, monks, and several important
women.[40] It is scarcely believable that a charismatic, informal
movement of this kind, a potential breeding-ground for heresy,
would have been allowed to flourish, unregulated and unsuper-
vised, right under the nose of the patriarchal church. The anomaly
of Basil's, and Gregory's, lack of monastic affiliation is rendered all
the more striking by the author's perfunctory attempt to give their
story a monastic beginning and end. How Basil had become a
monk, he says, was one of those details of his early life, along with
his parentage and childhood, of which the holy man had never

---

[35] *Vita Basilii*, ed. Vilinskij, 311.   [36] Ibid., 339-40.   [37] Ibid., 329-36.

[38] Ibid., 339-42. John is mentioned earlier in the text as a servitor in the imperial household, whom Basil delivered from the machinations of one of his female
slaves: *Vita Basilii*, ed. Veselovskij I, 69-72.

[39] *Synaxarium Ecclesiae Constantinopolitanae*, ed. H. Delehaye, *Propylaeum ad AASS
Novembris* (Brussels, 1902), 1-939, at col. 713: the commemoration of St Andrew
the Fool (28 May) is listed only in one late recension of the text. Cf. A. P. Khazdan
et al. (eds.), *Oxford Dictionary of Byzantium* (Oxford, 1991), iii, 1991.

[40] *Vita Basilii*, ed. Vilinskij, 290-1, 299-318; Veselovskij I, 51-76.

spoken and no one else knew.[41] He says that Basil, in his final exhortation, urged him to take monastic vows, but whether he has done so at the time of writing is not clear.[42] This vagueness confirms the impression that Gregory is casting himself and his hero as temporary outsiders to the normal structures of contemporary religious vocation. In other words, even if Basil was real, he had more in common with an imaginary fifth-century holy fool than with his sainted monastic contemporaries, such as Luke the Stylite, of whom more later.

There are further indications that the two texts were products of the same cultural milieu and written in close association. Although a tenth-century work on a tenth-century subject, the *Life of Basil*, like the *Life of Andrew*, shows an interest in early hagiography. It contains what appear to be echoes of the *Life of Symeon the Fool*, the *Life of John the Almsgiver*, and the *Life of Isaac the Recluse*.[43] The two violent confrontations which mark the turning points in Basil's career—his horrific interrogation and torture by the *parakoimomenos* Samonas, which provides him with his début in Constantinople,[44] and his maltreatment by the *magistros* Romanos Saronites,[45] which precedes his introduction to the houses of the rich and powerful—are modelled on the passions of early Christian martyrs.[46] Both hagiographies refer to the church of St Anastasia as a kind of lunatic asylum, where the insane were kept in chains.[47] This is a good indication of a tenth-century date for the *Life of Andrew*, not only because of a further reference in another tenth-century text,[48] but also because at earlier and later dates, other churches performed this function: St Panteleimon in the seventh century,[49] and St Niketas

---

[41] *Vita Basilii*, ed. Vilinskij, 284.   [42] Ibid., 332.

[43] Angelidi, Ό Βίος, 78–9, 96–8; Rydén, 'The *Life* of St Basil the Younger', 579–80.

[44] *Vita Basilii*, ed. Vilinskij, 285–8.   [45] Ibid., 296–9.

[46] Angelidi, Ό Βίος, 72 ff.

[47] *Vita Andreae*, ed. Rydén, 18–21, 26–9; *Vita Basilii*, ed. Veselovskij I, 68, 70. Cf. L. Rydén, 'A Note on Some References to the Church of St Anastasia in Constantinople in the Tenth Century', *Byzantion*, 44 (1974), 198–201.

[48] *Vita Irenae*, ed. Rosenqvist, 68.

[49] *Miracula Sancti Artemii* (BHG 173), § 18 (ed. A. Papadopoulos-Kerameus, *Varia sacra graeca* (St Petersburg, 1909; repr. Leipzig, 1975), 1–75, at 20); the text is reproduced with an English translation by V. S. Crisafulli and J. W. Nesbitt, *The Miracles of St Artemios* (Leiden, 1996), 114–15. The author of the miracle story does add, however, that 'it happened at that time that there were a very large number of possessed in many churches'.

in the twelfth.[50] Both texts accord a certain prominence to St John the Evangelist. Soon after Andrew pretends to go insane, the apostle appears to him in a vision and strengthens his resolve.[51] Epiphanios cites St John and asks questions about him.[52] St John is presumably the unnamed evangelist and apostle who conducts Epiphanios in his vision of Andrew at the court of the heavenly king;[53] and he appears in the retinue of the Mother of God in the vision at the Blachernae church.[54] The *Life of Basil* twice states that people thought Basil to be St John the Apostle in person.[55] In case we are puzzled by this statement, the *Life of Andrew* provides the explanation: to a question by Epiphanios about Elijah, Andrew replies that not only are Elijah and Enoch alive and waiting to fulfil their appointed roles in the Last Things, but 'John the Theologian also lives and is in the world, like a pearl in the mud'.[56]

Most telling are the positive references to holy fools in the *Life of Basil*. Not only does Basil himself practise holy foolishness as a protective cover against vainglory,[57] but in the narrator's preview of the Last Judgement, the *saloi* are among the saved.[58] The remarkable thing here is that no other type of asceticism is singled out for commendation. An author with a sympathetic interest in early sainthood might have been expected to make special mention of

---

[50] See Theodore Balsamon on canon 60 of the Quinisext Council: *PG* 137, col. 716; G. Ralles and M. Potles, Σύνταγμα τῶν θείων καὶ ἱερῶν κανόνων, iv (Athens, 1852), 442.

[51] *Vita Andreae*, ed. Rydén, 22–5.   [52] Ibid., 208–9, 214–17.

[53] Ibid., 126–7. The venerable old man in question holds a Gospel in his right hand and a papyrus scroll in his left, the standard iconographical attributes of evangelists and apostles respectively.

[54] Ibid., 254–5.

[55] *Vita Basilii*, ed. Vilinskij, 311; Veselovskij I, 50–1.

[56] *Vita Andreae*, ed. Rydén, 218–19. The belief goes back to the version of the apocryphal *Acta Johannis*, § 115 (ed. E. Junod and J.-D. Kaestli, 2 vols., *CC Series Apocryphorum*, 1–2 (1983), i, 336, 343), according to which the Apostle did not die normally, but his body was taken away in a *metastasis*. According to another variant of this tradition, he was taken up to heaven like the Virgin Mary, but the view that he would remain on earth until the reign of Antichrist was shared by other Byzantine authors, including Andreas of Caesarea, and, significantly for this study, the tenth-century rewriter of hagiography, Symeon Metaphrastes (*PG* 116, col. 703), which strengthens the possibility that the author or authors of the *Vita Andreae* and the *Vita Basilii* were associated with the official hagiographical projects of the mid-tenth century. See further M. Jugie, *La mort et l'Assomption de la Sainte Vierge*, Studi e Testi 114 (Vatican City, 1944), 716–19.

[57] *Vita Basilii*, ed. Vilinskij, 311; Veselovskij I, 50.

[58] Ibid., II, 74–5.

stylites.[59] But if St Symeon the Stylite and his imitators make it to heaven in Gregory's book, they do so without special distinction, as part of the band of righteous monks whose black habit now shines dazzling white.[60] They are numerous, but the angel who guides the narrator through the vision leaves him in no doubt as to the fate of the majority. 'Brother, in the consummation of the age, the whole generation of monks has proceeded to perdition, apart from a few, who have chosen to assume spiritual hardship and pain and toil.'[61] The damned include many who possess basic qualifications for sainthood—they have kept themselves celibate, prophesied, and cast out demons.[62] The church hierarchy fares no better: Gregory sees 'an exceedingly great multitude of bishops, deacons, sub-deacons, readers, and chanters' condemned to eternal torment.[63] Thus, the perfect sanctity of the unconsecrated *salos*, which is invisible to the eyes of the world, contrasts with the corruption underlying the officially consecrated and highly visible sanctity practised by the vast majority of clergy and monks. Such a contrast is not to be found in the *Life of Symeon the Fool*, but it features in two episodes of the *Life of Andrew*, where Andrew, through his divine insight, perceives the secret sins of an adulterous deacon and a mercenary monk who pockets the money given to him by penitents.[64] In both cases, Andrew delivers a sermon on the high responsibility of a life consecrated to God; in both cases, it takes a fifth-century holy fool to teach the monks and clergy the error of their ways, which the *Life of Basil* identifies as a matter of serious concern to tenth-century society.

It is, indeed, this critique of the religious establishment which reveals the vital link between the two texts and provides the key to

---

[59] *Vita Andreae*, ed. Rydén, 134–7, briefly shows Andrew in collaboration with St Daniel the Stylite, although the episode has the function of establishing Andrew's credentials as the contemporary and equal of a saint who was consulted by Emperors.

[60] *Vita Basilii*, ed. Veselovskij II, 66. [61] Ibid., 103–4.

[62] Ibid., 102. The idea that the gifts of the Spirit will not in themselves guarantee salvation is based on Matthew 7: 22–3, and is developed in the seventh-century *Quaestiones* of Anastasios of Sinai: *PG* 89, col. 520. This is one of several points of agreement between the author of *Vita Basilii* and Symeon the New Theologian: *Catachèses*, ed. Krivochéine [see n. 119 below], ii, 100.

[63] *Vita Basilii*, ed. Veselovskij II, 97 ff.

[64] *Vita Andreae*, ed. Rydén, 142–53, 193–9. The monk corresponds exactly to those in the *Vita Basilii*, ed. Veselovskij II, 102, 'who kept their virginity intact, but hankering after mercenary and stingy ways, perished miserably at the end'.

understanding the unconventional model of sanctity common to
both. Andrew and Basil are presented as outsiders to the norms of
clerical and monastic holiness because this gives them the spiritual
insight and moral authority to preach repentance by making
revelations about the supernatural dimensions that envelop the
material world: revelations of heaven, hell, and the end of time; revelations about the guardian angels and malign demons that battle
for the possession of every human soul; revelations that are hidden
from even the most saintly of contemporary monks and churchmen,
compromised as they are by a lingering attachment to the things of
this world. Criticism of monks and clergy is only a part of the message, which in both texts is directed against sinful laymen and
includes a virulent attack on the Jews.[65] But if both works signal
an ulterior purpose, this is to reform the quality of Christian leadership. Both saints entrust their disciples with a mission. Andrew
prophesies that Epiphanios will become Patriarch of Constantinople,[66] and this prophecy makes functional sense of many
episodes, both those in which the young man is shown fighting the
demon of fornication, asking theological questions of the saint, and
learning to see through the pleasant exteriors of his worldly friends,
and those in which the Devil punishes Andrew for depriving him of
his prey. Epiphanios is clearly in training to be a better pastor than
the Patriarchs who do not have holy fools 'to advise them on the
state of the Church'.[67] The tenth-century Patriarchs who figure in
the *Life of Basil* are all portrayed as flawed individuals: Nicholas I
because of his perjury and inhumanity to Constantine Doukas and
his followers; Euthymios because of the 'scandal' of the Emperor Leo
VI's fourth marriage; and Theophylact (933–56) as the uncanoni-
cally elected 'son of bigamy'; the only priest with whom Basil is
shown in close contact is one who refuses to celebrate the liturgy
in protest against these goings on.[68] Basil does not foresee a sacer-
dotal future for his disciple, but he does tell Gregory to be a *good*
monk, and the angel who takes Gregory through his frightful vision
of the Last Judgement tells him repeatedly to report all he has seen

---

[65] *Vita Andreae*, ed. Rydén, 222–5; *Vita Basilii*, ed. Veselovskij II, 3, 6–12, 29–30,
35–6, 63, 126–42.

[66] *Vita Andreae*, ed. Rydén, 118–21.

[67] Ibid., 120: ἤρξατο ὁ μακάριος παραινεῖν τὸν Ἐπιφάνιον περὶ τῆς ἐκκλησ-
ιαστικῆς καταστάσεως.

[68] *Vita Basilii*, ed. Vilinskij, 292–5; Veselovskij I, 63–4.

'to the churches and all those in charge of them', as well as to the heads of monasteries.[69] Gregory takes this instruction very seriously, for he worries, as soon as he comes out of the vision, 'what churches and what bishops did he mean?'[70] In neither Life, significantly, is the saint's behaviour prescribed as a model for others to follow. There is no question of laymen finding salvation outside the framework of organized worship. Churchmen have to improve because they make the rules that laymen have to follow. Both Lives insist that people must go to church and stay until the end of the service.[71] The *Life of Andrew* is in the spirit of the clerical regulation of lay morality introduced by the Quinisext council (691–2),[72] and the *Life of Basil* ends on a comforting but classically clerical note: people can secure their salvation if they 'make friends from the Mammon of unrighteousness' by donating their surplus wealth to the poor and to the churches of the saints who will intercede for them.[73]

Both saints, therefore, are on a mission to restore credibility to the religious establishment of Constantinople by teaching the things the licensed, institutional, holy men cannot preach, partly because the latter are corrupt and lacking in the grace of the Spirit, but partly, too, because the teachings in question are apocryphal. Since the truths revealed by Andrew and Basil about the end of the world and the afterlife had no basis in the Scriptures and the Fathers, they could not be proclaimed by the apostolic hierarchy, vital though they were for every Christian's salvation. Only a latter-day apostle with a fresh mandate could speak with authority. And Andrew and Basil are indeed cast as apostles in disguise, not only by their lives of absolute, apostolic, poverty, but in more explicit ways. Andrew bears the name of the 'first-called' apostle, and in choosing that name, the author of the *Life of Andrew* was surely aware of the legend which made St Andrew the founder of the see of Constantinople.[74] When, in one of the Life's supposedly fifth-century

---

[69] *Vita Basilii*, ed. Veselovskij II, 167–70.   [70] Ibid., 174.

[71] *Vita Andreae*, ed. Rydén, 122–3; *Vita Basilii*, ed. Veselovskij II, 173.

[72] J. Grosdidier de Matons, 'Les thèmes d'édification dans la Vie d'André Salos', *Travaux et mémoires*, 4 (1970), 277–328, esp. 322 ff.; Mango, 'St Andrew the Fool Reconsidered', 309. On the Council, see G. Dagron in *Histoire du christianisme*, iv (Paris, 1993), 60–9.

[73] *Vita Basilii*, ed. Vilinskij, 343–5, quoting Luke 16: 9.

[74] F. Dvornik, *The Idea of Apostolicity in Byzantium and the Legend of the Apostle Andrew* (Cambridge, Mass., 1958), 234–5.

moments, Andrew sees a vision of a church in the magnificent form in which it will be rebuilt by Justinian, the church is not Hagia Sophia but that of the Holy Apostles,[75] where relics of St Andrew, St Timothy, and St Luke had been deposited by Constantius II.[76] The church of Constantinople further claimed apostolic authority through its jurisdiction over the church of Ephesus, founded by St John the Evangelist.[77] As we have seen, Andrew has a close relationship with St John, who, he tells Epiphanios, will remain on earth until the end of the world. We have also seen how the *Life of Basil* applies this belief to Basil.[78] Although the author records the belief as a popular opinion which causes Basil some embarrassment, he registers his approval by mentioning it twice, and by making St Stephen say of Basil, 'I think God has placed him in the ranks of the apostles'.[79]

The affinities between the Lives are so fundamental that one of them, at least, must have been written with knowledge of the other. This would still allow for the theory that the *Life of Andrew* was written long before the *Life of Basil*. But in addition to the other indications of a tenth-century context for both texts, there are important respects in which the edifying purpose of each work is incomplete without the other. First, there is a perceptible division of visionary labour. The former describes the battle between angels and demons for the human soul before death, while the latter charts the fortunes of the soul after death. Although both texts present visions of the afterlife, only the *Life of Andrew* gives a special tour of the dungeons of hell. When it comes to eschatology, the division is very clear: the *Life of Andrew* describes the course of events leading up to the Second Coming, and the *Life of Basil* takes up the story at that point. Secondly, each Life deals with a different aspect of the secular urban space of Constantinople, with Andrew inhabiting public places and Basil confining himself to the private world of the secular house-

---

[75] *Vita Andreae*, ed. Rydén, 132–5. The church at the centre of the vision of the New Jerusalem in *Vita Basilii*, ed. Veselovskij II, 152, is described as a cruciform building with four domes, which is again more reminiscent of the Holy Apostles than of Hagia Sophia.

[76] C. Mango, 'Constantine's Mausoleum and the Translation of Relics', *Byzantinische Zeitschrift*, 83 (1990), 51–63, at 52–3; repr. in idem, *Studies on Constantinople* (Aldershot, 1993), no. V.

[77] Dvornik, *Idea of Apostolicity*, 238 ff.   [78] See n. 55 above.

[79] *Vita Basilii*, ed. Vilinskij, 324.

hold, the *oikos*.[80] There is some crossing of the boundaries, for Andrew pays one visit to Epiphanios in his house, and, in the process of moving between private locations, Basil has to traverse a lot of public space, including the whole of the processional route from the Golden Gate to the Great Palace, which gives his life the structure of an imperial *adventus*.[81] But on the whole, Andrew is cast as the apostle of the squares and porticoes and Basil as the apostle of private homes. The significance of this demarcation goes well beyond the contrast between the public setting appropriate to the existence of a fifth-century holy fool and the domestic priorities of tenth-century society. The Constantinople of the *Life of Andrew* is a gloomy, sordid place, symbolic of perdition, lacking in greenery or grandeur; the porticoes where Andrew defecates,[82] lives among filth and is treated like filth, shunned even by dogs and beggars,[83] are the material manifestation of a demonic world where everything is coated in faeces, from the souls of sinners to the depths of Hades.[84] By contrast, the network of *oikoi* which make up the Constantinople of Basil the Younger is on the whole a model of salvation, for even the houses where Basil suffers persecution contribute to his sanctity. In his second residence, Basil is attended by a circle of devotees who form a spiritual family.[85] Apart from the houses where he resides, Basil has relations with many other households, especially with their domestic staff, almost to the point of becoming the patron saint of household slaves.[86] The *Life of Basil* is remarkable as a source for the 'downstairs' social life of the Byzantine household.[87] It is even more remarkable for the way it projects the model of the *oikos* into the afterlife. When Gregory is transported out of his body in his first two visions, he finds himself

---

[80] On the significance of the term and the unit, see P. Magdalino, 'The Byzantine Aristocratic *oikos*', in M. Angold (ed.), *The Byzantine Aristocracy, IX-XIII Centuries*, British Archaeological Reports, International Series, 221 (Oxford, 1984), 92–111; repr. in idem, *Tradition and Transformation in Medieval Byzantium* (Aldershot, 1991), no. II.

[81] See G. Dagron, *Empereur et prêtre: Étude sur le 'césaropapisme' byzantin* (Paris, 1996), 79–85, 93–5.

[82] *Vita Andreae*, ed. Rydén, 94–5. [83] Ibid., 40–1, 44–5.

[84] Ibid., 34–5, 164–7, 176–7, 190–1, 230–1, 238–9.

[85] *Vita Basilii*, ed. Vilinskij, 300–1, 306–12; Veselovskij I, 54, 55–6, 57–8, 62.

[86] Ibid., 51–5, 56–7, 58–76.

[87] See also ibid., 31–2, and Chr. Angelidi, 'Δούλοι στην Κωνσταντινούπολη τον 10° αιώνα. Η μαρτυρία του Βίου του οσίου Βασιλείου του Νέου', *Σύμμεικτα*, 6 (1985), 33–51.

in Basil's heavenly palace, where, he learns on the second visit, the saint comes to visit his spiritual children who predecease him.[88] It is here that Basil's late maidservant Theodora tells him about her experience after death; how, having passed through the toll gates on the air-way to heaven, she was presented to the heavenly court, then led through the dwellings of the saints and given a glimpse of hell, before being delivered to Basil's spiritual abode.[89] The dwellings of the saints are described as 'incomparable palaces spiritually constructed of multicoloured mosaics and variegated marbles'; each type of saint has a different style of palace, and the area they occupy is one hundred times the size of Constantinople.[90]

The *oikos* again appears as the basic unit of the New Jerusalem where the righteous are settled after the Last Judgement. In his preview of this event, Gregory notices that when the saints have all marched in and concluded the inaugural celebrations, they ask Christ to create for them a multiplicity of churches and residences, such as they had been used to on earth, 'and lo, everywhere were houses, palaces, apartments, churches and walled estates.' There were even suburban villas, just as in Constantinople—but there were no public buildings or monumental public spaces.[91]

Basil's heavenly house makes a third and final appearance at the very end of the *Life of Basil*, after the death of John, the faithful eunuch who had arranged for the burial of the saint and waited on his tomb. A fellow disciple of the saint and close friend of John wonders what has happened to the latter in the afterlife. One night he is granted a vision in which he sees himself standing outside 'an awesome royal palace', with great gilded gates, and above them an inscription which reads 'Eternal dwelling and repose of my faithful servant Basil the Younger'. A young man throws open the gates to reveal Basil in great glory, surrounded by a 'royal suite', with John standing next to him, 'and a further multitude of glorious retainers'. A voice proclaims that this is the reward of those who love and honour God and his servants.[92]

The roles, and the disguises, of Andrew and Basil as latter-day apostles were shaped by the close relationship of their Lives, and by interaction with other texts and trends of the tenth century. By

---

[88] *Vita Basilii*, ed. Vilinskij, 323-4; Veselovskij I, 12 ff.
[89] Ibid., 32-48.   [90] Ibid., 39.
[91] *Vita Basilii*, ed. Veselovskij II, 159-61.
[92] *Vita Basilii*, ed. Vilinskij, 342-3.

looking at their points of contact with their tenth-century context, we can arrive at a more precise understanding of the choices made by their authors, and we can better appreciate the significance of, as well as their contribution to, the debate in which they were engaged.

The visions of heaven and hell which figure so prominently in both Lives have their counterparts in two free-standing visionary accounts from the same period. One is dated to 963 and records the vision which Kosmas, the late abbot of a monastery in Bithynia, had seen during a serious illness thirty years earlier.[93] The other is the *Revelation* of the nun Anastasia, who is said to have lived in the sixth century, although the text clearly post-dates the death of John I Tzimiskes (976).[94] The very existence of these texts is important as confirmation that speculation about the afterlife was intense during the tenth century, when apocalyptic expectations ran high with the advent of the middle of the seventh millennium since the creation of the world;[95] the corruption of the clergy, which exercised the author of the *Life of Basil*, was seen by a slightly earlier hagiographer as a sure sign that the end was nigh.[96] As a pair, the two visionary pieces form an interesting parallel to our Lives, with one text firmly grounded in tenth-century realities and the other set much earlier. A comparative analysis of the visions in all four texts is beyond the scope of this essay, but I will note two points in the *Vision of Kosmas the Monk* which show that the comparison should be instructive.

Kosmas, first, is taken into heaven and shown around by two venerable men whom he recognizes, from their icons, as the apostles Andrew and John. The editor of the text notes that these apostles are nowhere else mentioned or depicted as psychopomps, and asks whether they figure as such in this vision because the soul they are accompanying comes from a living body.[97] The answer is probably yes, given that the latter-day apostles Andrew the Fool

[93] Ed. Chr. Angelidi, 'La version longue de la vision du moine Cosmas', *AB* 101 (1983), 73–99.

[94] Ed. R. Homburg, *Apocalypsis Anastasiae* (Leipzig, 1903).

[95] See P. Magdalino, 'The History of the Future and its Uses: Prophecy, Policy and Propaganda', in R. Beaton and C. Roueché (ed.), *The Making of Byzantine History: Studies dedicated to Donald M. Nicol* (London, 1993), 3–34, at 24–6.

[96] Ed. L. G. Westerink 'Niketas the Paphlagonian on the End of the World', in *Essays in Memory of Basil Laourdas* (Thessaloniki, 1975), 177–95, at 194–5.

[97] Angelidi, 'La version longue', 84, 94 n. 92.

and Basil the Younger effectively act as guides to the afterlife to their disciples Epiphanios and Gregory.

Secondly, as Kosmas and his apostolic guides proceed from the outer gate of heaven to the inner city and palace of God, they pass through a large olive grove, 'whose trees, as I consider, were more than the stars of heaven'. Under each tree are a tent and a couch, and on each couch reclines a man. Kosmas recognizes many people he had known in the palace, in Constantinople, and in his monastery and its neighbourhood. When he asks his guides to explain, they chide him for asking a silly question: is it not obvious that these are the 'many mansions' (John 14: 2) in God's house? Yet in the heaven of the *Life of Basil*, these same 'mansions' are elaborate *oikoi*.

Was the *Vision*'s pairing of the apostles Andrew and John influenced by knowledge of the neo-apostolic duo Andrew the Fool and Basil the Younger, and was its picture of a relaxed, alfresco heaven a retort to the *Life of Basil*'s vision of a super-Constantinople of aristocratic *oikoi*? Without knowing the exact order in which the texts were composed, we cannot tell which author was reacting to which. But we can be reasonably sure that they were writing close to each other in time and place, for Constantinopolitan readers. This makes it very likely that at least one author was writing with the other, or others, in mind. Two important conclusions follow: first, Andrew and Basil were recognized as a duo in the 960s, which strengthens the case for a common or co-ordinated authorship of their Lives; secondly, the religious literature to which the Lives belonged did not represent a seamlessly united evangelical front, but represented differences of position and emphasis in a debate about what salvation meant and how it was to be achieved. When we turn to other religious texts of the period, we see that the terms of this debate went beyond speculation about the afterlife and covered a variety of questions concerning the quest for personal sanctification. Should monks remain in one place? Should they live as solitaries or in communities? Did holy men belong in the city? Was it possible to meet a living saint, and how was he to be recognized? What were the role and the qualifications of a spiritual father?[98]

---

[98] See in general R. Morris, *Monks and Laymen in Byzantium, 843-1118* (Cambridge, 1995); B. Flusin, 'L'hagiographie monastique à Byzance au IXE et au X[E] siècle: modèles anciens et tendances contemporaines', *Revue bénédictine*, 103 (1993), 31-50.

It might seem as though the Lives of Andrew and Basil give impossibly extreme answers to these questions, always privileging the charismatic at the expense of the canonical. But as we have seen, the unconventional holiness of Andrew and Basil is meant to validate their special apostolic mission, and their act is not meant to be followed. The disciples who benefit from their charisma are normal members of society who will follow normal institutional careers. By their very lack of formal consecration, and by keeping to the secular space of Constantinople, Andrew and Basil avoid endorsing extremism or individualism within the monastic environment, and cast doubt on the possibility of achieving old-style sanctity by the normal paths of solitary asceticism.

The place of Andrew and Basil within the spectrum of holiness that was on offer in tenth-century Constantinople becomes clearer when we compare their Lives with the evidence for two contemporary holy men who were advertised as the equals of the saints of old. Both lived close in time and place to the literary construction of Andrew and Basil and were almost certainly known to the latters' hagiographer or hagiographers. Luke the Stylite lived on a column at Chalcedon, in the Asiatic suburbs of Constantinople, from 935 to 979.[99] During that time he was undoubtedly the most famous holy man in the region of the capital, attracting crowds of visitors and an élite metropolitan clientele that included a subdeacon of the Great Church,[100] a cleric of the Nea Ekklesia,[101] and the Patriarch Theophylact,[102] of whom the author of the *Life of Basil* disapproved so strongly. It is hard to imagine that the latter had forgotten about Luke when he failed to make honourable mention of stylites among the company of the blessed. It is equally likely that Luke's hagiographer, writing in 980 or shortly thereafter, had the Lives of Andrew and Basil in mind when extolling the stylite life as the ultimate in saintly perfection, whose practitioners were 'rare and exceeding few'.[103] Luke is introduced as the fifth in a line of great stylites, after the Elder and Younger Symeon, Daniel, and Alypios;[104] he is presented as a Job figure,[105] angelic as well as

[99] *Vita S. Lucae stylitae* (BHG 2239), ed. with introductory commentary and French translation by F. Vanderstuyf, *Vie de Saint Luc le Stylite (879-979)*, PO 11/2 (1914), cols. 189-287.
[100] Ibid., § 48 (243).
[101] Ibid., § 56 (256).
[102] Ibid., §§ 45-7 (241-3).
[103] Ibid., § 5 (193).
[104] Ibid., §§ 6-7 (194-6).
[105] Ibid., § 8 (196); § 10 (200).

apostolic,[106] with solid credentials of the kind that Andrew and Basil conspicuously lack. He is properly tonsured and ordained,[107] and before setting up in the suburbs of the big city—with the blessing of the local bishop[108]—he serves a full rural apprenticeship, proceeding to the stylite life by degrees: first a spell of asceticism and philanthropy in the world, then a spell of communal life in a lavra on Bithynian Olympos, where he pretends to be deaf and dumb (but not insane).[109] This is in pointed contrast to Andrew and Basil who not only reveal but, to a great extent, earn their sainthood in the city-centre. Although it is Basil's previous career as a desert 'grazer' that is said to give him his spiritual powers,[110] much greater prominence is accorded to his persecution at the hands of Samonas and Saronites, which makes him, in effect, a confessor, qualified to convert the aristocratic *oikos* from a place of profane torment to a place of salvation. Andrew similarly qualifies for confessor status by his callous treatment at the hands of sadistic passers-by.

Yet while Luke's hagiographer is careful to show that his holiness was canonical, he is also at pains to play up its individual, heroic traits and to play down any sense of routine conformity. By introducing Luke as the imitator of the early stylites, he disregards the obvious fact that Luke was following the example of the monk who had tonsured him, and whose spiritual children had converted him to the religious life.[111] In other words, Luke was not an exceptional throwback to early asceticism, for stylites were a regular feature of the Byzantine religious landscape of the ninth and tenth centuries.[112] For his hagiographer, however, the obvious precedent for Luke was Daniel the Stylite, and he may well have been following the *Life of Daniel* in claiming that Luke did not come to Constantinople of his own volition, but was guided there by a divine

[106] *Vita Lucae stylitae*, § 12 (202); apostolicity is also hinted at in § 42 (236).

[107] Ibid., §§ 12–13 (201–3).

[108] Ibid., § 26 (217).

[109] Ibid., §§ 14–24 (203–15).

[110] *Vita Basilii*, ed. Veselovskij I, 47. See also ibid., 68, where an expelled demon calls Basil a 'herb-eating desert-dweller'.

[111] *Vita Lucae stylitae*, ed. Vanderstuyf, §§ 11–12 (201–2).

[112] This is also clear from *Vita S. Lucae iunioris* (*BHG* 994), § 43 (ed. D. Sophianos, *The Life of Hosios Loukas of Steiris*, 2nd edn. (Athens, 1993), 125–89, at 149), which mentions stylites at Patras and Zemena in the Peloponnese. The edition by G. Kremos, *Phokika*, i (Athens, 1874), is reproduced and translated into English by C. L. and W. R. Connor, *The Life and Miracles of St Luke of Steiris* (Brookline, Mass., 1994), 2–142: see § 35 (55).

revelation, which also told him where to find his column.[113] That the story was not so simple seems evident from the text's later information that Luke was buried in the city monastery of St Bassian, which he had refounded at the patriarch's behest.[114] The editor of the Life infers, reasonably, that Luke had lived at St Bassian before moving across the Bosphoros, and it is thus probable that he was invited to Constantinople by the patriarch to undertake the restoration. The hagiographer may have suppressed the information because the patriarch in question was the notorious Theophylact, who could be shown as beholden to the saint, but not as his spiritual superior. What is generally clear is that the hagiographer has no primary interest in Luke's role as a monastic leader, which was evidently considerable, for not only was he the 'new founder' of St Bassian, but there was a monastic community close to his column at *ta Eutropiou*.[115] He is not even interested in developing the theme of Luke's qualities as a spiritual director, of which he had first-hand experience.[116] Contemporary opinion was open to the idea that a saint was holy by virtue of his moral leadership, his role as a teacher and saver of souls. Luke's hagiographer chose not to canonize his hero in this way, but instead to ground his sainthood on conformity to ancient models, on superhuman *askesis*, and on the performance of numerous miracles. In taking this option, he seems to have ignored the parallels offered by contemporary ascetics who were revitalizing the spiritual life of the European provinces,[117] in favour of responding to the urban challenge posed by the newly created reputations of Andrew the Fool and Basil the Younger. Or was he responding to the growing reputation of the other urban holy man who was acquiring a very ambitious and publicity-conscious disciple at the time when the Lives of Andrew and Basil were being written?

[113] *Vita Lucae stylitae*, ed. Vanderstuyf, § 25 (215–16). Cf. *Vita S. Danielis stylitae* (*BHG* 489), § 10 (ed. H. Delehaye, *Les saints stylites*, SHag. 14 (Brussels, 1923), 1–94, at 10–12). The association was enhanced by the fact that Luke died on the same day as Daniel: see *Vita Lucae stylitae*, ed. Vanderstuyf, § 79 (277–8).

[114] Ibid., § 80 (278–80).

[115] R. Janin, *Les églises et les monastères des grands centres byzantins* (Paris, 1975), 34. The author of *Vita Lucae stylitae*, § 83 (ed. Vanderstuyf, 283), refers to the monastery as if it had nothing to do with Luke, but he also mentions a group of monks in attendance on the stylite, § 52 (250).

[116] Ibid., § 9 (198–9), § 33 (225–6).

[117] Notably Saints Athanasios the Athonite, Luke of Steiris, Nikon Metanoeite: see Morris, *Monks and Laymen*, chs. 1–4.

That other holy man was Symeon the Studite or Symeon the Modest (*Eulabes*), and the disciple was a young Paphlagonian eunuch in imperial service called George, later to become famous as St Symeon the New Theologian. The latter, according to his own hagiographer, got in trouble with the authorities for instituting a cult of his spiritual father, complete with an icon and an annual feast day.[118] Unfortunately, the hagiography he wrote for this cult has not survived, and we have to rely on what we can piece together from allusions in his sermons to the monks of the monastery of St Mamas in Constantinople, where he became abbot.[119] It may not be immediately obvious what these high-minded spiritual discourses, with their sometimes mystical emphasis on inner regeneration, their educated Greek, and their scrupulous adherence to bona fide scriptural and patristic teachings, have in common with the popular and apocryphal sensationalism of the Lives of Andrew and Basil. Yet there are four basic similarities between the heroes of these Lives and Symeon the Studite as evoked by the New Theologian:

(1) *Sainthood in the city*   Symeon was one of those saints who had lived a heavenly life in the thick of urban society, 'who shone like a sun in the midst of the famous monastery of Studius', close to the cares and temptations of the world.[120] He was considered a fool; he had let himself be humiliated and oppressed, abused, dismissed, and insulted as a worthless, deranged, and common vagrant . . . like one of the disabled beggars on the squares and streets of the city; like Christ, he was said to be possessed by a demon, and accused of consorting with publicans and sinners.[121] This combination of traits

---

[118] Niketas Stethatos, *Vita S. Symeonis novi theologi* (*BHG* 1692), §§ 72–93 (ed. I. Hausherr and G. Horn, *Un grand mystique byzantin: Vie de Syméon le Nouveau Théologien (949–1022) par Nicétas Stéthatos*, Orientalia Christiana 12/45 (1928), 1–228, at 98–129). The Patriarch called upon Symeon 'to prove that you are acting in accordance with the teaching of the Fathers and the apostles, in thus celebrating the memory of your father on a par with the saints of old'.

[119] Symeon's prose works have mostly been published with French translation in the Sources Chrétiennes series: *Chapitres théologiques, gnostiques et pratiques*, ed. J. Darrouzès, SC 51 (Paris, 1957); *Catachèses*, ed. B. Krivochéine and tr. J. Paramelle, 3 vols., SC 96, 104, 113 (Paris, 1963–5); *Traités théologiques et éthiques*, ed. J. Darrouzès, 2 vols., SC 122, 129 (Paris, 1966–7).

[120] *Catachèses*, ed. Krivochéine, ii, 26–8, 140–2. A few pieces have been translated into English with a useful introduction by P. McGuckin, *Symeon the New Theologian: The Practical and Theological Chapters and the Three Theological Discourses*, CStud. 41 (Kalamazoo, Miss., 1982).

[121] *Catachèses*, ed. Krivochéine, ii, 38–40, 86 f.

has led more than one scholar to believe that Symeon simulated foolishness, which the *Life of Andrew* and the *Life of Basil* present as the highest form of asceticism.[122] Certainly, it seems that if Symeon consciously took after any illustrious namesake, this was Symeon the Fool rather than either the Elder or the Younger Symeon Stylites. While the New Theologian says that saints live in caves, mountains, cells, and city centres, he does not mention suburban columns; elsewhere he writes that monks will not achieve salvation by the mere act of escaping to the tops of columns or mountains, or to caves or cells.[123]

(2) *The 'saints of old'* Most people did not recognize Symeon's sainthood, because they wrongly thought it impossible to encounter a saint in their own day, and this is why the author says that he was so grateful to have discovered Symeon.[124] The Lives of Andrew and Basil similarly present their heroes as ancient hagiography made real, to the surprise and delight of the spectator. 'What we heard in the Lives of the saints we have seen with our own eyes', exclaims a boy who sees Andrew levitate.[125] Basil's narrator, Gregory, declares, 'Until that moment I had never met a clairvoyant man, and I had only read about them in the Lives of the saints of old.'[126]

(3) *Eschatology* Though Symeon the New Theologian avoids the lurid apocalypticism of the Lives of Andrew and Basil, his message, like theirs, is a call to repentance in preparation for the Last Judgement, and the call is aimed, above all, at monks who have outwardly renounced the world but remain attached to it.[127]

(4) *Spiritual fatherhood* The relationship between spiritual father and spiritual child is central to the New Theologian's message of salvation, whether he is talking about his own conversion under the guidance of Symeon the Studite or applying this experience to his own pastoral role as father of the monks of St Mamas.[128] The

---

[122] Cf. Déroche, *Études sur Léontios de Néapolis*, 207–10.

[123] *Catachèses*, ed. Krivochéine, i, 26–8; *Traités*, ed. Darrouzès, ii, 172.

[124] *Catachèses*, ed. Krivochéine, i, 422, 442; ii, 142, 164, 176, 306, 310

[125] *Vita Andreae*, ed. Rydén, 100–1: ἄπερ ἐν τοῖς Βίοις τῶν ἁγίων ἠκούομεν, ταῦτα οἰκείοις ὀφθαλμοῖς ἑωράκαμεν.

[126] *Vita Basilii*, ed. Vilinskij, 306.

[127] *Catachèses*, ed. Krivochéine, i, 374–466; ii, 188–90; *Traités*, ed. Darrouzès, i, 236–388.

[128] See H. J. M. Turner, *St Symeon the New Theologian and Spiritual Fatherhood* (Leiden, 1990).

narratives of the Lives of Andrew and Basil are largely built around the disciple–teacher relationships of Nikephoros and Gregory to Andrew and Basil respectively. In the *Life of Basil* at least, the relationship is more than a perfunctory narrative device, for it is introduced as the answer to the narrator's prayers after his previous spiritual father has died. He insists on the importance, and the difficulty, of finding the right spiritual father, and he goes to his first meeting with Basil with the clear intention of testing the holy man's charisma.[129] As we have seen, Basil's hagiographer elevates the model of the spiritual *oikos*, composed of the saint and his spiritual progeny, into a heavenly microcosm, the vital building-block of the Kingdom of God.

The ostensible difference is that whereas Andrew and Basil are not held up for imitation, Symeon the Studite is prescribed to the monks of St Mamas as an example of the imitation of Christ that they should take to heart. If Basil the Younger was a real contemporary figure, Symeon might be seen as the canonical monastic response to Basil's uncanonical example. However, if Basil, like Andrew, was an edifying fiction and known as such to Symeon the New Theologian, there is no difficulty in seeing all three holy men as products of the same workshop, as representatives of an ideal of holiness that was to be cultivated in inner spirit rather than in literal detail. What Symeon advocated was the *principle* of total self-abasement and poverty, the *principle* of living sainthood, the *principle* of personal dependency on the head of a spiritual family. He intended these principles to reinforce, rather than subvert, the communal discipline of the Studite monastic rule.[130] Where he departed from contemporary practice was in his emphasis on spiritual over blood relations, and on ties of service as opposed to those of kinship. He himself did not imitate the more controversial aspects of Symeon the Studite's behaviour, and it is doubtful whether he expected the monks of St Mamas to do so. What he required was

---

[129] *Vita Basilii*, ed. Vilinskij, 305 ff. Gregory says that his previous director was a saintly monk called Epiphanios at the monastery of *ta Maximines*.

[130] See D. Krausmüller, 'The Monastic Communities of Stoudios and St Mamas in the Second Half of the Tenth Century', in M. Mullett and A. Kirby (eds.), *The Theotokos Evergetis and Eleventh-Century Monasticism* (Belfast, 1994), 67–85, and esp. J. A. McGuckin, 'Symeon the New Theologian (d. 1022) and Byzantine Monasticism', in A. Bryer and M. Cunningham (eds.), *Mount Athos and Byzantine Monasticism* (Aldershot, 1996), 17–35.

frequent and total confession of 'thoughts', and total obedience to himself as abbot. The functions of Andrew and Basil as charismatic spiritual directors were compatible with this purpose, and Basil's network of interlocking secular and spiritual *oikoi* was in harmony with Symeon's tendency, which has been identified as the essence of his programme, to structure the monastic *koinobion* along the lines of the aristocratic *oikos*.[131] Symeon himself pointed out the structural similarities,[132] in addition to making the point indirectly by his use of household and palace images to illustrate the relationship between man and God.[133] The difference is essentially one of refinement: Symeon's palatial heaven is highly centralized, with the apartments of the saints all opening on to a single foyer.[134] In this way, the *Life of Basil* functions as a trial sketch for the cenobitic model that Symeon wanted to impose on the monks of St Mamas. If this reading is correct, it helps to explain the otherwise puzzling fact that although Basil is cast as St John the Evangelist in disguise, the apostle of the secular *oikos*, he bears the name of St Basil of Caesarea, who was revered as one of the founding fathers of communal monasticism. St Theodore the Studite, the great medieval Byzantine reinventor of the cenobitic ideal, was said to have been inspired by his reading of St Basil.[135]

But the name Basil had further connotations for tenth-century Byzantines. It is unlikely, though not impossible, that contemporary Constantinopolitans had heard of Basil Digenes Akrites, the legendary frontier warrior who operated in the eastern borderlands where Basil the Younger was arrested as a spy.[136] However, they had all heard of the Emperor Basil I the Macedonian, the founder of the dynastic succession, which, despite the damaging minority of Constantine VII, was becoming the longest that Constantinople had

[131] Ibid., 32–3.   [132] *Catachèses*, ed. Krivochéine, i, 440.
[133] See, for example, *Catachèses*, ed. Krivochéine, i, 226–8, 290, 380, 400; ii, 284–6; iii, 140, 354; *Traités*, ed. Darrouzès, i, 180; ii, 22–3, 166. Cf. A. Kazhdan, 'Das System der Bilder und Metaphern in den Werken Symeons des Neuen Theologen', in P. Hauptmann (ed.), *Unser ganzes Leben Christus unserm Gott überantworten: F. von Lilienfeld zum 65. Geburtstag* (Göttingen, 1982), 221–39; A. J. van der Aalst, 'The Palace and the Monastery in Byzantine Spiritual Life *c.* 1000', in A. Davids (ed.), *The Empress Theophano* (Cambridge, 1995), 314–36.
[134] *Traités*, ed. Darrouzès, i, 222, 244.   [135] *PG* 99, col. 245.
[136] For the textual evidence, recent commentary, and previous bibliography, see E. M. Jeffreys, *Digenis Akritis: The Grottaferrata and Escorial Versions* (Cambridge, 1998); R. Beaton and D. Ricks (eds.), *Digenes Akrites. New Approaches to Byzantine Heroic Poetry* (Aldershot, 1993).

ever known. Around 950, Constantine commissioned a laudatory biography of his grandfather which has a strong hagiographical flavour.[137] Rydén has detected echoes of this text in the *Life of Andrew*, and there are perhaps even stronger echoes in the *Life of Basil*. The scene is set with a paragraph about Basil I and his sons.[138] St Basil the Younger, like the young Basil I, enters Constantinople from the south-west and penetrates to the centre of power at the eastern end of the city, along the route taken by arriving Emperors, by attaching himself to increasingly important households. The house which becomes his final residence is said to be near a church which Basil I had built in expiation of his murder of Michael III.[139] Both Basils tamed horses that others could not control.[140]

The author of the *Life of Basil* probably wrote in the knowledge that the future of Basil I's dynasty was assured by the young Basil II, born in 958 and crowned as co-Emperor to his father Romanos II in 960. He was certainly writing at a time when political life in Constantinople was influenced, if not dominated, by another homonym, the eunuch Basil the *parakoimomenos*, the illegitimate son of the Emperor Romanos I by a 'Scythian' (Russian?) slave-girl. Right-hand man of Constantine VII before 959, and power behind the throne of three Emperors from 963 to 985, Basil was a munificent patron of culture and religion, closely involved in the 'encyclopaedism' of the mid-tenth century. He commissioned a treatise on naval warfare, the *Naumachica*, and is believed to have been responsible for compiling the *Book of Ceremonies*. He paid for the production of luxury manuscripts, precious reliquaries, and liturgical vessels. Most interestingly for us, he founded a magnificent monastery in Constantinople, which was dedicated to St Basil—an uncommon dedication—and of which an early, probably the first, abbot, was also called Basil.[141]

---

[137] *Theophanes Continuatus*, ed. I. Bekker (Bonn, 1838), 211–353; P. Alexander, 'Secular Biography at Byzantium', *Speculum*, 15 (1940), 194–209, which is repr. in his *Religious and Political History and Thought in the Byzantine Empire* (London, 1978); cf. I. Ševčenko, 'Re-reading Constantine Porphyrogenitus', in J. Shepard and S. Franklin (eds.), *Byzantine Diplomacy* (Aldershot, 1992), 167–95, at 184–5.

[138] *Vita Basilii*, ed. Vilinskij, 284–5.   [139] Ibid., 307.

[140] *Theophanes Continuatus*, 230–1; *Vita Basilii*, ed. Veselovskij I, 60–1.

[141] W. Brokkaar, 'Basil Lacapenus', *Studia Byzantina et neohellenica Neerlandica* (Leiden, 1972), 199–234; L. Boura, ''Ο Βασίλειος Λεκαπηνὸς παραγγελιοδότης ἔργων τέχνης', Κωνσταντῖνος Ζ' ὁ Πορφυρογέννητος καὶ 'Η Ἐποχή Του (Athens, 1989), 397–434; Ševčenko, 'Constantine Porphyrogenitus', 185. On the monastery,

There is important circumstantial evidence to link both the Life of Andrew and that of Basil to Basil the *parakoimomenos*. In the case of the *Life of Basil* it consists of the information that Basil the *parakoimomenos* lived in the house 'of the Barbarian', which it is reasonable to identify with the house of the *primmikerios* Constantine, 'whom everyone called Barbarian', where Basil the Younger is said to have spent most of his life in Constantinople.[142] Where the *Life of Andrew* is concerned, the evidence consists of the fact that the majuscule script of the earliest known manuscript fragments of the Life (preserved as the flyleaves of Monacensis graecus 44) closely resembles that of a manuscript copied, as its colophon reveals, for Basil the *parakoimomenos* by the scribe (*notarios*) Nikephoros in July 955 (Athos, Dionysiou 70).[143] Rydén has argued that the fragments are from the original manuscript, and that the use of antique, Alexandrian, majuscule was meant to contribute to the illusion of fifth-century composition. That Basil the *parakoimomenos* had a taste for majuscule is certainly clear from the New Testament lectionary (St Petersburg/Leningrad 55) which he commissioned for the monastery of St Basil in 985.[144] When we look at certain elements of the *Life of Andrew* in the light of these comparisons—the author calls himself Nikephoros, Andrew comes to Constantinople as a Scythian slave, and serves as a *notarios* before pretending to go mad—the case for the patronage of the half-'Scythian' *parakoimomenos*, who 'loved and collected holy things',[145] becomes compelling if not conclusive.

The obstacle to seeing Basil as the patron of the Lives of both Andrew and Basil is that the author of the latter reveals political attitudes which would not have pleased the *parakoimomenos*. He is hostile to the Patriarch Theophylact, Basil's half-brother; this and his strictures on ecclesiastical corruption suggest that he supported the reforming policy of Theophylact's successor, Polyeuktos, whom

see Michael Psellos, *Chronographia*, ed. E. Renauld (Paris, 1926), i.13; for the Abbot Basil, see Boura, '*Βασίλειος Λεκαπηνός*', 401; for the location, see now A. Berger, 'Zur Topographie der Ufergegend am Goldenen Horn in der byzantinischen Zeit', *Istanbuler Mitteilungen*, 43 (1995), 156-7 n. 48.

[142] Cf. Porphyrogenitus, *De administrando imperio*, ed. Gy. Moravcsik and tr. R. Jenkins (Washington, DC, 1967), 190. Cf. Ševčenko, 'Constantine Porphyrogenitus', 191.

[143] Rydén, *St Andrew*, i, 72-81; see Boura, '*Βασίλειος Λεκαπηνός*', 401.

[144] Ibid., 401-4.

[145] τὰ θεῖα καὶ ποθεῖ καὶ συλλέγει, quoted from the dedicatory epigram of the St Petersburg manuscript: ibid., 404.

Basil the *parakoimomenos* tried to have deposed.[146] We have already
suggested that the controversy over Theophylact underlay the
unstated antagonism between stylites and holy fools that emerges
from comparison of the *Life of Basil* with the *Life of Luke the Stylite*;
here we may note that the *parakoimomenos* revered St Symeon the
Stylite.[147] The positive way in which the author of Basil's Life refers
to the Gongylios brothers suggests that he was sympathetic to the
eunuch administration of the Empress Zoe during her regency for
Constantine VII between 914 and 919.[148] This is certainly consis-
tent with the differences between his conception of heaven and that
described in the *Vision of Kosmas the Monk*, whose connections were
with the regimes of Zoe's opponents, the Emperors Alexander and
Romanos I. If the author of the *Life of Basil* liked the Gongylioi, he
may well have been linked with the Paphlagonian faction among
the eunuchs at the imperial court, and therefore with Joseph
Bringas, the great political rival of Basil the *parakoimomenos*. One
Paphlagonian eunuch who fell with Bringas when Basil made a
come-back at the death of Romanos II in 963 was George, the
future St Symeon the New Theologian.[149]

The political alignment of the *Life of Basil* would thus seem to
mark it as a critique rather than a creation of the religious patronage of Basil the *parakoimomenos*. Yet in religious terms, criticisms
could be given and taken in a spirit of charity, and in political terms
there was much to be gained from magnanimity. After his decisive
come-back in 963, Basil could afford to be magnanimous and to
listen to constructive admonition from imaginary holy men
with whom he was invited to identify. The young George the
Paphlagonian was able to resume his worldly career for a further
seven years, so perhaps the author of the *Life of Basil* was able to
interest Basil the *parakoimomenos* in Basil the Younger as a worthy
complement to Andrew the Fool, and as a magnate of the Kingdom
of God, holding court in his heavenly *oikos* just as the *parakoimo-*

---

[146] John Skylitzes, *Synopsis historiarum*, ed. J. Thurn (Berlin and New York,
1973), 244.

[147] He commissioned a silver casing for the crown of Symeon's skull: see Boura,
'Βασίλειος Λεκαπηνός', 407–9.

[148] *Vita Basilii*, ed. Veselovskij I, 57; cf. P. Magdalino, 'Paphlagonians in
Byzantine High Society', in S. Lampakis (ed.), *Byzantine Asia Minor (6th–12th cent.)*
(Athens, 1998), 141–50.

[149] Ibid. The changes of personnel that accompanied changes of regime in the
early tenth century are recorded in some detail in *Theophanes Continuatus* and by
Constantine Porphyrogenitus, *De administrando imperio*, 242 ff.

menos dispensed patronage in the house where the saint had lived on earth. As we have seen, the *Life of Basil* ends on a comforting note, holding out the promise of salvation to all who make themselves friends from the Mammon of unrighteousness—which the *parakoimomenos* did by gifting a costly monastery to St Basil the Elder. Is it coincidence that Gregory, in his second vision, sees himself arriving at Basil the Younger's heavenly *oikos* by the route which led to the monastery?[150]

This essay began with the truism that hagiographers reveal more of themselves than of their holy men. As we take our leave of Andrew the Fool and Basil the Younger we may wonder whether the truism is entirely true. The affinities which link the *Life of Andrew* to the *Life of Basil*, and both texts to other pieces of Byzantine literature, certainly allow us to place them in a recognizable historical context. Their authors emerge as evangelical spirits of the mid-tenth century, steeped in the hagiography of an earlier age, and formed by the culture of the Byzantine aristocratic *oikos*, which informs their vision of spiritual relationships on earth and of social order in heaven. They were clearly connected with the powerful eunuch bureaucrats of the age of Constantine Porphyrogenitus, and in particular with Basil the *parakoimomenos*. Their worldly connections, and their evident interest in the 'saints of old', suggest that they were involved in the official, 'encyclopaedic' hagiographical projects of the day, the *Synaxarion* and the *Menologion* of Symeon Metaphrastes. They lived at a time when the end of the world seemed imminent, and expectancy was no doubt heightened by news of victories in the east which brought the prospect that the holy lands of early Christianity, the lands where the saints of old had trod—perhaps even Jerusalem itself, were about to return to the Christian empire. Yet for our authors, the centre of the world which was reaching its finale was the New Jerusalem, Constantinople. Their hagiographical creations enriched the Reigning City with new holy men, just as recent emperors had enriched it with important new relics, such as the sacred Mandylion of Edessa (944) and the

---

[150] *Vita Basilii*, ed. Veselovskij I, 11–12. Leaving Basil's normal residence at Arkadianai, Gregory follows the road to the Blachernae church until he suddenly finds himself in a steep uphill passage. For the location of the monastery near the Golden Horn, see Berger, 'Zur Topographie'.

hand of St John the Baptist (956).[151] Indeed, Andrew and Basil set the seal on the holiness of Constantinople by sanctifying, through their apostolic presence, the secular space surrounding the churches and monasteries. Their hagiographers wrote to bring the clergy, the monastic establishment and the lay magnates who exercised religious patronage, an apostolic message of salvation more urgent and more far-reaching than the debate over the relative merits of communal and solitary asceticism.

This much we can infer from our texts; more than this, however, their authors do not reveal of themselves. In the end it is they, 'Nikephoros' and 'Gregory', who remain faceless and anonymous, masked by the holy men whom they invest with historical personae. It is the holy men, rather than the hagiographers, who are active and interactive. Andrew and Basil are hagiographical constructs, but this does not mean that they are merely edifying mouthpieces or teasing literary pastiches. They are there to remind us that saints will turn up when and where we least expect them. The construction of their holiness is integral to the message they convey, and the manner of their construction reveals the enduring validity of two structural features of the role model proposed by Peter Brown: the saint as patron and the holy man as outsider. And the timing of their construction is significant, coinciding as it does with the formative years of Symeon the New Theologian. By reinforcing the example he made of his spiritual father, Symeon the Studite, their inspiration may even have passed into the mainstream of Orthodox spirituality.

---

[151] John Skylitzes, *Synopsis Historiarum*, 31, 245. Cf. I. Kalavrezou, 'Helping Hands for the Empire: Imperial Ceremonies and the Cult of Relics at the Byzantine Court', in H. Maguire (ed.), *Byzantine Court Culture from 829 to 1204* (Washington, DC, 1997), 53–79, esp. 67–77.

PART III

The cult of saints in Western Christendom

6

Demystifying the role of sanctity in Western Christendom

PAUL ANTONY HAYWARD

In the Stenton and Haskell Lectures, delivered in 1976 and 1978, Peter Brown completed the project he began with the publication of the 'Holy Man' article in 1971.[1] Whereas the earlier paper examined the rise and function of the cult of saints in the Roman Empire's eastern half, these lectures addressed the cult's rise and function in its western half, where the veneration of the dead saint bulked larger in the sources than the activities of the living holy man. Here, apparently, the cult was centred upon the bodily remains of past heroes of the Church, who continued to preside over everyday life, directing good fortune to those who had attended to their requirements and bad fortune to those who had not. The aim of this essay is to discuss some strengths and weaknesses of Brown's analysis and to identify insights upon which scholars might continue to build. It is useful to begin by elucidating the intellectual origins of Brown's position.

FROM EDWARD GIBBON TO MARY DOUGLAS

Much of Peter Brown's work was written in opposition to Gibbon, and his treatment of the cult of the saints in Latin Christianity was no exception. For Gibbon, the rise of the cult was a symptom of the Empire's decline.[2] The martyrs and the more distinguished

---

[1] That is, *RSS* and *CS*. I would like to express my gratitude to Paul Fouracre, Philip Rousseau, and to my co-editor, James Howard-Johnston, for their comments and advice. They bear, of course, no responsibility for the views I express.

[2] Edward Gibbon, *The History of the Decline and Fall of the Roman Empire*, 6 vols. (London, 1776–88); ed. D. Womersley, 3 vols. (Harmondsworth, 1994), ii, 90–7, 428–9. For evidence of Brown's approach to Gibbon, see also his 'Gibbon's Views on Culture and Society in the Fifth and Sixth Centuries', *Daedalus*, 105 (1976), 73–88, repr. in G. W. Bowerstock, J. Clive, and S. R. Graubard (eds.), *Edward Gibbon and the*

confessors deserved the 'grateful respect' of Christians, but the practice of venerating them as though they were minor deities corrupted the 'pure and perfect simplicity of the Christian model'. Christianity was brought down from 'the contemplation and worship of the Universal Cause' to the level of the vulgar imagination: 'If, in the beginning of the fifth century, Tertullian or Lactantius had been suddenly raised from the dead, to assist at the festival of some popular saint, or martyr, they would have gazed with astonishment, and indignation, on the profane spectacle, which had succeeded to the pure and spiritual worship of a Christian congregation.' Men were tempted to fraud and credulity, while the lights of history and of reason were extinguished, all because of the episcopate's ambition to convert the masses: 'The most respectable bishops had persuaded themselves that the ignorant rustics would more cheerfully renounce the superstitions of Paganism if they found some resemblance, some compensation, in the bosom of Christianity.'

Brown's view is almost exactly opposite. Far from being a 'compromise' with the senses, the cult represented the realization of the highest spiritual aspirations of the age. The belief that worldly success depended upon one's right-standing in the eyes of the deity was as intrinsic to polytheism as it was to Christianity, but the insertion of human mediators added a new dimension of personal intimacy with the divine. Paganism did have its deified heroes, but, Brown argues, they were conceived as 'gods', as beings whose immortality made them entirely other. The martyrs, on the other hand, had a special relationship with God and yet remained approachable to ordinary humanity. They enjoyed a tie of shared experience with Jesus, since he had partaken of human mortality through his Incarnation and death and since they had suffered martyrdom after his example.[3] By bridging the gap between heaven and earth with human beings as opposed semi-divine angels and demons, Christians were able to articulate their relationships with these intercessors in terms of the intimate bonds of everyday life—to treat them, that is, as their kinsmen, as their dear friends, or as their preferred patrons: 'The need for intimacy with a protector with whom one could identify as a fellow human being, relations with whom could be conceived of in terms open to the nuances of known

Decline and Fall of the Roman Empire (Cambridge, Mass., 1977), 37–52, and in *SH*, 22–48.

[3] *CS*, 5–6.

human relations between patron and client, is the hallmark of late fourth-century Christian piety.'[4] In no sense superficial, the cult of saints worked its way outwards and downwards, 'slowly and deeply into the lives of Mediterranean men of all classes and levels of culture'.[5] A learned and Christian élite, including figures such as Sulpicius Severus and Paulinus of Nola, took a leading role in articulating its deepest sentiments. It brought about a wholesale reorganization of the social landscape, not least in breaking down the segregation of the living and the dead that had been an intrinsic feature of civic life in the ancient world.[6]

Brown stresses the ways in which saints' cults facilitated social life for people of all types. The cult offered 'a distinctive system of religious beliefs, often expressed with great power and beauty, which hung together in such a way as to leave considerable play for precise forms of social manoeuvring'.[7] Shrines offered women places of refuge from the rigidities of family life, the pressure to bear and raise children for husbands they were not free to choose.[8] Peasants could escape the oppression of their lords, by committing themselves, while seeking a cure at a shrine, to serve the saint for the rest of their lives rather than return to their masters.[9] At the other end of the social spectrum, cults helped to solidify episcopal authority. Bishops were able to manifest proof of divine approval by presiding over the translation of a saint's remains. A critical factor was the public unity which the arrival of the relics could elicit and manifest. Public consensus was seen as a miracle of divine making. Public hostility, by the same token, was a sign of divine disapproval, and bishops were anxious to mitigate their vulnerability to its appearance. The stable holiness of the relic 'high-lighted and orchestrated the personal and, so, fragile holiness of the other'.[10] The cult represented, in short, an entirely new order of social life: 'new forms of the exercise of power, new bonds of human dependence, new, intimate, hopes for protection and justice in a changing world'.[11] It served the interests of both the individual and the community more effectively, and sometimes more justly, than had former mechanisms of public life.

The cult of saints reached a peak of refinement in the late sixth century, by which time it had come to mean a highly structured,

[4] Ibid., 61.   [5] Ibid., 21.   [6] Ibid., 1–12. See also 'Holy Man', 151.
[7] *RSS*, 242–3.   [8] *CS*, 44.   [9] Ibid., 122–3.
[10] *RSS*, 240.   [11] *CS*, 22. See also *RSS*, 127.

but rewarding, approach to everyday existence. The categories *reverentia* and *rusticitas* denoted its moral absolutes in the writings of Gregory of Tours (d. 593 or 594):

Reverentia implied a willingness to focus belief on precise invisible persons, on Christ and his friends the saints—the *amici domini*—in such a way as to *commit* the believer to definite rhythms in his life (such as the observation of the holy days of the saints), to direct his attention to specific sites and objects (the shrines and relics of the saints), to react to illness and to danger by dependence on these invisible persons, and to remain constantly aware, in the play of human action around him, that good and bad fortune was directly related to good and bad relations with these invisible persons. *Reverentia*, therefore, assumed a high degree of social and cultural grooming. It was not a luxuriant undergrowth of credulity or neo-paganism. It involved learning an etiquette toward the supernatural, whose every gesture was carefully delineated. Hence the importance for Gregory of its antithesis, *rusticitas*, which is best translated as 'boorishness', 'slipshodness'—the failure, or the positive refusal, to give life structure in terms of ceremonious relationships with specific invisible persons.[12]

This representation of the cult of saints refutes Gibbon exactly. The cult's rise remains closely bound up with the process of Christianization, but a revolution has occurred in the way its origins, role, and effects are conceived. The cult has become the primary means by which late antiquity achieved the dream of an ideal community that eluded the classical world.

Brown's approach is also indebted to a long-standing but essentially non-Christian tradition of apology for the cult of saints whose development has owed much to Oxford historians. James Anthony Froude, Fellow of Exeter College (1842–9) and Regius Professor of Modern History (1892–4), offered a similar argument in an early essay on the Lives of the Saints.[13] Like Brown, Froude was respond-

---

[12] *CS*, 119. The passage is derived, in almost the same words, from *RSS*, 230, and the same ideas appear, more briefly stated, in Brown's recent work, *RWC*, 102.

[13] First published in the first series of his *Short Studies on Great Subjects*, 2 vols. (London, 1850), ii, 243–69. Froude's attempts to grapple with the significance of the cult of saints were part of a crisis in his own (Anglican) faith, occasioned by Newman's attempt to involve him in his aborted project for the publication of a series of biographies of some seven hundred British saints and worthies (for which, see J. H. Newman, *Apologia pro Vita Sua*, ed. I. Ker (Harmondsworth, 1994), 282–301, and I. Ker, *John Henry Newman: A Biography* (rev. repr. Oxford, 1995), 281–2). But Herbert Paul, *The Life of Froude* (London, 1905), 33–5, and Lytton Strachey, *Eminent Victorians* (London, 1918), 35–7, are quite misleading when they take Froude's misgivings as evidence of a purely dismissive view of the cult of saints. In fact, the

ot(done)

ing to Gibbon and his dismissal of the cult as evidence of medieval credulity and superstition.[14] 'The legends grew, and were treasured up, and loved, and trusted, and alas!', he wrote, 'all which we have been able to do with them is to call them lies, and to point a shallow moral on the impostures and credulities of the early catholic.' Froude made no attempt to deny Gibbon's charge that the texts themselves had all the 'fiction, without the genius, of poetry'.[15] His strategy, like that of Brown, was to argue that the cult was an exercise in the imaginative construction of life in the light of a sincere, if somewhat extravagant, ideal. The cult was 'a singular mythology'. When seen in its proper place as an historical phenomenon, it is 'every bit as remarkable as any of the pagan mythologies'. The Lives of the Saints were 'written as ideals of a Christian life'. They lack intrinsic beauty, but they are 'always good'. Their historical inconsistencies reflect the devotion inspired by the hero himself. Bede's account of Cuthbert was not a lie, because it put forward a picture of life which he considered admirable and excellent, and which he was genuinely concerned to make his own. The achievement, moreover, was to establish a repertoire of positive role models, something without which education cannot succeed:

To try to teach people how to live without giving them examples in which our rules are illustrated, is like teaching them to draw by the rules of perspective, and of light and shade, without designs to study them in; or to write verse by the laws of rhyme and metre without song or poem in which rhyme and metre are seen in their effects. It is a principle which we have

preface to the Legend of St Neot which Froude produced for Newman puts forward, in an earlier form, the same argument as the essay discussed here: see J. H. Newman and J. Toovey (eds.), *Lives of the English Saints*, 16 vols. (London, 1844–5), ii, 73–83. The development of Froude's view of the cult of saints is best approached through the autobiographical documents and commentary in W. H. Dunn, *James Anthony Froude: A Biography*, 2 vols. (Oxford, 1961–3), i, esp. 72–85. On the subsequent direction of Froude's historical opinions, which boil down to a faith in the moral use of power, see J. W. Burrow, *A Liberal Descent: Victorian Historians and the English Past* (Cambridge, 1981), 231–85—esp. p. 237.

[14] Froude, *Short Studies*, ii, 245, attributes to Gibbon the charge that the sixty-six Lives of St Patrick 'must have contained at least as many thousand lies', and he repeats it elsewhere: see Dunn, *Froude*, i, 86 and 220. But Gibbon makes no such criticism in *Decline and Fall*, and neither I nor David Womersley (to whom I am grateful for help with this point) have been able to locate the claim in any other of his published works. Froude's position owes more, it seems, to the trajectory of his own personal development than to any close acquaintance with the arguments of his iconic opponent.

[15] Gibbon, *Decline and Fall*, ii, 428.

forgotten, and it is one which the old Catholics did not forget. We do not mean that they set out with saying to themselves, 'we must have examples, we must have ideals'; very likely they never thought about it at all; love for their holy men, and a thirst to know about them, produced the histories; and love unconsciously working gave them the best for which they could have wished.[16]

Like Brown, Froude offered a subtle justification of the cult of saints which posited a 'true' purpose that was a mystery even to its makers. (Froude knew full well from his study of the Lives of St Neot that many hagiographers professed an historical purpose of giving a factual account of what had actually happened.) His identification of this hidden function reflects, moreover, the values of his own age. It takes no interpretative finesse to spot the appeal to the Victorian anxiety about moral example and the debt to Carlyle: 'For fourteen centuries', he writes, 'the religious mind of the catholic world threw them out as its form of hero worship, as the heroic pattern of a form of human life which each Christian within his own limits was endeavouring to realise.'[17] The Lives of the Saints were an instructive and timely lesson in how morality could be taught, even if the stories of ascetic self-mortification that featured in many were incompatible with the world-devouring spirit of the Victorian Age.[18]

Brown spoke to a similar constituency, but his rhetoric was that of the 1970s. He appealed, for example, to the reappraisal of popular culture which the rise of democracy had encouraged and, more subtly, to the modern cult of 'the intimate' at almost every turn.[19] He was indebted, moreover, to E. E. Evans-Pritchard, for an awareness of the role of the problem of evil in religious systems,[20] and to his pupil, Mary Douglas, for a sense of the 'interdependence' between different types of 'religious symbolism' and specific forms of

---

[16] Froude, *Short Studies*, ii, 258. See, likewise, Froude's comments in *Lives of the English Saints*, ed. Newman and Toovey, ii, 80–1.

[17] Froude, *Short Studies*, ii, 254. See, of course, T. Carlyle, *On Heroes, Hero-Worship, and the Heroic in History: Six Lectures* (London, 1841).

[18] See further Froude, *Short Studies*, ii, 140–6.

[19] For two very different discussions of the phenomenon, see Richard Sennett, *The Fall of Public Man* (London, 1986), and Anthony Giddens, *The Transformation of Intimacy: Sexuality, Love and Eroticism in Modern Societies* (Cambridge, 1992).

[20] See 'Sorcery, Demons and the Rise of Christianity: From Late Antiquity into the Middle Ages', in M. Douglas (ed.), *Witchcraft Confessions and Accusations*, Association of Social Anthropologists Monographs 9 (London, 1970), 17–45, repr. in *RSoc.*, 119–46, at 119–20 and 131–2, where Brown offers due praise to E. E. Evans-Pritchard, *Witchcraft, Oracles and Magic among the Azande* (Oxford, 1937).

'social structure'.[21] The latter debt is revealed by his use of the word 'grid' in various formulations:

The *grid* becomes noticeably weaker as the distance increases from the controls exerted by the life of a Catholic town. . . . In all strata of society, however, the Catholic *grid* met with forms of unwillingness to participate fully in its controls; and, in the minds of most, it had to co-exist uneasily with alternative systems of explanation.[22]

[There arose] a Mediterranean landscape covered, in its most settled parts, with a *grid* of shrines.[23]

The spread of Christian *reverentia* made final the processes by which the indigenous cultures of the western Mediterranean had been imperceptibly eroded by a slow but sure pressure from on top exercised through the *grid* of administration and patronage relationships that had reached ever outwards over the centuries from the country villas of the great.[24]

This word derives from Douglas's *Natural Symbols*, which Brown read in 1969 while it was still in manuscript.[25] Here the terms 'grid' and 'group' are used to distinguish two different kinds of social discipline. 'Grid' applies to cultural codes generated in the wider social context—to the representations of reality promoted by, say, the State or the Church. 'Group' applies to pressures generated in the immediate social context—to the actual demands put upon the individual by, say, the family or the tribe. Late antiquity appears in this scheme as a 'highly classified society' in which both grid and group are strong. A steady pattern of social control generates a clearly defined and coherent set of 'classifications' or 'symbolic categories'.[26] Douglas's argument is that there is a close correspondence between symbolic systems and the level and character of social control. (It is a variation on Durkheim's theory that the function of religion is to give human beings a representation of the societies to which they belong that will invest their lives with meaning and purpose.)[27] In highly classified societies, acts of piety become routine and are directed towards authority and its symbols, while

---

[21] *CS*, 177 n. 102: the acknowledgement is well-hidden, but crucial. See also 'Holy Man', 135 n. 164, and the autobiographical narrative in 'Exemplar', esp. 11.
[22] *RSS*, 231.   [23] *CS*, 11.   [24] Ibid., 121.
[25] Douglas acknowledges his help in the preface to her *Natural Symbols: Explorations in Cosmology*, 1st edn. (London, 1970); 3rd edn. (London, 1996), p. vii.
[26] Ibid., 58–62.
[27] E. Durkheim, *The Elementary Forms of Religious Life*, tr. J. W. Swain, 2nd edn. (London, 1976), esp. 219–29.

misfortune is always interpreted in ways which reinforce social discipline: 'These people use the incidence of misfortune to uphold the moral law. Disease and suffering are either attributed to moral failures or invested with nobility in a general metaphysical scheme that embraces suffering as part of the order of being.'[28]

Brown regards the cult of saints as a cultural phenomenon of this kind—that is, as a symbolic system that relates to a concise social structure. The idea that the cult of saints offered a symbolic representation of the actual social order had already figured prominently in the article on sorcery which Brown published in 1970. Here the rise of the cult of saints is related to the emergence of a more 'stable and defined' society: 'In the West, the triumph of the great landowners ensured that senatorial blood, episcopal office, and sanctity presented a formidable united front: any form of uncontrolled religious power received short shrift in the circle of Gregory of Tours.'[29] The rise of a more 'regimented society' can be 'seen more clearly' in the cosmology of the age than in other records:

The correlation between Christian imagery and the social structure of the Later Empire is a fact almost too big to be seen: we meet it in every detail of the iconography of the Christian churches. By the sixth century the image of the divine world had become increasingly stable. Angels were the courtiers and bureaucrats of a remote Heavenly Emperor, and the saints, the *patroni*, the 'protectors', whose efficacious interventions at court channelled the benefits of a just autocrat to individuals and localities. . . . We have entered the tidy world of the Middle Ages.[30]

Brown adapted from Mary Douglas a method which enabled him to present the trends revealed in the religious literature (which forms the bulk of the surviving textual record) as a measure of empirical social change: namely, the establishment of an urban, binding, and hierarchical social ethos throughout Latin Christendom. The implication, furthermore, is that the cult of saints enabled Christianity to triumph over the various pagan alternatives because it added a new symbolic structure that was more akin, in a metaphorical sense, to social life as people knew it. A closer correspondence between religious symbolism and social reality helped to make Christianity more seductive than its rivals. Brown sees the cult as a healing delusion distinct from the decivilizing obsession that Gibbon diagnosed, but he implicitly accepts Gibbon's view that it was driven by mental

---

[28] Douglas, *Natural Symbols*, 110. See also ibid., 63.   [29] 'Sorcery', 131.
[30] Ibid., 142. See, likewise, *WLA*, 109–10.

forces operating outside the realm of rational thought. It is as though the rise of the cult of saints were the inevitable outcome of the all-pervasive influence of the late Roman city upon the unconscious minds of its citizens. The effectiveness of Brown's approach is the subject of the next section of this essay.

THE POLITICS OF SANCTITY

Brown's argument is so indebted to British social anthropology and it overturns Gibbon so neatly that it invites suspicion. It needs to be stressed, therefore, that it makes better sense of the surviving sources than many other theories. Latin hagiography provides, for example, much less support for the theory that the cult of saints existed in order to supply models of holiness than Froude and many scholars since have supposed. The vast majority of saints' Lives are difficult to construe as serious attempts to provide instruction for would-be saints. It is true that their prefaces often claim that they were written in order to preserve an example of virtue for future generations. But this is a standard prefatory topos, frequently derived, ultimately if not directly, from the *Life of St Martin of Tours* by Sulpicius Severus. It works alongside the usual humility topos (where the author protests the meagreness of his literary talents all the while belying his or her statements with a display of grammatical prowess) to demonstrate a worthiness to write such an important text. The exemplar-topos is itself belied by the content of the narrative. There is rarely any sense of how the subject developed into a saint. Although the authors often recount scenes from childhood and note the subject's educational attainments, the saint is already completely sanctified at birth or even in the womb. The crises and trials in his or her life demonstrate the presence of holiness rather than the method of its acquisition. The use of hagiography to provide examples for imitation may well have been more prevalent in the Greek-speaking world,[31] but it seems to have played little part in the work of Western hagiographers.

---

[31] Brown himself offered an up-dated version of the 'moral-imitation' argument in his 'Exemplar' article of 1983, where he argued that the cult of saints played a crucial role in disseminating certain 'central' models of holiness. It is significant, however, that almost all of his examples derive from Greek texts. As will emerge further below, positive admiration for the achievements of a saint rarely seems to have been the driving force behind the development of cults in the West.

The functions that Brown highlights agree, moreover, with emphases taken by the texts themselves. The hagiographers often extract from their miracle stories the point that they demonstrated divine approval for their subjects and they almost always show their subjects exercising an entirely effective and just kind of power: with the help of God's miracles the saint wins the recognition of a consensual populace in the end. The problem is that the polemical character of the texts renders any attempt to read their portraits of sanctity in action as figural representations of the actual organization of power in post-Roman society problematic. For the texts were not simply passive witnesses to the historical action, they were deeply involved in it in ways which distort their presentation of the cult of saints. Most saints' Lives present themselves as completely reliable accounts of what really happened, but they were in reality a kind of propaganda, making it difficult to distinguish the shared belief-system on which they depend from the new concepts that were being recommended for belief. Many have no explicit purpose other than to win recognition for the merits of a particular saint or relic, but behind such efforts lay struggles to defend the faith and to legitimize the authority of particular persons and groups within the Christian community that shaped the ways in which they defined the nature of sanctity itself.

The works of Gregory of Tours, on whom Brown relied heavily, seem, for example, to exaggerate the importance of relic-centred veneration at the expense of other forms of cult. They describe how Gregory promoted the cults of his patron saints by fostering devotion to their relics and shrines, while recounting the deeds and mainly posthumous miracles of many other 'enshrined' saints.[32] He certainly believed in the holiness of these phenomena, but it suited his interests to define himself as an advocate of these saints. Gregory was responding, as Raymond Van Dam has shown, to the difficult political situation in which he found himself at Tours, a situation which was not helped by the fact that the majority of St Martin's miracles were taking place not in his cathedral but at the saint's tomb on the outskirts of the city.[33] He needed visible evidence of

[32] e.g., Gregory's *Liber in gloria confessorum*, ed. B. Krusch, *MGH SS rer. Merov.*, i (1885), 744–820 (cited hereafter as *GC*), where all but 23 of the 107 extant chapters concern such saints and refer to miracles at tombs.

[33] *Saints and their Miracles in Late Antique Gaul* (Princeton, NJ, 1993), esp. 66–8, 128–35. See also Paul Fouracre's contribution below.

divine approval which he obtained by, among other things, adding an oratory to the bishop's residence and placing in it relics of St Martin, St Saturninus, St Julian, and St Illidius.[34] That other sixth-century religious leaders were engaged in similar attempts to manipulate relic cults is not in doubt. Radegund (d. 587) used her royal connections to obtain, for example, a finger of St Mammas from Jerusalem and relics of the True Cross from Constantinople. Their arrival helped her to protect her convent from the interference of Maroveus, Bishop of Poitiers.[35] What is in doubt is the extent to which this culture of tomb-centred sanctity, in which claims to power were legitimized through the acquisition of relics and the development of shrines, was representative of all that sanctity did and meant in sixth-century Gaul. There are grounds for thinking, for one thing, that living holy men may have had a more important place in sixth-century society than the scant attention given to them in Gregory (and Brown) would suggest. Saints of this kind, living alone on the margins of human settlement but providing cures and spiritual advice, become much more prominent in eleventh- and twelfth-century records, but there must be a suspicion that such people had been there from soon after the arrival of Christianity in Gaul, in far greater numbers than the sources suggest, and performing much the same tasks as they did in the Greek-speaking East.[36] Gregory was sufficiently interested in other kinds of sanctity to cover a few hermits, some of whom seem to have enjoyed widespread fame for their powers. He mentions, for example, a miracle-working recluse called Eusicius whom King Childebert (511–58) stopped off to visit while *en route* to Spain.[37] Whether such holy men became the subjects of saints' Lives may well have depended upon whether sufficiently well-funded churches

[34] *GC*, § 20.

[35] Baudonivia, *Vita S. Radegundis* (BHL 7049), §§ 14 and 16 (ed. B. Krusch, MGH SS rer. Merov., ii (1888), 377–95, at 387–9); Gregory of Tours, *Liber in gloria martyrum*, § 5 (ed. B. Krusch, *MGH SS rer. Merov.*, i (1885), 484–561, at 489–92). See also *RSS*, 239, and Van Dam, *Saints and their Miracles*, 30–41.

[36] One might emphasize here the medical functions that have been explored in different ways by A. Rousselle, *Croire et guérir: La foi en Gaule dans l'Antiquité tardive* (Paris, 1990), and P. Horden, 'Disease, Dragons and Saints: The Management of Epidemics in the Dark Ages', in T. Ranger and P. Slack (eds.), *Epidemics and Ideas: Essays on the Historical Perception of Pestilence*, Past and Present Publications (Cambridge, 1992), 45–76.

[37] *GC*, § 81. See also ibid., §§ 23, 33, 80, 85, 96, 97, 101.

acquired their relics and a desire to promulgate this evidence of their own righteousness.[38]

It was clearly in the interests of different groups to foster, moreover, variations on the cult of saints which permitted them to legitimize their own authority with the least difficulty. Some bishops were clearly able to present a plausible claim to religious authority on the basis of personal asceticism. William Klingshirn has argued quite convincingly that Caesarius of Arles (d. 542) adopted the role of the holy man, dressing in 'rags' rather than 'linen' and delivering 'cures' which were widely reported in his own lifetime.[39] Though he delivered sermons in honour of various local saints, Caesarius is never said to have promoted their cults through the translation of relics or the erection of shrines. It must have been difficult for many bishops, however, to assume an ascetic mantle without manifest hypocrisy. The promotion of relic cults offered them a solution to the problem of securing visible proof of holiness. What we see in Gregory of Tours is his embrace of this culture of tomb-centred sanctity. His works contributed to its development and promotion at the same time as they articulated his own claim to membership of the select group that was validated by it. Other bishops seem to have gone as far, moreover, as to suppress alternative forms of sanctity which might have diverted attention from their shrines, not to mention their own claims to holiness. Gregory recounts, for instance, how a group of unnamed bishops prevented the Lombard Wulfelaic setting himself up as a stylite in the region of Trèves. They admonished him to come down from his column on the basis that the local climate was too harsh to permit such self-mortification. This he did. Later one of them induced him to visit a distant estate and smashed the column to pieces while he was gone.[40] Without Gregory's interest in this man's story—which

---

[38]   e.g., the conflict over the remains of Desideratus: *GC*, § 85.

[39]   *Caesarius of Arles: The Making of a Christian Community in Late Antique Gaul*, Cambridge Studies in Medieval Life and Thought, 4th ser. 22 (Cambridge, 1994), 159–70. The evidence derives from Cyprian of Toulon *et al.*, *Vita S. Caesarii* (*BHL* 1508–9), ed. B. Krusch, *MGH SS rer. Merov.*, iii (1896), 457–501, a work which was modelled on the earlier *vitae* of Honoratus and Martin of Tours, but the argument seems plausible enough.

[40]   Gregory of Tours, *Libri historiarum X*, viii.15 (ed. B. Krusch and W. Levison, *MGH SS rer. Merov.*, i.1 (2nd edn., 1937–51), 335–6). For a similar interpretation of this episode, see P. J. Geary, *Before France and Germany: The Creation and Transformation of Merovingian Gaul* (Oxford and New York, 1988), 137–9.

appears to have been occasioned by their shared devotion to Gregory's patron, St Martin of Tours—this hint of an alternative style of sanctity in sixth-century Gaul might well have gone entirely unrecorded, such is the domination of the hagiographical record by the Lives of leaders of well-endowed churches.[41]

Of course, Brown never denied the ideological nature of the sources. The problem is that he treats them as a general form of propaganda for a uniform religious ethos when they are more likely to represent much more narrowly based and contentious cultures of sanctity. Gregory's culture of tomb-centred veneration is unlikely to have penetrated Gallic society to quite the extent that Brown maintains. Widespread acceptance of the underlying cosmology—belief, that is, in the existence of saints, that they exercised some kind of conscious presence through their relics, and in the divine origin of their miracles—seems almost certain for the nobility, even if most aristocrats cultivated different ways of winning each other's respect. Otherwise it becomes difficult to explain why bishops and abbesses invested such energy in articulating claims of this nature. But considerable doubt hangs over the extent to which this culture and the belief system upon which it depends embraced the population as a whole.

There have been strenuous attempts to show that hagiography was aimed at a broad Christian audience, but the evidence is quite ambiguous and tends, if anything, to point the other way. Most Lives are preserved in manuscripts which show that they were used to supply readings during the celebration of their subject's feasts, but the codicological evidence is skewed by the capacity of the great monastic establishments to resist the vicissitudes of history rather better than most noble households and is properly understood as a record of how saints' Lives were used within ecclesiastical institutions. Many *Vitae* may have originated within aristocratic households and begun their lives as historical entertainments to be read

---

[41] Though the method of their collection is extremely doubtful, the statistics set out in H. F. Muller, *L'époque mérovingienne: Essai de synthèse de philologie et d'histoire* (New York, 1945), 82–3, offer some illustration: he identifies some 175 'fifth-century' saints, 123 of whom were bishops and 8 of whom were abbots. The figures for Italy are even more damning: see ibid., n. 37.

[42] e.g. M. Van Uytfanghe, 'L'hagiographie et son public à l'époque mérovingienne', *Studia Patristica*, 16/2 (1985), 54–62, esp. 56–61; K. Heene, 'Merovingian and Carolingian Hagiography: Continuity or Change in Public and Aims?', *AB* 107 (1989), 415–28.

out at private gatherings.[43] The linguistic evidence is less inconclusive but only somewhat so. Popular audiences may have been able
to comprehend simple Latin as late as the ninth century, but almost
every text contains elements which play to a select audience and the
use of *sermo humilis* can be seen as one of them. The simple Latin of
the Bible was often held out as the only style capable of conveying
the ineffable in sanctity,[44] but many hagiographers did not write in
a plain style even when claiming to do so,[45] and it was always standard practice to write the preface in the most elevated manner that
the author could achieve. The attention given to these stylistic distinctions, ranging as it did from mere lip-service to scrupulous adherence, is probably best explained as being intended to engage the
approval of those who shared an awareness of such generic rules.
The rhetoric of *rusticitas* which Gregory deployed to denigrate resistance to cults appealed to the same kind of prejudice.[46] Given that a
typical purpose of such totems is to distinguish the groups who
appreciate them from those who do not, it seems unlikely that many
saints' Lives were composed with a broad social audience in mind.

   This is not to deny that the custodians of the major monastic and
cathedral shrines and those who had recourse to their saints communicated their beliefs to one another. The point is that various
groups interpreted the phenomena of sanctity in ways divergent
enough to undermine Brown's notion of a uniform culture of sanctity driven from above. Miracle collections do record the cures
which peasants and townspeople received, but the reporting of such
events was affected by the need to show that they replicated the
recognized patterns for such proofs of sanctity, resulting in a kind
of censorship of oral reports. Even the language of intimacy which

---

[43] As argued long ago by M. Heinzelmann, 'Neue Aspekte der biographischen und
hagiographischen Literatur in der lateinischen Welt (1-6. Jahrhundert)', *Francia*, 1
(1973), 27–44, esp. 40–2.

[44] Thus, Braulio, *Vita S. Aemiliani* (BHL 100), ed. L. Vazquez de Parga (Madrid,
1943), 3–38, at 4–5: 'Quo circa dictaui, ut potui, et plano apertoque sermone, ut
in talibus rebus decet haberi, libellum de eiusdem sancti vita.' On the theory of *sermo
humilis*, see further E. Auerbach, *Literary Language and its Public in Late Latin Antiquity
and in the Middle Ages*, tr. R. Manheim (London, 1965).

[45] Caesarius of Arles certainly simplified the language of his sermons in the belief
that his message would reach all sections of his audience, but note his complaints
about bishops whose preaching was accessible only to the cultivated: e.g. *Sermo*, 1, §
20 (ed. G. Morin, *CCSL* 103–4 (1953), 16–17). See also Klingshirn, *Caesarius*, 148–9.

[46] e.g. GC, § 29. On the meaning of the word, see Van Dam, *Gregory of Tours:
Glory of the Confessors*, Translated Texts for Historians, Latin ser. 4 (Liverpool, 1988),
12–13; idem, *Saints and their Miracles*, 124 n.

Brown took as evidence of the cults' deep appeal demands scrutiny. Paulinus of Nola and Gregory of Tours may well have invested their narratives with the heartfelt intimacy of their relations with saints, but such talk was part of a recognized form of social discourse which the educated listener knew as the proper way to speak to the powerful. Whether the expressions of *amicitia* which come out of the mouths of the protagonists in miracles stories accurately reflect the attitudes of humbler people towards their saints is debatable. Love may well have been overcome by fear, not least because some miracle collections seem almost designed to make people contemplate the grisly punishments they would suffer if they usurped the saints' rights and property. Most hagiographers seem, however, to have been exploiting the experiences of humbler devotees rather than attempting to modify popular belief and practice.[47] Indeed, one reason why some bishops did not recommend recourse to shrines may well have been because this form of cult was implicated in a tacit compromise with popular enthusiasms. This might explain why the condemnations of festive excess on saints' days that feature in the sermons of Caesarius of Arles[48] scarcely figure in the works of Gregory of Tours.[49] The possibility that tomb-centred cults did in fact feed upon polytheistic tendencies among the wider population cannot be excluded. The stance of the texts is emphatically monotheistic,[50] but monotheism was crucial to the political point that many were intended to make.[51] Their ability to win widespread

---

[47] J. M. H. Smith, 'Oral and Written: Saints, Miracles and Relics in Brittany, *c.* 850–1250', *Speculum*, 65 (1990), 309–43, esp. 326, 335–8, argues for the peaceful coexistence of several distinct cultures of sanctity: her hagiographers, far from being antagonistic to 'folkloric' devotions at sacred spots in the landscape, exploit the oral traditions associated with them for cultic and pedagogical purposes internal to their religious communities. Brown, *RSS*, 125, on the other hand, argues that 'rural' modes of religion succumbed to an urban culture of sanctity.

[48] e.g. Caesarius, *Sermones*, 55, § 2 (ed. *CCSL* 103–4, 242), and 225, §§ 5–6 (ed. ibid., 891).

[49] Festive drinking at the feast of St Cyricus is reported without condemnation, for example, in Gregory of Tours, *Liber vitae patrum*, iii.1 (ed. B. Krusch, *MGH SS rer. Merov.*, i (1885), 661–744, at 673). Cf. H. Magennis, 'Water-Wine Miracles in Anglo-Saxon Saints' Lives', *English Language Notes*, 23 (1986), 7–9.

[50] Note, for example, how Caesarius is denoted as *vir plenus Dei* and as *servus Christi* at almost every opportunity: *Vita Caesarii*, ii.7, 11, 18, 19, and so on.

[51] The role of God, however conventionalized, was crucial to the ideological message: see further M. Van Uytfanghe, *Stylisation biblique et condition humaine dans l'hagiographie mérovingienne (600–750)*, Verhandelingen van de Koniklijke Academie voor Wetenschappen, Letteren en Schone Kunsten van België, Klasse der Letteren, 49/120 (Brussels, 1987).

approval for their communities and the style of Christianity they
represented depended upon the premise that the shared deity of society as a whole had supported the saint before and after death. But
since miracles were also necessary to make the point, few custodian
communities are likely to have turned away 'rustics' who believed
that healing power resided in the saint himself.[52] It is necessary, in
short, to make provision for a far more complex relationship
between the élites who sponsored tomb-centred cults and their
devotees than either Brown or Gibbon allowed for.

The objection that Brown exaggerated the élite's control over the
cult of saints is, of course, nothing new,[53] but the implications for
his argument run deeper than is generally recognized. For Brown's
notion of the symbolic function of sanctity is critically undermined
by his reliance on sources which distort its role in Gallic society.
That relations between God, the saints, and humanity were understood in the light of the behaviour found in contemporary society,
that people projected their social experiences into their understanding of how these supposedly sentient intermediaries with the divine
acted, is plausible enough. But if different groups disagreed in their
interpretation of these relations, the images of routinized piety and
saintly power provided by the hagiographical tradition cannot be
seen as a guide to how this society actually worked. This aspect of
their contents is probably better understood as a projection of how
certain sections of the élite felt social life *ought* to be conducted—of
the kind of loyalty, obedience, and efficiency they hoped for. This
'ideal' is likely, moreover, to have been defined in the face of social
realities which were much less 'tidy' than Brown would suggest.
Then, as now, the role and purpose of authority were subject to
constant redefinition and renewal. The evidence should be seen,
therefore, as contradicting Mary Douglas: far from being the product of a highly ordered society, the hagiographical idea of cosmic

---

[52] Andrew of Fleury, *Miracula S. Benedicti* (BHL 1126), v.6 (ed. E. de Certain, *Les
miracles de saint Benoît* (Paris, 1848), 173–271, at 203), openly admits having to rework the account of a vision of St Benedict that a peasant had given him. See
T. Head, *Hagiography and the Cult of Saints: The Diocese of Orleans, 800–1200*,
Cambridge Studies in Medieval Life and Thought, 4th ser. 14 (Cambridge, 1990),
176.
[53] See J. Fontaine, 'Le culte des saints et ses implications sociologiques: Réflexions
sur un récent essai de Peter Brown', *AB* 100 (1982), 17–41, esp. 24 and 37–40;
A. C. Murray, 'Peter Brown and the Shadow of Constantine', *JRS* 73 (1983),
191–203, at 201; R. Van Dam, 'Images of St Martin in Late Roman and Early
Merovingian Gaul', *Viator*, 19 (1988), 1–27, at 16–18.

order was the fantasy of an élite threatened by violence and competition.[54] None of this need mean that the capacity of the cult of saints to provide a hook upon which images of social behaviour could be hung did not make a contribution to the rise of Christianity. The cult of saints may well have helped it to become all things to all people by enhancing its ability to accommodate the social projections of different personalities and types. This, however, is all that can be inferred from the evidence.

BELIEF, NECESSITY, AND THE LOGIC OF SANCTITY

The political functions of tomb-centred sanctity can, moreover, be reconciled with the manifest sincerity of its sponsors without recourse to obscure psychological factors. Much evidence points, as this section will now show, to the existence of a much less mysterious dynamic in which intellectual ingenuity, working in dialogue with perceived realities and received dogma, played a decisive role in breaking new ground. The process involved is usefully likened to practices that have been observed in modern science—if care is taken to distinguish the actual methods of science from its representation of itself as a purely rational form of inquiry.[55] Here the production of new knowledge often proceeds through efforts to explain anomalous phenomena: features of the real world which contradict a paradigm as understood from within its categories and classifications.[56] The process is one of vigorous attempts to stave off

[54] On 'clerical fantasies of consensus', see B. Abou-El-Haj, 'The Audiences of the Medieval Cult of Saints', *Gesta*, 30 (1991), 3–15.

[55] See S. B. Barnes, 'A Comparison of Belief Systems: Anomaly versus Falsehood', in R. Horton and R. Finnegan (eds.), *Modes of Thought: Essays on Thinking in Western and Non-Western Societies* (London, 1973), 182–98, esp. 182–6.

[56] The relativism recommended here takes as its fundamental ground the premise that thinking is channelled by the *a-priori* categories from which it sets out. Many discussions of the relativity of cultural systems take an all-or-nothing approach to the problem, but a relativist epistemology of this kind need not entail a deeper *cognitive* relativism. As Horton and Finnegan point out in the introduction to their *Modes of Thought*, 26–7, it may well be the case that in terms of actual procedures the thinking *processes* of human beings remain constant while diverse representations of thinking come and go as different groups of 'knowers' seek to fence off and privilege species of learning exclusive to themselves—actual scientific method may be no different from actual poetic method. It follows that cultural relativism in some spheres need not rule out the existence of some, possibly many, universal patterns in others. See also G. E. R. Lloyd, 'Science in Antiquity: The Greek and Chinese Cases and their Relevance to the Problems of Culture and Cognition', in D. R. Olson and

the impending failure of the received paradigm, though belief in it is often so well-entrenched that the possibility of its collapse is never contemplated. The perception is that here is something that needs to be explained, that has still to be accounted for. The development of the cult of saints seems, likewise, to have proceeded through intellectual efforts to reconcile the Christian belief-system with realities that generated problems when seen from within its own 'world-view'. The cult of the Holy Innocents, the infants of Bethlehem aged two or less whom Herod was said to have slaughtered in a vain attempt to destroy the Messiah, provides a nice illustration of the process involved and of one problem in particular that many cults seem to have arisen to answer—the problem of evil.

The origins of the cult are, admittedly, quite obscure. The infants seem to have been regarded as saints from the third century at the latest. Cyprian of Carthage (d. 256) cites them as examples of 'martyrdom for justice'.[57] Fuller information about how the cult was understood in the West appears with the emergence of the Latin sermon tradition in the fifth century.[58] These sermons strongly suggest that a driving force in the cult's development was a need to vindicate Jesus Christ from certain theological implications of the massacre. The problem was that the event's inclusion in Matthew's Gospel had, regardless of whether it had actually happened,[59] made

N. Torrance (eds.), *Modes of Thought: Explorations in Culture and Cognition* (Cambridge, 1996), 15-33, esp. 28-9, and idem, *Demystifying Mentalities* (Cambridge, 1990), esp. 27.

[57] *Epp.* no. 58, §§ 5-6 (ed. G. de Hartel, *CSEL* 3/2 (1871), 661). The evidence for the celebration of an annual feast on 28 December accumulates from the first decades of the fifth century: see F. Scorza Barcellona in *Encyclopaedia of the Early Church*, ed. A. di Berardino and trs. A. Walford, 2 vols. (Cambridge, 1992), i, 410.

[58] I discuss these sermons more extensively, to different effect, in my 'Suffering and Innocence in Latin Sermons for the Feast of the Holy Innocents, *c.* 400-800', in D. Wood (ed.), *Church and Childhood*, SCH 31 (Oxford, 1994), 67-80. On the Western tradition, see also F. Scorza Barcellona, 'La celebrazione dei Santi Innocenti nell'omiletica latina dei secoli IV≈VI', *Studi Medievali*, 3a ser. 15 (1974), 705-67; J. Lemarié, 'Sermon africain inédit pour la fête des saints Innocents', *AB* 96 (1978), 108-16. On the Eastern tradition, which appears to have originated after that in the West, see F. Scorza Barcellona, 'La celebrazione dei Santi Innocenti nell'omiletica greca', *Bollettino della Badia greca di Grottaferrata*, n.s. 29 (1975), 105-35.

[59] R. T. France, 'Herod and the Children of Bethlehem', *Novum Testamentum*, 21 (1979), 98-120, attempts to uphold the historicity of the massacre, but the usual position of modern theologians, that the story was invented in order to liken Jesus to Moses, is reasserted in W. D. Davies and D. C. Allison, *A Critical and Exegetical Commentary on the Gospel According to Saint Matthew*, 3 vols. (Edinburgh, 1988-), i, 264-5.

the Incarnation of Jesus indirectly responsible for a massacre of helpless children and for the suffering of their parents. If Jesus were the son of a just and all-powerful god, ought he not to have prevented these children suffering such an awful fate which they could not have deserved? An awareness of the story's damaging implications is indicated by the apocryphal *Acts of Pilate*, a work which may date from the second century. Here the elders of the Jews are said to have accused Jesus in Pilate's presence of having brought death to the children of Bethlehem.[60] The only solution was to argue that Jesus had in fact done them a favour by deigning to grant them the gift of martyrdom. It mattered not that the event was probably a rhetorical invention, for it had become an established part of the Christmas story. One of the earliest Latin sermons for the feast, *Herod and the Infants* by Peter Chrysologus, Archbishop of Ravenna (d. *c.* 450),[61] offers a clear insight into the underlying issues. Chrysologus turns explicitly to the charge that Jesus abandoned these 'soldiers of his innocence' whom he knew were being hunted down and martyred in his place midway through the text. Christ did not condemn his soldiers, he argues, he promoted them. He allowed them to partake of the glory of martyrdom without having to suffer the ordeal of an entire life. The infants and their mothers were blessed by their passion, because it conferred on them all the grace of both baptism and martyrdom:

They live, they live, who die for the truth, who are worthy to die for Christ. Blessed are the wombs that carried such as them; blessed are the breasts which gave suck to such as them. Blessed are the tears which were shed for them and conferred on the weeping ones the grace of baptism. For, by one gift, but in different ways, the mothers were baptized in their tears and the infants in their blood; the mothers suffered in the martyrdoms of their sons. For the sword which cut off their sons' limbs, reached the hearts of the mothers: thus it is inevitable that they will be consorts in their reward, as they were companions in their passion.[62]

Chrysologus even suggests that the infants, in their *naïveté*, rejoiced at the arrival of their executioners. The point was that the massacre was not an injustice against helpless children and parents which Christ ought to have prevented, but a wondrous miracle that redounded to their benefit.

---

[60] Ed. E. Hennecke and W. Schneemelcher, *New Testament Apocrypha*, tr. R. L. Wilson, 2 vols. (London, 1963), i, 453.

[61] Ed. A. Olivar, *CCSL* 24B (1975–82), 947–57.   [62] Ibid., § 8.

That the problem was not easily overcome but continued to drive the development of the cult is evident from its ongoing discussion in the sermon tradition. Caesarius of Arles finds it necessary, for example, to argue that the anniversary of the massacre of the infants is an occasion not for grief but to honour those who were killed for Christ's sake, not to weep but to give due veneration.[63] Rachel, who was said to have wept for the infants in Matthew 2: 18, 'did not need to be consoled', not because she was inconsolable, but because she was not sorry for them. It is only the foolish who think that Israel (for which Rachel was a symbol) was left bereft by the loss of its infants: rather, Israel was blessed by this, and she never lamented her sons. Bede (d. 734) addresses the subject from the same angle, though with rather more sympathy and intelligence.[64] Rachel's laments do not show that 'she wished the infants to return to the world, so that they might bear its strife with her'. In heaven, moreover, 'Rachel will not bewail her children, but "God will wipe away every tear from her eyes", and give them the voice of joy and of eternal salvation in their tabernacles'. We should not, he goes on, feel sorry about the infants' deaths (some manuscripts read 'unjust' deaths)[65] as much as we should rejoice that they have attained the palm of righteousness. It was only at a late stage in the development of the Western sermon tradition, from the late seventh century, that the homilists began to turn to the spiritual and allegorical significance of the Innocents' sanctity directly without first having to dispose of these questions of theodicy and divine justice.[66]

Belief in the infants' sanctity seems to predate the emergence of a regular feast by at least three centuries, but the rhetoric of the sermons suggests that it was required from the start in order to explain away inconsistencies between the Christmas story and fundamental tenets of Christian doctrine.[67] The authenticity of the Gospels and

[63] *Sermo* 222, §§ 1–2 (ed. *CCSL* 103–4 (1953), 877–8).

[64] *Homeliarum Evangelii libri III*, i.10 (ed. D. Hurst, *CCSL* 122 (1955), 68–72).

[65] Ibid., i.10, line 120 and its apparatus.

[66] See, for example, the early medieval sermon tradition discussed by J. E. Cross, 'The Insular Connections of a Sermon for Holy Innocents', in M. Stokes and T. Burton (eds.), *Medieval Literature and Antiquities for Basil Cottle* (Cambridge, 1987), 57–70. A somewhat different tradition, deriving from Cyprian, prevailed within the heretical Churches of North Africa: e.g. Maximinus the Arian, *Sermones de sollemnatibus*, 8 (ed. R. Gryson, *CCSL* 87 (1982), 69–72).

[67] Augustine, *De libero arbitrio*, iii.23.68 (ed. W. M. Green, *CCSL* 29 (1970), 315), is tantalizing but ultimately unhelpful: 'Non enim frustra etiam infantes illos, qui, cum dominus Iesus Christus necandus ab Herode quaereretur, occisi sunt, in honore martyrum receptos commendat ecclesia.'

belief in the justice and omnipotence of God were at stake. As has been observed in modern science,[68] analogy and metaphor were as important as reason and debate in the elaboration of a solution to the problem. Chrysologus likens the infants to regular martyrs by denoting them as *milites Christi*—as soldiers of Christ. From the tears and the blood of the infants and their mothers he draws, moreover, an analogy to the salvific sacrament of baptism. Bede, similarly, conjures up an evocative image of Rachel being consoled by God himself. The problem was generated by logical scrutiny of received history in the light of the established paradigm, but solved with the help of poetry as well as reason. Each new suggestion helped, moreover, to enlarge the notion of what sanctity comprised, to extend the repertoire of hagiological explanations or 'models' in a new direction. Solving the problem of the massacre of the innocents broadened the notion of martyrdom to incorporate a new category of persons who had never testified for the faith in the conventional sense. A certain kind of opportunism was doubtless one effect of the expansion of 'hagiology' in new directions such as this one, as 'impresarios' reviewed events in order to discover 'neglected saints' around whom cults might be fostered for economic or political gain. But just as the expansion of the notion of sanctity seems to have been driven by the need to solve pressing problems, so also the majority of cults seem to have arisen out of moments of genuine crisis. The emergence of a cult was typically a tentative and unpredictable affair in which hope and imagination contended with reality. The slightest disruption in the flow of miracles at a shrine might cast doubt over the whole enterprise. Powerful needs were necessary in order to persuade people to take the many risks involved, emotional as well as political. The hagiographical record, biased as it is towards the concerns of élites, indicates that the loss of leaders at critical moments was a frequent cause of such situations.

Stephen the Priest's *Life of St Wilfrid* provides a particularly fine example of how the loss of the leader might occasion the search for signs of sanctity. Writing soon after the Archbishop's death in 709,

---

[68] On the role of the poetic imagination in science, see Barnes, 'Belief Systems', 187–90, and on its ideological uses, E. P. Thompson, 'Anthropology and the Discipline of Historical Context', *Midland History*, 1 (1971–2), 41–55, esp. 49. See also, more generally, C. Shelley and P. Thagard, 'Mythology and Analogy', in *Modes of Thought*, ed. Olson and Torrance, 152–83.

Stephen uses the following speech to describe how his abbots and monks, afraid that their old enemies would seize the opportunity to attack them now that their once powerful patron was dead, persuaded themselves that he could continue to protect their interests:

> While the outstanding head of our way of life lived, we often endured various trials from the kings and princes of Britain, on all of which it was usual to impose a worthy outcome on account of the holiness and wisdom of the bishop and the support of [our] many friends. But now it is for us to believe fully and completely that our intercessor has been made equal through the sign of the holy cross to God's apostles, Peter and Andrew, whom he loved utmost and to whom with his subjects he dedicated his substance, [and] that, in the sight of God, he figures as the constant guardian of our security.[69]

On the first anniversary of the Archbishop's death, a great white arc appeared in the sky to assure the saint's followers that their *familia* was indeed protected by a 'wall of divine support'. The speech doubtless summarizes a much more complex series of discussions, but Stephen is unlikely to have misrepresented the process involved given that his immediate audience included many who had been parties to it. Wilfrid's followers were encouraged, of course, by their patron's saint-like actions in life: his 'holiness' and his success in defending his followers while he was still alive—itself a sign of divine support. Notice also that the debate was confined to the circle of Wilfrid's followers at this early stage in the cult's development. Their enemies no doubt ascribed an entirely different meaning to the 'great white arc'. Having persuaded themselves, furthermore, that Wilfrid's cause had and always would be supported by God and having found sufficient signs to confirm this belief, the

---

[69] *Vita S. Wilfridi episcopi Eboracensis* (BHL 8889), § 68 (ed. B. Colgrave, *The Life of Bishop Wilfrid by Eddius Stephanus* (Cambridge, 1927), 2–148, at 146): 'Quamdiu vixit optimum caput vitae nostrae, frequenter a regibus et principibus Britaniae varias temptationes sustinuimus, quibus omnibus propter sanctitatem pontificis et sapientiam multorumque amicorum subsidium finem venerabilem semper imponere consuevit; nunc autem nostrum est plene perfecteque credere, intercessorem nostrum per signum sanctae crucis coaequari apostolis Dei Petro et Andreae, quos maxime diligebat et substantiam suam cum subditis dedicavit, in conspectu Dei sine cessatione nostrae defensionis tutorem existere'. Cf. Eadmer's version of Stephen's *Life*, probably written during the first decade of the twelfth century, *Vita et miracula S. Wilfridi* (BHL 8893), §§ 60–1 (ed. and tr. B. J. Muir and A. J. Turner, *The Life of Saint Wilfrid by Edmer* (Exeter, 1998), 8–161, at 140), and the laments for St Radegund written soon after her death in *GC*, § 104, and in Baudonivia, *Vita Radegundis*, § 22 (392).

abbots and monks set about convincing others through the composition and circulation of the Life.

The significant element for present purposes is that reflection on the consequences of Wilfrid's not-being-a-saint preceded the search for evidence of his sanctification by God. In this example the search was driven by the sense of desolation and anxiety brought on by the sudden loss of a powerful patron,[70] but in many cases the search seems to have been driven by the implications of the leader's sudden death for the righteousness of his cause. Such misfortune could easily be seen as a sign of divine disapproval, but signs of sanctity might be prevailed upon to overturn this reading of events. They could be said to demonstrate that God was providing for the leader's followers in a new way: by transforming their former patron into a more powerful and permanent protector in heaven.[71] At other times it was simply a less precisely defined need to convert defeat into victory. Bede admits, for example, that the Great Persecution was, on the face of it, an unmitigated disaster for the early Church. An entire generation of leaders had been wiped out. But that reversal was turned into victory, he explained, when the miracles of those who had been martyred brought others to the faith. Indeed, the martyrs worked miracles in both life and death and the common effect was to bring about the conversion of unbelievers, sometimes the very persecutors themselves.[72] The identification of saints often seems to have been driven by the idea that it would be unthinkable if God had not conferred this honour in particular circumstances. Notions of sanctity were enlarged when the received body of hagiological knowledge was insufficient to solve these problems.

Similar processes were at work in the interpretation of events identified as miracles performed through the agency of saints. Commenting on a column of light that an abbot observed rising heavenwards from the lips and head of a praying monk, Gregory of Tours offers, for example, the following exegesis:

---

[70] This much was recognized by the twelfth-century historian Orderic Vitalis: cf. *Historia Ecclesiastica*, ed. M. Chibnall, 6 vols., OMT (Oxford, 1968–80), iv, 310–11.

[71] See further the works of Fouracre and Gerberding and of Hayward cited in n. 75 below.

[72] Bede, *In Ezram et Neemiam prophetas allegorica expositio*, § 3 (ed. D. Hurst, *CCSL* 119A (1969), 235–392, at 377–8). For a systematic treatment, see W. D. McCready, *Miracles and the Venerable Bede*, Pontifical Institute of Medieval Studies, Studies and Texts 118 (Toronto, 1994), 112.

I think that this fire contains a mystical sacrament, but the darkness of my senses cannot understand how as it becomes visible it produces such light but does not burn anyone. I know this one thing, that these fires appear to just men or above just men. For a fire appeared to Moses in the thorn bush and to the other patriarchs in a burnt offering. A fire also burst from the top of the blessed Martin's head and entered the heights of the heavens. Often I have heard Abbot Bracchio tell a story, as I wrote in the book of his life. [He said that] while he was celebrating nocturnal vigils in the church of the aforementioned bishop [Martin], relics of saints were brought by pilgrims and placed on the altar. Suddenly a ball of fire rose up from the relics and seemed to climb all the way to the rafters of the church. But, as he himself claimed, the fire did not appear to many people. Thus also it appeared during the dedication of my oratory, as I set down above.[73]

Here and in his account of the dedication of his oratory, Gregory adopts the posture of the dispassionate inquirer, but the underlying point is emphatic and quite political: he is himself one of the righteous, because he has received a miracle of a kind that only the just receive. The final premise is left unstated, but there is no doubting the thrust of Gregory's inductive logic. The argument was required, furthermore, because the received paradigm was inadequate for Gregory's needs: it was an established premise of patristic thought that evil people could and sometimes did perform miracles.[74] Driven by political need, in short, Gregory attempts to push the interpretation of the miraculous beyond its received limits.

Processes of this kind, in which reason and imagination attempted to reconcile the needs of the present with the precise implications of events, seem largely sufficient to explain the evolution of the cult of saints, and explaining the development of cults in these terms has a number of advantages over Brown's approach. Cults are seen as fiercely political and sincerely pious but without denying their rationality at the same time—as operating within an alien cultural framework but in accordance, typically, with the natural, observable, processes of the human mind. The intersections between political and religious practice are thrown into much sharper relief. Saints' legends are seen as a serious kind of history, as the products of urgent attempts to engage with the 'facts' and

[73] *GC*, § 38. The translation is adapted from Van Dam, *Gregory of Tours: Glory of the Confessors*, 50.

[74] See Augustine, *De Trinitate libri XV*, iii.7-9 (ed. W. J. Mountain and F. Glorie, *CCSL* 50 (1968), 138-45); idem, *De diversis quaestionibus octoginta tribus*, § 79 (ed. A. Mutzenbecher, *CCSL* 44A (1975), 227-9).

their implications rather than as expressions of collective creativity whose success depended upon their engagement with the mysterious needs of the human unconscious. In Brown's approach, devotees seize upon historical figures and project their values on to them almost as though the past they represented were an inert substance, a meaningless vacuum waiting to be filled with fresh ideas and aspirations. His communities leap, for example, upon almost any old unjust execution 'with gusto', converting it into a 'reassuring' narrative in which an 'unambiguously good power, associated with the amnesty of God and the *praesentia* of the martyr', overcomes the ever-present power of evil.[75] Yet by seeing cults as attempts to answer difficult questions about the precise fates of persons of great importance to particular communities, it is possible to make much better sense of the effort and risks involved in assertions of sanctity, of the relationship between the many improbable and inexplicable cults which Western Christendom produced and the defiant devotion of their adherents.

---

[75] *CS*, 101–2. In support of this point, Brown, ibid., 169 n. 88, cites the intriguing case of the so-called 'Innocents of Milan': five State servants, including the former head of the State treasury in Illyricum and three attendants of the deputy governor of Italy, who were venerated as martyrs in Milan having been unjustly executed by Emperor Valentinian I in about AD 365. The forces which generated this cult are almost beyond explication, since the only narrative source of near-contemporary origin, Ammianus Marcellinus, *Historiae*, xxvii.7.5–6, provides no access to the devotees' view, excepting the clue that the Milanese Christians call the place where they are buried 'the tomb of the Innocents'. It seems quite likely that the cult represents an early example of the sanctification of murdered leaders as 'innocent martyrs', a phenomenon whose Merovingian manifestations have recently been illuminated by P. Fouracre and R. Gerberding, *Late Merovingian France: History and Hagiography, 640–720* (Manchester and New York, 1996), 166–300, and whose Anglo-Saxon examples are the subject of my book, *Kingship, Childhood and Martyrdom in Anglo-Saxon England* (Cambridge, forthcoming). The cult is probably best understood, like the Anglo-Saxon and Frankish cases, as an attempt to avoid the providential implications of the precise historical event which was the victims' unjust execution. See also H.-I. Marrou, 'Ammien Marcellin et les "Innocents" de Milan', *Recherches de science religieuse*, 40 (1951–2), 179–90, and A. Vauchez, *La sainteté en Occident aux derniers siècles du moyen âge*, Bibliothèque des écoles françaises d'Athènes et de Rome 241 (Rome, 1981), now tr. J. Birrell under the title, *Sainthood in the Later Middle Ages* (Cambridge, 1997), 152, who, like Brown, treat the cult as a 'popular' response to injustice driven by emotional rather than theological (i.e. ideological) forces.

CONCLUSION

To comment on the rise and function of the cult of saints in Western
Christendom is to confront an intricate complex of problems for
which there will probably never be an entirely satisfactory solution.
Brown's pioneering attempt to provide a comprehensive explanation was an important breakthrough, above all for its perception
that one of the cult's primary functions was to legitimize the power
of élites by manifesting evidence of divine approval for the persons
and institutions through whom and for whom miracles were performed. Every eventuality was full of imminent danger when the
passage of events was seen through the prism of immanent justice.
Misfortune could easily lead to public denunciation and the loss of
social support, since it could be construed as a manifestation of
God's judgement upon hidden sins. Élites in particular were faced
with the constant problem of asserting divine approval in the face
of contingency. Saints' cults held out a number of different solutions, though none that was invulnerable to further twists of fate.
The implications of personal misfortune could be overturned, for
example, by submitting oneself to the public ritual of obtaining forgiveness at a saint's shrine.[76] The implications of a leader's
untimely death could be reversed with evidence that God had
merely chosen this point in time to turn him into a saint. The cult
of saints offered, in short, various solutions to the many 'legitimation problems'[77] that arose from the way in which 'events' were
understood from the Christian world-view.

   Brown turned our attention towards this fundamental point. Yet
problems arise from his attempt to present the cult, for all its collaboration with the structures of power, as a liberating phenomenon. Brown portrays the cult of saints as a compulsive system of
religious symbols which, having captured the hopes of all sections
of society, worked to ameliorate its worst excesses. The obligations
that bound men to serve their patron saints 'might seem hard . . .
to us', Brown explains, 'but it was through these that late Roman
men hoped to gain that freedom of action from which the miracle

---

[76] See further Van Dam, *Saints and their Miracles*, 89.
[77] For this concept, see Jürgen Habermas, *Legitimationsprobleme im
Spätkapitalismus* (Frankfurt, 1973); tr. T. McCarthy under the title *Legitimation Crisis*
(London, 1976).

of justice, mercy, and a sense of solidarity with their fellow human beings might spring'.[78] As attractive as this idea is, it rests upon a reading of a hagiographical record that skirts around the many conflicts, social as well as intellectual, that these sources were attempting to overcome. The underlying problem is that the cult of saints was always a phenomenon of doubtful authenticity. Brown would deny the need to investigate the cult's truth status, but it has to be asked how it could have brought lasting happiness into people's lives if, as his argument implicitly admits, its fondest moments were not genuine intimacies with responsive, animate, living beings, but projections of the mind—if the 'very special dead' were not alive in their shrines, but quite defunct. Brown suggests that saints' cults gave people the self-confidence and assurance that came from knowing that they had a reliable and all-powerful protector, but it could equally well be argued that it gave them a hopeless fear of suffering from which they might otherwise have been free.[79] The many discrepancies between ideal and reality cannot be ignored, not least because the arguments contained in the sources reveal that the participants were themselves struggling to cope with the problems they caused. It is difficult, therefore, to avoid the conclusion that the cult was fraudulent to some degree, even if it was as much a matter of self-deception as of the seduction of others.

The reality seems to lie somewhere between, and yet also beyond, Gibbon and Brown. Gibbon's approach to cultic phenomena is much more convincing than Brown's when, commenting upon the reactions of the pagans to the destruction of the Egyptian idol Serapis, he explores the dialogic relationship between contingency and belief.[80] But Brown rightly removed the cult from the realm of the sensual to that of the higher imagination, asserted the role of the aristocracy in its development, and rightly redeemed its sponsors from the charge of wholesale mendacity: relic-centred sanctity evolved to answer the genuine needs of an educated élite rather than to pander to the sensuality of the masses. Yet in his heavy reliance on psychological factors Brown permits Gibbon's charge of irrationality to escape unchecked. Far from 'shutting out the light of reason', the cult of saints evolved through logic and

---

[78] *CS*, 126–7.
[79] Compare A. R. Radcliffe-Brown, 'Taboo', in his *Structure and Function in Primitive Society: Essays and Addresses* (London, 1952), 133–52, esp. 149.
[80] *Decline and Fall*, ii, 85.

intellectual effort. Acknowledging the cult's 'rationality' demands, however, that we also recognize what Brown wished to diminish: just how deeply self-serving the cult of saints would seem, from the textual record, to have become.

7

The origins of the Carolingian attempt to regulate the cult of saints

PAUL FOURACRE

IN an important article published in 1990, Julia Smith contrasted cultures of sanctity in Celtic regions in the early Middle Ages with those patterns of sanctity which had been influenced by Carolingian practices.[1] Whereas in the Celtic areas the response to cults was determined by a strong oral tradition which fed off places and objects associated with holy men and women, in the Frankish areas, she argued, cults were more tightly controlled by written hagiography which stressed the importance of corporeal relics under the guardianship of proper authorities. The Franks, in other words, had their saints under control in ways which reflected the theocratic flavour of their government, for Frankish rulers attempted to intervene in spiritual life in order to achieve some level of social control through the harnessing of supernatural power. The power of the saints thus fed the power of rulers, not just in Francia, but quite clearly, and just as effectively, in Ottonian Germany, and Anglo-Saxon England, and, at a slightly later date, in what Gabor Klaniczay terms the 'peripheral areas' of Scandinavia and Central Europe.[2] As Smith suggested, when these other areas moved to control cults for political ends, this was done in imitation of Carolingian practice.

To illustrate how control of spiritual life and Carolingian power and influence grew together in mutual reinforcement, let us take the example of Bavaria in the eighth century. Here we begin with that honorary Carolingian, Boniface, for whom uncontrolled cults

---

[1] 'Oral and Written: Saints, Miracles and Relics in Brittany, c. 850–1250', *Speculum*, 65 (1990), 309–43.

[2] 'From Sacral Kingship to Self-Representation: Hungarian and European Royal Saints in the 11th–13th Centuries', in his *The Uses of Supernatural Power*, tr. S. Singerman (Cambridge, 1990), 79–94, at 83–6.

and unrestrained holy men were anathema.[3] In the decade after
738 Boniface demanded that Bavaria receive a proper diocesan
structure,[4] and that the church there reject the baptisms of those
Bavarian priests who had not been properly trained, which meant,
in effect, trying to undo independent missionary efforts in the
region.[5] Boniface also requested the pope to restrain the activity of
Bishop Virgil, a charismatic holy man who was his chief rival in
Bavaria.[6] Then, in the next generation we see Bavarian bishops
being pulled into a Frankish orbit with a downplaying of cults associated with the pre-Carolingian evangelization of the region. Finally,
thanks to the rich material of the charters of Freising, in the late
eighth and early ninth centuries we can see the Bishop of Freising,
backed by the Archbishop of Salzburg, Charlemagne's principal
agent in the region, asserting Freising's control over local monasteries and churches.[7] This involved taking over property, rights,
and resources, but the moral basis for the appropriation was the
bishop's rightful control over local cults: property given to the local
patron saint had become his moral responsibility. The political
agenda in Carolingian Bavaria is equally clear, for the donors who
lost control over the cults they had endowed were said to have
made their gifts in the time of Tassilo, the last Duke of Bavaria, who
was possibly Charlemagne's most dangerous opponent before he
was deposed in 787. Removing cults from the control of the local
nobility was thus part of the process of sweeping away the remains

---

[3] Boniface expressed his views in his letters, complaining, for example, about the activities of one Adalbert whom Boniface regarded as a charlatan, but who otherwise looks like a classic Brownian holy man: *Epistolae*, no. 59 (ed. M. Tangl, *MGH Epp. Sel.*, i (1916), 111–12). See also *CS*, 123–4 and n. 93.

[4] Boniface, *Epp.*, no. 45 (Oct. 739): Pope Gregory III responds to Boniface's report on the Bavarians, whom the missionary had found *extra ordinem ecclesiasticum viventes*.

[5] Boniface, *Epp.*, no. 68 (July, 746), which letter contains the famous line on the Bavarian priests who were so ignorant that they had been baptizing people *in nomine patria et filia et spiritus sancti*. The papacy here refused Boniface's demand that such people be rebaptized. Boniface returned to the demand in May of 748 (ibid., no. 80).

[6] Boniface, *Epp.*, no. 80.

[7] See *Die Traditionen des Hochstifts Freising*, ed. T. Bitterauf (Munich, 1905), nos. 142, 143, 145, 147, 169, 171, 183–7, 193, 197, 223, 227, 231–2, 235, 242, 251, 258, 275, 277, 284, 288, 299. These charters record disputes in which Bavarians contested the imposition of Freising's control over their proprietary churches and monasteries. See also P. Fouracre, 'Carolingian Justice: The Rhetoric of Improvement and Contexts of Abuse', in *La Giustizia nell' Alto Medieovo (secoli V–VIII)*, Settimane di Studio del Centro Italiano di Studi Sull'alto Medioevo 42 (Spoleto, 1995), 784–6.

of Tassilo's regime. Similar measures were attempted throughout the empire. Local cults were brought under the control of bishops who were themselves to be subject to metropolitan authority, and as Charlemagne's capitularies make abundantly clear, discipline in the Church was a primary concern of government.[8] Charlemagne frowned upon the idea of new saints being created, and since at the same time he insisted on the use of relics when oaths were taken, and commanded that all altars contain relics,[9] there was in consequence an explosion in the demand for relics from long-dead saints, preferably martyrs.

This, therefore, is the background to Smith's model of a relic-based Frankish sanctity, in which relics were boxed, labelled, distributed, and dispensed with episcopal sanction. This form of sanctity, which reinforced the social power of an aristocratic ecclesiastical hierarchy as a way of strengthening social control, Peter Brown traced right back to the sixth century. By the time of Pope Gregory the Great the holy was, wrote Brown, 'securely vested in men who knew what it was to rule, and who lived in a society where few men were prepared to rule as they were'.[10] In Brown's mind there was here a strong contrast between the Western style of relic-based cults controlled by bishops and the cults of the living holy man in the East. The Eastern holy man he notably showed to be an outsider and patron of village communities, a figure in competition with, rather than in support of, the hierarchy of Church and State.[11] There is surely a great deal of sense in Brown's contrasts, but they were intuitive rather than based in detailed analysis of contemporary materials, especially where the West is concerned. As Paul Hayward explains in this volume, Brown's approach to the text was shaped by anthropological models which he applied in an impressionistic fashion. Further, in supposing that Western sanctity assumed definitive social form in the sixth century, Brown did not consider the history of sanctity in the seventh

[8] For the first of many examples, see Herstal Capitulary of 779, §§ 1–5 (ed. A. Boretius, *MGH Legum*, sect. 2, *Capitularia Regum Francorum*, vol. 1 (Hanover, 1883), 47–8; tr. P. D. King, *Charlemagne: Translated Sources* (Kendal, 1987), 203).
[9] On oaths, see *Admonitio Generalis* of 789, § 64 (ed. Boretius, *MGH Capitularia Regum Francorum*, i, 58; tr. King, *Charlemagne*, 215). On the importance of relics to the Carolingians in general, see P. Geary, *Furta Sacra: Thefts of Relics in the Central Middle Ages*, 2nd edn. (Princeton, 1990), 28–43.
[10] 'A Parting of Ways', 193.
[11] 'Holy Man', esp. 115–41.

and eighth centuries, which is the time in which living saints made something of a comeback in the West, and in which the cult of the saints spread into new areas and amongst different groups of peoples. In what follows I shall focus on the living or recently dead saints of the seventh and eighth centuries, and on the relationship between power and sanctity in this period which lies, as it were, between Brown and Smith. This will permit a more precise explanation of the evolution of Carolingian attitudes towards sanctity in terms of a reaction against the saintly power held by their predecessors and rivals, the Neustro-Burgundian leaders of later Merovingian Francia.[12]

THE RISE OF THE HOLY IN THE SIXTH AND SEVENTH CENTURIES

Many of Brown's contrasts between the holy in Eastern and Western Christendom are open to doubt. His location of the holy in the particular dynamic of rural social development in Syria and Asia Minor seems to rest upon snapshots of village life taken from tendentious and highly coded sources, upon which he placed a great deal of weight.[13] Brown's view of the Frankish West rests overwhlemingly on the writings of Gregory of Tours, and he likewise takes Gregory at his word.[14] In the light of recent scholarship,

---

[12] P. Riché noted that the Carolingian preference for long-dead saints was in sharp contrast to Merovingian practice, but he did not really attempt to explain the phenomenon: see, for example, his 'Les Carolingiens en quête de sainteté', in J.-Y. Tilliette (ed.), *Les Fonctions des Saints dans le Monde Occidentale (III-XIIIe siècle)* (Rome, 1991), 217–24.

[13] In 'Holy Man', it is above all the skilful use of Theodoret which makes Brown's images of the Syrian holy man so vivid. He acknowledges that Theodoret had his own point of view (ibid., 120), but then uses his narrative without further *Quellenkritik*, rather as historians of early Iceland use saga material. More than twenty years later, in *AS*, Brown did of course address this question and acknowledged that in 'Holy Man' he had been 'following almost too closely the grain of our principal sources' (p. 59), thus taking too literally their picture of the importance of the holy men (now, 'holy persons'). Though this leads him to nuance his picture of the holy person's role in society, he remains wedded to a composite picture made up of anecdotes from a series of sources, still without making a critical evaluation of his material.

[14] In 'A Parting of Ways', 190, Brown makes the contrast 'between the exuberant and optimistic world of East Rome and the grim and depleted Gaul of Gregory of Tours'.

Gregory was not such a good example to choose.[15] Rather than using relics to maintain social control, Gregory was, as Van Dam has argued, hanging on to his job by the hem of Martin's cloak, forced out of his dilapidated cathedral to try and get in on the action at the shrine of St Martin in the suburbs.[16] Martin Heinzelmann's work on episcopal epitaphs would, in fact, have provided Brown with more reliable material with which to illustrate the accommodation of sanctity within late Roman aristocratic values, with the *virtus* of the noble Roman transforming into a manifestation of holiness, or sanctity itself.[17] But although one can trace the conventions of the epitaph into the nobility *topos* of early medieval hagiography, this is not to say that the sixth-century bishops wielded the same degree of power, through relics or otherwise, as did their later counterparts. Brown, to be fair, did hint at this.[18]

Recent work by Yitzhak Hen has re-emphasised that the later sixth century was a period in which sanctoral cycles in Gaul were rapidly being established.[19] The cycles themselves tend to show an early phase which established the feasts of universal saints, such as the apostles, followed by an increasing proportion of local saints, that is, local martyrs of Diocletianic vintage, and early bishops. These saints would provide the bedrock of a culture of sanctity throughout the Middle Ages.[20] Relatively few newcomers would subsequently join the ranks of these long-dead heroes, but in the seventh and early eighth centuries those who did join were

[15] One of the first studies to question the credibility of Gregory's historical narrative was I. N. Wood, 'Gregory of Tours and Clovis', *Revue Belge de Philologie et d'Histoire*, 63 (1985), 249-72. The seminal critique of Gregory's writing is W. Goffart, *The Narrators of Barbarian History* (A.D. 550-800): *Jordanes, Gregory of Tours, Bede, and Paul the Deacon* (Princeton, 1988), 112-234. See now, in addition, the analysis by M. Heinzelmann, *Gregor von Tours* (538-594), 'Zehn Bücher Geschichte': *Historiographie und Gesellschaftskonzept im 6 Jahrhundert* (Darmstadt, 1994).

[16] R. Van Dam, *Saints and their Miracles in Late Antique Gaul* (Princeton, 1993), 69-81.

[17] M. Heinzelmann, 'Neue Aspekte der biographischen und hagiographischen Literatur in der lateinischen Welt (1.-6. Jahrhundert)', *Francia*, 1 (1973), 27-44; idem, *Bischofsherrschaft in Gallien. Zur Kontinuität römischer Führungsschichten vom 4 bis zum 7 Jahrhundert. Soziale prosopographische und bildungsgeschichtliche Aspekte*, Beihefte der Francia, 5 (Zurich, 1976); idem, ' "Sanctitas" und "Tugendadel": zur Konzeptionen von "Heiligkeit" im 5 und 10 Jahrhundert', *Francia*, 5 (1977), 741-52.

[18] The hint is present in *RSS*, 246-7 n. 98, where he criticizes the work of F. Prinz.

[19] *Culture and Religion in Merovingian Gaul*, A.D. 481-751, Cultures, Beliefs and Traditions. Medieval and Early Modern Peoples 1 (Leiden, 1995), 82-120.

[20] I am grateful to David Ganz for impressing this point upon me.

important contemporary leaders, whose sanctity would become a clearly political issue. Later, partly as a result of the Carolingian shift in preference, and partly simply due to a fading memory of Merovingian history, many of their cults would lapse into obscurity.[21] This does not mean, however, that such leaders were not famous in their own time. Although relics were essential to the establishment of the cults of the more ancient saints, it may be a fair impression that in the sixth century the relic stock was still being built up. Without Gregory of Tours' particular and rather personal emphasis upon the importance of relics, we would actually hear about them much less in the sixth than in the seventh century, and it was undoubtedly in the latter period that the translations of local saints got going. We may therefore accept that the forms which sanctity would take were indeed established by the end of the sixth century, in terms both of models of behaviour expressed in hagiographical convention, and of the intercessionary value placed on relics. On the other hand, before sanctity could become a source of significant social and political power, local cults had first to become widespread throughout Frankish Gaul, and the episcopate had, second, to be drawn from amongst the most powerful in society to a degree that it had not been in the sixth century.[22] The centralizing tendency in Carolingian sanctity was in great part a response to the political ramifications of these developments, and in particular it was a reaction to the sanctification of other powerful magnates which took place in the course of the seventh century.

The seventh century opened with the arrival in Francia of what appears at first sight to have been a radically new form of sanctity, in the form of Irish holy men. These newcomers were outsiders, very much alive, and made a point of challenging rulers. This impression is formed by one highly influential source, the *Life of Columbanus* which focused upon the conflict between Columbanus

---

[21] The cult of St Praejectus provides a good example. A Bishop of Clermont murdered in 676, he became the focus of a martyr cult based on his tomb in a family monastery at Volvic, outside Clermont. After his body was moved to Flavigny by Abbot Widerad in 755, the monastery disappeared and Volvic is now much better known for its mineral water than for its native saint, Praejectus.

[22] For a general account of this process, see P. Fouracre and R. A. Gerberding, *Late Merovingian France: History and Hagiography, 640–720*, Manchester Medieval Sources Series (Manchester and New York, 1996), 43–52.

and the queen Brunhild,[23] and its narrative of Columbanus's part in Brunhild's downfall was taken up with gusto in the *Fourth Book of the Chronicle of Fredegar*.[24] But after the conflict with Brunhild, which had its own political logic, the so-called 'Columbanan movement' rapidly became a vehicle for the spread of a culture of sanctity amongst the Frankish aristocracy. The point here was that Columbanus's spiritual athleticism was monastic in inspiration, and in order to safeguard its purity he insisted that his monastery of Luxeuil be free of outside interference, whether by rulers or by bishops. This provided a model of monasticism which proved highly attractive to independently minded powerful people. There followed a wave of monastic foundations in the style of Columbanus's establishment at Luxeuil, and around the middle of the seventh century other Irish holy men arrived on the scene, helping to keep up enthusiasm for this form of religious devotion. This is all textbook stuff,[25] and it hardly needs to be rehearsed in detail here, but it is worth stressing that the relationship between power and sanctity did take a new turn at this time with the involvement of leading families outside the traditional Gallo-Roman centres represented in the sanctoral cycles of the previous century. That members of such families then came to be included amongst those venerated as saints is equally well documented, although it still needs saying that this multiplication of cults did not amount to a process of 'aristocratic self-sanctification' in which families of Germanic extraction found a new, Christian, form of charisma.[26] The reason for reiterating this point is not merely to pile more scorn on the now long-discredited notion of Germanic charisma,[27] but also to indicate the way in

---

[23] Jonas, *Vita Columbani et discipulorum eius* (BHL 1898), ed. B. Krusch, *MGH SS rer. Merov.*, iv (1902), 64–108.

[24] Fredegar, *Chronica*, §§ 36 and 42 (ed. J. M. Wallace Hadrill, *The Fourth Book of the Chronicle of Fredegar and its Continuations*, Nelson's Medieval Texts (London, 1960), 23–9 and 34–6).

[25] See, for instance, the account of Columbanus's activity and influence in P. J. Geary, *Before France and Germany: The Creation and Transformation of Merovingian Gaul* (Oxford and New York, 1988), 171–8. For a more critical view of the traditional picture, see I. N. Wood, *The Merovingian Kingdoms 450–751* (London, 1994), 181–97.

[26] The idea of 'aristocratic self-sanctification' (*Adelsselbstheiligung*) was formulated by F. Prinz, *Frühes Mönchtum in Frankenreich: Kultur und Gesellschaft in Gallien, den Rheinlanden und Bayern am Beispiel der monastischen Entwicklung (4. bis 8. Jahrhundert)* (Munich, 1965), 489–93. For further qualifications on the usefulness (or otherwise) of this concept, Fouracre and Gerberding, *Merovingian France*, 38–9, 46–52.

[27] F. Graus was the first to discredit it in his *Volk, Herrscher und Heiliger im Reich der Merowinger: Studien zur Hagiographie der Merowingerzeit* (Prague, 1965).

which access to the holy had become a normal part of élite culture, that is, a normal attribute of power. Far from being the preserve of any one ethnic group, it had actually become a principal element in the integration of people from different backgrounds into a single élite, and in the course of the seventh century a common investment in cults would become an important plank in the construction of a non-ethnic Frankish identity. By the late eighth century, in the Long Prologue to the *Lex Salica Karolina*, the Franks' patronage of martyr cults was claimed as one of their most distinguished features, and one which made them superior to the Romans of old who had persecuted the very saints whose bodies the Franks now decorated with gold and silver.[28] This largesse towards the saints was also associated in the Prologue with the search for wisdom and justice which was the second quality in Frankish superiority. The third was success in battle, which the first two merits earned them. The need to preserve these qualities was seen as the duty of the rulers, a duty which positively necessitated their intervention in religious life. The Carolingians may have had theocratic pretensions, but they always worked within existing custom and by manipulating aristocratic consensus. Control over cults was achieved largely by leading patronage away from saints associated with their opponents and back towards the martyrs of old.

One important reason why the sixth century looks rather different to the seventh century not just in terms of attitudes towards the supernatural, but also in terms of politics and power in general, is that whereas for the sixth we are dependent upon a single, concentrated narrative, that of Gregory of Tours, which argues for the operation of the divine in the world of men, for the seventh century we have an increasingly diverse range of sources which take that operation for granted. It is now clear, if it was not before, that sanctity has entered the grain of social and political life, and the miraculous requires less emphasis in the political narrative. One source for this impression is the *Fourth Book of the Chronicle of Fredegar*, compiled probably *c.* 660, and it is an important source because its references to the cult of saints are usually incidental, rather than hagiographical or proprietorial. Take, for instance, Fredegar's last word, the conclusion of a story about the struggle for power in

---

[28] Ed. K. A. Eckhardt, *Lex Salica: 100-Titel Text*, Germanenrechte, neue Folge (Weimar, 1953), 86–90; tr. K. F. Drew, *The Laws of the Salian Franks* (Philadelphia, 1991), 171.

Burgundy between two leaders, Flaochad and Willebad.[29] Willebad was killed in battle, but his vanquisher, Flaochad, died of fever shortly after: 'Many believed', wrote Fredegar, 'that since Flaochad and Willebad had time and again sworn mutual friendship in places holy to the saints (*loca sanctorum*) and in addition had both greedily oppressed and robbed their people, it was God's judgement that delivered the land from their overweening tyranny and laid them low for their faithlessness and lying'. Elsewhere too, Fredegar refers to *loca sanctorum* in political contexts: they were where oaths were taken and fidelity tested. Interestingly, apart from condemning the theft of church property, oath-breaking, and oppression, he comments very little on other aspects of behaviour, including violence, even when this takes place close to sanctuaries. No comment is offered, for example, on the behaviour of King Clothar when he had an opponent, one Godinus, conducted on a tour of *loca sanctorum*, 'on the pretext of having him swear lifelong fidelity, but in fact only with the object of finding a suitable place to kill him', which he duly did.[30] Fredegar's view of Clothar, sounded earlier in the *Chronicle*, would not in fact have looked out of place as an episcopal epitaph, or as the opening of a saint's life. He was 'strong minded and educated in letters, God fearing, a munificent patron of churches and priests, an almsgiver to the poor, kindly disposed to all and full of piety'.[31] It was clearly possible to be all these things as well as being a bloodthirsty Merovingian.

THE POWER OF SANCTITY

One might in this context argue that sanctity was progressively debased by the attentions of the powerful, that it was, in effect, secularized as it was subjected to political needs. But by the same token, sanctity could be an effective agent in the reinforcement of power only if there was a genuine belief in its efficacy, for this was the basis upon which it attracted widespread support. As we have seen, in the course of the seventh century new saints were created as cults multiplied and spread, these new recruits typically being drawn from the founders of monasteries and from the episcopate. These men, and some women, were often active in politics,

[29] Fredegar, *Chronica*, § 90.   [30] Ibid., § 54.   [31] Ibid., § 42.

sometimes violent politics. Hagiography written not long after the
heat of the moment does not hide this fact, but interprets careers in
the light of convention, and with hindsight, that is, in the certainty
that what all these leaders did on earth was in fact leading towards
heaven.[32] Were such people really regarded as holy, or was there a
kind of cultural conspiracy to think good of the great, or at least of
those great in whom institutional interests were vested? This is a
question hard to answer given that nearly all of our source material was, of course, produced in support of those same institutional
interests, and was framed by the conventional view of sanctity as
an all-important principle of social as well as religious life. Peter
Brown in effect chose to accept this convention as a true reflection
of social life. Can we?

If we are to treat sanctity as having a political importance derived
from a genuine belief in the holiness of contemporary leaders and
in the efficacy of supernatural power, we must look hard for material which can verify that belief. Because he supports no identifiable
institutional interest, Fredegar is one source we *can* use for more
neutral (though still conventional) comment on sanctity. The *Liber
Historiae Francorum* is another, but not quite so useful because
being written in the 720s there was time for its author to be influenced by the *Vitae* composed in the late seventh century.[33]
Fredegar, writing about the events of the year 636, referred in passing to the reputation of the referendary Dado, whose company the
God-fearing Breton leader Judicael preferred to that of the dissolute
King Dagobert.[34] Judicael recognized that Dado, the later St
Audoin, led a religious life (*sanctam religionem sectantem*), and the
reference provides a unique confirmation that Dado (Audoin) really
was regarded as holy when a young man at court, as his *Vita*
claimed.[35] Moreover, we can be absolutely certain that this reference was independent of hagiographic tradition because it must
have been made at a point at which Audoin still had at least twenty

[32] On the framing of careers and conflict within hagiographical conventions, see
Fouracre and Gerberding, *Merovingian France*, 42–8.
[33] *Liber Historiae Francorum*, ed. B. Krusch, *MGH SS rer. Merov.*, ii (1888),
215–328. See also the translation of chs. 43–53 with commentary in Fouracre and
Gerberding, *Merovingian France*, 79–96.
[34] Fredegar, *Chronica*, § 78.
[35] *Vita Audoini episcopi Rotomagensis* (BHL 750), §§ 3–4 (ed. W. Levison, *MGH SS
rer. Merov.*, v (1910), pp. 553–67; tr. Fouracre and Gerberding, *Merovingian France*,
155–6).

years of life left in him, for he did not die until 684. When, on the other hand, the *Liber Historiae Francorum* waxes lyrical on Audoin's reputation, we may suspect that its author was responding to a written account of the saint's virtues.[36] Independent confirmation of Audoin's reputation is particularly important because he was just the sort of saint who was up to his neck in the power struggles of the day, and an accessory to violence. Another confirmation of a hagiographer's claim that his or her hero had holy power which others acknowledged, can be found in the *Passio Praejecti*.[37] This is less clear-cut in terms of dating, but it is in a way more impressive because it concerns a hagiographer's acceptance of an opponent's claim to sanctity, and as this admission seems to run counter to the author's purpose of building up the prestige of her or his subject, it is all the more believable. The *Passio Praejecti* was composed soon after the murder of its hero, Praejectus, Bishop of Clermont, which took place in January 676.

Another saint, Leudegar, Bishop of Autun, had been involved in the events leading up to the murder of Praejectus, and our author refers to his part in them in critical terms, saying that they were a stumbling block or *scandalum* on Leudegar's path to martyrdom. But she, or he, goes on to say that later Leudegar 'grasped the palm of martyrdom and now he is strong in the performance of holy miracles'. Leudegar's death took place sometime in the years 677–9, and it is reasonable to suppose that the earliest version of his *Passio* was composed in the very early 680s, so the *Passio Praejecti* and the *Passio Leudegarii* were written down at roughly the same time.[38] It was Bruno Krusch's view that the *Passio Praejecti* was the first to be written, and if this was the case, then the work backs up the claim made in the *Passio Leudegarii* that people recognized Leudegar's miraculous power soon after his burial. Without this cross-reference one would be tempted to dismiss the latter claim as merely conventional. With it, we have to take the claim seriously, and with

[36] *Liber historiae Francorum*, § 47; Fouracre and Gerberding, *Merovingian France*, 92.

[37] *Passio Praejecti episcopi et martyris Averni* (BHL 6915–16), ed. B. Krusch, *MGH SS rer. Merov.*, v (1910), 225–48; tr. with commentary in Fouracre and Gerberding, *Merovingian France*, 254–300.

[38] *Passio Leudegarii episcopi et martyris Augustodunensis* (BHL 4849b), ed. B. Krusch, *MGH SS rer. Merov.* v (1910), 282–322; tr. with commentary in Fouracre and Gerberding, *Merovingian France*, 191–253. On the relationship between the *Passiones* of Leudegar and Praejectus, see ibid., 225 n. 118.

Leudegar we are dealing with a saint who, like Audoin, was involved in a violent struggle for power. In fact, the two of them lined up on opposite sides of the same power struggle. Leudegar lost. It is a happy coincidence that the only two people whose saintly reputations we can confirm in this way happened to be two of the most powerful men on the Frankish political scene. So, although we have pathetically little information to go on, the question of whether or not there was a genuine belief in the holiness of such people should, on the available evidence, be answered in the affirmative.

Evidence for the importance of sanctity in Frankish culture in more general terms (as opposed to belief in the holiness of specific individuals) is of course ubiquitous, since all of our written sources have passed through a clerical medium, although archaeology might suggest that the victory of Christian culture was not as early nor as complete as its writers proclaimed. As suggested earlier, the basic forms of this written culture can be traced back at least into the sixth century, and the distinction of the seventh century tends to lie in degree rather than in kind. Where charters are concerned we have no surviving examples from the sixth century, but plenty (several hundred, that is) from the seventh and early eighth centuries. Guy Halsall has argued that in the seventh century there was an increasing concern to keep the written records of property ownership and transfer, a concern which reflects a more permanent ownership of land.[39] Halsall's contrasts between the sixth and seventh centuries may be overdone, given the similarities between later Roman and Merovingian diplomatic which seem to indicate unchanging concepts of ownership, but what does seem to be new in the seventh century is the development of the charter of immunity, and what may not be new but which dominates the charter content is the giving of gifts to monasteries and churches, envisaged as giving to *loca sanctorum* and to the saints who inhabited the *loca*. Behind this activity no doubt lay expression of all manner of power relationships, exchanges, and transactions, now lost to us because usually we have only the one link in what usually must have been a longer chain of dealings. But it is clear that the form in which these transfers of property took place was the gift to the holy, and if we take the charter *arenga* seriously, the point was to merit supernatural reward. We may see here a tendency to turn supernatural

[39] G. Halsall, *Settlement and Social Organization: The Merovingian Region of Metz* (Cambridge, 1995), 46–8.

power into a commodity. Although such power could not be bought or sold, it could be earned by honouring a saint with gifts. Royal charters which conferred immunity on churches and monasteries express the point of the gift most clearly.[40] Rulers granted rights and resources to chosen institutions to pay for the burning of lamps, that is, in order to pay for an important spiritual service which symbolized eternity. Sometimes the grants would also be intended to pay for food or alms, which like the oil in lamps, could be consumed and could thus convert the material into the spiritual. The hoped-for counter-gift is vague: eternal reward, 'mercy', future salvation, or just 'benefits'. Indeed, the exchange looks so rhetorical that it has usually been seen as a mere vehicle for a privilege which was essentially political in nature and which had constitutional implications in that kings granted away so much in this manner that the consequence was a significant loss of royal power. I have recently argued that it is a false impression that immunities had this effect in the longer term, but it still remains striking that rulers were prepared to invest so heavily in salvation and the prospect of supernatural aid, whether via immunities or by simple grants of property. The same goes for the other powerful who made substantial gifts to the holy. There are two obvious points to be made here. First, the extent of gift-giving to the holy confirms the impression that there was a very strong, not just rhetorical, belief in the efficacy of supernatural power. Second, the giving meant that the patrimonies of the saints were massively built up in this period. It was the combination of the power which came from property and the spiritual prestige which came from an association with the saint to whom that property had been given that made access to sanctity so essential to leading families.

A politicization of sanctity was the natural consequence of the involvement of the powerful. Such people were in cultural and political terms rather different from Brown's late antique and sixth-century Gallo-Roman bishops and abbots who were 'born to rule', but who were, in the main, local leaders rather than national figures. The seventh-century saints, on the other hand, were members of a political élite which identified itself as 'Frankish' and which was

---

[40] On charters of immunity and their religious and historical significance, see P. Fouracre, 'Eternal Light and Earthly Needs: Practical Aspects of the Development of Frankish Immunities', in W. Davies and P. Fouracre (eds.), *Property and Power in the Early Middle Ages* (Cambridge, 1995), 53–81.

active in the affairs of the royal palace, and was thus involved in politics at a supra-regional level. This involvement is why, around the middle of the seventh century, we begin to see saints caught up in conflict when palace politics turned to violence. Conflict also had the effect of refreshing established models of sanctity with contemporary examples. In particular, the seventh century saw a reinvention of martyrdom, with five, possibly six, martyrs being created in the later Merovingian period.[41] In addition, abbots, abbesses, bishops, and rulers who died more peacefully were included amongst the new saints. It is indeed worth considering whether the grounding of models in the lives of contemporary leaders may have been crucial in keeping up interest in the traditions of much older saints. Certainly, the making of new martyrs and the search for old ones went hand in hand. What we see, therefore, is a burgeoning culture of sanctity with investment in the cults of saints of different types and of different vintages, with the new stimulating an interest in the old, and vice versa. Let us now turn to the political history which directly influenced Carolingian attitudes towards sanctity, namely their preference for old over new saints, and their wish to control the spread of cults.

THE USES OF SANCTITY IN POLITICAL LIFE

As we have seen, the two most politically powerful saints of the seventh century were Audoin and Leudegar, and they were on opposite sides of a struggle for power in the Neustro-Burgundian regime which dominated Francia for much of the seventh century. It was the leading families of this kingdom which were overwhelmingly involved in setting up new cults, endowing older ones, and founding monasteries. There was, of course, similar activity in Austrasia, with the Pippinid family at the forefront, but it is in Neustria-Burgundy that we see the closest conjunction of sanctity and power. Here one can detect the Merovingian rulers attempting more sys-

---

[41] The five certain examples are Aunemund, Bishop of Lyons (d. *c.* 660), Germanus, Abbot of Grandivalle (d. *c.* 675), Praejectus (d. 676), Leudegar (d. 677 × 679), and Lambert, Bishop of Tongres-Maastricht (d. 705 × 707). Ragnebert, a layman executed at some point between 659 and 680, may represent a sixth example, but his ninth-century *Passio* (BHL 7058), ed. B. Krusch, *MGH SS rer. Merov.*, v (1910), 209–11, leans so heavily on *Passio Leudegarii* that one must doubt that it contains any authentic detail about the seventh century.

tematically to reinforce themselves with supernatural power by building up the patronage of St Denis, by trying to gather a store of relics in the palace, and by issuing immunities to the most prestigious churches and monasteries. Queen Balthild, who was regent from 657 to about 664, is the first Western ruler modern historians speak about as having had a *Klosterpolitik*, and this amounted to taking control of the kingdom's premier cult sites, the *seniores basilicas*.[42] Balthild, of course, became a saint herself. One of her principal advisers was Audoin, and she is said to have promoted Leudegar to the see of Autun. On the downside, she is also said to have had Bishop Aunemund of Lyons killed, and if we believe Stephen the Priest's *Life of Wilfrid*, she had another nine bishops put to death.[43] In this period the Neustro-Burgundian élite seems to have been divided into two factions, which were not always at loggerheads, but which, despite cross-factional marriage ties, did eventually attempt to exterminate each other. One side was led by the 'mayor of the palace' Erchinoald, who had brought Balthild to Francia and had provided her as royal bride. He died in 659. His son Leudesius, Balthild, and Leudegar became allies. The other side was led by Audoin, Ebroin (who was Erchinoald's successor as 'mayor'), and Agilbert, who became Bishop of Paris once Balthild was out of the way.

These groups (which were, of course, very much larger than the principals mentioned here) are usually studied for the history of their interfactional rivalry,[44] but I would here simply like to emphasize their power. Its heartland was in the Seine-Oise region, stretching up to the Somme and east towards Rheims, but they had connections throughout Francia. Erchinoald's relatives, for

---

[42] For Balthild's 'monastic policy', see E. Ewig, 'Das Privileg des Bischofs Berthefrid von Amiens für Corbie von 664 und die Klosterpolitik der Königin Balthild', *Francia*, 1 (1973), 62-114; repr. in his *Spätantikes und fränkisches Gallien*, Beihefte der Francia 3, 2 vols. (Munich, 1979), ii, 538-83. On the wider significance of Balthild's career, see J. L. Nelson, 'Queens as Jezebels: Brunhild and Balthild in Merovingian History', *Medieval Women*, ed. D. Baker, SCH: Subsidia 1 (Oxford, 1978), 31-77; repr. in her *Politics and Ritual in Early Medieval Europe* (London, 1986), 1-48. See also Fouracre and Gerberding, *Merovingian France*, 97-118.

[43] Stephen the Priest, *Vita S. Wilfridi archiepiscopi Eboracensis* (*BHL* 8889), § 6 (ed. B. Colgrave, *The Life of Bishop Wilfrid by Eddius Stephanus* (Cambridge, 1927), 12-15).

[44] The classic account of the politics of these groups remains E. Ewig, 'Die fränkischen Teilreiche im 7. Jahrhundert (613-714)', *Trierer Zeitschrift*, 22 (1953), 85-144; repr. in his *Spätantikes und fränkisches Gallien*, i, 172-230.

instance, appear as rulers of Provence in the eighth century, or Leudegar's as bishops of Poitiers.[45] Interestingly they also had an overseas dimension. Erchinoald is said to have married his daughter Emma to Eadbald of Kent, and later Kentish royalty, Eorconberht and Eorcongota, had names linked with his, so, more obviously, did the later Bishop of London, Eorconwald.[46] Erchinoald was also a patron of Irish monks, and it must have been through his insular contacts that he acquired the slave girl Balthild, herself being probably a royal captive.[47] On the other side, Ebroin's power was legendary and it may have derived much from Audoin's backing. Agilbert seems to have been related to Audoin.[48] As is well known, Agilbert had spent some time in Ireland before becoming Bishop of Dorchester upon Thames sometime after 646, holding the see until 663. He returned to Francia probably in 664, and it is tempting to imagine that he was effectively an exile in England during the ascendancy of first Erchinoald and then Balthild, returning when the latter was ousted from power. Agilbert's name is the Frankish form of Æthelberht, a name borne by the most famous of the Kentish kings, and Agilbert's nephew, Leuthere, who was Bishop of Winchester 670-6, also had a name very similar to that of a Kentish king, Hlothere. This name is in turn close to the Merovingian name, Clothar. Leuthere's name might thus suggest that he, and possibly Agilbert, were linked with the Merovingian royal family. Further name connections can be found between Berta, Abbess of Bath, and Bertila, one-time nun of Jouarre, a foundation of the Agilbert-Leuthere family.[49] Bertila was later Abbess of Chelles, Balthild's monastery. From the English side we have the later evidence of Bede that at this time several Anglo-Saxon princesses joined Frankish monasteries, all of which were either the foundations of, or were under the control of, this same group of people.[50] It has been argued that the Merovingians had at one time ruled southern England, and that it was as a client kingdom that Kent received a

[45] On Erchinoald's family, see P. J. Geary, *Aristocracy in Provence: The Rhône Basin at the Dawn of the Carolingian Age* (Stuttgart, 1985), 131-48. On Leudegar's family, Fouracre and Gerberding, *Merovingian France*, 196-8.

[46] For the Kentish connection, see Wood, *Merovingian Kingdoms*, 176-9.

[47] Fouracre and Gerberding, *Merovingian France*, 102-4.

[48] He was said to have been the cousin of Ado, who founded the monastery of Jouarre. Ado was Audoin's brother.

[49] P. Sims-Williams, 'Continental Influence at Bath Monastery in the Seventh Century', *Anglo-Saxon England*, 4 (1976), 1-10.

[50] Bede, *HE*, iii.8 (pp. 236-9).

rather low-status Frankish princess, Berta, as a bride for King Æthelberht.[51] For this there is no hard evidence, but we can say that leading Neustrian families, who were quite possibly related to the original Princess Berta, continued to have strong links with southern England throughout the seventh century. They enjoyed sufficient influence there to have their people made magnates in a foreign land, and one source of their influence seems to have been their spiritual prestige. It was they who controlled the leading monasteries in Francia, and they who filled the episcopal vacancies in the most prestigious places. It was above all this group of people who, alongside the Merovingian rulers who supported their aims and aided their efforts, had made sanctity a source of power. One cannot, however, go as far as Felice Lifshitz here in seeing sanctity as the basis of Neustrian identity, and Neustrian hagiography as the principal expression of opposition to rising Carolingian power.[52] The situation was rather more complex than this, given the violent factionalism within the Neustro-Burgundian élite. Nor can all texts of the eighth century be simply lined up on either side of a 'pro-' or 'anti-Carolingian' line. It nevertheless remains true that when the Carolingians sought to break the power of the old regime, the leading Neustrian families and their saints remained a power which had to be neutralized.

The leading Austrasian families were also involved in the spread of Columbanan monasticism, but they seem to have lagged a little behind the Neustro-Burgundian élite in building up cult centres. The Pippinid family got their new-wave Irish second-hand, as it were, for the band of holy men led by Foillan, brother of Fursey, moved on to Pippinid territory only after they had been expelled, rather mysteriously, by their patron the Neustrian mayor Erchinoald.[53] Part of the problem for the Austrasians was geography: they occupied areas which were peripheral to the most prestigious religious centres, which lay in what had been Gallo-Roman territory. Beyond the forest of Carbonaria, which divided the Neustrian from the Austrasian heartlands, monastic foundation

[51] Wood, *Merovingian Kingdoms*, 176–9.

[52] F. Lifshitz, *The Norman Conquest of Pious Neustria: Historiographic Discourse and Saintly Relics, 684–1090*, Pontifical Institute of Medieval Studies, Studies and Texts 122 (Toronto, 1995), 37–99.

[53] *Additamentum Nivialense de Fuilano*, ed. B. Krusch, *MGH SS rer. Merov.*, iv (1902), 449–51, at 449; tr. Fouracre and Gerberding, *Merovingian France*, 327. See also the commentary at ibid., 301–19.

was still at an early stage in the later seventh century. Indeed, the major centres which would later provide the Carolingian family with its spiritual credentials, that is, Echternach, Prüm, Lorsch, and Fulda, were not yet founded, or in the case of Metz, special connections with the cult of St Arnulf had not yet been established. Rheims, with its powerful cult of Remigius, famously closed its gates against the early Carolingians.[54] Cologne, on the other hand, did have a store of ancient martyr relics, presumably under the control of Pippin and his wife Plectrud, but according to the *Vita Audoini*, Audoin removed them to Rouen after visiting the city on a mission of peace in the early 680s.[55] The other problem for the Austrasians, as the experience of Cologne suggests, was their weakness in the face of Neustrian hostility. For most of the seventh century, the Austrasians either had no king of their own, or were ruled by Merovingians of Neustrian provenance. This may be why in Austrasia we see so few joint royal-aristocratic ventures in monastic foundation. Three Austrasian attempts to free themselves of Neustrian domination ended in disaster. First, the failure of an attempted coup by the Pippinid mayor Grimoald in the 650s meant that Austrasia's most powerful family had to sit on the sidelines for the next generation. The family as a result lost control of the important monasteries of Stablo-Malmedy, and their prime cult centre, Nivelles, struggled to survive.[56] Second, when the Neustro-Burgundian élite tore itself apart in feuding in the years 673–6, the King of Austrasia, Childeric, a son of Balthild who had been imposed on the Austrasians after Grimoald's demise, ruled briefly over all of Francia, but he was killed and his Austrasian followers driven out after he had challenged the privileged position of the Neustro-Burgundian élite. In fact, Leudegar's faction probably killed him, Audoin is said to have buried him, and Ebroin certainly took advantage of the confusion to return to power. Then, finally, sometime between 676 and 679, the Austrasians under the leadership

---

[54] *Vita Rigoberti* (BHL 7253), § 9 (ed. W. Levison, *MGH SS rer. Merov.*, vii (1919–20), 61–78, at 67).

[55] *Vita Audoini*, § 13; Fouracre and Gerberding, *Merovingian France*, 162.

[56] Loss of influence over Stablo-Malmedy is seen through the monasteries' charters which ceased to refer to the part played by the Pippinid 'mayor' Grimoald in their foundation and endowment: *Recueil des Chartes de l'Abbaye de Stavelot-Malmedy*, ed. J. Halkin and C.-G. Roland, vol. I (Brussels 1909), nos. 6 and 8. On the troubles at Nivelles, see *Vita S. Geretrudis* (BHL 3490), § 6 (ed. B. Krusch, *MGH SS rer. Merov.*, ii (1888), 453–74, at 459–61); tr. Fouracre and Gerberding, *Merovingian France*, 24.

of Pippin and one Duke Martin invaded Neustrian territory but were soundly beaten by Ebroin. According to the *Continuation of the Chronicle of Fredegar*, Martin was treacherously slain in the aftermath of the battle, and a chief agent in this was none other than Agilbert who, along with the Bishop of Rheims, gave Martin false promises of safe conduct over an empty relic box.[57] In the light of this history one can see why when the Austrasians did finally crush the Neustrians their leaders sponsored a kind of cultural revolution in which the focus of sanctity was relocated and redefined.

THE CAROLINGIANS AND THE CULT OF SAINTS

Following their victory over the divided Neustrians at the battle of Tertry in 687, Pippin and the Austrasians can be seen exercising influence over a series of monasteries and bishoprics which stretched in a great arc from Rouen in the west round northern Neustria through the Pippinid heartlands in Belgium down into the Champagne. Though they acquired control of Audoin's diocese and its monasteries by virtue of a marriage alliance with the leading family of the area,[58] the Pippinids were at first unable to displace the Neustro-Burgundian élite from their other centres in the upper Seine and Oise valleys. Crucially, St Denis, St Germain-des-Prés, and the other *seniores basilicae* eluded their grasp until the next generation when Charles Martel imposed his control on the area by military force. Then from around the second quarter of the eighth century, we begin to see a shift in attitude towards the holy. First, however, the Merovingian order did not go under without throwing up a few more saints who were largely the victims of the Pippinids or Carolingians. These include Ansbert of Rouen, Landibert of Tongres-Maastricht, Bonitus of Clermont, Rigobert of Rheims and most memorably, Eucherius of Orleans, whose *Vita* would become the basis for future condemnations of the behaviour of Charles Martel.[59] Thereafter, the construction of contemporary

---

[57] *Continuationes Fredegarii*, § 3 (ed. Wallace Hadrill, *Fredegar*, 83).

[58] Pippin's son Drogo married Anstrud, the daughter of one Neustrian mayor (Waratto) and the widow of another (Berchar).

[59] *Vita Eucherii Aurelianensis urbis episcopi* (*BHL* 2660), ed. W. Levison, *MGH SS rer. Merov.*, vii (1919–20), 46–53. The influence of this work is briefly reviewed in P. Fouracre, 'Frankish Gaul to 814', in R. McKitterick (ed.), *The New Cambridge Medieval History*, ii, *c. 700–c. 900* (Cambridge, 1995), 91–2. For other sanctified

religious leaders as saints tails off sharply. In its place, we have from the late eighth century a burst of hagiography which celebrated Carolingian missionary activity,[60] activity which lay, significantly, in the hands of outsiders, and which, naturally, took place well away from the traditional centres of sanctity. The Carolingians had, in effect, wiped the slate clean.

Other elements of change from the mid-eighth century involved the holding of church councils at which the sons of Charles Martel presented themselves as guardians of the Church charged with the responsibility of bringing it to order.[61] At the same time links between the Carolingian rulers and the papacy were built up. These changes had the effect of curbing the independence of bishops, but they also trumped the *seniores basilicas* in Francia by stressing the importance of Rome as spiritual leader. Similarly, insistence on the use of the Roman liturgy helped to undermine the traditions of the older cult centres which were based on the Gallican rite.[62] Finally, at the synod of Frankfurt in 794 Charlemagne decreed that 'no new saints are to be venerated'.[63] The sanctification of contemporary political figures was now no longer possible. But the Carolingians not only tried to suppress rival sources of spiritual prestige, they also appropriated the language of the Bible and of hagiography to describe, and to justify, their own exploits. This we see most clearly in the *Earlier Annals of Metz*, composed in 805 or 806 as an account of the family's rise to power.[64] This work begins

victims of the Pippinids, see *Vita Ansberti episcopi Rotomagensis (BHL* 520), ed. W. Levison, *MGH SS rer. Merov.*, v (1910), 618–41; *Vita Landiberti episcopi Traeiectensis vetustissima (BHL* 4677c), ed. B. Krusch, *MGH SS rer. Merov.*, vi (1913), 353–84; *Vita beati Boniti episcopi et confessoris (BHL* 1418), ed. B. Krusch, *MGH SS rer. Merov.*, vi (1913), 119–39; *Vita Rigoberti* (see n. 54 above).

[60] On the competing hagiographies in the missionary field, see I. N. Wood, 'St Wandrille and its Hagiography', in idem and G. A. Loud (eds.), *Church and Chronicle in the Middle Ages: Essays presented to John Taylor* (London, 1991), 1–14.

[61] Three councils, held between 742 and 744, set the agenda for Carolingian reform and called upon the sons of Charles Martel to provide protection and military leadership. See the canons of *Concilium Germanicum, Concilium Liftinense*, and *Concilium Suessionense*, ed. A. Werminghof, *MGH Legum*, sect. 3, *Concilia*, vol. 2.1 (Hanover 1908), pp. 2–4, 5–7, 33–6.

[62] On the replacement of the Gallican by the Roman rite, see *Admonitio Generalis* of 789, § 80 (ed. Boretius, *MGH Capitularia Regum Francorum*, i, 61; tr. King, *Charlemagne*, 218).

[63] Ed. Boretius, *MGH Cap. Reg. Franc.*, i, 77 (§ 42); tr. King, *Charlemagne*, 229.

[64] *Annales Mettenses priores*, ed. B. von Simson, *MGH SS rer. Germ.*, x (1905), tr. down to AD 724 with commentary in Fouracre and Gerberding, *Merovingian France*, 330–70.

with a description of the Pippinid family which is clearly hagiographic in inspiration. When the author moves on to the events leading up to the battle of Tertry in 687 he, or perhaps she, very cleverly focuses on the death of Leudegar as a symbol of Neustro-Burgundian iniquity. The hero Pippin in effect avenges Leudegar's death by taking power in Neustria and wiping out injustice. He is thereby presented as a worthy heir to Neustria's saint leaders, represented in the text by Leudegar, who had formerly been the self-proclaimed guardians of peace and arbiters of justice. It was from this lot, rather than simply from the ailing Merovingian dynasty, that the Carolingians 'took over'. The battle of Tertry itself is represented as God's judgement, and as the manifestation of God's decision that Pippin should take power in Neustria. Like a saint, Pippin treads a path ordained by God. The *Annals* continue in the same vein, thus carrying the argument that Carolingian power was based on saintly virtues. Their successes were, by implication, *virtutes*, manifestations of God's power and will. In their legislation too, the Carolingians used the language of God-driven duty, focusing on the path to salvation which would be achieved by moral correction. As with every word that ever came out of a Carolingian, calls for duty, correction, justice, and order all strengthened the hand of the ruler.

Metaphors of sanctity were appropriate here because sanctity had for so long been associated with power. It is important to remember that power, still in the image of Roman authority, was strongly hierarchical in nature. Sanctity could be used to subordinate others, with the use of violence if necessary, because the word of a saint could not, in theory, be challenged. The saints themselves, living or dead, or their spokespersons, might challenge opponents, might, therefore, be politically troublesome, but they were never remotely subversive, apart from one *topos* in which the saint reacts to the cruelty of the count and saves or frees prisoners. Otherwise, they were pillars of the *status quo*. It is impossible to find in the language of contemporary texts any sign of opposition to the established social order, although it was a convention of hagiography, and of Carolingian legislation, to care about widows, orphans, and the poor. The convention did not signal any intent to improve the position or rights of such people, but it was used as the moral justification for holding power. Sanctity and power were, however, most clearly linked through concepts of justice, for the pursuit of justice not only justified powerful actions, but also necessitated them.[65] It was, as we have seen, the *Earlier Annals of Metz* which most cleverly employed these conventions to justify the growth of Carolingian power, but it was in Merovingian hagiography that the connections were first made, and they were made here precisely because the later Merovingian saints were aristocrats of the highest rank. It was in the description and justification of their careers that we see an elision between the languages of power, law, and religion. Common concepts were 'right', 'judgement', 'sentence', 'battle'. The property which accumulated around cults in exchange for the saint's goodwill was, furthermore, itself a source of power. In this way the later Merovingian saints both prepared the way for the Carolingians to focus ideas of divinely sanctioned power upon themselves, and made it necessary for the Carolingians to break with the Merovingian habit of allowing contemporary leaders to be seen as saints—or, in other words, to switch away from the patterns of aristocratic sanctity established in Neustria-Burgundy. For too many of these saints were their opponents, or might become the focus of opposition. It was thus the developments of the seventh century which determined the direction Carolingian sanctity would take in the eighth, namely, the protection and exploitation of sanctity as a source of power for the new royal family and its allies alone. In practice, of course, most cults must have continued to develop with little or no interference from the rulers, for the Carolingians were always better at preaching than practice. But what is so striking about their writing is the coherent way in which they responded to the past.

CONCLUSION

It is important to understand, in short, how and why sanctity came in the Carolingian period to be marked by that tight control of cults and corporeal relics which Julia Smith has contrasted so concisely with models of a more decentralized sanctity from Brittany, Wales, and Ireland. The development of Carolingian modes of sanctity was not simply the result of a long-term transfer of power from Peter Brown's canny bishops of the sixth century to the theocratically inclined Frankish aristocrats in Charlemagne's following. The inter-

---

[65] Fouracre, 'Carolingian Justice', 773–4.

vening period, the seventh and early eighth centuries, was formative in that it was then that sanctity really came to terms with political power through the medium of active saints who were involved
in struggles for the control of the Neustro-Burgundian regime. And
it was a mark of the success these leaders had had in making sanctity a normal attribute of power that the Carolingians tried to bring
cults under their control, and to appropriate for themselves some of
the politically potent qualities of the saint. By the mid-ninth century
it is clear that the Carolingian rulers occupied the religious
imagination to an extent no Merovingian could have dreamt of.
Hagiography was written, and, importantly, rewritten to reorder
the past and to focus on the missionary activity sponsored by the
ruling family, and as Paul Dutton has recently shown, when
religious critics began to imagine the area between heaven and hell,
a kind of proto-purgatory, that space was filled with Carolingian
kings.[66] This phenomenon Dutton relates to the decline of
Carolingian power, but what the religious imagination more consistently shows is the importance of the supernatural in the maintenance of order, irrespective of the fortunes of particular rulers. In
this context one should place the issue of sanctity in the broader
perspective of social power. Just at the time when a culture of sanctity was spreading into every corner of the Frankish polity, other
resources of power were drying up. What measure of control rulers
did have was largely the fruit of consensus and compromise. Power
and authority increasingly became a complex cultural phenomenon
rather than a matter of fiscal resource and bureaucratic organization, and in this development sanctity played a key part, for not
only did it provide a justification for authority and a rationale for
power, sanctity was also an issue around which social support
could be mobilized. This lesson, so clear in Carolingian writing, is
first to be read in the hagiography of the later seventh century.

[66] P. E. Dutton, *The Politics of Dreaming in the Carolingian Empire*, Recent Studies
in Medieval Culture (London and Lincoln, Nebr., 1994).

8

The missionary Life

IAN N. WOOD

THE great tale of the evangelization of pagan peoples, which encompasses Europe east of the Rhine from the late seventh century, is usually seen as a succession of saintly histories. This is scarcely surprising for the tale itself has to be reconstructed in large measure from saints' *Vitae*.[1] These and a handful of related texts provide us with the vast majority of our narrative information for mission, at least from 750 until the eleventh century; and even if Adam of Bremen marks a change in the second half of that century, his account of the missions to Scandinavia before 900 is essentially a paraphrase of Rimbert's *Life of Anskar* and the anonymous *Life of Rimbert*.

For the historian of mission, therefore, the *Vitae* of missionary saints form a crucial chain, which allows the construction of a narrative of mission to the pagans.[2] Yet there may be a danger in

---

[1] See, for instance, K. Schäferdiek (ed.), *Kirchengeschichte als Missionsgeschichte*, vol. 2, *Die Kirche des früheren Mittelalters* (Munich, 1978). In the Anglophone world, see S. J. Crawford, *Anglo-Saxon Influence on Western Christendom 600–800* (Oxford, 1933), and now Brown himself in *RWC*, and R. Fletcher, *The Conversion of Europe* (London, 1997). For a very different view of evangelization east of the Rhine, built up entirely from linguistic evidence, see D. Green, 'The Influence of the Merovingians on the Christian Vocabulary of German', in I. N. Wood (ed.), *Franks and Alamanni in the Merovingian Period*, Studies in the History of Archaeoethnology 3 (Woodbridge, 1999), 343–61. What follows is a revision of a lecture given at a conference in York in 1997, and is essentially a sketch of part of a book I am currently writing on the hagiography of mission. For earlier explorations of part of this theme, see, in particular, I. N. Wood, 'Missionary Hagiography in the Eighth and Ninth Centuries', in K. Brunner and B. Merta (eds.), *Ethnogenese und Überlieferung: Angewandte Methoden der Frühmittelalterforschung*, Veröffentlichungen des Instituts für Österreichische Geschichtsforschung 31 (Vienna, 1994), 189–99.

[2] For the sake of clarity I am drawing a clear distinction between mission to the pagans and evangelization within a supposedly Christian world. The distinction was, of course, not as clear-cut as this stance may seem to imply, and, indeed, many early medieval ecclesiastics would have seen little difference between evangelization within the Merovingian, Carolingian, and Ottonian realms and mission beyond their borders.

following this chain of sources without a careful exploration of its nature. Many of these missionary Lives are linked by more than the supposed fact that they can be plundered to provide us with a reasonably coherent narrative: a substantial number build on one another, referring back to past saints, both explicitly and implicitly, drawing on earlier works of hagiography and even subverting them. Such a referential tradition raises considerable problems for the historian intent primarily on the reconstruction of a grand narrative or even of the biography of a single saintly individual. My intention, however, is simply to investigate these sources as a chain of narratives: I will begin by sketching out its main strands, one of which will take us away from any standard hagiographical form. In so doing I shall limit myself largely to those *Vitae* which were written within a half century of the saint's death. This chronological limitation allows some insight into developments within both mission and its presentation, and also allows me to bypass the very different issues which are raised by some of the more challenging recreations of a distant past.

Having explored the chains of hagiography which stretch from Boniface to Bruno of Querfurt, I shall turn back briefly to ask about the origins of this missionary hagiography: clearly some earlier *Vitae* do describe episodes in the history of mission, especially if one decides to make no real distinction between evangelization within officially Christian areas (such as that performed by Martin) and mission to pagan peoples. If one were to include *Vitae* written at some considerable date after their subject's death, the *Lives of Patrick* would provide full, if legendary, accounts of a missionary career in a pagan society. Yet none of the texts relating to such figures as Martin or Patrick belongs to a stream of interrelated hagiographical narratives as sustained as those following Willibald's *Life of Boniface*.[3] Nor is it enough to argue that there was little in the way of a tradition of evangelization before the Gregorian mission to England and the subsequent work of Anglo-Saxon missionaries on the continent. The histories of Palladius and Patrick point to fifth-

---

[3] Wood, 'Missionary Hagiography', 189. One should, however, note the important grouping of Anglo-Saxon Lives identified by W. Goffart, *The Narrators of Barbarian History* (A.D. 550–800): *Jordanes, Gregory of Tours, Bede, and Paul the Deacon* (Princeton, 1988), 256–96: see also J. M. Picard, 'The Purpose of Adomnán's *Vita Columbae*', *Peritia*, 1 (1982), 160–77, and M. Herbert, *Iona, Kells and Derry: The History and Hagiography of the* Familia *of Columba* (Oxford, 1988), for the Columban tradition of hagiography.

century notions of mission,[4] and however much one may doubt Columbanus' significance as a missionary,[5] the next generation of Columbanian saints were extraordinarily active on the fringes of Francia, among which one may include Anglo-Saxon England.[6] The fact that the creation of a solid tradition of portraying saints first and foremost as missionaries emerges only in the eighth century is an issue that cannot be avoided.

To begin, however, with the relatively clear: the reactions to Boniface. Not that Boniface's career was dominated by missionary work to the same extent as were the careers of those who followed him: his years in Frisia, at the start and end of his continental work, apart, Boniface was primarily a reformer and organizer. The evidence for Bavaria, Hesse, and Thuringia is unequivocal in showing that these areas had already been Christianized, however superficially, and that what was needed was the creation of a church organization capable of strengthening and supervising the nascent Christian religion.[7] To be fair, Willibald does not present Boniface as a lifelong missionary, although that appears to be what the saint yearned to be.[8] Apart from some misrepresentation of the religious positions of Theobald and Hetan, and of the state of the Bavarian Church, almost certainly for political reasons, Willibald presents an accurate picture of his hero. This, at first sight,[9] is hardly surprising, given the fact that he was writing within fourteen years of the martyr's death: that is, before 768, and given the extent to which the hagiographer was working from the Mainz archive.[10]

Yet Willibald's *Vita Bonifatii* met with almost immediate hostility. For the time being I shall leave on one side the earliest response to Willibald's work, that by Arbeo of Freising, but instead look to the

[4] T. M. Charles-Edwards, 'Palladius, Prosper, and Leo the Great: Mission and Primatial Authority', in D. N. Dumville (ed.), *Saint Patrick*, A.D. *493-1993*, Studies in Celtic History 13 (Woodbridge, 1993), 1-12.

[5] For a recent assessment, see I. N. Wood, *The Merovingian Kingdoms, 450-751* (London, 1994), 312-3.

[6] Wood, *Merovingian Kingdoms*, 312-15; idem, 'Ripon, Francia and the Franks Casket in the Early Middle Ages', *Northern History*, 26 (1990), 1-19, at 11.

[7] Wood, *Merovingian Kingdoms*, 307-9.

[8] See Boniface, *Epistolae*, ed. M. Tangl, *MGH Epp. Sel.*, i (1916), nos. 38, 46, 48, 65, 66, 67, and 75.

[9] Though chronological and personal proximity to one's subject is by no means a guarantee of factual accuracy: see below, on Liudger's *Vita Gregorii*.

[10] Willibald, *Liber S. Bonifatii archiepiscopi* (BHL 1400), ed. W. Levison, *MGH SS rer. Germ.*, lvii (1905), 1-58.

responses among members of the Bonifatian tradition. Some forty years after Boniface's martyrdom Eigil wrote what is known as the *Life of Sturm*, but which is better described as a 'double Life' of both Boniface and Sturm.[11] Again Eigil does not present Boniface primarily as a missionary, but rather as the inspiration behind the discovery of the site and foundation of the monastery of Fulda. As monastic founder Eigil's Boniface is set deliberately against Willibald's creation, involving a defamation of Lull, to make a point about Fulda's independence from the Church of Mainz.[12] Not that mission is unimportant to Eigil, but he associates it more closely with Sturm than with Boniface.[13]

The development of the presentation of Boniface himself as a largely missionary figure was to come not from Mainz or Fulda but from the third centre of his cult, Utrecht. It finds its fullest expression in the anonymous *Vita Altera* of Boniface, which almost entirely bypasses the saint's career outside Frisia, to make him not only the companion but also the explicit successor of Willibrord.[14] The dating of the *Vita Altera* is much disputed; but it, or a lost work containing some of the same information, was used by Altfrid in his *Life of Liudger*, written between 825 and 849.[15] Not that it matters in terms of dating the emergence of the missionary presentation of Boniface, for this was achieved in Liudger's *Life of Gregory of Utrecht*, another double Life, whose first half is largely devoted to Boniface.[16] Liudger wrote his piece of hagiography between 786 and 804, and the latter date must, therefore, mark the latest possible moment for the emergence of Boniface as a totally missionary figure.

The developing presentation of Boniface was only one strand in the emergence of a missionary hagiography. More important in certain respects were Alcuin's twinned *Lives of Willibrord*, in prose and verse, and sermon on the same saint, written in 796.[17] As an

[11] *Vita S. Sturmi abbati* (*BHL* 7924), ed. P. Engelbert, *Die Vita Sturmi des Eigil von Fulda*, Veröffentlichungen der Hist. Kommission für Hessen und Waldeck 29 (Marburg, 1968), 131–63.

[12] Eigil, *Vita Sturmi*, §§ 16–20 (149–56).

[13] Ibid., §§ 15, 22–5 (147–9, 156–62).

[14] *Vita altera S. Bonifatii* (*BHL* 1401), ed. Levison, *Vitae Bonifatii*, 62–78.

[15] *Vita S. Liudgeri episcopi* (*BHL* 4937), i.5 (ed. W. Diekamp, *Die Vitae S. Liudgeri*, Die Geschichtsquellen des Bisthums Münster 4 (Münster, 1881), 1–53).

[16] *Vita S. Gregorii abbati Traeiectensis* (*BHL* 3680), ed. O. Holder-Egger, *MGH SS*, xv.1 (1887), 66–79.

[17] *Vitae et homilia S. Willibrordi* (*BHL* 8935–9), ed. A. Poncelet, *AASS Novembris*, iii (Brussels, 1910), 435–57. W. Levison edited the prose Life alone (*BHL* 8935–6)

account of the saint this cycle of texts is notoriously uninformative, and that, despite the fact that Alcuin was related to his subject, as well as to the dedicatee of the work, Beornrad, Bishop of Sens and Abbot of Echternach—Willibrord's main monastery and resting place. Alcuin's decision not to include much in the way of a historical narrative must therefore have been deliberate. So too must his decision to omit any reference to Boniface, despite the known connections between the two missionaries. In fact Alcuin's work is essentially a piece of pastoral and missionary theory: it divides clearly into two halves—indeed it is announced as so doing in the very middle of the text.[18] The first half concerns preaching, the second wonderworking. It is a blueprint for a pastor and evangelist, and being Alcuin's blueprint it is firmly opposed to force. Effectively it should be read along with the exactly contemporary letters of Alcuin to Arn:[19] it is a critique of Charlemagne's earlier missionary policy, which had foundered, as Alcuin had predicted, in Saxony. Although it is nowhere stated who were the authors of the failed policy, all the indications point to Lull and Sturm: Boniface's rival disciples.[20] There was, therefore, good reason for Alcuin to omit Boniface from his account of Willibrord.

Boniface, however, could not be dropped from the representation of mission: as we have seen, Liudger, who had extremely close connections with Alcuin, went out of his way to write a double *Life of Boniface and Gregory of Utrecht*. Liudger's work is, indeed, an extremely complex creation, in certain respects the shape of things to come. For the historian who would use it to help reconstruct the

in *MGH SS rer. Merov.*, vii (1919-20), 113-41, as has H.-J. Reischmann in *Willibrord—Apostel der Friesen* (Sigmaringendorf, 1989). The verse Life (*BHL* 8938-9), which is an integral part of the cycle, was previously edited by E. Dümmler in *MGH Poetae lat.*, i (Berlin, 1881), 207-20.

[18] *Vita Willibrordi*, § 14 (ed. Poncelet, 443).

[19] Alcuin, *Epp.* 107, 112, 113, 184, 207, and also *Ep.* 99: all ed. E. Dümmler, *MGH Epp.* iv (1895).

[20] For Sturm, see Eigil, *Vita Sturmi*, §§ 22-5 (pp. 156-62); the role of Lull has to be reconstructed from his founding of the missionary monastery of Hersfeld: see Lampert of Hersfeld, *Vita S. Lulli episcopi* (*BHL* 5066), §§ 15-18 (ed. O. Holder-Egger, *MGH SS rer. Germ.*, xxxviii (1894), 307-40, at 328-31). For the importance of Hersfeld, see H. Büttner, 'Mission und Kirchenorganisation des Frankenreiches bis zum Tode Karls des Großen', in W. Braunfels (ed.), *Karl der Große: Lebenswerk und Nachleben*, 5 vols. (Düsseldorf, 1965-72), i, 454-87, at 474, 486. Lull has also been seen as the author of the *De conversione Saxonum Carmen*, ed. E. Dümmler, *MGH Poetae lat.* i (Berlin, 1881), 380-1: see P. Godman, *Poets and Emperors: Frankish Politics and Carolingian Poetry* (Oxford, 1987), 41.

careers of either Boniface or Gregory one alarming aspect of this text is its degree of fraudulence, and this despite Liudger's own connections with Gregory:[21] Boniface's three years in Frisia between 718 and 721 are turned into thirteen, and this is no slip of the copyist, since the places in which the saint worked throughout those thirteen years are enumerated.[22] With such basic errors one has no reason to accept any of the detail in the text which is not substantiated elsewhere: above all, Liudger's presentation of Gregory as Boniface's favoured disciple, which has no support in the martyr's letter collection, must be regarded as sheer hype. On the other hand some of Liudger's falsifications undoubtedly had a purpose: like the Boniface of his imagination, the author was himself a missionary: indeed, his Boniface worked in areas where Liudger would start his own missionary career. It is difficult to avoid the conclusion that Liudger was using hagiography not only to set out a past for Utrecht, but also to explore his own personal missionary concerns. Such 'displaced autobiography' will become a recurrent aspect of missionary hagiography.

If we turn to the *Life of Liudger* himself, however, we are faced with a text which was written not by a disciple of the saint but by his nephew, Altfrid, a later incumbent of his see of Münster. Whereas family interests scarcely affect Alcuin's *Life of Willibrord*, except in its Preface and Epilogue, they run throughout Altfrid's *Vita Liudgeri*, which provides us with the most compelling account of a family's involvement in the evangelization of an area that we have: for Altfrid, it was his ancestors who had done more to evangelize Frisia than anyone: one might take the claim with a pinch of salt, but as a picture of the way in which a family could further the cause of Christianity the *Life of Liudger* is unrivalled.[23] By comparison with the almost abstract qualities of Alcuin's *Life of Willibrord*, to which it is formally indebted in its bipartite structure,[24] Altfrid's work presents a living community: it has a quality of here-and-nowness, resulting from close contact with both the subject and the landscape in which he had worked. This here-and-nowness, which

[21] On a parallel problem of accuracy in Merovingian hagiography, see I. N. Wood, 'Forgery in Merovingian Hagiography', *Fälschungen im Mittelalter*, MGH Schriften 33, 5 vols. (Hanover, 1988), v, 369–84.

[22] Liudger, *Vita Gregorii*, § 2 (67–70).   [23] Altfrid, *Vita Liudgeri*, i.1–7.

[24] This is obscured by Diekamp's division of *Vita Liudgeri* into two books: the real division in the work comes at i.25, which specifically echoes Alcuin, *Vita Willibrordi*, § 14 (ed. Poncelet, 443).

is prefigured in Liudger's *Vita Gregorii*, may be seen as reflecting a growing awareness of the realities of life in a frontier zone.

The question of a hagiographer's use of hagiography to express his own psychological concerns, which appears in Liudger's *Life of Gregory*, was very much to the fore in the neighbouring diocese of Hamburg–Bremen, where Anskar wrote an account of the miracles worked around 860 at the tomb of his predecessor at Bremen, Willehad, which are explicitly presented as divine reassurance in the face of disaster.[25] And indeed the 850s had proved disastrous for Anskar, with setbacks to his missionary work caused by Viking activity and challenges to the ecclesiastical amalgamation of Hamburg and Bremen from the Archbishop of Cologne. Yet more psychological insights are at the heart of the *Vita Anskarii*, written by the saint's pupil, Rimbert, between 865 and 876.[26] Of all the works of missionary literature this is among the most elaborate. Its form declares it to be an apologetic work: quite out of chronological place Rimbert inserts the letter of Pope Nicholas sanctioning the amalgamation of the dioceses of Hamburg–Bremen in the very middle of the text.[27] It is also apologetic in that it faces the problem of the conflict between Benedictine *stabilitas* and mission. In its portrayal of mission it clearly reflects the ideas of Rimbert as much as those of Anskar, although it should be said that the two men were very much of one mind. If, that is, one takes Anskar in his last years. His initial involvement in mission is likely to have been far more optimistic than Rimbert suggests,[28] but then the missions of the 820s and 830s essentially predated the upsurge of Viking activity. Rimbert's sombre narrative, like that of Liudger and Altfrid, reflects realities of the missionary life of which Alcuin had no cognizance. That Rimbert was accurately reporting Anskar is clear enough from his account of the saint's visions, which appeared not

---

[25] Anskar, *Miracula S. Willehadi episcopi* (BHL 8899), ed. A. Poncelet, *AASS Novembris*, iii (Brussels, 1910), 847–51.

[26] Rimbert, *Vita S. Anskarii episcopi* (BHL 544), ed. W. Trillmich, *Quellen des 9. und 11. Jahrhunderts zur Geschichte der hamburgischen Kirche und des Reiches*, Ausgewählte Quellen zur Geschichte des Mittelalters 11 (Darmstadt, 1961), 16–132. See further I. N. Wood, 'Christians and Pagans in Ninth-Century Scandinavia', in B. Sawyer, P. H. Sawyer, and I. N. Wood (eds.), *The Christianization of Scandinavia* (Alingsas, 1987), 36–67.

[27] Rimbert, *Vita Anskarii*, § 23 (74–6).

[28] For the initial enthusiasm for the Danish mission, see Ermold the Black, *In honorem Hludowici pii christianissimi caesaris augusti*, lines 1882–2513 (ed. E. Faral, *Ermold le Noir: Poème sur Louis le Pieux*, 1st edn. (Paris, 1932), 144–90).

to have come true: only some quick-witted theology explains what they really meant.[29] Further, we know from the *Vita Rimberti* that Rimbert himself used Anskar's visions as guiding principles in his own career.[30]

One other point should perhaps be noted: in the *Vita Anskarii* the miraculous never occurs when the saint is present: that is, it is not a factor in Anskar's work of evangelization, but rather it is usually something which is crucial to those the saint has already converted after he has departed. In this sense the miraculous in the *Vita Anskarii* acts as divine consolation, as did the miracles at Willehad's tomb. This represents a revolution in the understanding of the function of the miraculous in a missionary situation. Gregory the Great, from his knowledge of the Bible, had expected the miraculous to flourish in the process of conversion,[31] and this notion is still present in Alcuin's *Life of Willibrord*.[32] Some missionaries (although not Augustine of Canterbury) came to learn from personal experience that this was not so, but that the miraculous was God's consolation for the converted in the face of crisis.

The *Life of Rimbert* is the last text in a particular chain, begun by Willibald. This chain would not be picked up again until the eleventh century, and then by Adam of Bremen, and for purposes other than the psychological understanding of mission. There are, however, other chains. For the sake of brevity, I shall pass over the *Vita Wulframni*, St Wandrille's reply to Alcuin's *Life of Willibrord*,[33] and instead turn back to another response to Willibald: that of Bavaria. This begins with Arbeo's straightforward attack on Boniface's claims relating to his work in Bavaria, which are repeated by Willibald. In his Lives of Corbinian (written in *c.* 769) and Emmeram (written in 772) Arbeo quite simply denied that Boniface had founded the sees of Freising and Regensburg,[34] and he

---

[29] Rimbert, *Vita Anskarii*, § 40 (122–4).

[30] *Vita Rimberti* (BHL 7258), § 19 (ed. G. Waitz, *MGH SS rer. Germ.*, lv (1884), 81–100, at 96).

[31] See I. N. Wood, 'The Mission of Augustine of Canterbury to the English', *Speculum*, 69 (1994), 1–17, at 13–15.

[32] e.g. Alcuin, *Vita Willibrordi*, §§ 10, 14 (ed. Poncelet, 441, 443).

[33] I. N. Wood, 'St Wandrille and its Hagiography', in idem and G. A. Loud (eds.), *Church and Chronicle in the Middle Ages: Essays presented to John Taylor* (London, 1991), 1–14, at 13–14.

[34] *Vita S. Haimhrammi episcopi et martyris* (BHL 2539) and *Vita S. Corbiniani episcopi* (BHL 1947), both ed. B. Krusch, *MGH SS rer. Germ.*, xiii (1920), 26–99 and 188–232. See further Wood, *Merovingian Kingdoms*, 307–9.

did so while asserting a very much more muscular and sexy view of Christianity than Boniface allowed. A *Life of Rupert of Salzburg* was written at approximately the same time.[35] Thus of the four Bavarian dioceses which Boniface claimed to have created, three were given earlier histories, quite rightly, while the fourth, that of Passau, was known to have been a papal foundation.[36] Thus began the most cantankerous and radical chain of hagiography to stem from Willibald. It was not, however, Arbeo's writings which were central: indeed within a generation his attitudes were found to be too earthy by his copyists.[37] More important was the earliest *Life of Rupert,* which was used in two texts from the time of Arn of Salzburg, the *Notitia Arnonis,* written between 788 and 790,[38] and the *Breves Notitiae,* written between 798 and 800.[39] Here Rupert's career was integrated into texts which were primarily to do with the holdings and jurisdiction of the see of Salzburg. Evangelization could be seen in legal terms.

This reading of mission was to provide the Church of Salzburg with a model for its great conflict with Methodius. Essentially the form of the *Notitia Arnonis* and the *Breves Notitiae* was to be copied by Salzburg in its account of its evangelization and organization of Bavaria and Carinthia, the *Conversio Bagoariorum et Carantanorum,* prepared in the context of or just after the trial of Methodius before Louis the German in Regensburg in 870.[40] Again Rupert is of significance, but otherwise the document is almost entirely concerned with the history of ecclesiastical jurisdiction and church foundation, except for a short anecdotal chapter on the priest Ingo.[41] Hagiographical narrative and law had been combined: and to judge by the fate of Methodius, successfully so.

---

[35] *Gesta Hrodberti episcopi* (BHL 7390), ed. W. Levison, *MGH SS rer. Merov.,* vi (1913), 157–62.

[36] Boniface, *Epp.,* nos. 44, 45.

[37] See, for instance, Arbeo, *Vita Corbiniani,* § 22 (212–14).

[38] *Notitia Arnonis,* ed. F. Lošek, '*Notitia Arnonis* und *Breves Notitiae*: Die Salzburger Güterverzeichnisse aus der Zeit um 800: Sprachlich-historische Einleitung, Text und Übersetzung', *Mitteilungen der Gesellschaft für Salzburger Landeskunde,* 130 (1990), 5–192, at 80–96.

[39] *Breves Notitiae,* ed. Lošek, 'Die Salzburger Güterverzeichnisse', 102–40.

[40] F. Lošek, *Die Conversio Bagoariorum et Carantanorum und der Brief des Erzbischofs Theotmar von Salzburg,* MGH Studien und Texte 15 (Hanover, 1997), 5–8.

[41] *Conversio Bagoariorum et Carantanorum,* § 7 (ed. Lošek, *Die Conversio,* 90–134, at 112–14).

The Churches of Bavaria continued to keep an eye on Moravia and then Bohemia. Regensburg and Passau had attitudes similar to those of Salzburg, although they did not branch out into hagiographical texts which have survived, except in the case of Regensburg's possible involvement in the propagation of the cult of St Wenceslas. Determining the exact order of the composition of works on Saints Ludmilla and Wenceslas, and what is the relation of the Latin to the Slavonic texts, is almost impossible.[42] Suffice it to say that the *Life of Ludmilla*, in one version or another, provides a tenth-century account of the Christianization of Bohemia,[43] while the history of her grandson Wenceslas prompted a new development in hagiography. Although the *Life of Wenceslas* does not present the earliest picture of a pious martyr king—that honour must go to the *Life of St Sigismund*[44]—it played a role in transforming what had hitherto been an uncommon hagiographical form, the passion of the martyred king, into a relatively popular one.[45] Which text was responsible for this transformation is unclear, but one contender must be the Bavarian recension of the earliest Latin *Life of Wenceslas*, *Crescente Fide*:[46] again we may be seeing Bavaria as a driving force in changes in hagiography—albeit this time not of a missionary saint, but of a model Christian ruler in a period of Christianization.[47]

The most famous and controversial *Life of Wenceslas* is the so-called *Legenda Christiani*, which purports to have been written by one Christian of Scala for Bishop Adalbert of Prague.[48] The authen-

---

[42] There is a very useful survey, together with a translation of most of the major texts, in M. Kantor, *Origins of Christianity in Bohemia: Sources and Commentary* (Evanston, Ill., 1990).

[43] *Passio S. Ludmille martyris = Fuit in Provincia Boemorum* (BHL 5026), ed. V. Chaloupecký, 'Prameny X. století', *Svatováclavský Sborník*, ii (Prague, 1939), 467–81.

[44] *Passio S. Sigismundi regis et martyris et sociorum eius* (BHL 7717), ed. B. Krusch, *MGH SS rer. Merov.*, ii (1888), 333–40.

[45] Another important text of roughly the same date which deals with a martyred king is Abbo of Fleury, *Passio S. Eadmundi* (BHL 2392), ed. M. Winterbottom, *Three Lives of English Saints*, Toronto Medieval Latin Texts (Toronto, 1972), 67–87.

[46] For the Bavarian recension of *Crescente Fide* (BHL 8823), which omits the translation and miracles, see Chaloupecký, 'Prameny X. století', 495–501.

[47] Strictly speaking, the *Passio Ludmille* (*Fuit in Provincia Boemorum*) is a text more concerned with mission than is the *Crescente Fide*.

[48] *Vita et passio S. Vencezlaui et eius avie Ludmilae* (BHL 8825 + 2075 + 5028), ed. J. Pekar, *Die Wenzels- und Ludmila-Legenden und die Echtheit Christians* (Prague, 1906), 88–125, and more recently by J. Ludvíkovský, *Kristiannova Legenda* (Prague, 1978), 8–102.

ticity of this text has been much under discussion for most of this century. Suffice it to say that the general outline, although not all of the detail contained in the *Legenda Christiani*, can be found in unquestionably tenth-century texts,[49] and that there is nothing provably late about the work. Further, Adalbert is known from other sources to have been involved in the cult of Wenceslas: indeed in the early eleventh century he was even thought to have organized the translation of the martyr's body to Prague.[50] Although Laurentius of Montecassino is quite wrong to have made this assertion, and can scarcely have received information about Wenceslas from Adalbert, the latter is almost certain to have been involved in the promotion of the king's cult in Italy.[51] This does not prove, however, that the *Legenda Christiani* was indeed addressed to Adalbert: the text could be a forgery of the first decades of the eleventh century.[52] In any event, the fate of Wenceslas hung over Adalbert, twice driven out of Prague, in 989 and 995, and martyred in Prussia in 997. Adalbert's family, the Slavniks, clearly championed the cult of the dead king, against the Premyslid Boleslav II, who was actually Wenceslas' nephew. The killing of the Slavniks by Boleslav II is depicted by Bruno of Querfurt, in his *Passio Adalberti*,[53] as emulating the killing of Wenceslas by Boleslav I.

In other respects, however, the hagiography relating to Adalbert of Prague deals with the question of Christianization differently from texts concerned with Ludmilla and Wenceslas. The *Life of Adalbert*, written in 999 or 1000 by John Canaparius or a monk of the monastery of Saints Boniface and Alexius in Rome where Adalbert himself had stayed, sets out the basic facts of his career.[54] Perhaps not surprisingly for a member of a community dedicated to St

[49] Kantor, *Christianity in Bohemia*, 18.

[50] See Laurence, monk of Montecassino and Archbishop of Amalfi, *Passio S. Wenceslai regis* (*BHL* 8824), lectio 12 (ed. F. Newton, *MGH*, *Die deutschen Geschichtsquellen des Mittelalters 500–1500*, vii (Weimar, 1973), 23–42, at 38).

[51] Also important was Gumpold, Bishop of Mantua, who wrote *Passio S. Vencezlaui martyris* (*BHL* 8821), ed. J. Emler and tr. into Czech by F. J. Zoubek, *Fontes rerum Bohemicarum*, 4 vols. (Prague, 1873–84), i, 146–66, for Otto II.

[52] It can scarcely be much later, because an illustration in the Wolfenbüttel manuscript of Gumpold's *Vita Vencezlavi* appears to derive from information in *Legenda Christiani*, § 7 (ed. Ludvíkovský, 64–74): see the reproduction in Kantor, *Christianity in Bohemia*, 191.

[53] Bruno of Querfurt, *Vita S. Adalberti episcopi* (*BHL* 38), § 21 (ed. Emler and tr. J. Truhlář, *Fontes rerum Bohemicarum*, i, 266–304, at 288–90).

[54] Johannes Canaparius, *Vita S. Adalberti episcopi* (*BHL* 37), ed. Emler and tr. Truhlář, *Fontes rerum Bohemicarum*, i, 235–65.

Boniface, the author tries to engage with the saint's mission and to understand his final dealings with the Prussians. Equally, the author has a strong visionary and contemplative streak, which may well reflect the character of Adalbert himself.

Canaparius' account was to some extent modified by Bruno of Querfurt, who wrote a second *Life of Adalbert* in 1004, revising it while he himself was waiting in Poland to evangelize the Prussians in 1008.[55] The changes made by Bruno relate in part to his attitude towards the Italian and Polish policies of the Ottonians. Unlike Canaparius or the author of the first *Vita*, he is distinctly critical of Otto II and III.[56] But equally he departs from his source at the end, presenting a modified view of the saint's martyrdom, which includes the statement of a new missionary strategy that involved going native.[57] Since there were eyewitness accounts of the death of Adalbert, Bruno may have been recording the martyr's ideas: on the other hand similar ideas crop up in other of Bruno's works,[58] and also in Peter Damian's account of Bruno in his *Life of Romuald of Benevento*.[59] It may have been Bruno rather than Adalbert who was the true author of this new approach to evangelization.

That Bruno was using hagiography to work out his own ideas, as had Liudger and Rimbert, is even clearer from his *Vita Quinque Fratrum*: an account of five missionaries, led by Benedict and John, who were killed by thieves before they could get to Prussia, because Bruno himself had delayed obtaining papal permission for them to preach. This text has two narratives: one is a narrative of boredom, as Benedict, John, and their three companions wait for their licence: the other is a narrative of Bruno's fear, and his failure to get that licence. The text is essentially confessional, and is an outpouring of Bruno's guilt. Bruno followed this with an explicitly autobiographical work, the Letter to Henry II, in which he described his mission

---

[55] R. Wenskus, *Studien zur historisch-politischen Gedankenwelt Bruns von Querfurt* (Münster and Köln, 1956), 3.

[56] Compare, for example, Canaparius, *Vita Adalberti*, § 8 (241), with Bruno, *Vita Adalberti*, § 9 (270-1).

[57] Bruno, *Vita Adalberti*, § 26 (294-5): see the discussion of this in I. N. Wood, 'Pagans and Holy Men, 600-800', in P. Ní Chatháin and M. Richter (eds.), *Irland und die Christenheit: Bibelstudien und Mission / Ireland and Christendom: The Bible and Missions* (Stuttgart, 1987), 347-61, at 358-9.

[58] Bruno, *Vita quinque fratrum Poloniae* (BHL 1147), § 10 (ed. R. Kade, *MGH SS*, xv.2 (1888), 716-38, at 725-7).

[59] Peter Damian, *Vita S. Romualdi abbati* (BHL 7324), § 27 (ed. G. Tabacco, *Fonti per la storia d'Italia* 94 (Rome, 1957), 3-116, at 56-61).

to the Pechenegs.[60] By this time he had clearly lost the fear that had engulfed him when he failed to secure the licence for Benedict and John. This fearlessness is equally apparent in the eyewitness account of his death by Wipert,[61] and in the account of his career which Peter Damian incorporated into his *Life of Romuald of Benevento*.[62]

With Bruno we have returned to the growing autobiographical elements of ninth-century hagiography: the missionary as hagiographer again prompted a particular type of self-analysis, which flatly contradicts any assertion that it was the twelfth century which saw the discovery of the individual. With Damian's account of Bruno we also come to another closure in the history of missionary hagiography, which, as I hope I have shown, took all sorts of interesting paths, but which in many respects forms a series of chains which take us back to Willibald's *Life of Boniface*. The problem is, what came before Willibald? This is a less easy question to answer than one might suppose. Of course there were perfectly good models for missionary history, most notably the Acts of the Apostles. There were also models for missionary hagiography: the legendary apostles to Gaul, for instance, were the subject of hagiographical texts,[63] and in the seventh century Armagh and Kildare developed a type of missionary hagiography relating to Patrick not unlike that which Salzburg would later formulate.[64] Further, Patrick himself provides us with a missionary autobiography of the first order[65]—although of course this had no immediate impact, nor did the later Armagh texts outside Ireland and Iona. Indeed, when all is said and done, what texts there are fail to coalesce into a tradition of writing about missionaries in the way that such a tradition emerged in the late eighth century.

---

[60] Bruno, *Epistola ad Heinricum II Imperatorem*, ed. W. von Giesebrecht, *Geschichte der deutschen Kaiserzeit*, 4th edn., 2. vols. (Braunschweig, 1874–5), ii, 689–92.
[61] *Passio S. Brunonis martyris* (BHL 1471), ed. G. H. Pertz, *MGH SS*, iv (1841), 579–80.
[62] Peter Damian, *Vita Romualdi*, § 27 (56–61).
[63] Cf. L. Duchesne, *Fastes Épiscopaux de l'Ancienne Gaule*, i (Paris, 1894), 45–59.
[64] Cf. Herbert, *Iona, Kells and Derry*, 146.
[65] Patrick, *Confessio* (BHL 6492), ed. most recently by D. R. Howlett, *The Book of Letters of St Patrick the Bishop* (Dublin, 1994), 52–92.

Even the Lives of those fourth- to seventh-century saints who are thought of nowadays as missionaries really amount to *Vitae* in which there are solitary chapters on mission. The *Life of Martin*, for instance, has a small, but immensely famous, group of chapters on the saint's dealings with pagans,[66] but mission is in no sense the driving force of the Life. Jonas' *Life of Columbanus* presents a similar problem: the saint comes across pagans in the region of Bregenz, but mission is not a dominant issue in the text.[67] In some respects this is particularly puzzling, for in his account of Eustasius, in the second book of the *Vita Columbani*, Jonas does refer to the organization of missions to the Bavarians, and the renegade Agrestius is even revealed as a failed missionary.[68] Further, Jonas himself was a missionary, working with Amandus, as he reveals in the preface to his *Life of Columbanus*. Here one might have expected to find a missionary exploiting hagiography to face the problems of mission, much as Liudger, Rimbert and Bruno of Querfurt did later. That he did not is probably in part a reflection of the fact that Columbanus was not primarily a missionary: as the Leinsterman explains in one of his letters he decided not to evangelize the *gentes* because of their lukewarmness.[69] He was essentially a *peregrinus pro Christo,* and if he converted some people by chance that was all to the good.

On the other hand, one should also note that Jonas had no model for writing the hagiography of a near-contemporary missionary. Other texts of the same period, for instance the first *Life of Richarius*[70] and what can be reconstructed of Audoin's *Life of Eligius,*[71] are similar in not making mission to the pagans their central theme. One exception is likely to have been the *Vita Amandi*:

---

[66] Sulpicius Severus, *Vita S. Martini* (*BHL* 5610), §§ 12–15 (ed. J. Fontaine, *Sulpicius Sévère Vie de Saint Martin*, 3 vols., SC 133–5 (Paris, 1967–9), i, 278–87). Cf. R. M. Price's contribution below.

[67] *Vita Columbani et discipulorum eius* (*BHL* 1898–9), i.27 (ed. B. Krusch, *MGH SS rer. Merov.*, iv (1902), 64–152, at 101–4).

[68] Ibid., ii.8–9 (121–6).

[69] Columbanus, *Epp.* 4, § 5 (ed. G. S. M. Walker, *Sancti Columbani Opera*, Scriptores Latini Hiberniae 2 (Dublin, 1970), 30–1). This does, of course, reflect a biblical position: Matthew 10: 14.

[70] *Vita S. Richarii abbati* (*BHL* 7245), ed. B. Krusch, *MGH SS rer. Merov.*, vii (1920), 444–53.

[71] 'Audoin', *Vita S. Eligii episcopi* (*BHL* 2474), ed. B. Krusch, *MGH SS rer. Merov.*, iv (1902), 663–741. On this text, see M. Banniard, 'Latin et communication orale en Gaule franque: Le témoignage de la *Vita Eligii*', in J. Fontaine and J. N. Hillgarth (eds.), *The Seventh Century: Change and Continuity* (London, 1992), 58–79.

that text does not survive in its earliest form,[72] but the fragments of the earliest known Life of the saint already portray him as a missionary[73]—and in any case the subject's claim to sanctity was so entirely bound up with his missions that to have downplayed them would have been perverse.[74] That historians have difficulties in piecing together the history of evangelization before the age of Boniface (except, significantly, in England) is, thus, an exact reflection of the problem posed by the absence of any real tradition of missionary hagiography in the seventh century or before.

The Christianization of England, of course, presents a major exception. Not that Bede wrote his *Ecclesiastical History* in the seventh century, but that in that *History* he provides a narrative history of mission unequalled until Adam of Bremen's *Gesta Hammaburgensis ecclesiae Pontificum*. Bede's history is essentially missionary history, and in certain respects it is missionary biography: the second half of Book I of the *Ecclesiastical History* is largely an account of Augustine and his mission: the first half of Book III can be read as an account of Aidan, and Book IV, together with the *Vita Cuthberti*, presents Cuthbert as the ideal pastor.

It is worth considering whether the development of the traditions of missionary hagiography which I have traced was an accidental spin-off from Bede's *Ecclesiastical History*. There are a number of indications to suggest that that was indeed the case. First, although Willibald lies at the head of so many hagiographical debates, his *Life of Boniface* is not, in essence, the Life of a missionary saint, neither is Eigil's *Life of Sturm*, despite its reflections on mission to the Saxons. Mission comes to the forefront of hagiography in Alcuin's *Life of Willibrord* and Liudger's *Life of Gregory*. That Alcuin knew his Bede is unquestionable; after all he had already versified the *Ecclesiastical History*.[75] Although the text of Liudger's *Life of Gregory*

[72] For the earliest complete text, see *Vita S. Amandi episcopi* (*BHL* 332), ed. B. Krusch, *MGH SS rer. Merov.*, v (1910), 428–49.

[73] See J. Riedmann, 'Unbekannte frühkarolingische Handschriftenfragmente in der Bibliothek des Tiroler Landesmuseums Ferdinandeum', *Mitteilungen des Instituts für Österreichische Geschichtsforschung*, 84 (1976), 262–89; J. Riedmann, 'Die ältesten Handschriftenfragmente in der Bibliothek des Museum Ferdinandeum', *Veröffentlichungen des Tiroler Landesmuseum Ferdinandeum*, 56 (1976), 129–39.

[74] On Amandus' importance in missionary history, see W. H. Fritze, '*Universalis Gentium Confessio*. Formeln, Träger und Wege universalmissionarischen Denkens im 7. Jahrhundert', *Frühmittelalterliche Studien*, 3 (1969), 78–130.

[75] Alcuin, *The Bishops, Kings and Saints of York*, ed. P. Godman, OMT (Oxford, 1982).

does not immediately reveal a dependence on Bede, it is unlikely that, having studied in York with Alcuin, the author had not read the *Ecclesiastical History*. Later missionary texts like the *Vita Willehadi* and the *Vita Lebuini* are explicitly dependent on Bede.[76] So too are the earlier works of Hugeburc, tangential although they are to the main development of missionary hagiography.[77]

If we accept that Bede is central to the developing tradition of missionary hagiography, we may also accept that the Gregorian ideology of mission was transmitted not only through Gregory the Great's own works, but also through the *Ecclesiastical History*. In particular, the portrayal of missionaries as living like the apostles may have been a model transmitted primarily by Bede.[78]

This, I would suggest, is of more than literary importance—if Bede provides the stimulus for much missionary hagiography, he may also explain the recurrent emphasis on the importance of the English and of Anglo-Saxon England for the evangelization of Europe east of the Rhine. This is not to say that, *de facto*,[79] the accounts of English activities are necessarily wrong, but rather that they receive more emphasis than they warrant, and that one of the reasons the English have been so emphasized, by comparison with others, is that Bede, the literary model for much missionary hagiography, instituted an in-built bias towards the contribution of the English on the Continent. One might also add more generally that Bede has defined for us what mission is.

Bede and the *Ecclesiastical History* may explain something of the origins of our representation of mission, but what I would wish to emphasize more is the importance of remembering that the history of mission and of missionary saints is a history of texts: further, this history may best be seen as presenting us with a 'delayed narrative'[80]—that is, one may look with more certainty at the ideas of writers than at the actions of their subjects: when we read a narrative we are always looking at the author's generation's reading of

---

[76] *Vita S. Willehadi* (BHL 8931), ed. A. Poncelet, *AASS Novembris*, iii (Brussels, 1910), 842–6; *Vita S. Lebuini antiqua* (BHL 4810b), ed. A. Hofmeister, *MGH SS*, xxx (1934), 791–5.

[77] *Vita S. Willibaldi episcopi* (BHL 8931) and *Vita S. Wynnebaldi abbati* (BHL 8996), both ed. O. Holder-Egger, *MGH SS*, xv.1 (1887), 86–106 and 106–17.

[78] e.g. Bede, *HE*, i.26 (76–9).

[79] Though that could be the implication of Green, 'Influence of the Merovingians on the Christian Vocabulary of German' (see n. 1 above).

[80] The phrase was suggested to me by Paul Hyams.

events: sometimes the new generation was simply following the model of its predecessor, sometimes ideas about mission had changed. I would stress, therefore, that the chain of missionary hagiography presents an immensely rich history of developing ideas and of fragmentary autobiographies, culminating in the writings of Bruno of Querfurt, who, like Liudger, Anskar, and Rimbert, used hagiography as a form of confessional literature. In one sense all this undermines any simple reading of missionary hagiography and of its subject matter: at the same time, those texts which one might regard as constituting 'displaced autobiography' bring us closer to the thoughts, and thus to the inner life, of a missionary than does any attempt to recreate a narrative of mission. One might add that autobiography is a form which is otherwise largely absent from literature between the *Confessiones* of Augustine and the *Confessio* of Patrick on the one hand, and the High Middle Ages on the other. Given the hostile reactions to Willibald's *Life of Boniface* and to Alcuin's *Life of Willibrord*, and given the inaccuracies of Liudger's *Life of Gregory*, it is perhaps safer not to concentrate on any narrative, whether of mission as a whole or of a single missionary, but to think first and foremost about what an author regarded as constituting the proper experience of a saint in the field of mission.

PART IV

The cult of saints in medieval Rus'

9

Holy men and the transformation of political space in medieval Rus'

PAUL A. HOLLINGSWORTH

POLITICAL power in medieval Rus' was intensely intimate and contingent. It relied on the constant creation and cultivation of an extensive network of personal relationships through which wealth, social standing, and political authority could be acquired and sustained. This was true for the Scandinavian warlords who moved along the waterways between the Baltic, Black, and Caspian Seas in the ninth and tenth centuries and established themselves among the native, mainly East Slavic tribes. It was no less true for their Slavicized descendants of the eleventh and twelfth centuries, especially the proliferating descendants of Volodimer I of Kiev (c. 980–1015), who had established his family as the princely dynasty of Rus'. Although standard histories of medieval Rus' focus on the formation of governing institutions and bureaucracies in the East Slavic principalities that arose in the pre-Mongol period, as Simon Franklin and Jonathan Shepard recently pointed out in an important and much-needed corrective to the traditional misleading emphasis on 'state building', rulership was in fact dependent on a series of interlocking ties between princes, retainers, and townsmen that required continual calculation, brokerage, affirmation, and management.[1]

The most immediate concern of the warlord-prince was the hiring and retention of a retinue. For, as German envoys were said to have told Prince Sviatoslav Iaroslavich of Kiev in 1075, 'it is better to have a retinue than [gold, silver, and fine cloth], for with men you can acquire even more wealth.'[2] A reliable body of retainers

[1] S. Franklin and J. Shepard, *The Emergence of Rus'*, 750–1200, Longman History of Russia (London and New York, 1996), 193–7.
[2] The so-called *Tale of Bygone Years* (*Povest' vremennykh let*), commonly referred to as the Primary Chronicle, which was compiled in the Kievan Caves Monastery c. 1115, lacks a critical edition. References therefore are given to its two oldest copies—

was essential for successful rulership. With a strong and satisfied retinue a prince could secure new territory and fresh sources of revenue through campaigns and diplomacy, exploit established streams of revenue by collecting tribute and levying taxes, extend authority by placing trusted men as representatives in towns under his sway and giving sons over to trustworthy fosterers, and protect his towns and domain from external attacks, particularly from the nomadic tribes of the steppes. A prince also needed to develop strong ties to the leading men of his main town, which was the critical base of support within his region or domain. This was particularly urgent for a prince who had been newly assigned to a town by an elder kinsman and who might not have any pre-existing links with the town. Failure to foster relations with the most significant townsmen could lead to requests for the prince's removal or to violent efforts to expel him. Deprived of the protection of a stockaded town and its potential sources of wealth and manpower, a prince had few choices other than turning to his kinsmen for a new town or attempting to seize one by force. Finally, a strong warband and a firm group of urban supporters were essential to a prince for defining his relations *vis-à-vis* the other princes in the ruling family. This was the key issue as Volodimer's dynasty expanded rapidly, enlarging the field of 'legitimate' claimants to authority in Kiev and other subject domains. Would a prince be satisfied with the town or domain which he had inherited or to which he had been assigned, or would he seek to change his status and authority by asserting his claim to another domain or town? If he chose the latter course, would he press his case through negotiations or through violence?

This dilemma became acute in the last half of the eleventh century. Inter-princely fratricide had left Volodimer as the sole ruler of Rus' from *c.* 980 to 1015 and his son Iaroslav as sole ruler from 1036 to 1054. Iaroslav had followed tradition and settled his sons in the main towns of Rus', but after his death Iaroslav's sons and grandsons carried on a dual struggle to defend the patrimonial domains based on the main towns in which they had resided under Iaroslav and to assert a claim to Kiev, in which Iaroslav had resided. Scholars have long asserted that there was a clear-cut system of succession to the throne of Kiev and the other towns of the Middle Dnieper region. In their opinion, this system is reflected in the so-called 'Testament of Iaroslav' found in the Primary Chronicle's entry for the year 1054, which depicts Iaroslav as assigning on the basis of seniority Kiev to Iziaslav, Chernigov to Sviatoslav, Pereiaslavl' to Vsevolod, Volodimer to Igor', and Smolensk to Viacheslav, and in the treaty of Liubech in 1097, which after three decades of intermittent warfare confirmed Iziaslav's son Sviatopolk in Kiev, Sviatoslav's sons in Chernigov, and Vsevolod's son Volodimer Monomakh in Pereiaslavl'.[3] It appears more likely, however, that the inter-princely conflicts that plagued Rus' after 1068, when Iaroslav's sons had their first falling out, arose precisely because there was no definitive system in operation within this young and expanding dynasty, and that both Iaroslav's 'Testament' and the arrangement of Liubech should be regarded not as reflections of an actual system of succession and assignments but rather as important moments in the rough and often violent process by which the princes attempted to sort out competing claims as to how the main towns of Rus' should be shared out.[4]

Once successfully negotiated, a prince's relations with his supporters, allies, and even potential rivals needed to be acknowledged visibly and acted out socially through various public rituals and with the help of gestures familiar to any reader of such 'northern' works as *Beowulf* and the *Heimskringla*. For the prince, for example, the open giving of gifts to retainers and townsmen was essential; these gifts could be as grand as a grant of a town with its revenues or as intimate (but no less symbolically significant) as a piece of jewellery. So too a prince was required to bolster his standing within his towns by conspicuous acts of generosity, such as the holding of feasts in his *dvor*—the fenced complex of buildings that included the Rus' equivalent of the mead hall. For their part, retainers and townsmen were obliged to provide services, such as campaigning with the prince, accompanying him to collect tribute (the Rus' version of the 'royal progress'), acting as his local representatives, and raising his sons.

---

the fourteenth-century Laurentian Chronicle, *Polnoie sobraniie russkikh letopisei* (hereafter *PSRL*), vol. 1, 2nd edn. (Leningrad, 1926), and the fifteenth-century Hypatian Chronicle, ibid., vol. 2, 2nd edn. (St Petersburg, 1908). For this entry, see ibid., i, 198–9; ii, 189–90.

[3] The most nuanced and persuasive argument for this point of view is given by N. Kollmann, 'Collateral Succession in Kievan Rus' ', in F. E. Sysyn (ed.), *Adelphotes: A Tribute to Omeljan Pritsak by his Students = Harvard Ukrainian Studies*, 14 (1990), 377–87.

[4] Franklin and Shepard, *The Emergence of Rus'*, 245–9, 265–6.

During the processes by which these relationships were arranged
and acknowledged the various parties jockeyed to articulate and
project their expectations of proper behaviour on each other, hoping to lock in their achievements through the social performance of
the negotiated contract. Although obligations were created on all
sides, the prince in particular was enmeshed in a complex network
of expectations as he confronted the relentless and constant pressure to define his network of supporters. Paradoxically, the very
relations necessary for rulership also worked to restrain his freedom
of action. The prince was expected to 'love his retinue greatly and
spare them neither property nor drink nor food'.[5] A prince who did
not show ambition in pressing his claims against other princes
risked abandonment, as happened to Boris when he chose the path
of negotiation and subordination and not of confrontation with his
elder half-brother Sviatopolk following the death of their father
Volodimer in 1015.[6] A prince risked desertion by his retainers for
not keeping his promises, showing appropriate generosity, or being
sensitive to their public honour, as happened to Volodimer, who
seized Kiev in about 980 from his brother Iaropolk, and then saw
his retainers depart for Constantinople when he failed to pay them.[7]
A prince was expected to strive for consensus in decision-making by
consulting with his retainers before taking action and heeding their
counsel and interests, as Igor' did with his retinue in 944 before
making peace with Byzantium,[8] and as Volodimer did with his retinue and the town elders in 988 before rejecting Islam, Judaism,
and Latin Christianity in favour of accepting Christianity from
Byzantium.[9] A prince was expected to safeguard his town and
domain from external attack, particularly from the nomadic tribes
of the steppes, otherwise he risked expulsion for failure to deal with
the threat adequately, as happened to Prince Iziaslav of Kiev in
1068, when 'the men of Kiev' drove him out after he refused to arm
them during a raid by the Cumans.[10]

The coming of Christianity to Rus' did not fundamentally alter
the nature of rulership in East Slavic territory. Princes still needed
to create warbands and to foster relations with townsmen. But the

---

[5] Thus, the necrology for Prince M'stislav of Chernigov in the Primary
Chronicle's entry for the year 1036: *PSRL* i, 150; ii, 138.

[6] Ibid., i, 132; ii, 118.   [7] Ibid., i, 79; ii, 66.

[8] Ibid., i, 45–6; ii, 35.   [9] Ibid., i, 106; ii, 93.

[10] Ibid., i, 170–1; ii, 160.

growing presence of churchmen in their towns reshaped the societal space in which acts of rulership took place by adding a new and enduring network of relations and a fresh and extremely powerful set of expectations that an East Slavic prince had to take into consideration as he sought to define his circle of supporters and solidify and extend his authority in his town or domain.

At heart, the relations between princes and churchmen were fundamentally distinct from those between princes and retainers, and in ways that permanently reshaped Rus' society. In the first place, of course, the churchmen represented the holy. Unlike retainers in a warband, who relied largely on the ambitions and generosity of the prince for wealth and status, the churchmen enjoyed prestige and an independent social status derived from the charisma of representing the sacred. Moreover, the churchmen represented that notion of the holy behind which the ruling dynasty had thrown its prestige and patronage. Volodimer's baptism in 988 in Cherson, immediately followed by his destruction in Kiev of the shrine of the pagan god Perun and the erection of a church dedicated to St Basil, emphatically signalled the reorientation of the ruling family's religious beliefs from paganism to Christianity. This at once placed the Byzantine churchmen whom Volodimer brought back to Kiev from Cherson and all of their successors, Byzantine and Rus', at the heart of what Edward Shils defines as the 'zone of values and beliefs' and the 'realm of action' that define and govern a society's centre,[11] and henceforth made them partners with the princes in bearing the central belief system of Rus' society.

This partnership was mutually reinforcing. On the one hand, the vitality of Christianity in the Middle Dnieper region depended on princely patronage. From the moment that Volodimer built the Church of the Mother of God in the 990s, gave it over to the Byzantine Bishop Anastasios, and endowed it with a tithe of his revenues, the pattern was established whereby the churchmen would be supported primarily out of the princes' wealth. So too the spread of Christianity beyond Kiev depended in great measure on princely promotion. As excavations of gravesites have revealed, Christianity flourished in pre-Mongol Rus' primarily where bishops appeared with their capacity for local promotion and organization,[12] but

---

[11] *The Constitution of Society* (Chicago, 1982), 93.
[12] Franklin and Shepard, *The Emergence of Rus'*, 228.

bishoprics were usually created in those towns that were made prestigious enough by the presence of a strong and significant member of the dynasty.

On the other hand, the presence of these bishops played an important role in solidifying the position of the Rus' princes in their towns. Christianity entered Rus' at a time when Volodimer's dynasty was only beginning to establish itself in East Slavic territory. Volodimer had settled his twelve sons in various towns, but due to premature deaths and the inter-princely fratricide of 1015–19, it was only under Iaroslav that princes began to create lasting ties to specific towns. The coming of Christianity offered a prince very public ways to put his stamp on his new town and to put it on the map of Rus'. Volodimer set the example immediately after his baptism by building the Tithe Church and by being buried in it. His sons followed his lead: Iaroslav built the magnificent Church of St Sophia in Kiev, in which he and his son Vsevolod (prince of Kiev from 1078 to 1093) were buried, while M'stislav erected the stone Church of the Transfiguration in Chernigov, in which he was buried in 1036 and Iaroslav's son Sviatoslav too in 1076. As Iaroslav's sons and grandsons spread throughout East Slavic territory, they too founded masonry cathedrals in the 'downtowns' of their domains and made them 'family' churches through burials. Excavation has shown that the foundation of such masonry churches usually coincided with the reign of a powerful prince and the initiation of a programme of monumental construction, including strong ramparts, which often had more to do with the prince's desire for prestige than with the town's economic importance.[13] By erecting these churches and patronizing the churchmen who staffed them, the princes were not simply announcing that they were throwing their prestige and authority behind the newly embraced religion, they also were making plain their enduring commitment to that particular town and its region.

Second, as representatives of the holy, the churchmen controlled the ascendant sacred space of Rus' towns. As the ecclesiastical hierarchy of Christianity spread throughout East Slavic territory, it acquired a fixed physical presence in the towns of Rus' in the form of churches and monasteries. Churches built of timber were most common, but the erection of large masonry churches was a partic-

---

[13] P. A. Rappoport, *Building the Churches of Kievan Russia* (Aldershot, 1995), 208.

ularly powerful statement of permanence and prominence in towns consisting of earthen ramparts and dotted by one- and two-storey wooden buildings. These foundations made the holy accessible and salient on an unprecedented scale. We know little of pagan sanctuaries in pre-Christian Rus'. Yet one need only compare Volodimer's first known statement of religious adherence, a series of wooden statues of pagan gods erected on a hill near his *dvor* in Kiev, with his son Iaroslav's greatest building project, the Cathedral of St Sophia, a masonry church located in Kiev's central square, to see an emphatic statement of aspiration and eminence on behalf of the new religion. Its size (54.6 × 41.7 metres) and height (28.6 metres) were unmatched by any other local building. Nor was the holy confined within the walls of churches and monastic enclosures. The churchmen could move out of their fixed establishments and create sacred space—by, for example, temporarily sacralizing the streets of a town with a procession. Finally, this sacred space was also mobile: it could be brought into secular space in the form of a living holy man, such as the monastic superior Feodosii who frequented the *dvory* of several Kievan princes and notables, or in the form of a cross, which figured so prominently in ceremonies of oath-taking.

Third, the churchmen of Rus' possessed a sense of community that transcended kin groups, towns, and domains. A retainer or townsman had to negotiate one-on-one with a prince, drawing for social leverage on his own personal authority, sources of wealth, or ability to mobilize other men; he might even represent a large kin group, a network of merchants, or perhaps even a town. A churchman, in contrast, was always integrated within a community of clerics, who had a sense of collectivity within Rus' and who also felt themselves, even though they had been converted 'at the eleventh hour' and in a land remote from the Mediterranean, to be part of Christian history and Christian geography. Baptism and tonsure, participation in the liturgical hours, journeys to Mount Athos, and pilgrimages to the Holy Land—in these and many other ways the churchmen of Rus' acquired a shared religious language, set of symbols, and interests, and formed collectively a strong sense of self-identity and solidarity.

This community had leadership and an organizational framework without precedent in Rus'. By the early twelfth century the ecclesiastical structure of Rus' consisted of the Kievan metropolitan and bishops in Chernigov, Pereiaslavl', Novgorod, Belgorod,

Volodimer (Volhynia), Iur'iev, Rostov, and Turov,[14] to which should be added the superiors of the main monasteries of East Slavic territory, most of which were clustered in the eleventh century in the area of Kiev. These church leaders knew each other; many had been tonsured or educated in the same monasteries. Their ties were reinforced on key occasions such as church councils, translations of relics, and funerals of prominent princes and clerics. The solidity of these links and the ability to tap into the full range of Christian symbols and ceremonies and to mobilize other churchmen allowed the churchmen to project expectations corporately and consistently across the towns of Rus'.

Finally, the churchmen had an agenda: the reshaping of Rus' society. A retainer's negotiations with a prince revolved around his own interests or those of his family, clan, guild, or town. The relationship could account for social change, perhaps in wealth or status or position, but this was individualized change, which depended on being acted out within a larger unchanged status quo. The churchmen, however, were very consciously trying to create a Christian society in Rus', as seen in the *Sermon on Law and Grace*, an optimistic and enthusiastic panegyric to Volodimer written and delivered in about 1050 by the native Rus' churchman Ilarion ('Behold Christianity growing!').[15] In pursuit of that goal, they had at their disposal an impressive array of physical spaces, liturgical rites, and social rituals for defining and expressing membership in the Christian community.

Not surprisingly, much of their proselytizing efforts, or at least as much as we see in the sources, focused on the princes and their retainers. There is little evidence that the churchmen conducted active missionary work among the pagans of East Slavic territory, but there is a great deal of evidence that they worked hard to Christianize the Christians of Rus', particularly the princely family on whose authority they depended to define and back up their income base, legal status, ecclesiastical jurisdiction, and social standing. Certainly they hoped that their work would produce princes like Iaroslav, who 'loved ecclesiastical statutes and greatly

[14] A. Poppe, 'Die Metropoliten und Fürsten der Kiever Rus' ', in G. Podskalsky, *Christentum und theologische Literatur in der Kiever Rus' (988–1237)* (Munich, 1982), 280–321, at 281.
[15] Now available in the excellent translation by S. Franklin, *Sermons and Rhetoric of Kievan Rus'*, HLEUL 5 (1991), 3–29.

loved priests, especially monks', and like Volodimer Monomakh, who 'loved the metropolitan, bishops, and superiors, especially the monastic rank'[16] and who advised his sons to go to church first thing in the morning before taking counsel with their retainers, rendering justice, or hunting; to patronize churchmen and pray nightly; to abide by oaths taken on the cross; to care for people in need, widows, orphans; and to kill no Christian.[17]

As the churchmen, aided by the patronage of the princes, developed their own urban social networks, worked out and promoted their own local privileges and concerns, and took on the role of safeguarding the welfare of the faithful who rallied to their parish churches and monasteries, they came to represent a formidable presence within a prince's town that he could not afford to neglect, lest they become rallying points that could undermine his authority. For example, a prince pursuing unpopular economic goals could find a churchman being asked by townsmen to act as a focal point for opposition, or a prince who encroached on another prince's town or seized it by force could find himself confronted by the resistance of a local churchman who had patronage ties with the offended or expelled prince. This posed particular problems for the prince when the opposition came from a holy man, who could ground his criticism in the charisma of the sacred and back it up with the support of his own 'retainers', including laymen tied to the monastery by family (many monks were locals and from notable families) or acts of devotion. This is best attested in the sources for the relations between a succession of princes of Kiev and the holy men of the Caves Monastery, which was located a short walk south of Kiev's ramparts, just far enough into the 'wilderness' to be outside the prince's main urban space but close enough to Kiev and the princely residence at Berestovo to exert a strong gravitational pull on events in Kiev and the court. In 1073, for example, the superior Feodosii condemned Prince Sviatoslav Iaroslavich of Chernigov for expelling his elder brother Iziaslav from Kiev and refused his invitation to have dinner in the prince's *dvor* and 'take part in their unrighteous deliberations', thereafter criticizing Sviatoslav as a 'brother-hater' through intermediaries and letters.[18] Three decades

---

[16] For Iaroslav, see *PSRL* i, 151; ii, 139. For Volodimer Monomakh, see ibid., i, 263; ii, 238.   [17] Ibid., i, 245–7.
[18] *Kyjevo-Pechers'kyi Pateryk*, ed. D. Abramovych (Kiev, 1930), 66–7; tr. M. Heppel, *The Paterik of the Kievan Caves Monastery*, HLEUL 1 (1989), 74–6.

later the monk Prokhor's ability to turn ashes into salt and to distribute it to the population directly undercut revenue from the salt monopoly that Prince Sviatopolk Iziaslavich of Kiev (1093–1115) had acquired and was exploiting, and stirred the prince (who had already imprisoned one monastic superior for publicly accusing him of avarice when he was prince in Turov) into plotting against him.[19]

As acted out socially, the construction of relations between the princes and the churchmen flowed along the same lines as the formation of ties between princes and retainers and townsmen. The links between princes and the churchmen who resided in or near their urban space were built up through direct, face-to-face contacts and then affirmed through visible displays of patronage and gift-giving, such as the erection of churches, the granting of lands and the endowment of monasteries, and the funding of artistic decorations. This could be expressed in an overarching act of patronage, such as the issuance of church statutes (the first are attributed to Volodimer and Iaroslav) that established the church's revenues based on the tithe. More often in the sources it is depicted in the form of gifts to individual churchmen. This usually required the prince to leave his *dvor* and come to the churchman. Once again this is best documented with regard to the Caves Monastery, the *Paterik* of which contains a series of scenes in which the princes are depicted as fostering relations with individual monks through personal attention, conspicuous gift-giving, and public displays of solicitous piety. Such a commitment of time, resources, and public honour was particularly important if a prince wanted to defuse the · opposition of a holy man to the very fact of his rulership or to unpopular aspects of it. Sviatoslav, for example, after seizing Kiev from Iziaslav sought to mollify Feodosii's anger by personally visiting him at the Caves Monastery and facilitating the construction of its great masonry Church of the Dormition—Sviatoslav provided the land and personally helped to dig the foundations.[20] Sviatopolk too eventually won over the monk Prokhor through patronage of the monastery and made plain his display of penitence, the solidity of their reconciliation, and his hope for a continued relationship after Prokhor's death by carrying the monk's body to its grave.[21] For

---

[19] *Kyjevo-Pechers'kyi Pateryk*, ed. Abramovych, 151–4; tr. Heppel, 172–4.
[20] Ibid., ed. Abramovych, 67–9; tr. Heppel, 76–8.
[21] Ibid., ed. Abramovych, 154–5; tr. Heppel, 174.

their part, the churchmen responded with services, including acting as spiritual fathers and blessing hunting expeditions and campaigns against the nomads, and so on. The 'Testament' attributed to Volodimer Monomakh neatly encapsulates the relationship: 'Receive in love blessings from bishops, priests, and monastic superiors, and do not keep distant from them, but love and tend to them as much as you can, so that you will receive a prayer from God through them.'[22]

By patronizing the churchmen the princes opened themselves up to a new and highly demanding set of religious expectations, which the churchmen reinforced through their personal contacts and during the princes' participation in liturgical life. Moreover, the princes committed themselves to manifesting their support for Christianity in social acts. This too slipped comfortably into the customary ways in which a prince attempted to foster and maintain his reputation and authority within his town. Volodimer, for example, is said to have kept up his custom of hosting banquets but he took to holding them on Sundays, inviting to his *dvor* his retainers and the town notables (presumably after liturgy at the Tithe Church, which was built alongside his court).[23] (Even these Christianized banquets could not avoid the realities of social status based on public displays of the prince's favour: on one occasion, according to the chronicle, Volodimer's retainers complained because they had been given wooden and not silver spoons with which to eat.)

In the political sphere this resulted in a reformation and widening of the traditional physical and psychic spaces in which the princes calculated, contested, and repaired the main relationships of rulership. This process is reflected most visibly in the prominent role played by churchmen in mediating and defusing secular conflict, especially inter-princely rivalry. Pre-Christian Rus' society did not differ from other northern societies: this was a world of blood feuds. Note the opening article of the first Rus' law code, which is attributed to the reign of Iaroslav (1019–54): 'If a man kills a man [the following relatives of the murdered man may avenge him], the brother is to avenge his brother; the son, his father; or the father, his son; and the son of the brother [of the murdered man] or the son of his sister, [their respective uncle].'[24] New feuds could arise suddenly, or long-simmering rivalries and resentments could flare

---

[22] *PSRL* i, 245.   [23] Ibid., i, 126; ii, 110–11.
[24] Tr. G. Vernadsky, *Medieval Russian Laws* (New York, 1979), 26.

up without warning. Even small feuds could have great consequences. For example, Prince Iaropolk of Kiev (973–80) was said to have attacked and killed his brother Oleg after being egged on by his retainer Sveinald, who was seeking vengeance for Oleg's murder of Sveinald's son over a hunting dispute.[25] The passionate inventiveness and cruelty with which Princess Ol'ga, regent of Kiev (c. 945–62), was said to have taken vengeance on the Derevlianian prince and nobles who had murdered her husband, Igor', should not surprise any reader of *Njal's Saga*.[26]

Churchmen throughout the 'northern world', in societies as seemingly distinct as medieval Iceland and modern Montenegro faced the same harsh social realities that they confronted in Rus'.[27] They did not, of course, understand these conflicts, like modern anthropologists, as mechanisms for the regulation of status and wealth in premodern societies. Instead, they focused on the dangers of unchecked feuding among the princely kinsmen, which took a heavy toll on the towns and villages of Rus' and posed a constant direct threat to the harmony of the artificial kin group formed by the Christians of Rus'. As important, they also saw the feuding as an impediment to the collaborative effort needed from the princes to confront the external threats to Rus', especially from the nomadic Turkic tribes of the steppes. For these reasons, the surviving literary sources for pre-Mongol Rus' history are dominated by the churchmen's concern over princely rivalries and their efforts to maintain harmony among the princes and their retinues. The churchmen successfully introduced themselves into this sphere of society because they took on the traditional roles of broker and peacemaker—customary and necessary functions in a society marked by feuding. As pagans the Rus' had looked to the holy to bear witness to oaths, so it is not surprising that as Christians the princes, retainers, and townsmen looked to churchmen and the new holy that they represented to mediate disputes and validate settlements aimed at ending cycles of violence. For the churchmen, however, this was a matter, not simply of performing a vital social function, but also of attempting to contain and even end the cycles of violence generated by personal or princely feuds, as seen in their involvement in

[25] *PSRL* i, 74; ii, 62.   [26] Ibid., i, 58–9; ii, 46–8.
[27] J. Byock, *Medieval Iceland: Society, Sagas, and Power* (Berkeley, 1988), 154.

revising the law codes of the Rus'.[28] Although Iaroslav's law code had allowed for blood feuds, the law code promulgated by his sons in 1072 outlawed them, substituting instead fines for offences to persons, property, and honour.

The efforts of the churchmen to mediate rivalries and conflicts and work toward reconciling princes took two main forms. First, the churchmen actively entered princely space, putting their own prestige on the line and introducing the holy into the political calculations. The presence of churchmen in negotiations created considerable pressure on the parties to reach an accommodation or else face the social consequences of being seen to be rejecting the churchmen's counsel and, by extension, the will of God. So in 1096, Sviatopolk Iziaslavich of Kiev and Volodimer Monomakh of Pereiaslavl' asked their cousin Oleg Sviatoslavich of Chernigov to come to Kiev and to agree 'before the bishops, monastic superiors, men of our fathers, and townsmen' to conduct a campaign against the nomads, to which Oleg retorted, 'it is not fitting for me to be judged by bishops, superiors, and commoners'.[29] In 1066, the townsmen of Tmutorokan' sent the monastic superior Nikon to intercede with Sviatoslav of Chernigov so that the latter would send his son Gleb to them as prince (Nikon himself escorted Gleb back to Tmutorokan').[30] In 1097, the townsmen of Kiev sent Metropolitan Nicholas to conduct negotiations with Volodimer Monomakh to end the princely feuding that had flared up after Sviatopolk of Kiev had blinded Vasil'ko of Terebovl'.[31] In 1127, the monastic superior Grigorii of St Andrew's Monastery convened a church council that successfully negotiated a settlement between Prince M'stislav Volodimerovich of Kiev (1125–32) and Prince Vsevolod Ol'govich, despite pressure on M'stislav from his cousin Iaroslav, who had been driven out of his town of Chernigov by Vsevolod.[32]

Second, the churchmen made their sacred space available as a means to avoid disputes, prevent further ones, and to provide a forum for expressions of co-operation. Monasteries, for example, became 'neutral' territories for princes who opted out, or were opted out, of princely rivalries. In 1059, Iaroslav's three sons liberated

---

[28] See *Kniazheskiie ustavy i tserkov' v drevnei Rusi*, ed. Ia. N. Shchapov (Moscow, 1972), 307–11.
[29] *PSRL* i, 229–30; ii, 220.
[30] *Kyjevo-Pechers'kyi Pateryk*, ed. Abramovych, 45; tr. Heppel, 51.
[31] *PSRL* i, 263; ii, 237.   [32] Ibid., i, 297; ii, 291.

from prison their uncle Sudislav of Pskov (their grandfather Volodimer's last surviving son) and had him enter a monastery.[33] In 1106, Sviatosha, the oldest son of Prince David Sviatoslavovich of Chernigov (1096–1123) and once prince in Lutsk, removed himself from the succession politics of his domain by entering the Caves Monastery.[34] In 1093, Volodimer Monomakh met his cousin Sviatopolk Iziaslavich at the Monastery of St Michael in Kiev, where they set aside their recent differences over Kiev (Sviatopolk had succeeded in Kiev after the death of Volodimer's father, Vsevolod) and vowed to campaign jointly against the nomads.[35]

The efforts of churchmen personally to mediate conflict and to draw on the holy to affirm harmony can be seen most visibly in the accounts of the ritual of the kissing of the cross. The very frequency with which 'cross-kissing' appears in the sources for eleventh- and twelfth-century Rus' testifies to the profound need within Rus' society for mechanisms to contain the threat of violence or to defuse it. It is noteworthy that this ceremony occurs in the sources in tandem with the first reliable mention of a Christian community on the Dnieper River. In 907, according to the oldest Rus' chronicle, Prince Oleg led the other chieftains of East Slavic territory on a campaign against Byzantium, which ended in a treaty affirmed in keeping with Byzantine diplomatic practice by oaths taken according to the religion of each side: the Byzantine Emperors Leo VI and Alexander swore by the Cross and the pagan Rus' warlords swore by their weapons and their gods of thunder and cattle, Perun and Volos, respectively.[36] Yet two generations later, following an attack on Byzantium led by Prince Igor' and other Rus' warlords, the subsequent treaty stipulated that the Rus' leaders could swear in Kiev to observe the treaty in either the traditional pagan manner at the sanctuary of Perun or the Christian ceremony of cross-kissing at the Church of St Elijah.[37]

Here in the mid-tenth century, therefore, we see all the elements that would come to the fore in the eleventh and twelfth centuries. One of the most important social rituals of pagan Rus' society—the formal sealing of an agreement through the public swearing of oaths—had been recast in a Christian context: God had been sub-

---

[33] *PSRL* i, 162; ii, 151.
[34] *Kyjevo-Pechers'kyi Pateryk*, ed. Abramovych, 131; tr. Heppel, 131.
[35] *PSRL* i, 219; ii, 210.   [36] Ibid., i, 32; ii, 23.
[37] Ibid., i, 52–4; ii, 41–2. The origins and precise location of the Church of St Elijah in Kiev are unknown.

stituted for Perun and the cross for the sword in a ceremony mediated by a Christian cleric and occurring in a fixed point of Christian sacred space. In committing their public honour to the new arrangement, both parties wanted to stress the seriousness of their declaration by invoking God as a witness. In so doing, they were acknowledging the central message that the churchmen brought to all their mediating efforts, namely that the parties should recognize and react appropriately to the primacy of divine power. This message is articulated most forcefully in the chronicler's effort to explain why in 1068 Prince Iziaslav Iaroslavich was expelled from Kiev by his two brothers, Sviatoslav of Chernigov and Vsevolod of Pereiaslavl', and why shortly thereafter the nomadic Cumans conducted a devastating raid on Kiev:

God manifested the power of the Cross, inasmuch as Iziaslav had kissed the cross and yet had imprisoned [Vseslav of Polotsk]. Therefore God provoked the pagans' incursion, from which the venerable Cross plainly delivered us. For on the day of the Exaltation [of the Cross] Vseslav sighed and said, 'O venerable Cross, inasmuch as I have believed in you, deliver me from this abyss!' God showed the power of the Cross as an admonition to the land of Rus' that he who kisses the cross should not transgress it. If anyone transgresses it, he shall be punished here and eternally in the world to come. For great is the power of the Cross. Through the Cross demonic forces are defeated. Through the Cross our princes are aided in battle. With the sign of the Cross the faithful drive away the devil's minions. For the Cross swiftly delivers from misfortune those who call upon it with faith. Nothing terrifies demons as much as the Cross.[38]

The transformation effected at the centre of Rus' society by the intersection of the traditional bearers of political power and the new representatives of the holy and by their shared efforts to manage political violence was propelled and even accelerated by the first and most widespread saints' cult of Rus', which arose in the first generations after Volodimer's decision to embrace Christianity. The cult originated in a typical incident of secular strife in the northern world. Volodimer, a very successful warlord and diplomat, reportedly had twelve sons from seven wives. When he died in 1015, he was succeeded in Kiev by his eldest surviving son, Sviatopolk (born of one of Volodimer's two Greek wives), who moved to increase his chances of holding Kiev by murdering his various half-brothers, who had been settled in Volodimer's main towns. He succeeded in killing Boris of Murom and Gleb of Rostov (full brothers by Volodimer's Volga Bulgar wife) and Sviatoslav (born of Volodimer's Czech wife) before being vanquished himself in 1019 by Iaroslav of Novgorod (a son from Volodimer's first wife, the daughter of a Scandinavian warlord who had settled in Polotsk). According to all the sources, Boris and Gleb, upon learning of their father's death, were faced with the options of contesting the throne of Kiev or of accepting the claims of their elder kinsman Sviatopolk. Although urged by their retainers to press their own claims and possessing the force to do so (at least in the case of Boris, who was returning from campaigning with Volodimer's retinue), they chose to make peace with Sviatopolk and were murdered for their efforts.

Although the precise origins of the cult of Boris and Gleb remain obscure, there is no doubt that by the middle of the eleventh century some sort of recognition that Boris and Gleb were not merely victims of a fratricidal struggle for the Kievan throne but rather martyrs present at God's court had crystallized in connection with their graves near the Church of St Basil in Vyshegorod (modern Vyshhorod), a princely residence ten kilometres north of Kiev. Their status as holy men was publicly affirmed by the leading princes and clerics of southern Rus' first in 1072, when their relics were translated into a wooden church dedicated to them in Vyshegorod, and then again in 1115, when their relics were translated into a large masonry church built in their name. The hagiographic image of Boris and Gleb was fully articulated in a number of contemporaneous literary works, including three chronicle entries describing their martyrdom and the two translations of their relics, three full-length hagiographic works describing their martyrdom and posthumous miracles, and a liturgical office. An icon of Boris and Gleb is mentioned in one of the hagiographic works written in about 1080, and archaeologists have found numerous bronze *enkolpia* and lead seals with their image dating from the medieval period. Eleven churches dedicated to Boris and Gleb, at least seven of which were made of stone, are known to have existed in Rus' before the Mongol devastation of 1240, and four feast days in their memory were fixed in Rus' liturgical calendars.[39]

[39] The most useful starting points for studying the cult of Boris and Gleb are P. Hollingsworth (tr.), *The Hagiography of Kievan Rus'*, HLEUL 2 (1992), which

Many different theories have been offered to explain why the first and most significant saints' cult in medieval Rus' arose around the veneration of two princes murdered in an internecine secular struggle, but all of them share a 'two-tiered' model of Rus' society put forth in the hagiographic sources themselves. In this paradigm, the veneration of Boris and Gleb is an example of 'popular religion': the 'people' spontaneously responded to marvellous signs and miraculous occurrences at the graves of Boris and Gleb and propelled the emergence of a cult, with the support of pious secular leaders (first Iaroslav and later his son and successor, Iziaslav) and in opposition to the initially disbelieving clerical authorities (the Byzantine-appointed Kievan metropolitans Ioannes and later Georgios), who eventually were won over by receiving accounts of miracles or by observing evidence of the princes' sanctity themselves.

In general, scholars fall into one of two groups depending on which 'tier' of the model they stress. On the one hand are scholars who treat the cult as a phenomenon of 'veneration from below'. This approach arose as early as the 1850s, along with the first efforts to publish critical editions of the hagiographical texts, and basically repeated the account of the sources themselves. It was developed most fully in pre-Revolutionary Russian historiography in the monumental church history of Evgenii Golubinskii and his full-length survey of East Slavic saints, which quickly became established as the authoritative works on the subject.[40] This 'bottom up' approach was given a brilliant and extremely influential twist by George Fedotov, a church historian who left Soviet Russia in 1925 to teach in France and then in the United States until his death in 1951. Eschewing Golubinskii's stress on the institutional framework for saints' cults in favour of focusing on the 'Russian religious consciousness' that created them, Fedotov asserted that the coming of Christianity into East Slavic territory, 'the shock of the Gospel', sparked fresh forms of sanctity within 'the old and ossified Byzantine tradition' and created new types of saints, namely 'passion-sufferers' (*strastoterptsy*) whose voluntary deaths for

---

contains English translations of the main hagiographic works, G. D. Lenhoff, *The Martyred Princes Boris and Gleb: A Socio-Cultural Study of the Cult and the Texts*, UCLA Slavic Studies 19 (Columbus, Ohio, 1989), and A. Poppe, 'La naissance du culte de Boris et Gleb', *Cahiers de civilisation médiévale*, 24/1 (1981), 29–53.

[40] *Istoriia russkoi tserkvi*, 2nd edn., 2 vols. (Moscow, 1901–4), and idem, *Istoriia kanonizatsii russkikh sviatykh*, 2nd edn. (Moscow, 1903).

Christ's sake and not for faith in Christ revealed a uniquely Russian
devotion to non-resistance.[41] On the other hand are scholars who
emphasize that the cult of Boris and Gleb was an example of 'canonization from above'. Most of these scholars accept the account of
the sources that the veneration originated at the grassroots level,
but argue that princely and/or clerical authorities quickly channelled and manipulated popular sensibilities for their own interests.
A smaller group of scholars asserts that the cult was essentially an
official creation that was then played back to a receptive popular
audience. Different motives are attributed to different possible
orchestrators. Most often, it has been suggested that Iaroslav fostered the cult of Boris and Gleb in order to bolster his own position
on the throne by blackening the name of Sviatopolk from whom he
had seized Kiev, or to legitimize his own budding dynasty, or to
assert the ecclesiastical autonomy of Rus' from Byzantine cultural
hegemony, or simply as part of his programme to Christianize Rus'.

Now this 'two-tiered' model contains none of the hostility toward
saints' cults found in the 'two-tiered' model that, in Peter Brown's
opinion, long characterized Western approaches to the cult of
saints.[42] Although both have a vertical view of society and regard
the cult of saints as essentially a 'popular' phenomenon operating
at a lower social level distinct from élite or official culture, no student of Rus' history would share the Enlightenment view of Hume
and Gibbon that saints' cults were a phenomenon of cultural deca-
dence which marked the lamentable end of a grand historical
period. On the contrary, the great majority of scholars of East Slavic
religious history consider the appearance of holy men in Rus' very
positively and indeed as a point of pride, since for them the appearance of the cult of saints helped bring forth Christian Rus' culture
and thus marked the entry of the East Slavs onto the historical
stage. Since the field of East Slavic hagiology has been framed and
defined largely by Russian scholars or by scholars with cultural or
historical ties to Russia, many analyses of the cult of Boris and Gleb
are closely tied to the desire to see in it the first signs of native 'originality' and 'uniqueness' in early Russian cultural institutions.
(Soviet scholars frequently expressed an ambivalence toward the
cult of Boris and Gleb, noting the gullibility and pliability of the

---

[41] *The Russian Religious Mind*, vol. 1, *Kievan Christianity* (Cambridge, Mass.,
1946).
[42] *CS*, 12–22.

'masses' in the face of princely or clerical manipulation of popular sensibilities while simultaneously hailing the appearance of local saints as examples of a distinctive native Kievan culture independent of Byzantium and an important impetus to the formation of a specifically Russian society and State.)

The prevalence of the 'two-tiered' model is also due to the fact that almost no compelling challenges to it have emerged from within modern East Slavic historiography. In general (and for this reason the exceptions clearly stand out) medieval East Slavic religious studies have remained untouched by the intellectual developments in late antique and Western medieval historiography that have made possible the robust scholarly discussion on the role of the holy man in the Mediterranean world, to which Peter Brown's famous 'Holy Man' article belongs. The writings of Brown and his supporters and critics on notions of holiness in late antiquity are informed on all sides by the willingness to appropriate new historical methods, draw on other disciplines, and exploit the results of investigations in neighbouring fields in order to ask fresh questions of old sources and to suggest novel answers to long-standing questions. Yet one could sift through the entire corpus of modern scholarly works on saints' cults in pre-Mongol Rus' and find hardly a trace of creative influence from the Annales school, social anthropology, or religious sociology and scarcely a meaningful mention of Norman Baynes, A. J. Festugière, Arnaldo Momigliano, Évelyne Patlagean, or Peter Brown, much less references to Mary Douglas and Victor Turner and to cults of Islamic holy men in North Africa. It is instructive that in 1975, four years after the appearance of Brown's 'Holy Man' article, such a distinguished historian as Dimitri Obolensky published an article characterizing the 'popular cult of saints' ('the vision of sanctity . . . seen partly through the eyes of simple folk') as the highest of four levels of 'Russian medieval religion'.[43]

Hemmed in by its own self-imposed historiographical isolation, scholarly work on medieval Rus' saints' cults has tended to focus on revisiting long-standing points of controversy and not posing new questions or examining the truly momentous shifts in orientation that occurred when Christianity entered Rus' society. In 1970,

---

[43] 'Popular Religion in Medieval Russia', in A. Blane (ed.), *The Religious World of Russian Culture: Essays in Honour of G. Florovsky*, Russia and Orthodoxy 2 / Slavistic Printings and Reprintings 260/2 (The Hague, 1975), 43–54.

for example, A. P. Vlasto devoted thirteen of the fifty-nine pages dealing with Rus' in his lengthy survey of the Christianization of the Slavs to the long-standing controversy about the organizational status of the Rus' church hierarchy between 988 and 1036 (was it autocephalous or dependent on Bulgaria or on Constantinople?) and only a half-page to the cult of Boris and Gleb (merely recapitulating Fedotov's interpretation).[44] Scholarship dealing with Boris and Gleb has focused heavily on sorting out the complex literary problems of the main hagiographic sources, which share a great deal of material in common and which cannot be dated absolutely or even relatively to within less than fifty years with much confidence. For the past four decades, for example, Andrzej Poppe has assiduously devoted his considerable talents to determining exactly when in the eleventh century the cult of Boris and Gleb arose, not with the goal of understanding the meaning and social role of the cult but with the aim of establishing at least a relative chronology for the appearance of the sources so that the century-old dispute about the priority of the three main hagiographic texts can be put to rest.[45] Only a small handful of works has focused in recent decades on the hagiographic image of Boris and Gleb.

This state of affairs, all too common for medieval East Slavic hagiology,[46] calls to mind the comments made two decades ago by Hans-Georg Beck, who praised Byzantine studies for their high level of 'industry', but asked if the field would not benefit more from discovering new perspectives than from publishing yet more scholarly editions of sources.[47] At least in the field of medieval East Slavic hagiology it is clear that efforts to shed new light on old issues by casting a wider historical or historiographical net pay dividends. It

---

[44] *The Entry of the Slavs into Christendom: An Introduction to the Medieval History of the Slavs* (Cambridge, 1970), 266–7 (on Boris and Gleb), 268–81 (on the status of the church).

[45] A. Poppe, 'O vremeni zarozhdeniia kul'ta Boris i Gleba', *Russia mediaevalis*, 1 (1973), 6–29, at 6; idem, 'La naissance', 38. Poppe reiterates his arguments about the cult of Boris and Gleb, first announced in his doctoral thesis in 1960, again in 'O zarozhdenii kul'ta svv. Borisa i Gleba', *Russia Mediaevalis*, 8 (1995), 21–68.

[46] In the last two decades seven different scholars have produced eleven scholarly works on the century-old dispute regarding the date (945 or 957?) when Princess Ol'ga travelled to Constantinople and regarding the location (Constantinople or Kiev?) of her baptism, while only one significant work has been devoted to her hagiographic image: see the works cited in J. Featherstone, 'Ol'ga's Visit to Constantinople', in Sysyn (ed.), *Adelphotes*, 293–312.

[47] *Byzantinistik heute* (Berlin and New York, 1977), 13.

is no coincidence that the firm position enjoyed in large portions of Western scholarship by Fedotov's anachronistic views about the existence of the 'Russian soul' in eleventh-century Kiev began to be undermined when Norman Ingham compared the veneration of Boris and Gleb to the cults of murdered princes elsewhere in non-Mediterranean Europe and found strong similarities between them.[48]

Put directly, the 'two-tiered' model long employed in East Slavic hagiology does not tell us very much about the cult of Boris and Gleb and is in fact a major impediment to drawing any sort of nuanced picture of the dynamic role of the cult in both reflecting and shaping the process by which a Christian society was formed in medieval Rus'. The problem with the 'veneration from below' explanation is that it is formed of a series of hagiographic commonplaces that were drawn from an entirely different social milieu, that is, the Mediterranean world in which the traditions of Byzantine hagiography arose. Scholars have appropriated the 'two-tiered' model of the sources without first asking if it reflects what we know about the Christian community of Rus'. To be sure, Rus' society was stratified, but what exactly would 'popular' mean in eleventh-century East Slavic society, which was not urbanized in a Mediterranean sense (despite the claims of scholars who have characterized the towns of Rus' as 'classic city-states')?[49] How justified are we in speaking of strata within the Christian community of Rus' when it was still in the very process of being formed and which the sources depict as being composed of princes, prominent townsmen, and churchmen? Even if one accepts the 'bottom up' account for the appearance of the veneration of Boris and Gleb, it does not explain why the cult took such root in Rus' society and bulked so large in Rus' political life of the eleventh and twelfth centuries.

The 'canonization from above' approach is slightly more sophisticated in that it draws our attention to the need to focus on the parties to the cult of Boris and Gleb. As many modern works have pointed out, saints' cults do not originate by themselves but require advocacy and response, promoters and a receptive audience. Certainly somebody had to order and pay for the churches built at the gravesite of Boris and Gleb in Vyshegorod. Somebody had to

---

[48] 'The Sovereign as Martyr: East and West', *Slavic and East European Journal*, 17 (1973), 1–17.

[49] e.g. G. Vernadsky, *Kievan Russia* (New Haven, Conn., 1948), 174.

commission the hagiographic works and icons that created and projected the saints' image. Somebody had to organize the ritual pro-
cessions and translations of their relics that made public the
response to that image. And so on. But very few scholars embracing the 'canonization from above' theory move beyond the simplis-
tic assumption that princes and senior clerics have the ability to
fashion saints' cults in their own interests and then successfully to
foist on the 'people' their self-interested presentation of a holy man.
In other words, they focus on promotion without investigating the
audience or apparently understanding that the promoters were part
of the audience themselves. (Soviet scholarship on the whole was
particularly crude in regarding saints' cults as forms of social and
political control and often treated hagiographic sources as vehicles
for inculcating princely propaganda among the masses.) Finally, as
with the 'veneration from below' theory, even if one accepts the
notion that a specific prince or churchman invented the cult and
succeeded in persuading the other princes and churchmen to promote it, this too would not account for the widespread appeal of the
image of Boris and Gleb in medieval Rus'.

At heart, the 'two-tiered' model as embraced in Rus' historiography fails because it stresses tension and not consensus in viewing saints' cults. Yet, as Pierre Delooz points out, saints are saints
both for other people and by other people.[50] In other words, the
emergence and maintenance of a cult requires a creative interaction
between those who initiate and promote a saint's claims to holiness
and by those who accept, validate, and work out the expressions of
that claim. Understanding a cult's appearance and vitality requires
identifying the interested parties to a given cult and thoroughly
investigating and analysing the expectations that they bring to it.

The challenge, therefore, in analysing the rise and function of
saints' cults in medieval Rus' is acting on Peter Brown's advice that
'beliefs must be set precisely against their social context'.[51] This is
not easily done. We have relatively little evidence for the development of Christian Rus' in the eleventh century, at least nowhere

[50] 'Pour une étude sociologique de la sainteté canonisée dans l'Eglise catholique',
Archives de Sociologie des Religions, 13 (1962), 17–43; tr. J. Hodgkin, 'Towards a
Sociohistorical Study of Canonized Sainthood in the Catholic Church', in S. Wilson
(ed.), *Saints and their Cults: Studies in Religious Sociology, Folklore and History*
(Cambridge, 1983), 189–216, at 194–9.
[51] *CS*, 48.

near the depth and breadth of information that has allowed Brown and others to debate so carefully the social role of holy men and saints' cults in late antiquity. But what little evidence we have indicates that we should look for the social setting of the first Rus' saints' cult not in tension between the 'people' and the 'authorities', but rather in the consensus about the holy that developed at the centre of East Slavic society as it became Christianized and how that society was shaped as the parties worked out in social ways their commitment to that consensus. Put more sharply, scholars should study the veneration of Boris and Gleb against the backdrop of how the mutual interaction between the princes and the churchmen led to the formation in a Christianizing society of a religious language for expressing the desire for political harmony and the social mechanisms for trying to attain it.

At its secular core the story of Boris and Gleb encapsulates the essential tension of medieval East Slavic politics by providing two models of princely behaviour. On the one hand is Sviatopolk, the elder prince who at a critical moment of dynastic change must decide how to consolidate his authority in Kiev and work out a *modus vivendi* with his princely kinsmen residing in other towns. In the portrayal of the hagiographers Sviatopolk clearly articulates his choices and then chooses secretly to form a retinue and send it to kill his brothers. On the other hand are Boris and Gleb, junior princes who must decide whether to press a claim to Kiev or to negotiate an arrangement that would affirm them in their current towns or elevate their status by giving them more prestigious ones. They too clearly articulate their options, which in the case of Boris is made even more plain by the encouragement of his retinue to move against Sviatopolk, and then act by dismissing their retainers and proceeding toward Kiev to express their willingness to hold Sviatopolk 'as their father' and to negotiate a new arrangement. Boris and Gleb, therefore, declare and act out the very fundamental links of Rus' political life that Sviatopolk denies and violates. As rulers, they are satisfied with the individual domains assigned by their father and opt to negotiate with the senior prince to confirm this arrangement, while Sviatopolk wants the entirety of Rus' for his domain and opts to negotiate deceitfully while he murders secretly. As brothers, they submit to their elder kinsman, while he aims to murder his younger relations. As warband leaders, they consult with their retainers and ultimately preserve their lives and social status by relieving them of their service obligations, while Sviatopolk plots with retainers in secret and ultimately risks their lives and social status by involving them in fratricide and exposing them to a blood feud.

The power of the hagiographic image of Boris and Gleb is generated by the fact that in making this 'correct' choice Boris and Gleb appropriate for themselves the charisma of martyrdom and place their decision squarely within a religious context. They earn the martyr's crown and turn their secular deaths into a heavenly victory by self-consciously redirecting the ultimate focus of their loyalties. In dismissing their retinues and deciding to parley with Sviatopolk, Boris and Gleb affirm their loyalty to their divine Lord, proclaiming that it is God who calls Christians to be faithful and to be submissive to kinsmen, even if this means giving one's life. As the hagiographers point out in describing the posthumous miracles worked by Boris and Gleb, as martyrs the murdered princes received a far greater reward and much more authority in death than that which they were denied in life, namely the status of intercessors for Rus' at God's court and the ability to work miracles on behalf of their newly converted countrymen and to aid their princes in defeating the attacks of the nomads.

The influence of this image on Rus' political life reveals how deeply it summed up and tapped into the desires of the princes and churchmen of eleventh- and twelfth-century Rus' for a shared expression of that perfect harmony in political relations that had always eluded them. The hagiographical narratives of course were composed by churchmen, and so all the elements of the cult—the liturgical office, the icons, the Lives and miracle accounts, the church building, the translations of the relics—must be regarded against the larger backdrop of the effort of churchmen to project into the princely sphere their hopes for political stability and to appropriate and make available the holy to create the social pressures that might bring about that harmony. As Janet Nelson has pointed out regarding similar cults in Western Europe, 'royal saints, manipulated by the living, provided not just a model but a yardstick of kingly conduct and performance in office'.[52] Yet it is very important to note that the basic messages of the cult of Boris and Gleb

---

[52] 'Royal Saints and Early Medieval Kingship', in *Sanctity and Secularity: The Church and the World*, ed. D. Baker, SCH 10 (Oxford, 1973), 39–44, at 43–4.

were not politically partisan: they did not make an argument for any particular succession arrangement or promote the claims of one dynastic line over another. They simply called upon the princes of Rus' to be 'brother-lovers' in the image of Boris and Gleb and to respect the rights of other princes, especially senior ones.

The princes of Rus' could not live up to the standards set by the image of Boris and Gleb, but perhaps for that very reason they rallied so forcefully around a cult that presented in such a religiously distilled fashion their own unattainable wishes for ideal political relations. The 'neutrality' of the cult gave it widespread appeal, since its language, themes, and spaces could be appropriated without regard for a particular prince or line. This much is illustrated by the cult's ability in its first decades to attract as its greatest patrons those very princes for whom expressions of concord were so necessary, namely Iaroslav's sons and grandsons. According to the sources, Iaroslav built the first church for Boris and Gleb, commissioned their first icon, and participated with Metropolitan Ioannes in translating their relics. His son Iziaslav built another church and then in 1072 joined his two brothers, Sviatoslav and Vsevolod, and Metropolitan Georgios in translating the relics. In 1115, Volodimer Monomakh joined his cousins David and Oleg Sviatoslavichi and Metropolitan Nikephoros in translating the relics into a huge masonry church founded by David's father Sviatoslav and finished by his brother Oleg.

The strong magnetic attraction of the cult-site further reshaped the political space of the princes of southern Rus'. For the graves of Boris and Gleb, just a few hours' walk north of Kiev and located within the princely town of Vyshegorod, became a permanent and potent feature on the Rus' political map as a focal point for expressions of concord and reconciliation. For example, the translation of 1072 was staged on 2 May, the third anniversary of the return to the throne of Kiev of Iziaslav, who had been expelled by his brothers Sviatoslav and Vsevolod. In 1150, the Kievan Prince Iziaslav M'stislavich ceded the throne to his uncle Viacheslav Volodimerovich, and they sealed the transfer of power by kissing the cross at the tomb of Boris and Gleb,[53] and the first thing that Volodimerko of Galich did after he had expelled both Iziaslav and Viacheslav from Kiev later that year was to worship at the Church

[53] *PSRL* ii, 399.

of Boris and Gleb before making the rounds of the other three great local religious landmarks—St Sophia, the Tithe Church, and the Caves Monastery.[54]

The potency of the image of Boris and Gleb, praised in the sources as patrons of all of Rus', was not limited to Vyshegorod. Any of the many churches built in their name could serve as an expression of a commitment to reach an accommodation and not to carry on a feud or claim. When, for example, in 1220 Prince Vsevolod came from Smolensk to Novgorod and attempted forcibly to remove the lieutenant (*posadnik*) Tverdislav, the latter sought protection in the Church of Boris and Gleb, whereby Vsevolod asked the bishop to intercede and negotiate a settlement—Tverdislav entered a monastery.[55] The image was also not linked to physical space: the feast days of Boris and Gleb too created opportunities for political settlements. When, for example, in 1093 Volodimer Monomakh was besieged in Chernigov by his cousin Oleg Sviatoslavich, he chose to hand over the town and depart on 24 July, the primary feast day of Boris and Gleb.[56]

One episode in particular associated with the cult of Boris and Gleb illustrates how traditional expectations and projections of power were reorientated and recast as the coming of Christianity to the northern world of East Slavic territory created a dynamic consensus among the chief political actors of Rus' and the chief bearers of the new Christian culture. For this episode shows just how fleeting, and therefore just how needed, were the restraints on princely feuding. In 1101, Prince Sviatopolk Iziaslavich of Kiev attacked his nephew Iaroslav Iaropolkovich at Brest' and brought him to Kiev in chains. Metropolitan Nicholas and several monastic superiors interceded and persuaded Sviatopolk to release Iaropolk, which he did by going with the churchmen to Vyshegorod and unshackling him at the tomb of Boris and Gleb.[57] Here we have all the elements: the warring princes; the clergy trying to restrain them; the use of a Christian setting to seal an oath; and the involvement specifically of the cult of Boris and Gleb to make a public

---

[54] *PSRL* ii, 403

[55] *Novgorodskaia pervaia letopis' starshego i mladshego izvodov*, ed. A. N. Nasonov (Moscow and Leningrad, 1950), 60, 262.

[56] So according to Volodimer's 'Testament', in *PSRL* i, 249. The historical circumstances are found in ibid., i, 226; ii, 217.

[57] Ibid., i, 274–5; ii, 250.

demonstration of reconciliation between feuding kinsmen. Yet it is a very telling postscript to this episode that within a month of his departure from Kiev Iaroslav was recaptured by Sviatopolk's son and returned in chains to Kiev, where he died the following year.

The holy man and Christianization from the apocryphal apostles to St Stephen of Perm

RICHARD M. PRICE

PETER Brown's article on 'The Rise and Function of the Holy Man in Late Antiquity', first published in 1971, immediately added a new dimension to the study of the ascetic movements within the Christian Empire, by drawing attention to the ways in which holy men could contribute to the easing of social relations, as well as of the anxieties of individuals, in a time of rapid economic and political change. One change that the holy man could certainly assist was the process of Christianization. This essay will explore the ways in which the holy man, as represented in the Lives of the saints, could make a distinctive contribution to this process. I shall use a wide range of hagiographical narratives, which will extend in time from the apocryphal Acts of the late second century, through the hagiographical literature generated by the monastic movement, to texts from the late medieval period, and in location from Egypt to Ireland, and from the Loire to beyond the Volga. The texts vary enormously in their historicity, extending from the reliable to the wholly fictitious. I hope to show how this literature, despite its huge range, shows striking continuity in ideology and narrative motifs, and how texts from widely different times and countries can be mutually illuminating.

EARLY MISSIONARY LIVES

Ramsay MacMullen, in a study of the Christianization of the Roman Empire, begins with a scene from the fifth century at the foot of the column of St Symeon Stylites, where the saint is surrounded by hundreds of Arab tribesmen, who had made a journey of 250 miles or more to break their idols and embrace the Christian faith under the eyes of the holy man.[1] What was their motivation? MacMullen opines that they came in quest of an immediate source of super-natural power. Certainly, the account in Theodoret's *Religious History* lays stress on the miracles of healing that Symeon wrought on their behalf. But does this really mean that they renounced their ancestral faith simply in order to have access to the miraculous, with little thought of 'conversion' beyond that? The story can be read differently. The Arab tribesmen of the Syrian desert who were confederates of the empire had many motives for embracing Christianity at a time when the Eastern Empire was developing a new identity as a specifically Christian State (in contrast to its fourth-century character as a State whose emperors promoted Christianity). Why did they come all the way to Symeon's column to make their act of faith? It was, most simply, a way of maximizing publicity. To this the miraculous powers attributed to the holy man could contribute powerfully. If a miracle was deemed to occur, it would serve to dramatize their conversion, and to express in memorable form the new status of the tribe as part of God's holy people, under his immediate protection. Everyone was to gain—the converts who achieved a resonant expression of their new status, the holy man who proved his power, the pilgrims round the column who were the fortunate witnesses of so stirring an event, and the monastery and pilgrimage centre serving St Symeon and his visitors, which doubtless received a generous contribution from the grateful tribesmen.[2] In any event, the story illustrates the drawing power of the most static of holy men, and the way in which the unique status of the man of God, displayed in his miraculous powers, made him a prime agent in the process of Christianization.

This can be illustrated from further material in Theodoret, such as his account of the fifth-century Thalelaeus of Gabala in Syria.[3] Thalelaeus set up his monastic cell by a great pagan shrine on a hill not far from the city. The demons tried to scare him away by wailing at night and waving torches; once they uprooted five hundred trees in a single storm. Theodoret heard of this from the peasantry of the surrounding plain, who were gradually converted to

---

[1] R. MacMullen, *Christianizing the Roman Empire*, A.D. 100–400 (New Haven and London, 1984), 1–3, citing Theodoret, *HR*, xxvi.13–14 (ii, 190–3).

[2] The financial interest of the pilgrimage centres in promoting recourse to holy men is noted by Peter Brown, *AS*, 63–4, as a factor he omitted in the 'Holy Man' article of 1971.

[3] Theodoret, *HR*, xxviii (ii, 224–31).

Christianity as they witnessed the holy man's indifference to demonic attack and his ability to cure the animals whose ailments were attributed to demonic malice.

The link between Christianization and the miraculous powers of the holy man had received a strong emphasis as early as the second century in the developing corpus of the apocryphal Acts. The *Acts of Andrew*, as they survive in Gregory of Tours' epitome, have a whole series of stories in which the apostle achieves the conversion of his hearers through raising their dead and liberating them from demons. A particularly striking story occurs in the *Acts of John*.[4] On the great feast day of Artemis of the Ephesians, St John enters her shrine wearing the colour of mourning; the enraged bystanders seize him and try to murder him. At this he challenges Artemis to strike him dead, while he prays to his own God to display his power. The altar of Artemis shatters into pieces, and half the temple falls down, killing the pagan priest. This spurs the people to demolish the rest of the temple themselves, while John further manifests his power by raising the priest to life. What has this rather crude and wholly fantastic story to tell the historian? It illustrates the link between miracles as manifesting the power of holy men and belligerent Christianization through the destruction of pagan shrines. It also contains a mass of related motifs which recur in later Lives of saints: the attempt to kill the holy man which, in an unexplained way, comes to nothing; the formal ordeal, in which the saint, representing Christ, is pitted against the heathen and the demons they serve; the proof of the weakness of the idols in their inability to defend themselves; the mercy shown by the holy man to the enemy he has now no reason to fear. We shall find all these motifs again in later and less legendary Lives.

Christianization through the smashing of idols, demolition of temples, and cutting down of sacred trees was more than a commonplace of pious fiction: however distasteful it may be to modern susceptibilities, it recurs repeatedly in the Lives of historical saints famous as missionaries. What kind of Christianization does it imply? As Peter Brown has brought out well, for fourth-century Christians the triumph of Christ was in the first place a victory not over men's souls but over the demons who for millennia had dominated the

---

[4] *Acta Joannis*, 38–47, in *The Apocryphal New Testament*, ed. J. K. Elliott (Oxford, 1993), 322–4.

cosmos.[5] The destruction of their earthly shrines was a continuation of the supernatural victory of Christ over the powers of darkness. Numerous Christian texts that celebrate the destruction of idols echo the Old Testament denunciation of idols that neither see nor hear, but the actual belief of Christians was that pagan statues and temples were the abode of real spirits with (for the unprotected) terrifying power. The demolition of the objects of pagan cult was therefore a direct act of defiance against Satan and his angels, and only God's true warriors could undertake it with impunity. This made the smashing of temples and idols an end in itself. We have seen how texts as early as the apocryphal Acts celebrate the destruction of temples, but of course they are fictitious. How soon were Christians able to act out in reality this form of spiritual warfare?

In the Acts of the Martyrs the voluntary martyr, who brings about his own arrest and death, is a prominent figure. Although there are stories of martyrs who after their arrest insult or overturn idols when ordered to sacrifice in front of them,[6] there is a dearth of stories of voluntary martyrs destroying idols as their initial act of defiance. This reflects the general attitude to idolatry of the Christians of the first three centuries, which was simply to remain at a distance from it: thereby they maintained their own purity, without attempting to change the world. The story of St John's destruction of the Temple of Artemis discussed above dramatizes a conflict between Christians and the demonic which in actual fact was fought out not as yet in pagan shrines but in the more domestic setting in which were celebrated the rites of exorcism.[7] From the fourth century we may observe a change. Take for example the *Life of St Abercius of Hierapolis*—a fictitious fourth-century account of a historical figure of the second century. In a dream he receives from Christ a rod with which to destroy the idols of the heathen, which he proceeds to do in temple after temple. The pagans are dumb-

---

[5] *AS*, ch. 1.

[6] A common variant in later legends is for martyrs after their arrest to agree to go to a temple, where they destroy the idols through the power of prayer: see H. Delehaye, *Les passions des martyrs et les genres littéraires*, SHag. 13b, 2nd edn. (Brussels, 1966), 190.

[7] MacMullen, *Christianizing the Roman Empire*, 27, notes the stress in Christian writers of the second and third centuries on the observed power of Christian exorcism as a public proof of the truth of the gospel.

founded by the inability of their gods to defend themselves, and there are numerous conversions.[8]

In a famous fourth-century text from the pagan side, the orator Libanius protested against a wave of attacks on rural temples by Syrian monks in the mid-380s, which deprived the peasantry of the symbols both of their sense of community and of their trust in the divine.[9] As described by Libanius, these attacks were notable for their wanton destructiveness, as ancestral shrines, one after another, were recklessly destroyed without anything taking their place. He bears witness to a 'Christianization' that consisted of proving the impotence of the demons by destroying their abodes, rather than implementing a programme of evangelization in which the demolition of temples was simply one stage in the work of converting countryfolk to the Christian faith.

The text from this time best known for the destruction of shrines as an act of spiritual warfare is Sulpicius Severus' *Life of St Martin*, written in the 390s, a decade after Libanius' protest. In a series of episodes, Martin pits himself dramatically against the idols and shrines of paganism. The prominence of miraculous motifs in this as in other sections of the work has excited scepticism among twentieth-century critics, but the systematic analysis of the text in Jacques Fontaine's massive commentary shows how we can discern, under the dramatization and symbolism that the miraculous elements confer, a solid bedrock of historical fact, firmly rooted in the distinctive features of Gallic paganism and of the spirituality of Martin himself.[10] A good case in point is the episode of the destruction of the temple at Levroux, one of the most important sanctuaries of the Celtic tribe of the Bituriges.[11] Martin found himself rudely repelled by the local population when he endeavoured to demolish this great sanctuary. He withdrew out of danger's way, and prayed in sackcloth and ashes for three days. At the end of this time two angels, armed with lances and

---

[8] *Vita S. Abercii* (BHG 2), 6–24 (ed. T. Nissen (Leipzig, 1912), 6–19). This episode is the probable source of the similar story told in the legendary *Life of Abramy of Rostov* (a thirteenth-century text otherwise known as the *Story of the Establishment of Christianity in Rostov*), in which St John the Divine gives the saint a staff with which to smash the great idol of Volos in Rostov.

[9] *Oratio*, XXX.9 (ed. R. Foerster, *Libanii opera*, 12 vols. (Leipzig, 1903–27), iii, 92).

[10] Sulpicius Severus, *Vita S. Martini* (BHL 5610), §§ 12–15 (ed. J. Fontaine, *Sulpicius Sévère Vie de Saint Martin*, 3 vols., SC 133–5 (Paris, 1967–9), i, 278–87). Fontaine discusses the problems of historicity at length in ibid., i, 171–210.

[11] *Vita Martini*, § 14.3–7 (i, 284–5). See also Fontaine, *Vie de Saint Martin*, ii, 778–93.

shields, came to his assistance. While they (invisibly) held the crowd at bay, Martin demolished the altars and statues of the shrine. The bystanders realized that their failure to intervene was an act of God and a proof of the impotence of their idols; 'almost all', we are told, embraced the faith of Martin. Fontaine has suggested that we can demythologize the warrior angels as a troop of imperial soldiers: such humdrum support is explicitly mentioned in a similar episode narrated in another major work on Martin's life by Sulpicius, the *Dialogues*. The story is rich in biblical allusions, which we may accept as more than literary motifs, since they express what we may take to have been the understanding of Martin himself. The destruction of pagan shrines fulfilled the injunctions of the Lord to Moses (Leviticus 26: 30) and renewed the great deeds of Josiah (2 Kings 23: 8).[12] Martin's withdrawal to pray follows the dominical injunction of Matthew 17: 21 ('This kind never comes out except by prayer and fasting'), and at the same time invokes the theme of monastic withdrawal into the solitude of the desert.

The dominant theme of these chapters of the Life is that St Martin carried out his work of evangelization by means of spiritual combat against the powers of darkness. Sulpicius uses literary motifs from hagiography and even Virgilian epic to add dignity to his narrative, but the biblical models remain central: he presents Martin as a man in whom the great biblical events of the history of salvation could endlessly repeat themselves. Martin as a man of power continues and manifests the once-for-all victory of Christ over the demonic. This does not explain to the modern reader how Martin could achieve the destruction of pagan shrines and the partial conversion of rural populations. The historian must invoke his alliance with Christian landowners and the use of military force. But such demythologization should not be taken so far as to obscure Martin's own understanding of what he was about: we have no reason to doubt that the biblical motifs we have been considering were as dominant for him as for his biographer. Martin was concerned to achieve a real Christianization, as is evidenced by his programme of founding parishes in the countryside;[13] but this does not alter the

---

[12] *Dialogi* (*BHL* 5614–16), iii.8.6 (ed. C. Halm, *CSEL*, 1 (1866), 206). The importance of Josiah for Martin's circle is illustrated by his treatment in Sulpicius, *Chronica*, i, 52 (ed. ibid., 53).

[13] See C. Stancliffe, 'From Town to Country: The Christianization of the Touraine 370–600', in *The Church in Town and Countryside*, ed. D. Baker, SCH 16 (Oxford, 1979), 43–59.

fact that he shared an ideology that interpreted the destruction of pagan shrines as more than a preliminary to church-building in that it was the acting out of a spiritual battle against the demonic forces of evil.

There is no shortage of later material that provides further examples of this ideal of aggressive evangelization, linked to the theme of spiritual combat with the powers of darkness. One significant body of medieval Latin texts, which illustrate the influence of St Martin and his biographer, consists of the Lives of the eighth-century Anglo-Saxon missionaries in Germany—Lives which vary in historical reliability but which testify alike to the vitality of the Martinian ideal.[14] We read in Alcuin's *Life of St Willibrord* of an occasion when the saint smashed an idol and was miraculously protected when its custodian struck him on the head with his sword; the saint's companion rushed forward to avenge the blow, but he insisted that the man be left to go free.[15] The theme of the refusal of the holy man to punish his adversaries serves, here and elsewhere, to pinpoint that his true enemies are not the benighted pagans but the powers of darkness: 'for our struggle is not against flesh and blood, but against the principalities, against the powers, against the cosmic rulers of this present darkness, against the spiritual hosts of wickedness in the heavenly places' (Ephesians 6: 12).

The best-known of these works is Willibald's *Life of St Boniface*. The text betrays the influence of the *Life of St Martin*. We read how Boniface, at an early stage in his mission, 'destroyed pagan temples and shrines, and built churches and chapels',[16] though it is clear from the following chapter that his church-building was very gradual. One vivid episode is the cutting down of an oak sacred to 'Jupiter'. A great crowd of pagans stood around, 'bitterly cursing in their hearts the enemy of the gods'. To everyone's amazement, no

---

[14] For a balanced treatment see R. Fletcher, *The Conversion of Europe* (London, 1997), 193–227. *Vita S. Vulframni* (BHL 8738), ed. W. Levison, MGH SS rer. Merov., v (1910), 661–73, illustrates how religious houses could have an interest in disseminating dramatic stories of evangelization in Germany that were wholly fictitious, as pointed out by I. N. Wood, 'Saint Wandrille and its Hagiography', in idem and G. A. Loud (eds.), *Church and Chronicle in the Middle Ages: Essays presented to John Taylor* (London, 1991), 1–14, esp. 13–14.

[15] Alcuin, *Vita S. Willibrordi* (BHL 8935–6), § 14 (ed. W. Levison, MGH SS rer. Merov., vii (1920), 128); tr. C. H. Talbot, *The Anglo-Saxon Missionaries in Germany* (London, 1964), 12–13.

[16] Willibald, *Vita S. Bonifatii* (BHL 1400), § 6 (ed. G. H. Pertz, MGH SS, ii (1829), 341); tr. Talbot, *Missionaries*, 41.

sooner had he made a first shallow incision, than the whole tree, shaken by a mighty gust of wind, fell to the ground and broke into four great pieces. The pagans no less than Boniface, we are told, interpreted this event as proof of the power of the Christian God.[17]

An episode from the *Life of St Lebuin* (of dubious historicity) provides a particularly striking illustration of the belligerent spirituality we are exploring. Lebuin insists on attending a general assembly of the Saxons, despite warnings that he is likely to be roughly handled. He interrupts the assembly, and threatens the Saxons that if they do not renounce their ancestral idolatry God will subject them to alien rulers (that is, the Franks). The Saxons lose their patience, and a number of them pull stakes out of a nearby fence as weapons to use against Lebuin. But the saint suddenly vanishes from their sight, and the Saxons immediately repent of their murderous intent. This story is told plainly, but tellingly, in the original anonymous version of the Life.[18] But when Hucbald of St Amand came to write his more elaborate version of the text in *c.* 900, he added a number of details that bring out the meaning of the story.[19] Lebuin, as he arrives at the assembly, is described as 'a good soldier . . . clothed in the breastplate of righteousness . . . protected with the shield of faith, crowned with the helmet of salvation, armed with the sword of the Spirit'. He makes the sign of the cross 'like the advance standard-bearer of his King'. In the presence of the pagans he imitates, we are told, the zeal of Elijah the prophet (against the priests of Baal), and raises his voice like a trumpet. The Saxons react 'delirious with a demoniacal spirit, full of fury and madness'. Lebuin walks away unharmed through their ranks, like Christ escaping 'from the perfidious Jews'. He is proud of this divine protection, but disappointed to have been deprived of the crown of martyrdom. All these details are added by Hucbald, but they simply bring out more vividly what is already implicit in the original text. One of the characteristics of the late antique holy man was the frankness of speech

[17] *Vita Bonifatii*, § 8 (pp. 343–4); tr. Talbot, *Missionaries*, 45–6. This story is indebted to the famous episode of the felling of the sacred pine-tree in the *Vita Martini*, § 13 (on which, see below). It is itself echoed in the *Heliand*, a ninth-century Old Saxon paraphrase of the *Diatesseron*, which refers to the power of the gospel to 'fell every evil creature and work of wickedness' (tr. G. R. Murphy, *The Heliand* (Oxford, 1992), 4).
[18] *Vita S. Lebuini antiqua* (BHL 4810b), § 6 (ed. A. Hofmeister, *MGH SS*, xxx.2 (1934), 793–4); tr. Talbot, *Missionaries*, 231–3.
[19] *Vita S. Lebuini* (BHL 4812), ed. G. H. Pertz, *MGH SS*, ii (1829), 362–3.

with which he addressed those in authority; it was part of his role to speak, when appropriate, with the firmness of a mouthpiece of God. But in this story this frankness is raised to a higher level as a frontal attack against the demonic. The pagans, in their resistance to his words, take on the aspect of demons themselves, raging, maddened, and malicious. The holy man may die a martyr, or he may with God-given power render their fury impotent. In either event he makes present the victory of Christ, the crucified King.

Another form of the confrontation between the man of God and the powers of evil consists of a trial of strength between the holy man, as the representative of Christ, and pagan priests or sorcerers, as representatives of evil sources of supernatural power. There were biblical precedents for this in the tests of power between Moses and the magicians of Pharaoh and between Elijah and the priests of Baal; the example most cited by medieval writers, in both West and East, was the contest between St Peter and Simon Magus described in the vivid fiction of the late second-century *Acts of Peter*.[20]

The best-known fourth-century example is the following story from the *Life of St Martin*. On one of his missionary excursions Martin demolished a village temple, without any resistance from the villagers (cowed, perhaps, by the armed guard that generally seems to have attended Martin on these raids), but excited determined opposition when he set about cutting down a sacred pine-tree. (The contrast doubtless reflects the fact that sacred trees and wells had a longer history and a more central place in Celtic cult than temples, which were a Roman importation.) Agreement was reached that Martin should stand, bound, under the tree while the pagans themselves cut it down: if the tree did not strike Martin on its descent, that would be proof of the power of his God. With consummate art Sulpicius Severus describes the felling of the tree and Martin's all too predictable escape in a way that makes us share the excitement of the original onlookers:

And now the tree began to totter, and to look as if it were about to fall. The monks, standing a distance, grew pale, terrified as disaster drew near; they had lost all hope and confidence, and expected only the death of Martin. But he, trusting in the Lord, waited calmly. A loud crack had already been heard from the felled pine, it was already coming down and already crashing upon him, when he raised his hand against it and made the sign of the

[20] Exodus 7–9; 1 Kings 18: 20–40; the Vercelli *Acts of Peter*, 22–29, in *The Apocryphal New Testament*, ed. Elliott, 415–21.

cross. But then, as if driven backwards by some hurricane, it swept round to the opposite side—so much so that it almost crushed the peasants who had taken their places there in what had seemed a safe spot. Then indeed a great shout went up to heaven, the pagans were stunned by the miracle, while the monks wept for joy; all together extolled the name of Christ.[21]

One striking variant of this theme is the public trial of strength between a Christian holy man and a pagan sorcerer (or heretic), in which both submit to an ordeal which flesh and blood can only survive by miracle. The best early example is to be found in the *History of the Monks of Egypt*, a fourth-century Egyptian text widely disseminated in the East and influential in the West through Rufinus' translation. We read there of the monk Apa Copres who enters into debate with a Manichee.[22] When intellectual argument proves indecisive, they agree to undergo trial by fire: each in turn will walk onto a burning pyre. The Christian spends half an hour in the flames, sound and unharmed—like the three youths in Nebuchadnezzar's fiery furnace. The Manichee loses his nerve, and has to be pushed by the crowd into the flames, which give him burns all over his body.

A similar contest is described in Muirchú's *Life of St Patrick*, a text of the late seventh century. Patrick and a Druid are pressed by the King of Tara to undergo an ordeal of water and fire. The ordeal by water is to consist of throwing their sacred books into the water, to see which emerge undamaged. This test is rejected by the Druid on the ground that water is the Christian God (presumably a reference to baptism). So they agree to ordeal by fire. A wooden hut is constructed with two rooms, in one of which, made of green wood, stands the Druid, wearing Patrick's chasuble, while in the other, built of dry wood, is placed one of Patrick's boy acolytes (the future bishop Benignus), wearing the robes of the Druid; we are doubtless not meant to think that Patrick is being pusillanimous in putting a

---

[21] Sulpicius, *Vita Martini*, § 13.6–9 (i, 280–3). The story is not credible as it stands: why would the pagans be happy to cut down their most sacred object, even as a way of disposing of Martin? Fontaine, *Vie de Saint Martin*, ii, 747–8, pointed out that there was an annual feast of Cybele in which a pine-tree, bearing the image of Attis, was cut down, as a symbol of his sacrificial death. If such a feast was indeed the occasion, the cutting down of the tree becomes believable but now suffers from over-explanation. We begin to doubt whether Martin's presence under the falling tree (which is credible enough) was a formal trial by ordeal. It remains significant that this is how Sulpicius chose to present it.

[22] *Historia monachorum sive de vita sanctorum patrum*, ix.7.9–15 (ed. E. Schulz-Flügel, Patristische Texte und Studien 34 (Berlin, 1990), 320–1).

boy in his place. The hut is then set alight, and—the reader is surprised to hear—the green wood, the Druid, and his garb are consumed by the flames, while the boy and Patrick's chasuble are unharmed.[23] The credibility of these stories is not their strong point. Certainly the *Life of St Patrick* is agreed to be wholly imaginary, once we leave the material derived from Patrick's own writings. But a strikingly similar story, only far more credible, is told in the next work that will receive our attention—the *Life of St Stephen of Perm*, written near Moscow by Epifany Premudry in the late fourteenth century.

THE *LIFE OF ST STEPHEN OF PERM*

Epifany Premudry (Epiphanius the Most Wise) was a monk first in Rostov and later in the famous Trinity Monastery of St Sergius of Radonezh, whose life he was to write. The only one of his works that survives in its original form is the *Life of St Stephen of Perm*, written, it would appear, immediately after the death of the saint in 1396.[24] The work is notable for its highly rhetorical style, richly wrought to the point of monotony: the author loves strings of biblical citations, sequences of synonymous expressions, the collocation of different words from the same root, paratactic clauses that begin with the same word or end with words with the same termination. It is the style of the work that has won it close study from students of Old Russian literature, while its religious content has received scant attention.[25] It relates how Stephen, at first a fellow

[23] *Vita S. Patricii (BHL* 6497), i.19–20 (ed. L. Bieler, *The Patrician Texts in the Book of Armagh*, Scriptores Latini Hiberniae 10 (Dublin, 1979), 92–6). Note how in these stories the belligerent note so strong in accounts of the contests between holy men and the demonic is significantly modified by the comparative passivity of the holy man who submits patiently to an ordeal which might lead to his death. Here the theme of the holy man as akin to the martyr enriches the dominant theme of the holy man as warrior.

[24] *Zhitie sv. Stefana Episkopa Permskogo*, ed. V. Druzhinin (St Petersburg, 1897); repr. with an introduction by D. Čiževskij ('S-Gravenhage, 1959).

[25] The outstanding discussion is J. Børtnes, *Visions of Glory: Studies in Early Russian Hagiography*, tr. idem and P. L. Nielsen, Slavica Norvegica 5 (Oslo, 1988), 136–93. Much of this had been published before as 'The Function of Word-Weaving in the Structure of Epiphanius' *Life of Saint Stephen, Bishop of Perm*', in H. Birnbaum and M. S. Flier (eds.), *Medieval Russian Culture*, California Slavic Studies 12 (Berkeley and Los Angeles, 1984), 311–42. Børtnes offers a structuralist analysis that is illuminating on the themes as well as the style of the work. Other studies in English are

monk of Epifany's in Rostov, persuaded the Muscovite authorities to send him as a missionary to a group of Finno-Ugric tribes around Perm in the region north-east of Kazan towards the Ural Mountains. There he devoted the rest of his life to preaching the gospel, apart from periodic visits to Moscow, on one of which he was consecrated as the first bishop of Perm, and on another of which he died. His burial in Moscow did nothing to stimulate the development of a cult, since he was not a figure of lasting interest to the inhabitants of the capital. The Life lacks the stories of posthumous miracles that are a standard feature of Russian hagiography. It was Epifany's work that stimulated interest in Stephen and won his belated canonization in 1574.

How well did Epifany know his subject? They had been monks together in Rostov, but that was before Stephen's mission. Epifany claims to derive his material partly from what he learnt from Stephen's disciples, partly from what he saw with his own eyes (which cannot have been very much), and partly from what he himself heard from the saint.[26] Such claims are a hagiographical commonplace, but it is possible, indeed likely, that Stephen paid visits to Sergius's monastery when on his way to or from Moscow and did indeed speak with Epifany there. The general view of students of the Life is that, once we set aside the flamboyance of Epifany's literary style, there remains factual content that is sober and credible, and markedly free of obviously legendary elements; indeed the Life contains not a single miracle story. Far more of the text is devoted to developing biblical types and theological commonplaces than to narration, but since Epifany and Stephen came from the same milieu, and shared the same devotion to the literary inheritance from Greek Orthodoxy, we may presume that Epifany's interpretation of Stephen's mission is reasonably close to Stephen's own ideological world. Certainly, there was not the cultural distance between Stephen and Epifany as there was between, say, Symeon Stylites and Theodoret, or between Martin of Tours and Sulpicius Severus.

Doubts have been cast on the historical reliability of the Life in an article by Michael Dane which argues that Stephen as portrayed

F. C. M. Wigzell, 'Convention and Originality in the *Life of Stefan of Perm*: A Stylistic Analysis', *Slavonic and East European Review*, 49 (1971), 339–54, and F. C. M. Kitch, *The Literary Style of Epifanij Premudryj: Pletenije Sloves* (Munich, 1976).

[26] *Zhitie sv. Stefana*, 1.

in the Life is a very different figure from the historical Stephen revealed in a surviving example of his own writing, the *Tract against the Strigolniki*.[27] While the Stephen of the Life promotes the reading of Scripture (by translating it into Permian), adopts a life of voluntary poverty, and practises non-violence, the Stephen of the Tract regards the study of Scripture as dangerous, defends clerical wealth, and is ferocious in his denunciation of heretics. But surely these contrasts are forced. There is nothing incompatible in Stephen's promoting biblical study in Perm and yet at the same time deploring the way in which heretics interpret Scripture 'without meekness and humility'[28] in support of their own errors. We may admit that the Life's insistence on Stephen's poverty is partly a hagiographical stylization, since, as Dane points out, it is clear from the Life itself that he possessed funds for church-building and far-flung almsgiving. The defence of clerical property in the Tract was in any case necessitated by the claims of the Strigolniki that clerical wealth invalidated the sacraments of the official Church. Even so, Stephen's defence is hardly enthusiastic: he observes that, even if some of the clergy are accumulating estates, they should be left to the judgement of God.[29] Finally, so far from the Stephen of the Tract being a fanatical hounder of heretics, his tone is comparatively mild by the standards of medieval polemic, and there are no personal attacks on the heretical teachers; his main complaint is that their self-righteousness and censoriousness is Pharisaical and un-Christian. The tone is no different from the extended warnings against the dangers of heresy in the farewell discourses towards the end of the Life.[30] The Tract fills out our picture of Stephen by supplementing hints in the Life, such as Stephen's repeated visits to Moscow and his influence as a patron, that point to him as a powerful presence in the Russian church scene and not just a humble monk working in a backwater; but it is a mistake to use it to cast doubt on the reliability of the Life. Though hagiographical conventions reduce the individuality of Stephen in Epifany's account, they

[27] 'Epiphanius' Image of St. Stefan', *Canadian Slavonic Papers*, 5 (1961), 72–86. The *Pouchenie protiv Strigol'nikov* ('Tract against the Strigolniki') is to be found in N. A. Kazakova and Ya. S. Lur'e, *Antifeodal'nye Ereticheskie Dvizheniya na Rusi* (Moscow and Leningrad, 1955), 234–43.
[28] *Pouchenie*, 242.   [29] Ibid., 241.
[30] *Zhitie sv. Stefana*, 80–4. Note how the use of Galatians 1: 8 as a key anti-heretical text occurs in both this passage and the *Pouchenie*, 239.

do not exclude a quantity of reliable detail on the nature and conduct of his mission.[31]

The realism of the narrative is apparent in its description of the gradualness of the process of conversion. When Stephen builds a church, the Permians, we are told, are attracted at first simply out of curiosity and delight in the beauty of the architecture.[32] Stephen accompanied his preaching of the gospel (in the Permian language, his third after Russian and Greek) by that frontal assault on idolatry that we have found to be a standard feature in the Lives of missionary saints. The following text may serve as an example of Epifany's development of this theme, as well as of his baroque prose style:

He destroyed all their idols, and demolished their sanctuaries, and pulled down their altars, and overthrew their images, as one with great authority; and so with a clatter their memory perished from among men. The Permians were exceedingly amazed at another thing too, and said: 'How does he smash images and yet remain whole and immune? How does he day and night go among idols, casting them down, and yet stay whole and unharmed by them? Why can the images not harm him? Why can demonic spells not cause him any hurt or do him any ill?' In Perm up till this time, until they received baptism, their custom had been the following: if one of the Permians touched an image, or took any of the offerings given and presented to idols and assigned and destined for demons, or desecrated any of the sacrifices prohibited and forbidden to them, he would be cast down, broken and crushed, as their sorcerers attacked him with sorcery. Because of this no one ever dared to take anything, either openly or in secret, or to steal anything from the sanctuaries or from the offerings or from the sacrifices. But good Stephen, courageous victor as he was, felt no

[31] Dane relates the contrast, in his view, between the Life and the Tract to the conventional division of Old Russian spirituality into two sharply differentiated and opposing strands: the emphasis on love, interior religion, and renouncing wealth and power in the hesychast and 'kenotic' tradition, on the one side; and the emphasis on fear and external religion, and the avarice and power politics, of much of the church hierarchy, on the other. This schematization of the tensions in early Russian spirituality is far too crude. To Dane's scepticism, oddly endorsed by Børtnes, *Visions*, 141, contrast two highly regarded Russian treatments—V. Klyuchevsky, *Drevnerusskie Zhitiya Svyatykh* (Moscow, 1871), 88–112, and O. F. Konovalova, 'Printsip otbora fakticheskikh svedeniy v "Zhitii Stefana Permskogo" ', *Trudy Otdela Drevnerusskoy Literatury*, 24 (1969), 135–8—both of which acknowledge the reliability of Epifany's narration and claim that Stephen's own words are often apparent beneath Epifany's rhetorical embellishments, both generally in the account of Stephen's preaching and specifically in the narrative of his confrontation with the sorcerer Pam, discussed below.

[32] *Zhitie sv. Stefana*, 29–30.

anxiety, but without fear and without terror went round their sanctuaries day and night, through wood and field, without the people or in front of the people. He struck the idols on the forehead with the butt of an axe, shattered their legs, severed them with a hatchet, cut them into pieces, broke them into logs, divided them into faggots. He utterly rooted them out, and burnt them with fire, and incinerated them with flame. He himself stayed whole and remain unharmed; the idols could not harm him, the demons could cause him no ill. What could demons bring about, what harm could idols do, what could idol-worshippers effect, what could be accomplished by sorcerers, idolaters and magicians, when God protected his servant, watched over his devotee, and surrounded him with hosts of angels?[33]

Here again is the familiar theme that the pagans lose faith in their gods when these gods prove unable to defend themselves; but that this is more than a hagiographical commonplace is shown by the distinctive detail about the threat of sorcery to deter sacrilege. The effect of such spells on those who believed in their power can easily be imagined, and Stephen's imperviousness is indeed likely to have impressed the Permians. Another aspect of the matter was Stephen's refusal to appropriate the furs laid as offerings on the idols. Sacrilege that was not mere theft lay outside the mental horizons of the Permians, and we are told that this confirmed their growing sense that he was not an adventurer but the servant of God.[34]

As Stephen's mission bore fruit, he won a body of faithful followers who aided him in his work of desecration and could defend him from attack. But up till then he was highly vulnerable, and there is a series of three episodes in the Life when the pagans make a determined attempt to kill him.[35] In all three of them the saint's escape is very vaguely narrated or not narrated at all, while the text moves into top gear in eloquent passages of prayer, preaching, and biblical citation. This has been treated by literary historians as an artistic flaw, and as evidence of Epifany's only cursory interest in narrative. But, as we noted above in the context of the *Acts of Andrew*, the motif of the murderous attack on a saint that simply peters out was a traditional one. Indeed it has a biblical precedent in Luke's account of Christ's return to Nazareth: 'Rising up, they drove him out of the city, and led him to the brow of the hill on which their city was built, in order to cast him down headlong. But going through the midst of them he went on his way' (4: 29-30).

[33] Ibid., 36–7.   [34] Ibid., 35.   [35] Ibid., 19–28.

This passage is indeed directly echoed in one of these passages of Epifany.[36]

Stephen's evangelization of the Permians, as narrated by Epifany, was well advanced when it was interrupted by the return (after a strangely long interval) of their chief sorcerer, one Pam, who attempted (with minimal success, we are assured) to pervert Stephen's recent converts.[37] There followed a series of debates between Stephen and the sorcerer, which (Epifany admits with honesty) were utterly inconclusive. Some of Pam's arguments are strikingly distinctive, and are generally accepted as authentic and not the inventions of Epifany. He appeals to the Permians' resentment at Russian rule: 'What good can come to us from Moscow? Is it not from there that we receive heavy taxes and dues, and every kind of burden?'[38] Against the argument that the pagan gods have proved their impotence by failing to harm Stephen, Pam replies that the gods could have destroyed Stephen long ago but have chosen to be merciful. In an argument singled out by most commentators on the Life he insists that the Permians' success in hunting (their main source of livelihood) depends on the assistance of the many gods who haunt every part of the natural world, in contrast to the one, distant God of the Christians; for example, he adds, when one of our people goes bear-hunting he can kill a bear and skin it without any assistance, but when Russians go hunting, they need one or even two hundred hunters to catch a single bear, and even then the animal often escapes.[39] In contrast, Stephen's arguments, which simply repeat the commonplaces of Christian dogmatism, strike a modern reader as ineffective.

Finally, after a particularly prolonged debate over a whole day and night, attended by a great crowd of Permians, the two disputants agree to put their rival faiths to the test. Pam proposes that they should light a fire and both enter it together, to see which of them can come out unharmed. Ordeal by fire is to be followed by ordeal by water (we are reminded of the very similar ordeal in Muirchu's *Life of St Patrick*, treated above): the priest and the sorcerer are to descend, arm in arm, through an ice-hole in the river, and then after a watery perambulation re-emerge out of another

---

[36] *Zhitie sv. Stefana*, 28.
[37] The confrontation between Stephen and Pam (or Pan) is treated at length (ibid., 39–58) and is the narrative climax of the Life.
[38] Ibid., 40.   [39] Ibid., 46–7.

one. Stephen agrees to the test, hoping, we are told, in divine protection, but quite prepared to undergo a martyr's death. But it is the
sorcerer who now loses his nerve. Stephen takes him firmly by the
arm and tries to drag him into the fire. The tussle goes on for some
time, until a humiliated Pam admits his inability to cope with fire
and begs for mercy. He is then taken to the river, where a similar
scene follows, and the sorcerer is finally and totally defeated. Why
did Pam himself propose these two ordeals, and then refuse to go
through with them? Under pressure he reveals his reasons to
Stephen and the crowd. He had learnt from his father a whole
repertoire of spells and enchantments; earlier in the debate he had
mentioned that, in contrast to the Christians who need days to hear
what has happened at a distance, the traditional skills of the
Permians enable them to know at once what is happening even in
far-distant lands.[40] Pam's repertoire did not, however, contain
spells to control fire and water. But did the Christian know this?
When Pam first mentioned the possibility of an ordeal by fire and
water, Stephen had replied immediately; 'I don't know how to
enchant fire and water, I've never learnt how.'[41] It was this reply
that led Pam to insist on the ordeal: he too could not tame fire and
water, but Stephen did not know this, and therefore was bound to
admit defeat when pressed to undergo the ordeal. But, the sorcerer
continues, when Stephen insisted on going through with it, he
(Pam) realized to his horror that he had been tricked: manifestly
Stephen *did* know how to enchant fire and water. So, Pam ruefully
concludes, he has been defeated as a result of his own cunning. The
crowd now insist that the sorcerer must become a Christian or die.
Stephen, however, is more merciful, and simply banishes him for
ever from the land of Perm.

What are we to make of this memorable narrative, incomparably
the most lifelike and also the most skilfully narrated of all the stories of thaumaturgic contest that I have come across in the long
sweep of hagiographical literature? The narrative is convincing as
a piece of accurate reporting, deriving from Stephen himself. Of
course, it is partly a literary construction. Pam's exposition of his
train of thought reads like guesswork on the part of Stephen, when
later he narrated the episode to fellow churchmen in Moscow; but
Stephen's guesswork is likely to be close to the truth, certainly

---

[40] Ibid., 47.   [41] Ibid., 54.

closer to the truth than any alternative explanation that might occur to the modern scholar. The contrast that emerges between the holy man and the sorcerer is that, while the holy man is not a magician but knows that his God can do anything, the pagan sorcerer has only a limited repertoire of spells; consequently, once he is moved on to unfamiliar terrain he has no resources to put against the confidence of the man of God. In what is in reality a test not of thaumaturgic power but of self-confidence, this puts the holy man at a distinct advantage, quite apart from his freedom from fear of death and his readiness, if need be, to die for his faith. This, surely, is the real significance of the stories of trial by ordeal. Whether true, partly true, or wholly legendary, they express the strongest card in the hand of the holy man as missionary—a complete lack of fear, which is likely to impress both his companions and his intended converts as a sign of the presence within him of a power not of this world.

One common feature of early evangelization that reappears in the *Life of St Stephen of Perm* is that of intensified expectation of the End of the Age and the Second Coming of Christ, as part of a distinctive Christian vision of history. The first church that Stephen built in the land of Perm was dedicated to the Annunciation of Our Lady. This leads Epifany into a lengthy discourse on the significance of the Annunciation in relation to other events in the history of salvation which (according to tradition) may also be assigned to the month of March: these include the creation of the world, the Exodus, the entry into the Promised Land, the Passion and Resurrection of Christ, the Second Coming, the General Resurrection, and the Last Judgement.[42] The implication is that Stephen's building of a church, as the first decisive step in the conversion of the Permians, belongs to this great cycle.

Equally notable is Epifany's retelling of the parable of the Labourers in the Vineyard (Matthew 20: 1–16). After following the first part of the Gospel text closely, he expands the rest of it as follows:

At the eleventh hour he found others standing idle, and said to them, 'Why do you stand here all day idle, Permians? Has no one hired you?' And they answered, 'No one has hired us—that is, no one has taught us the Christian faith, no one has illuminated us with holy baptism, no one has

---

[42] *Zhitie sv. Stefana*, 23–4. Børtnes, *Visions*, 165, provides a translation of this passage.

led us into the rational vineyard, that is, the Law of God.' . . . But when our Saviour was well pleased, in the last days, at the end of the years, in the final times, at the close of the seventh millennium, the Lord had pity on them.[43]

This bold application of the parable may be related to a long disquisition of Epifany's on why the conversion of the Permians occurred so late in history. Why did the apostles not come to the land of Perm? In an apology for their neglect of this clearly essential part of their mission, Epifany lists the great missionary journeys that legend attributed to the apostles, commenting several times that this or that apostle 'did not come to the land of Perm'.[44] The clear implication, shameless in its boldness, is that the work of Stephen completes and redeems the labours of the apostles. This completion was linked in Epifany's mind (and doubtless in Stephen's also) to the expectation of the end of the world in the not so distant future. According to the traditional chronology that assigned seven thousand years to world history, the world, created in 5508 BC, was due to come to an end in AD 1492, less than a century after Stephen's death and the writing of the Life. This 'fact' is brought up several times by Epifany, once in the mouths of critics of Stephen's mission, who think that it is now too late to lay the foundations of a Christian culture in the land of Perm.[45] This belief was indeed so widespread in late medieval Russia that it could not but affect the perception of Stephen's mission.[46] Epifany's purpose remains clear: the conversion of the Permians is to be seen as the fulfilment of Christ's commission to the apostles to preach the gospel to the ends of the world. This makes the conversion of Perm virtually the climax of salvation history. Certainly, it places it firmly within that history and links it closely to the great events narrated in Scripture.

This eschatological dimension in missionary work had recurred repeatedly in the earlier history of Christian evangelization. It is a familiar fact that St Paul preached an imminent *parousia*, and saw his own missionary work as an essential prelude to the return of Christ.[47] The monastic movement of the fourth century (which had

---

[43] *Zhitie sv. Stefana*, 12–13.   [44] Ibid., 10–12.   [45] Ibid., 70.
[46] See Børtnes, *Visions*, 174–5, for the intensity of eschatological expectation in Russia at this time.
[47] See J. Christiaan Beker, *Paul the Apostle* (Edinburgh, 1980), 135–81, and J. W. Thompson, 'The Gentile Mission as an Eschatological Necessity', *Restoration Quarterly*, 14 (1971), 18–27.

such a decisive influence on the Christianization of Egypt and Syria) was accompanied by heightened eschatological expectation: we read in the *History of the Monks of Egypt* that for the fathers in the desert 'there is only the expectation of the coming of Christ in the singing of psalms'.[48] St Martin of Tours was convinced that he was living in the last days, and that already in his own lifetime the Antichrist had been born and was soon to manifest himself.[49] St Patrick (not the legendary figure of the Lives, but the authentic Patrick of the *Confessio*) wrote that he was preaching in the last days, that the coming of Christ was near, and that in preaching to the Irish just before the end of the world he was fulfilling the words of Christ, 'This gospel of the kingdom will be preached throughout the whole world, as a testimony to all the nations, and then will come the end.'[50] St Gregory the Great, in the wake of Augustine of Canterbury's mission to England, wrote to King Ethelbert of Kent that 'the end of the present world is now nigh and the reign of the saints is about to come'.[51] This eschatological theme was more than icing on the cake, a sort of homiletic extravaganza. We have to remember that evangelization was not central in the Church's mission until modern times. Citizens of the Roman Empire or of the Byzantine Empire, of sub-Roman Britain or of medieval Muscovy, had very mixed feelings about the spread of the faith to barbarians who were the enemies of Christian civilization and did not deserve the benefits of the gospel. The belief that missionary expansion could herald the completion of history and the return of Christ in glory was an important part of the motivation for evangelization.

Expectation of the End also contributed something to the spirit in which evangelization was carried out. The End was foreseen as the full manifestation of the powers of darkness, who would then be overcome by the forces of light led by Christ in glory. 'And then the lawless one will be revealed, and the Lord Jesus will slay him with

[48] *Historia Monachorum*, prol., § 8 (p. 245).
[49] Sulpicius Severus, *Dialogi*, ii.14 (pp. 197–8). See also idem, *Vita Martini*, § 24.1–3 (i, 306–7).
[50] *Confessio*, 4 ('adventum ipsius mox futurum'), 34 ('in novissimis diebus . . . ante finem mundi'), 41 (citing Matthew 24: 14). According to Joachim Gnilka, *Das Matthäusevangelium* (Freiburg, 1988), ii, 318, the meaning of the Matthaean text is not that worldwide evangelization is a sign of the End but that it is a precondition for it. The distinction is a fine one.
[51] Bede, *HE*, i.32 (pp. 110–15). For other passages where Gregory expresses this conviction, see G. R. Evans, *The Thought of Gregory the Great* (Cambridge, 1986), 19.

the breath of his mouth and destroy him by his appearing and his coming' (2 Thessalonians 2: 8). It was this scenario that stimulated the belligerent note in evangelization. The holy man who overcame the demonic powers through openly defying them was in the advance-guard that announced and anticipated the final victory of Christ.

CONTINUITY IN MISSIONARY HAGIOGRAPHY

The similarities between Epifany's view of mission and that of earlier Greek and Latin hagiography have turned out to be considerable. They are evidence of a degree of stability in Christian ideology in general and in Christian hagiography in particular. The narrative parallels between the *Life of St Stephen* and Western texts such as the *Life of St Martin* and the *Life of St Patrick* must be explained by a common source in the Greek tradition, since no Latin hagiography was known in Russia. Epifany's knowledge of the Greek tradition is likely to have been extensive. It has been pointed out that the rhetorical laments which conclude the Life are heavily indebted to Greek rhetoric and in particular to Gregory of Nyssa's *Funeral Oration over Meletius*.[52] The story of the trial by ordeal between Stephen and Pam has as its closest Greek parallel known to me the story of Apa Copres and a Manichee in the *History of the Monks of Egypt*, related above. It is therefore relevant to note that this text was available to Russians in a vernacular translation,[53] though in any case Epifany had direct knowledge of Greek texts, as did Stephen himself. The recurrence of narrative motifs through borrowing by hagiographers from their predecessors or the Scriptures often arouses doubts as to historicity—and quite rightly so, when the biographer is writing on some aspect of his subject's life where the historical facts were either unknown to him or incompatible with his ideal of sainthood. But we also have to reckon with latter-day holy men who consciously emulated their great forebears from

[52] For a detailed analysis, see Yu. A. Alissandratos in *Drevnerusskaya Literatura: Istochnikovedenie*, ed. D. S. Likhachev (Leningrad, 1984), 64–74.

[53] For the Old Slavonic translation of the *Historia Monachorum in Aegypto*, made as early as the ninth century, and the Old Russian recension of the eleventh or twelfth century, see D. S. Likhachev, *Slovar' knizhnikov i knizhnosti drevney Rusi*, vol. I (Leningrad, 1987), 305-6.

the early centuries of Christianity. We may recognize in Epifany's account of Stephen's mission something more interesting than hagiographical commonplace—namely, the work of a missionary who, without neglecting the needs of the present, hoped to fit into sacred history by imitating it.

The *Life of St Stephen of Perm* takes us, in one sense, a long way from our starting-point in the legends of the apostles and the missionary labours of Martin, Patrick, and Boniface in the early medieval West; but the similarities are extremely striking. Of course, the student of Christian texts living in a post-Christian society is not well trained in detecting varieties of paganism, and the texts themselves encourage us to see paganism, at whatever time and whatever place, as much of a muchness. For the early or medieval Christian paganism always represents the same thing. From the human side it represents a mindless traditionalism, uncivilized and irrational: *consuetudo*, as used by Sulpicius and others, takes on a markedly pejorative connotation in this context, and corresponds precisely to Epifany's use of its Russian synonym *poshlina*. But the texts lay heavy emphasis on the more sinister side of paganism: it is the cult of demons masquerading as gods. The pagans, in these stories, have no constant personality: they veer wildly and inexplicably (often within the same episode) from being childlike and amiable to being furious and bloodthirsty (as the victims and agents of demons) and then, to their own surprise, to becoming passive and docile under the sudden influence of the Spirit present in the holy man.

We may raise again a question we mentioned at the beginning: what concept of Christianization do these texts imply? Peter Brown, developing the insights of Robert Markus,[54] has recently pointed out how the ascetical movement of the fourth century came to view real Christianization as the creation of a wholly Christian culture, incompatible with the traditional civic values and customs of Greece and Rome; according to this model, Christianization is always partial and never complete. Earlier views of Christianization, in contrast, were content with a more superficial victory over the public manifestations of paganism. The hagiographical material we have been looking at rarely touches on the problem of a superficial evangelization that places a thin veneer of outward Christian profession

---

[54] *AS*, 1–26, after Markus, *End*, 1–43.

over an uneradicated paganism (though the *Life of St Boniface* is an exception); the texts are all too ready to narrate repeated episodes where a crowd of pagan onlookers are converted by some feat of a holy man, without answering our questions about how this 'conversion' was consolidated. The Christianization celebrated in these texts is rather that of the older model, with its emphasis on the manifestation on earth of a heavenly victory. The missionary enacts again and again the victory of Christ over the demonic, and the faith of the hagiographer and his audience in the completeness of this victory (in theological terms) excludes a sober assessment of the imperfections of the actual process of Christianization.

Missionary work has many aspects, only some of which appealed to the writers of hagiography. The texts we have examined do not provide a template to define the 'typical' missionary of antique or medieval times; and of course their historicity varies enormously. But what they do reveal is a long and continuous tradition in which the agent of evangelization is endowed with the characteristics of the holy man—independence of action, confidence before God, boldness before men. They present an interpretation of the work of a missionary in terms of the basic biblical mythology of the battle between light and darkness, a battle that has in essence already been won, so that there is no possibility of real defeat, even a temporary one. The holy man is essentially performing a mopping-up operation. He does so with urgency and zeal, because he knows that he has been entrusted with this final task that must be completed before Christ can return in a cloud of glory, to consummate the manifestation of his kingship.

St Martin once encountered on a country road a burial procession which he mistook for a pagan lustral procession. Charging in with the sign of the cross (Sulpicius makes use of military language), he brings the procession to an immediate halt, only to discover his mistake. Jacques Fontaine unkindly compares the St Martin of this episode to Don Quixote and the windmill.[55] The story certainly illustrates a spirituality that read life as a constant warfare of the spirit and was alert to detect the enemy behind every bush. It was a spirituality that interpreted the work of Christianization in terms of a closely related set of biblical images, in which (to borrow the language of Romans 13: 12) the armour of light is arrayed

---

[55] *Vie de Saint Martin*, ii, 720, on Sulpicius, *Vita Martini*, § 12.2 (i, 278).

against the works of darkness. These texts are more than literary stylization: missionaries of the early and medieval epochs possessed this mentality no less than their biographers. The ideology we have been exploring reveals the relevance of the figure of the holy man as warrior of Christ to early and medieval notions of evangelization.

PART V

The cult of saints in Islam

II

Prophecy and holy men in early Islam

CHASE ROBINSON

'To vest a fellow human being with powers and claims to loyalty associated with the supernatural, and especially a human being whose claim was not rendered unchallengeable by obvious coercive powers, is a momentous decision for a society made up of small face-to-face groups to make.'[1] If the typology of Brown's holy men has become considerably more complex in the last twenty years or so,[2] their ubiquity in the Mediterranean world has stood the test of time: holy men seem to have impressed themselves on the whole of this world, settled and pastoralist communities alike. Among the latter, the Arabs of the Fertile Crescent were no strangers to Christians and their claims, having come into contact with holy men in a variety of ways: crowding around the base of saints' towering pillars, camping at Christian shrines, gratefully receiving the curative blessings of itinerant preachers.[3] Still, to the cosmopolitan

---

As a set of suggestions intended for non-Arabists as well as Arabists, this essay is equipped with modest documentation, no Arabic diacritics, and only occasional references to Arabic texts; whenever possible, I have included translations. I am grateful to F. W. Zimmermann for reading a draft.

[1] *MLA*, 16.

[2] Thus M. Whitby, 'Maro the Dendrite: An Anti-Social Holy Man?', in M. Whitby, P. Hardie, and M. Whitby (eds.), *Homo Viator: Classical Essays for John Bramble* (Bristol, 1987), 309–17, at 316 ('The Holy Men of late antiquity were diverse, and their image was not static'); and J. D. Howard-Johnston's review of C. Galatariotou, *The Making of a Saint: The Life, Times and Sanctification of Neophytos the Recluse* (Cambridge, 1991), in the *Journal of Ecclesiastical History*, 45 (1994), 134 ('There were numerous gradations of holiness in men recognised as holy and several types, ranging from the withdrawn contemplative to the interventionist guru moving in high social circles').

[3] While the evidence for Christianity on the periphery of the Peninsula grows richer, the Hijaz remains all but uncharted in archaeological and epigraphical terms. There is still much to recommend in T. Andrae, 'Der Ursprung des Islams und das Christentum: I. Das Christentum in Arabien zur Zeit Muhammeds', *Kyrkohistorisk Årsskrift*, 23 (1923), 155–80; cf. R. Bell, *The Origins of Islam in its Christian Environment* (London, 1926). For Christianity outside of Arabia, see F. Nau, *Les Arabes Chrétiens de Mésopotamie et de Syrie du VIIe au VIIIe Siècle* (Paris, 1933);

cultures of the Near East, these Arabs remained outsiders as much as many of the holy men preaching amongst them; and if mission-izing amongst these barbarians brought them into closer contact,[4] it took Islam, in Brown's words 'the last, most rapid crisis in the religious history of the late antique period',[5] to move them on to the centre-stage of the Mediterranean world, to reconstitute, in the form of the Caliphate, Alexander's 'Mountain Arena'.[6]

In what follows I offer some tentative suggestions about this transformation and some of its consequences; I focus, in particular, on prophecy and social power. More precisely, I shall suggest that whatever Muhammad's debt to the late antique world made famil-iar to us by Brown, his movement was *sui generis*, and set a new paradigm of activist piety for Muslims, embedded as they were in what remained a predominantly non-Muslim Near East: some of the ingredients of Muhammad's message were no doubt familiar, but the recipe was altogether new. A holy man's 'sudden conglomera-tion' might survive only by heading on to the steppe, with the result that the townsfolk of Palmyra quickly shut their gates against Alexander the Sleepless and his band: 'for what they saw was the old curse of the Fertile Crescent in a new form—a Bedouinization of the ascetic life'.[7] Similarly, a fourth-century (?) saint named John the Arab might perform the standard miracles (curing the infirm, feeding the hungry, converting the Godless, exorcizing demons, and making barren women fertile); when invoked to do so, he might also appear on his horse, sword drawn, to send a hundred Bedouin bandits reeling away from the caravan they had threatened.[8] But

J. S. Trimingham, *Christianity Among the Arabs in pre-Islamic Times* (London and New York, 1979); I. Shahîd, *Byzantium and the Arabs in the Sixth Century*, vol. 1, pt. 2, *Ecclesiastical History* (Washington, DC, 1995), esp. 949 ff.; D. T. Potts, *The Arabian Gulf in Antiquity*, 2 vols. (Oxford, 1990), ii, 241 ff.

[4] Thus, the remark by the biographer of Ahudemmeh, the Monophysite bishop conventionally credited with converting the pastoral Arabs of northern Mesopotamia: 'There were many people between the Euphrates and Tigris in the land that is named "the Island"; they live in tents, and are barbarians and deadly . . . He [Ahudemmeh] saw that they were evil (*bish*) and their speech [literally, "tongue"] coarse.' See *Histoires d'Ahoudemmeh et de Marouta*, ed. and tr. F. Nau, PO 3/1 (1909), 21 f.

[5] *WLA*, 189.

[6] The phrase and idea are G. Fowden's: *Empire to Commonwealth: Consequences of Monotheism in Late Antiquity* (Princeton, 1993), 15 ff.

[7] 'Holy Man', 114.

[8] For the account, see S. Brock, 'Notes on Some Monasteries on Mount Izla', *Abr-Nahrain*, 19 (1980–1), 6–19.

none of this would have impressed Muhammad, who was proposing to turn the world upside down: he was not to lead a hungry band to beg at the doors of the Palmyrenes, but to lead an army to conquer their city.

MUHAMMAD AND HIS REVELATION

Precisely why Qurashi tribesmen of north-western Arabia came to believe that an otherwise undistinguished kinsman named Muhammad should serve as the locus of the supernatural remains unclear. Barring the fantastic discovery of new evidence, the 'problem of Muhammad', as Blachère aptly entitled his biography of Muhammad,[9] is a nut that Islamicists have so far been unable to crack. For the sources, Arabic and otherwise, conspire against us in a variety of ways: while contemporaneous or near-contemporaneous non-Islamic sources know too little of Muhammad to be of any real help,[10] much later Islamic accounts know altogether too much to be believable. That Muhammad was a God-fearing man who thought that others should fear Him too is clear enough; but precisely how he became so, how he expressed his fear in practice, and finally how these practices relate to late antique precedents, remains controversial for the simple reason that the sources—written as they were no less than a century and a half after his death—remain so controversial. It is true that the Qur'an can tell us several things, but aside from problems of dating and transmission, its rhetoric is discursive and allusive;[11] the voluminous *hadith* literature, which the tradition conventionally holds to be the repository of Muhammad's views on a wide variety of legal issues, more clearly reflects the opinions of late eighth- and ninth-century jurists than it does Muhammad's;[12] and the biographical tradition, which also

[9] R. Blachère, *Le problème de Mahomet: Essai de biographie critique du fondateur de l'Islam* (Paris, 1952).

[10] Which is very different from saying that they have no value for understanding early Islam more generally; for a recent survey, see R. Hoyland, *Seeing Islam as Others Saw It: A Survey and Evaluation of Christian, Jewish and Zoroastrian Writings on Early Islam* (Princeton, 1997).

[11] For a summary that remains valuable, see R. Paret, 'Der Koran als Geschichtsquelle', *Der Islam*, 37 (1961), 24–42.

[12] That Muhammad's example only emerged as paradigmatic for Muslim jurists during the second Islamic century was demonstrated by J. Schacht, *The Origins of Muhammadan Jurisprudence* (Oxford, 1950).

dates from the late eighth century, only occasionally embeds nuggets of authentic history in the midst of a very rich vein of legend.[13]

An example that illustrates the problems of evidence is an account appearing in Ibn Ishaq's *Sira* (Life) of Muhammad, recorded here in the recension of Ibn Hisham (d. 834) and in the monumental *Ta'rikh* (History) of Abu Ja'far al-Tabari (d. 921):[14] it describes Muhammad's first revelation, traditionally identified as Qur'an 96: 1–5. As is frequently the case in the historiographical tradition of this period, the account comes on the authority of a contemporary of Muhammad's, in this case 'Ubayd b. 'Umayr b. Qatada; it has a tripartite structure: (1) an opening, which locates the event in the context of Muhammad's regular practices of piety and spirituality (for example, solitary wanderings in the hills near Mecca; the giving of alms to the poor; circumambulation around the Ka'ba); (2) a dialogue between Muhammad and the angel Gabriel, flagged by a change of voice (from third to first), in which Muhammad only reluctantly consents to the act of reciting God's words as dictated by Gabriel; and (3) a return and denouement, initially signalled by the appearance on Mount Hira' of men who had been sent by Muhammad's wife Khadija, but only fully realized by a second dialogue, in which Khadija's cousin Waraqa b. Nawfal confirms that Muhammad's experience is authentically prophetic. The narrative thus has a clear design, and while some would understand material such as this in exclusively exegetical terms, others would discern a mixture of exegesis and historical material generated for reasons of its own; all would agree that several apologetic features make it difficult to interpret. For what is at issue is nothing less than the definition of true prophecy, and if the exact provenance of the account is indeterminate, prudence dictates that one allow for an Arabian and Near Eastern setting: here early and later

[13] See now L. I. Conrad, 'Abraha and Muhammad: Some Observations apropos of Chronology and Literary Topoi in the Early Arabic Historical Tradition', *BSOAS* 50 (1987), 225–40; P. Crone, *Meccan Trade and the Rise of Islam* (Princeton, 1987), 203–30; and cf. M. Lecker, 'The Death of the Prophet Muhammad's Father: Did Waqidi Invent Some of the Evidence?', *Zeitschrift der Deutschen Morgenländischen Gesellschaft*, 145 (1995), 10–27.

[14] See *al-Sira al-nabawiyya*, ed. al-Saqqa, i, 235 ff., which is translated into English by A. Guillaume as *The Life of Muhammad* (London, 1955), 105 ff., and al-Tabari, *Ta'rikh al-rusul wa'l-muluk* (Leiden, 1879–1901), i, 1149 ff., which is translated by W. M. Watt and M. V. McDonald as *The History of al-Tabari, VI: Muhammad at Mecca* (Albany, 1988), 69 ff.

material seems to have been intertwined by the eighth- and ninth-century historiographical tradition, which was as sophisticated and experimental as it was voracious.

In a cultural milieu such as the seventh-century Hijaz, where the visions and words of poets and soothsayers could express both the ecstatic and oracular, and where *jinns* took possession of unsuspecting tribesmen,[15] the distinction between true prophecy on the one hand, and magic and soothsaying on the other, had to be drawn, particularly since much of Muhammad's revelation was expressed in a poetic register.[16] Among Muslims, as among Christians, 'what was hotly debated was the difference between legitimate and illegitimate forms of supernatural power'.[17] The account's emphasis on the *written* character of Muhammad's revelation—Gabriel brings a 'coverlet of brocade whereupon was some writing', and in the wake of this first revelation 'it was as though these words were written on my heart' (Guillaume)—may have functioned to insulate Muhammad's experience from that of the poets and soothsayers. Muhammad's words certainly did so, for he is given to doubt his experience, anxious lest he be mistaken for something else: 'None of God's creation was more loathsome to me than poets and those possessed; I could barely set eyes on them. And so I said (to myself): "Such a person, he's a poet or possessed"—never shall the Quraysh speak thus of me!'[18] Although Muhammad is given to voice concerns about the character of his experience, it is left to Waraqa b. Nawfal to identify it conclusively as prophetic. For unlike Khadija, Waraqa is said to have possessed

---

[15] Thus, T. Fahd, *La divination arabe: études religeuses sociologiques et folkloriques sur le milieu natif de l'Islam* (Strasbourg, 1966), 63: 'dans une pensée arabe plus au moins syncrétiste, entre divination et prophétie, il existe une certaine continuité'; for more background, see R. Paret, *Mohammed und der Koran: Geschichte und Verkündigung des arabischen Propheten* (Stuttgart, 1966), 21 ff.

[16] On this Qur'anic language, see in general Paret, *Mohammed und der Koran*, 48 ff.; R. Bell and W. M. Watt, *Introduction to the Qur'an* (Edinburgh, 1970), 69 ff., and, more recently, A. Neuwirth, 'Der historische Muhammad im Spiegel des Korans—Prophetentypus zwischen Seher and Dichter?', in W. Zwickel (ed.), *Biblische Welten: Festschrift für Martin Metzger*, Orbis biblicus et orientalis 123 (Freiburg, Switz., 1993), 83–108.

[17] *MLA*, 60.

[18] That some quite naturally held that Muhammad belonged to the local tradition is made clear in the Qur'an itself: 'Remember (or Give warning): by God's beneficence, you are neither soothsayer nor possessed. Or do they say, "He is a poet, for whom we await the uncertainty of fate"? Say [then]: "Wait, and I shall wait along with you" ' (see Qur'an 52: 29–31; and cf. ibid., 68: 2, 69: 41–2).

monotheist credentials: a Christian who was literate and well read in the Torah and Gospels, he was deeply pious and credited with venerable practices of asceticism; he was thus one of the very few contemporaries of Muhammad qualified to render judgement on the character of his experience: 'Holy! Holy! There has come to him', Waraqa says, 'the greatest law (*namus*) that came to Moses.' These were the visions not of a lunatic or seer, but evidence of God's serial (if occasional) communication of His will; a new cycle of prophecy had begun.

In all of this one might fairly sense an apologetic concern, particularly since the tradition knows virtually nothing of Waraqa as an ascetically inclined Christian in his own right. Indeed, many themes of the Waraqa story clearly conform to biblical precedents.[19] This said, the tradition is ambivalent about Waraqa's own faith: while all accounts have him confirm the authenticity of Muhammad's prophecy, only rarely do they have him convert, *à la* Salman al-Farisi, Suhayb b. Sinan, and other (semi-legendary) contemporaries; rather, the consensus has him resist the kerygma announced by Muhammad, holding firm to his Christianity.[20] In sum, there does seem to have been an historical Waraqa,[21] one who belonged to the same clan as Khadija, with whom marriage seems to have been mooted; but whether he can clearly signal the penetration of Christianity into the heart of Meccan society, much less chart the passage of Christian ideas and practices to Muhammad, remains very hard to say.[22]

[19] For a discussion, see U. Rubin, *The Eye of the Beholder: The Life of Muhammad as Viewed by the Early Muslims* (Princeton, 1995), 103 ff.

[20] For the minority view that Waraqa was the first to convert, see al-Zurqani, *Sharh 'ala 'l-mawahib al-laduniyya* (Bulaq, 1278 A.H.), i, 257; Ibn al-Athir, *Usd al-ghaba fi ma'rifat al-sahaba* (Beirut, n.d.), v, 88 f., acknowledges confusion about his conversion. On Waraqa, see Rubin, *The Eye of the Beholder*, 103 ff.

[21] My conclusion here is anticipated by T. Andrae, *Mohammed: sein Leben und sein Glaube* (Göttingen, 1932), 91; tr. T. Menzel as *Mohammad: The Man and his Faith* (London, 1936), 111 f.

[22] For night-time vigils and recitations, see Qur'an 73: 2 and 25: 64. For some sense of the problems of interpretation, see the case of *tahannuth*, Muhammad's solitary worship that led to his first revelation, in M. J. Kister, '*Al-tahannuth*: An Inquiry into the Meaning of a Term', *BSOAS* 31 (1968), 223–36; and N. Calder, '*Hinth, birr, tabarrur, tahannuth*: An Enquiry into the Arabic Vocabulary of Vows', *BSOAS* 51 (1988), 214–39, esp. 234 ff. (where the variants adduced by Kister 'have of course nothing to do with historical facts, at least not historical facts of the seventh century', and the accounts betray nothing more than jurists' views of *c.* 800). In general, see E. Graf, 'Zu den christlichen Einflüssen im Koran', in *al-Bahit: Festschrift Joseph Henninger*, Studia Instituti Anthropos 28 (Bonn, 1976), 111–44.

It appears then that an Arabian setting for our account has not been entirely effaced; the account also betrays signs of its passage into the cosmopolitan Near East. In a cultural milieu such as Iraq in the late eighth and ninth centuries, where Muslims of various theological and legal stripes were honing their dialectical skills, and where Christians, Jews, and Muslims rubbed shoulders, formally and informally debating their faiths, the wrinkles of individual experience began to be ironed out; now, with authentic memory out of reach, Muhammad's personality and career took more legendary and apologetic shape. It is this context that explains why Muhammad, for whom miracles seem to have played only a very modest role early on, was now equipped with his definitive and most formidable evidentiary miracle, namely, the inimitability of the Qur'an.[23] And in this the dogma of his illiteracy plays a principal role, informing our text (Muhammad repeats Gabriel's dictation), and secondary scholarship too (since Waraqa was literate, he must have exercised a monotheistic influence on the unschooled Muhammad). Certainly, theological considerations moved the classical tradition to emphasize the auditory aspect of Muhammad's revelations at the expense of the visual.[24]

All this makes reconstructing Muhammad's life in real detail— that is, reaching sound conclusions about his precise debt to Arabian (or non-Arabian) Christianity, his practices of piety and holiness,[25] and the political context of his preaching—very difficult indeed, especially since authorities such as al-Tabari wrote as

---

[23] On the doctrine of *i'jaz*, see the English summary of al-Baqillani's views in *Miracle and Magic: A Treatise on the Nature of the Apologetic Miracle and its Differentiation from Charisms, Trickery, Divination, Magic and Spells*, ed. R. J. McCarthy (Beirut, 1958), 'analytical summary'; and G. E. von Grunebaum, 'i'djaz', in *EI²*, iii, 1018–20. For the apologetic milieu, see S. Stroumsa, 'The Signs of Prophecy: The Emergence and Early Development of a Theme in Arabic Theological Literature', *Harvard Theological Review*, 78 (1985), 101–14; C. Adang, *Muslim Writers on Judaism and the Hebrew Bible* (Leiden, 1996), esp. ch. 5; and H. Lazarus-Yafeh, *Intertwined Worlds: Medieval Islam and Bible Criticism* (Princeton, 1992), 79 ff.

[24] See R. Bell, 'Muhammad's Visions', *Muslim World*, 24 (1934), 145–54; and on the Prophet's so-called Night Journey (to Heaven), the collection edited by M. A. Amir-Moezzi, *Le voyage initiatique en terre d'Islam: Ascensions célestes et itinéraires spirituels* (Louvain, 1996); and J. van Ess, ' 'Abd al-Malik and the Dome of the Rock: An Analysis of Some Texts', in J. Johns and J. Raby (eds.), *Bayt al-Maqdis: 'Abd al-Malik's Jerusalem* (Oxford, 1992), 89–103.

[25] Cf. Andrae, *Mohammed*, 183: 'Hence what the traditions tell us about Mohammed's private life is comparatively worthless as a historical source.'

apologists as well as historians.[26] In fact, the now century-old
industry of biographies of the Prophet has failed to produce a full
reconstruction of his life that can withstand serious criticism;[27] and
much of the most important work now eschews historical reconstruction in favour of charting the course of a literary
Muhammad.[28] The interpretation proposed by W. M. Watt, which
put Meccan society in a social crisis brought on by the appearance
of a mercantile élite, was adopted by Brown himself;[29] but the historiographical girders of his reconstruction, as Brown acknowledged
in 1988, have now collapsed under P. Crone's wrecking ball.[30]
Crone herself has proposed that Muhammad's movement fits the
typology of a nativist movement, but she has also conceded that the
evidence required to trigger such a movement of defensive self-identity can be found on Arabia's periphery, rather than in the Hijaz
proper.[31] The argument therefore remains tentative, but it still
retains the great virtue of highlighting the radical character of
Muhammad's call. For in as much as both Watt's and Brown's
views can be called broadly functionalist—Muhammad, like the
archetypal holy man, repairs the breaches of a society under
stress—they underestimate precisely this radicalism. Muhammad

---

[26] Thus, he declares in the midst of his section on Muhammad's call to prophecy
that 'reports that can be adduced to prove his prophethood are innumerable; if God
wills it, a book (*kitab*) should be devoted entirely to it'; see al-Tabari, *Ta'rikh*, i, 1146;
tr. Watt and McDonald, *History of al-Tabari*, 67. C. Brockelmann, *Geschichte der arabischen Litteratur*, suppl. vol. 1 (Leiden, 1937), 218, counted this as a title, a point
disputed by F. Rosenthal, *The History of al-Tabari, I: General Introduction and From the
Creation to the Flood* (New York, 1989), 88 f.

[27] For a useful summary of what this industry produced to about 1980, see
M. Rodinson, 'A Critical Survey of Modern Studies on Muhammad', in M. L. Swartz
(ed.), *Studies on Islam* (Oxford and New York, 1981), 23–85; and, for a sobering
account of how little we know, F. E. Peters, 'The Quest of the Historical Muhammad',
International Journal of Middle Eastern Studies, 23 (1991), 291–315.

[28] Perhaps the best example is Rubin's *The Eye of the beholder* (see n. 19 above).

[29] *WLA*, 191: 'It was a stroke of genius on the part of Muhammad to turn this
foreign message [namely, fear of God] into a principle on which the conflict-ridden
society of the Hijaz could reorganize itself. He was called upon to cure the *malaise* of
an "emergent" society. In the towns, the tribal style of life was losing its hold on the
nouveaux riches of the merchant dynasties. Private and public standards of behaviour were being torn apart by new wealth . . .' For the inspiration, see W. M. Watt,
Muhammad at Mecca (Oxford, 1953); idem, *Muhammad at Medina* (Oxford, 1956); a
résumé of the two can be found in his *Muhammad, Prophet and Statesman* (Oxford,
1964).

[30] Brown, *WLA*, 213. For the demolition, see Crone, *Meccan Trade*, esp. the
'Introduction'.

[31] Crone, *Meccan Trade*, 245 ff.

was certainly an exemplar and a hinge man, but one of a very different sort: whereas Brown's holy men served to keep late Roman society in balance, Muhammad threw his into massive imbalance, creating a religious vortex into which the backward Arab pagans of Arabia and the Fertile Crescent tumbled, and out of which emerged Muslim Caliphs and armies who would rule much of the civilized world.

The wars of conquest outside of Arabia seem to have flowed directly from the so-called Wars of Apostasy within it, which broke out upon the Prophet's death, and they reflect more generally the revolutionary character of the Qur'an's demands on Muhammad and his community. Warfare against non-Muslims (polytheist and monotheist alike)—holy war (*jihad*), conducted 'in the path of God'—was the proving ground of belief and piety. One of the few pieces of documentary evidence we possess from this period—the 'Constitution of Medina', which Muhammad drafted soon after making the *hijra* (emigration) from Mecca to Medina in 622—shows us that the glue that was to hold the nascent polity together consisted largely in the 'help' (or 'support', *nasr*) that the tribesmen offered each other against the Unbelievers,[32] whom Muhammad fought in a string of battles, from Badr (year two of the *hijra*), through Uhud, al-Khandaq ('The Ditch'), al-Hudaybiyya, and Khaybar, to the conquest of Mecca (year eight).[33] The compact that binds Muslim to Muslim in the 'Constitution' mirrors the compact that binds God to his community, and since the stakes were highest on the battlefield, it was there that God kept up His end of the bargain. There is no room for sentimentality; as Qur'an 9: 111 puts it: 'God has bought from the believers their selves and their possessions in return for Paradise; they fight in the way of God; they kill and are killed—that is the promise incumbent upon Him in the Torah, the Gospel, and the Qur'an, and who is more true to His

---

[32] For an introduction to the text, see R. B. Serjeant, 'The "Constitution of Medina" ', *The Islamic Quarterly*, 8 (1964), 3-16; for detailed analysis and translation, see idem, 'The Sunnah Jami'ah, Pacts with the Yathrib Jews, and the *tahrim* of Yathrib: Analysis and Translation of the Documents Comprised in the so-called "Constitution of Medina" ', *BSOAS* 41 (1978), 1-42.

[33] For the Qur'anic evidence for these battles, see Paret, *Mohammed und der Koran*, 113 ff.; for the historical evidence, see J. M. B. Jones, 'The Chronology of the *Maghazi*—A Textual Survey', *BSOAS* 19 (1957), 245-80; and for a general reconstruction, see F. M. Donner, 'Muhammad's Political Consolidation in Arabia up to the Conquest of Mecca: A Reassessment', *Muslim World*, 69 (1979), 229-47.

promise than God?' Perceptions of the battle of Badr are preserved in Qur'an 3: 123 ('God had helped you at Badr, when you were but a handful; so fear God, and perhaps you will be thankful') and Qur'an 8: 9 ('When you appealed to God for help, and he answered (saying), "I will help you with a thousand of the angels, ranks upon ranks" '). The authenticity of the historical tradition of this period is considerably more controversial than the Qur'an, but here it seems faithful to the spirit underlying the Qur'anic evidence. On the eve of the battle, Muhammad is said to have beseeched God: 'If this band perishes, you will not be worshipped on earth'; according to a variant, 'he began to call out: "O God, fulfil what you promised me. O God, if this band perishes, you will not be worshipped on earth".'[34]

Whatever role the Prophet played in the genesis of Islamic law, there can be no question that the earliest stages of the tradition charted his career not so much as a law maker, but as a reforming monotheist battling the polytheists of the Peninsula; thus recording his *maghazi* ('raids') appears to have all but monopolized the writing of Prophetic biography until well into the eighth century.[35] The battlefield was where Muslims proved themselves to God; it was the crucible of belief during the earliest days, particularly before the tide had turned in favour of Muhammad and his believers.[36] This explains why early traditionalists show much less interest in the course of these battles than in exactly who participated in them: while the *Sira* creates only general impressions about what happened at Badr and Uhud, it records precise lists of those who fought, organized by tribe and membership in the *Muhajirun* (those who emigrated with Muhammad) and *Ansar* (those Medinans who joined him). For *jihad* was not simply a struggle for God, but an act of piety and holiness for which God rewarded those who survived with

---

[34] See the *Sira*, i, 626 f.; tr. Guillaume, *Life of Muhammad*, 300.

[35] For an overview, see the introduction to Guillaume, *Life of Muhammad*; and J. M. B. Jones, 'The Maghazi Literature', in A. F. L. Beeston *et al.* (eds.), *Arabic Literature to the End of the Umayyad Period* (Cambridge, 1983), 344-51. Cf. Serjeant's comment regarding the 'Constitution' ('The "Constitution of Medina" ', 15): 'It will be noted that, apart from general provisions about blood-money, etc., the documents really say virtually nothing about law.'

[36] Cf. D. Cook, 'Muslim Apocalyptic and *jihad*', *JSAI* 20 (1996), 66-104, in 75 ff.; and, more generally, Paret, *Mohammed*, 121: 'Wichtig ist, daß alle Geschichte, also auch das Zeitgeschehen, als Heilsgeschichte verstanden wird, d.h. also Geschehen, das sich nach dem Ratschluß Gottes vollzieht und den Menschen zum Heil dient'.

booty, and those who died with Paradise; it was to participate in God's design, to make an instrument of oneself. 'God conquered such-and-such land for the Muslims' (*fataha Allah ʿala yad al-muslimin*) is a phrase that appears and reappears throughout the conquest tradition, based on the (pre-conquest) Qurʾanic use of *f-t-h*, according to which God 'reveals' and 'delivers' blessings, mercy, and His judgement or reckoning;[37] it is in this last sense that the capitulation of Mecca was apparently understood, while Badr itself came to be called 'the day of Discrimination' (*al-furqan*).[38] When asked by Heraclius to describe the Muslims he knew only from afar, a former captive reported that they were 'horsemen by day, monks by night'; the account expresses an ethos underlying the well-known saying of the Prophet that 'every community has its monasticism; the monasticism of my community is holy war in the path of God'.[39]

Success on the battlefield thus underpinned Muhammad's authority and vouchsafed his revelation by making manifest God's favour towards his community of believers; in addition to the obvious material advantages, this probably explains why his successors pressed on, well after the conquest of Arabia proper, to carry the fight into the Fertile Crescent. Again, since what mattered was the meaning of His victories and the revealing in history of His will, rather than the precise course of these campaigns, anyone reading the tradition for military history is as disappointed with its coverage of military matters as he is impressed with the compilers' attention to the booty that the conquests generated. What could be more miraculous than the astounding wealth of Sasanian Ctesiphon falling into the Arabs' hands?[40] It should hardly surprise then that the Muslims' spectacular military success came to be adduced as an

[37] Orientalist discussions of the semantic range of the term have a long pedigree, but the most thorough discussions are R. Paret, 'Die Bedeutungsentwicklung von arabisch *fath*', in J. M. Barral (ed.), *Orientalia Hispanica sive studia F.M. Pareja octogenario dicata* (Leiden, 1974), 537–41; idem, *Der Koran: Kommentar und Konkordanz* (Kohlhammer, 1980), 167; and C. F. Robinson, 'Conquest', in *The Encyclopaedia of the Qurʾan* (Leiden, forthcoming).

[38] Qurʾan 8: 42, but cf. Crone, *Meccan Trade*, 226 ff.

[39] For the Heraclius account, see al-Tabari, *Taʾrikh*, i, 2395; for a recent discussion of the Prophetic saying, see S. Sviri, 'Wa-rahbaniyatan ibtadaʿuha: An Analysis of Traditions Concerning the Origin and Evaluation of Christian Monasticism', *JSAI* 13 (1990), 195–208.

[40] For the Ctesiphon accounts, see al-Tabari, *Taʾrikh*, i, 2444 ff.; it is translated by G. Juynboll, *The History of al-Tabari, XIII: The Conquest of Iraq, Southwestern Persia, and Egypt* (Albany, 1989), 24 ff.

evidentiary miracle for those (Christians, Jews, or others) who
remained unpersuaded of Muhammad's credentials. Although the
very early *Doctrina Jacobi nuper baptizati* takes issue with
Muhammad on precisely these grounds ('He is a false prophet, for
do prophets come with a sword?'),[41] it is unlikely to be a reflex of
Muslim claims; by the early ninth century, things are considerably
clearer. Thus the Muslim convert ʿAli Rabban al-Tabari argued not
only that Muhammad's victory over his oppressors qualifies as a
miracle, but so too the conquests 'in [every] region, horizon, sea
and land, from Sus [in the west] to the deserts of the Turks and
Tibet [in the east]' that followed.[42] Meanwhile, Christians and Jews
continued to argue the opposite: according to ʿAmmar al-Basri,
while Christianity abhors violence (*al-sayf*, literally 'the sword'), the
Torah and Islam condone it: 'So too the religion of Islam, when it
used the sword; rather than disavowing it, it gave accounts of it,
and explained its [Islam's] strength and its conquests of far-flung
lands by its use.'[43] Similarly, the ninth-century Jew Dawud b.
Marwan discusses several criteria by which authentic prophecy
may be judged; among these one finds the view that true prophets
defeat their enemies by supernatural means, rather than on the
battlefield.[44]

JIHAD AND PIETY

'The problems that late antique men faced', Brown has written,
'were not whether such [supernatural] power existed, nor whether
it rested solely in the Christian Church. The power had to be focused
and its apparently random distribution canalized trenchantly and

---

[41] *Doctrina Jacobi Nuper Baptizati*, v.16 (ed. V. Déroche, *Travaux et mémoires*, 11
(1991), 47–273, at 208–11). The text seems to have been composed in Palestine in
the early 630s: see Hoyland, *Seeing Islam*, 55 ff.

[42] ʿAli Rabban al-Tabari, *Kitab al-Din waʾl-dawla* (Beirut, 1977), 109; tr.
A. Mingana as *The Book of Religion and Empire* (Manchester, 1922), 58.

[43] See ʿAmmar al-Basri, *Kitab al-burhan*, in M. Hayek (ed.), *Apologie et controverses* (Beirut, 1977), 33 f. (for the Arabic); see also G. Tartar, *Dialogue Islamo-Chrétien
sous le calife Al-Maʾmûn (813–34)* (Paris, 1985), 159 ff., and A.-T. Khoury, *Polémique
byzantine contre l'Islam, VIIIe-XIIIe siècles* (Leiden, 1972), 136 ff. Cf. the *hadith*
(Prophetic sayings) adduced by Y. Friedmann, *Prophecy Continuous: Aspects of Ahmadi
Religious Thought and its Medieval Background* (Berkeley, 1989), 54.

[44] See G. Vajda, 'La prophétologie de Dawud ibn Marwan al-Raqqi *al-muqammis*,
théologien juif arabophone du IXe siècle', *Journal Asiatique*, 265 (1977), 227–35, at
233.

convincingly onto a definite class of individuals and a definitive institution.'[45] The problem early Muslims faced was how to contain the volcanic explosion of God's will that had erupted in early seventh-century north-western Arabia, represented first and foremost by Muhammad himself. In practice this meant trying to wrench shut the prophetic tap, and diluting the concentration of corporate piety and *jihad* that the Prophet had so spectacularly produced. We can begin with the second of these.

Understanding how the earliest Muslims understood frequent Qur'anic injunctions to 'fight [or struggle] in the path of God' requires that one look behind classical formulations produced in a social and political milieu radically different from that in which the text was originally produced and understood. According to Qur'an 9: 33 and 61: 9, Muhammad had been sent by God to make His religion prevail; Qur'an 2: 193 and 8: 39 instruct believers to fight until there is no *fitna* (which first seems to have signified the Meccans' opposition); and Qur'an 9: 29 holds that 'those who have received the Book' (which came to mean monotheists) are to be fought until they pay the *jizya* (classically, the poll tax). Now it seems that Muhammad and his contemporaries saw in these passages a prescription for ongoing and corporate warfare against non-Muslims. It seems, moreover, that after Muhammad many Muslims continued to think so too: the circulation of *hadith* that forbid the practice of *hijra* (emigration from garrison to garrison) suggests that the practice was ongoing for many Muslims, that is, that *jihad* in what Crone has called its 'open-ended' sense remained alive. In fact, we are now fortunate to possess two very different studies that converge in arguing that *jihad*, along with *hijra*, was central to early Muslim experience well beyond the period of the great conquests, even into the second third of the eighth century.[46]

Hadith that forbid post-prophetic *hijra* obviously have a twofold value: they can be adduced to infer its continuing practice, and they

---

[45] *MLA*, 64.

[46] See K. Y. Blankinship, *The End of the Jihad State: The Reign of Hisham ibn ʿAbd al-Malik and the Collapse of the Umayyads* (Albany, 1994), and P. Crone, 'The First-Century Concept of *Hiğra*', *Arabica*, 41 (1994), 352–87. Cf. M. Meeker, *Literature and Violence in North Arabia* (Cambridge, 1979), 93: 'The Bedouins, in other words, could perhaps understand the Koran as a book that was the basis of a politico-religious community, but they would be inclined to stress all those ways in which the Koran prescribed political actions rather than religious rituals' (a note referring to Kharijite warfare then follows).

can be adduced to infer the presence of a lobby—a strong, *hadith*-coining lobby—that was arguing that it should end. Whatever the precise relation between State and learning in the late Umayyad period, it is fair to say that both had an interest in reformulating Muhammad's message in terms compatible with the inexorable realities of settlement and assimilation; in other words, both had an interest in rationalizing in religious terms the shift from conquest society to empire. As far as *hijra* is concerned, the transformation was effected by coining and circulating *hadith* that promoted an antiquarian understanding, one that restricted its practice to the Prophet's lifetime;[47] as far as *jihad* is concerned, it was effected by promoting a conception that was individual and ethical, rather than corporate and political, and by institutionalizing the practice as Caliph-sanctioned warfare along the frontier.[48]

Insofar as empire building was predicated on settlement and the professionalization of irregular levies of nomad fighters into salaried, standing armies, the eclipse of the 'open-ended' *hijra* and *jihad* might be construed as almost inevitable; and given the long memories of some tribesmen and the short reach of State power, nor should it surprise that some pastoralists preserved the fusion of piety and warfare that had fuelled the conquests, holding to what Zimmermann has called 'the spirituality of the conquest society' that underlay the thinking of many of the State's opponents.[49] That what had been normative in the early seventh century was becoming subversive at the end of the century is made clear by the Kharijites (literally 'those who go out' or 'rebel'), sectarian revolutionaries who challenged Umayyad authority throughout the Marwanid period (685–750). The Kharijites challenged the Umayyads not only by threatening rural security and humiliating Umayyad generals, but by insisting that *jihad*, which in the earliest period was not necessarily directed against non-Muslims,[50]

---

[47] For a full discussion, see Crone, 'First-Century Concept'.

[48] The relatively conservative account in A. Morabia, *Le ǧihad dans l'Islam médiéval* (Paris, 1993) can now be contrasted with M. Bonner, *Aristocratic Violence and Holy War: Studies in the Jihad and the Arab-Byzantine Frontier* (New Haven, 1996), which argues with considerably more imagination.

[49] F. W. Zimmermann, 'Islam', in C. Jones *et al.* (eds.), *The Study of Spirituality* (London, 1986), 498–503, at 499 n. 5.

[50] Rather than against the enemies of God, which is a different thing altogether; see M. Bonner, 'Some Considerations Concerning the Early Development of *jihad* on the Arab-Byzantine Frontier', *Studia Islamica*, 75 (1992), 5–31, esp. 29.

remained a fundamental article of belief. They produced a number of apposite examples, men who combined asceticism, piety, and revolution, but one of the best is Salih b. Musarrih, who rebelled in about 695 in northern Mesopotamia.[51] In Salih we have nothing less than an early Muslim holy man who preached *jihad* on much the same Qur'anic grounds as had Muhammad: whatever his debt to some of the ingredients of late antique piety,[52] Salih no more fits a late antique pattern of social action than does Muhammad. Known widely for his piety and godliness, Salih inspired a succession of Kharijite outbreaks for over a century; and we read in several places that no Kharijite would rebel before cutting his hair at Salih's tomb.[53] In a surviving sermon he calls for 'fear of God, abstinence (*zuhd*) in this world, desire for the next, frequent remembrance (*dhikr*) of death, separation from the sinners, and love for the believers'. *Jihad* remains integral to true belief: 'So prepare yourself—may God have mercy on you—to fight (*jihad*) against these enemies aligned [against Kharijite Islam] and the oppressive leaders of error, and to go out from the transient to the eternal world, and to join our believing, resolute brothers who have sold this world for the next, and who have expended their wealth, seeking to please God in the hereafter.'[54]

Muhammad's fusion of piety and activism thus remained vital for some early Muslims, but already in Salih's rebellion, and more clearly in those of the later Umayyad period, there is a decidedly old-fashioned feel. Fewer and fewer Muslim tribesmen had any direct experience of the primitive kerygma of early Islam; and as Muslim Arabs settled and assimilated amongst non-Arabs busily converting to Islam, the ethnic and tribal dimension to Kharijism appeared *passé*. Muslims, in other words, were now less and less frequently Arab tribesmen in the sense that Muhammad was an Arab

[51] For a brief overview of Salih, see J. Wellhausen, *Die religiös-politischen Oppositionsparteien im alten Islam* (Göttingen, 1901), 42 ff.; tr. R. C. Ostle and S. M. Walzer as *The Religio-Political Factions in Early Islam* (Amsterdam, 1975), 69 ff.; and J. van Ess, *Theologie und Gesellschaft im 2. und 3. Jahrhundert Hidschra: eine Geschichte des religiösen Denkens im frühen Islam*, 6 vols. (Berlin and New York, 1991–7), ii, 460 ff.

[52] Cf. M. Morony, *Iraq after the Muslim Conquest* (Princeton, 1984), 475 ff.

[53] On the late antique precedents for saint worship in general, see I. Goldziher, 'On the Veneration of the Dead in Paganism and Islam', in idem, *Muslim Studies*, tr. S. M. Stern and C. R. Barber, 2 vols. (London, 1967–71), i, 209–38; for hair cutting, see the literature cited by van Ess, *Theologie und Gesellschaft*, ii, 461 n. 8.

[54] Al-Tabari, *Ta'rikh*, ii, 882 f., which is translated by E. Rowson as *The History of al-Tabari, XXII: The Marwanid Restoration* (Albany, 1989), 33 ff.

tribesman. In a late Umayyad and soon Abbasid world where the cultural values of the cosmopolitan and settled were increasingly in the ascendant, Kharijism—and with it, this form of the Prophet's legacy—consequently declined.

PROPHECY AND HOLY MEN

Of course Muhammad had been more than a God-fearer who fused Arab ethnicity with militant monotheism; he had also been an immensely charismatic and 'imaginative' visionary to whom God had revealed Himself.[55]

It was in this respect that his legacy was more enduring and more productive of holy men. The date and character of our source material make it difficult to describe how Muhammad's prophetic authority was routinized in the first two centuries. The classical view presents the scriptural élite (the *'ulama'*, those possessing knowledge of Muhammad's legal *dicta*) as the 'heirs of the prophets' from the earliest period itself, but it rather seems that the *'ulama'* claimed Muhammad's legal and religious inheritance at a secondary stage, affecting a decisive defeat of the Caliphs in the middle of the ninth century; having generated and codified a fixed Prophetic *sunna* ('way', 'paradigm'), they put an end to the Caliphs' legislative powers.[56] Since the goal was to define a body of law that was immutable and finite, and one which the *'ulama'*—and the *'ulama'* alone—would serve to safeguard, this meant insisting not only that Muhammad was the legislator prophet *par excellence*, but that he was the final prophet. Thus the dogma that prophecy had ended with Muhammad's death now crystallized, principally around an obscure Qur'anic passage (Qur'an 33: 40), which calls Muhammad the 'seal' (*khatam* or *khatim*) of the prophets, the phrase having meant a variety of things earlier on.[57]

[55] On 'imaginative' charisma, see the discussion in E. Shils, *Tradition* (London and Boston, 1981), 228 f.

[56] P. Crone and M. Hinds, *God's Caliph: Religious Authority in the First Centuries of Islam* (Cambridge, 1986).

[57] The fullest discussion is Y. Friedmann, 'Finality of Prophethood in Sunni Islam', *JSAI* 7 (1986), 177–215, but see also van Ess, *Theologie und Gesellschaft*, i, 29 ff.; C. Colpe, *Das Siegel der Propheten: historische Beziehungen zwischen Judentum, Judenchristentum, Heidentum und frühem Islam* (Berlin, 1990); G. Strousma, ' "Seal of the Prophets": The Nature of a Manichaean Metaphor', *JSAI* 7 (1986), 61–74; and J. Wansbrough, *Quranic Studies* (London, 1977), 58 f.

In systematizing along these lines, the *'ulama'* are readily comparable to the rabbis; and in leaving behind occasional pieces of discordant evidence, rabbis and *'ulama'* alike reflect the two traditions' ambivalence about how God was to reveal Himself in a post-prophetic age.[58] As Hodgson noted more than forty years ago, we should expect early Muslims to have held to the possibility of continuing prophecy;[59] that the evidence is generally late and associated with marginal features of the tradition more directly reflects the powerfully homogenizing force of Sunnism than it does the historical significance of those who believed that theirs remained an age of prophecy. At the fringes we find what the heresiographical traditions call the *ghulat*, Shi'ites who took their allegiance to the family of 'Ali (Muhammad's son-in-law and cousin) to 'extremist' positions. These include the Khattabiyya, at least some of whom apparently held that the sixth Imam (leader) of the Twelver Shi'ite tradition, Ja'far al-Sadiq (d. 765), was himself God, and that he had sent Abu'l-Khattab (d. 755) as a prophet.[60] They also include the Mansuriyya, who took their name from the Kufan Abu Mansur (d. *c.* 740), and who were infamous for strangling their victims amidst the din of barking dogs; they also held that the Imams of 'Ali's line were divinely inspired, and that prophecy continued for at least six generations after Abu Mansur.[61] One could adduce many more

[58] As P. S. Alexander, put it, 'The social structure and religious authority of the rabbinate are predicated on the assertion that prophecy has ceased: God no longer speaks directly to humanity; the Sages now determined his will by applying their rational faculties to the elucidation of sacred texts' (' "A Sixtieth Part of Prophecy": The Problem of Continuing Revelation in Judaism', in J. Davies, G. Harvey, and W. G. E. Wilson (eds.), *Words Remembered, Texts Renewed: Essays in Honour of John F. A. Sawyer* (Sheffield, 1995), 414–33, at 414); see also F. E. Greenspahn, 'Why Prophecy Ceased', *Journal of Biblical Literature*, 108 (1989), 37–89.

[59] M. G. S. Hodgson, 'How did the Early Shi'a become Sectarian?', *Journal of the American Oriental Society*, 75 (1955), 1–13, at 6: 'It is hardly surprising that the notion of prophecy as a recurrent (and not necessarily world-shaking) event should have survived the death of Muhammad. . . . After all, there is nothing very explicit in the Qur'an, apart from the ambiguous phrase about Muhammad's being the "seal" of the prophets, to debar even major prophets from appearing after him; to say nothing of God's speaking through minor figures to confirm the faith given as had admittedly happened among the Jews.' See also Strousma, ' "Seal" ', 74.

[60] On the Khattabiyya, see W. Madelung, 'Khattabiyya', in *EI²*, iv, 1132–3. A principal heresiographic treatment is al-Ash'ari, *Maqalat al-islamiyyin*, ed. H. Ritter (Leipzig, 1929), i, 10 f.

[61] The fullest treatment is W. F. Tucker, 'Abu Mansur al-'Ijli and the Mansuriyya: A Study in Medieval Terrorism', *Der Islam*, 54 (1977), 66–77; see also al-Ash'ari, *Maqalat*, i, 9 f.

examples, but it is more important to note that evidence from the
Twelver Shiʿite tradition demonstrates that these 'extremist' positions, far from being inspired by non-Islamic influences, only accen-
tuated what the mainstream suppressed. For in the doctrine of the
'spoken to (by an angel) Imam' (al-imam al-muhaddath), Twelver
Shiʿites clearly sought to rein in their Imams' ongoing communication with God.[62] Considering reports that ascribe (unfulfilled)
prophetic promise to Muhammad's son Ibrahim,[63] we might reasonably understand accounts describing the second Caliph, ʿUmar
b. al-Khattab, as the 'muhaddath of the community' as evidence for
authentically early conceptions, rather than Sunni reflexes against
Shiʿite claims.[64]

Prophecy thus closed because the 'ulamaʾ closed it, but the door
remained ajar;[65] and provided that the law was respected and politics quietist, there was room enough for the holy man to walk
through: in time the miracle-working saints (awliyaʾ, usually
'friends of God'),[66] would become 'the Prophet's flesh and blood';[67]

---

[62] Here it is worth noting that the proof text for this doctrine (the Shiʿite reading
of Qurʾan 22: 52, 'We have not sent before you any apostle [rasul] or prophet [nabi]
or muhaddath') is attested from the very early period. See E. Kohlberg, 'The Term
Muhaddath in Twelver Shiʿism', in Studia Orientalia: Memoriae D. H. Baneth Dedicata
(Jerusalem, 1979), 39–47; M. A. Amir-Moezzi, The Divine Guide in Early Shiʿism, tr.
D. Speight (New York, 1994), 70 ff.; van Ess, Theologie und Gesellschaft, ii, 280.

[63] The accounts usually take the form of 'had Ibrahim survived [his infancy], he
too would have become a prophet', less frequently 'had prophecy remained open,
Ibrahim would have survived'; for examples, see Ibn ʿAsakir, Taʾrikh madinat Dimashq
(Beirut, 1995-), iii, 134 f.; Friedmann, 'Finality of Prophethood', 187 ff.; and note
that according to al-Diyarbakri, Taʾrikh al-khamis (Cairo, 1302 AH), ii, 130 f., the
angel Gabriel greeted Ibrahim upon his birth. Cf. W. Madelung, The Succession to
Muhammad: A Study of the Early Caliphate (Cambridge, 1997), 16 f.

[64] Kohlberg, 'The Term Muhaddath', 44. Among the surviving pre-classical views
of ʿUmar can be counted several miracles: thus he is said to have uttered words in
the Arabian city of Medina that were heard by one of his commanders in Iraq,
informing him of the exact location of the enemy; for one version of the story, see
Ibn al-Jawzi, Sirat ʿUmar b. al-Khattab (Cairo, n.d.), 120 f. (fi dhikr karamatihi).

[65] Thus, in a number of different ways we are told that although prophecy has been
cut off, one of its forty-six (or seventy) parts does survive, and this in the form of
dreams; see Ibn Abi Shayba, Musannaf (Beirut, 1989), vii, 230 ff.; for more sources,
see L. Kinberg (ed.), Ibn Abi al-Dunya's Morality in the Guise of Dreams (Leiden, 1994),
35 f. For the view that one could see and speak with prophets, see F. Meier, 'Eine
Auferstehung Mohammeds bei Suyuti', Der Islam, 62 (1985), 20–58, at 51 f.

[66] Sing. wali, the inspiration of which is Qurʾan 10: 63 ('Surely, there is no fear
upon the friends of God (awliyaʾ Allah), nor are they sad'); for the term, see
I. Goldziher, 'Veneration of Saints in Islam', in his Muslim Studies, ii, 255–341, at
263.

[67] Gellner ('Koranic propriety emanates from their essence, as it were. Islam is
what they do. They are Islam'), as cited by C. Geertz, Islam Observed: Religious

and Islam in this respect is more comparable to late antique Christianity than it is to Rabbinic Judaism. The holy man would make a spectacular comeback.

Accounting for the emergence of the *awliya'* is now altogether more sophisticated than it used to be.[68] Earlier literature held that the saints arrived only late on the scene, and represented the recrudescence of 'popular' or 'folk' beliefs, which stood in stark contrast to (and were in some measure introduced to compensate for) the sterile transcendence of the lawyers' God.[69] Certainly, pre-Islamic practices of spirituality were integrated into Islam,[70] but the local Khurasani tradition identifies saints already in the middle of the ninth century, and the context is not foreign influence so much as recognizably Islamic piety and asceticism.[71] Meanwhile, some old-fashioned spade work in the textual tradition has shown that a doctrine of *wilaya* ('friendship with God') was articulated during the second half of the ninth century.[72] Far from developing at a

---

Development in Morocco and Indonesia (New Haven, Conn., 1968), 51. Cf. Brown, 'Exemplar', 9: 'Hence the crucial importance of the holy man as Christ-carrying exemplar. In almost all regions of the Mediterranean, from the third century onwards, he was far more than an exemplar of a previously well-organised and culturally coherent Christianity: very often, he quite simply was Christianity.'

[68] For criticisms (largely on textual grounds), see B. Radtke's acidic comments in 'Between Projection and Suppression: Some Considerations Concerning the Study of Sufism', in F. de Jong (ed.), *Shi'a Islam, Sects and Sufism* (Utrecht, 1992), 70–82; and also B. Radtke and J. O'Kane, *The Concept of Sainthood in Early Islamic Mysticism* (Guildford and King's Lynn, 1996), 7 f.; for a historian's criticisms, see J. Chabbi, 'Remarques sur le développement historique des mouvements ascétiques et mystiques au Khurasan', *Studia Islamica*, 46 (1977), 5–72; and, for both, see F. W. Zimmermann's review of Radtke, *Al-Hakim al-Tirmidhi* (see n. 76 below) in the *Journal of Arabic Literature*, 15 (1984), 139.

[69] Thus, Goldziher, 'Veneration of Saints', examples being 261 ('popular belief'), 300 ('the veneration of saints provided the cover under which surviving remnants of conquered religions could continue to exist in Islam'), and 332 ('a cultic trend in direct opposition to the cardinal doctrines of Islam'). See also his *Vorlesungen über den Islam* (Heidelberg, 1910), tr. A. and R. Hamori as *Introduction to Islamic Theology and Law* (Princeton, 1981), where a short discussion of the saints appears unceremoniously in the chapter on 'later developments', 238 ff. Goldziher was followed by B. Carra de Vaux, 'Wali', *EI*[1], iv, 1109–11: 'But Islam had to yield on this point to the pressure of popular sentiment, which by its traditions, its tendency to the marvellous and other psychological factors, is strongly inclined to this way of expressing its religious feelings.'

[70] See now O. Livne-Kafri, 'Early Muslim Ascetics and the World of Christian Monasticism', *JSAI* 20 (1996), 105–29.

[71] See Chabbi, 'Remarques'.

[72] Here I draw on Radtke's pioneering work on *al-Hakim al-Tirmidhi* (see n. 76 below).

secondary stage, it seems then that the saints emerged just as classical Islam was taking shape. In Brownian and functional terms, the
rise of the (individual) Muslim holy man thus relates to the ninth-
century collapse of God's Caliphate and the (collective) salvation it
promised.[73] With the office of the Caliphate now emptied of nearly
all of its religious and political authority, and the unified State
eclipsed by a commonwealth of Muslim dynasties only loosely tied
together by the use of Arabic (or Arabized languages) and a (more
or less) uniform Prophetic *sunna*, the saints once again came to
monopolize the holy.

The saints were embraced only after accommodations were
made. Suffice it to say that just as some had argued that Caliphs
ranked higher than prophets and angels,[74] some had argued that
the saints ranked higher too,[75] and it is against this view that al-
Hakim al-Tirmidhi (d. *c.* 910), a crucial figure in the systemization
of early Sufism, wrote.[76] Here, as in later Sunni creeds, the existence of saints' miracles was admitted; but they are said to rank
lower than prophets, in large part because they were unable to leg-
islate. Classical Islam thus settled on this and a number of other ter-
minological distinctions: *wahy* (true revelation mediated by angels)
came to be the preserve of prophets, while *ilham* (among other
terms) came to denote the saints' 'inspirations'; prophetic evidentiary miracles (*mu'jizat*) are described as supernatural acts prefaced
by a public announcement, while saints' miracles (*karamat*, such as
walking on water, flying, telepathy, and clairvoyance) were supposed to remain private. Al-Hallaj (d. 922, by crucifixion), the most

---

[73] See Zimmermann, 'Islam', and also Radtke and O'Kane, *Concept of Sainthood*,
8. An Eastern inspiration for ninth-century mysticism has long been posited; for an
alternative view, see C. Melchert, 'The Transition from Asceticism to Mysticism at
the Middle of the Ninth Century CE', *Studia Islamica*, 83 (1996), 51–70, at 62 f.

[74] See Crone and Hinds, *God's Caliph*; and W. M. Watt, 'God's Caliph: Qur'anic
Interpretations and Umayyad Claims', in C. E. Bosworth (ed.), *Iran and Islam*
(Edinburgh, 1971), 565–74, which is reprinted in idem, *Early Islam: Collected
Articles* (Edinburgh, 1990), 57–63.

[75] For one later example, see Goldziher, 'Veneration of Saints', 266 f.

[76] On al-Hakim al-Tirmidhi and his views on prophecy and sainthood, see the
work of B. Radtke: e.g. 'Der Mystiker al-Hakim al-Tirmidi', *Der Islam*, 57 (1980),
237–45; idem, *Al-Hakim al-Tirmidi: ein islamischer Theosoph des 3./9. Jahrhunderts*
(Freiburg, 1980), esp. 89 ff.; and 'The Concept of *wilaya* in Early Sufism', in
L. Lewisohn (ed.), *Classical Persian Sufism from its Origins to Rumi* (London, 1993),
483–96. On a much later Sufi, Ibn 'Arabi (d. 1240), see M. Chodkiewicz, *Seal of the
Saints: Prophethood and Sainthood in the Doctrine of Ibn 'Arabi*, tr. L. Sherrard
(Cambridge, 1993).

spectacular of all early charismatic mystics, seems to have got into trouble precisely for crossing the line that separated *karamat* from *mu'jizat*.[77] It is in large part because of the proliferation of saints' miracles that Muhammad's own portfolio grew dramatically in the classical period.[78] His charisma, which had earlier been squarely based on his political vision and success, now came to rest more and more on the miracles so familiar to students of late antique holy men (water flowed from his fingertips, and barley leaves multiplied at his hands).[79] For the mystics, Muhammad now appears as a Sufi master, 'sitting cross-legged in the midst of the deep ocean [of divine beauty], drunk, and in his hand a cup of wine from that ocean, which he drank'.[80]

The mystics pulled in their horns not only by toning down doctrines; they also set about compiling their own history during the late ninth century, stressing the complementarity of esoteric and exoteric Islam, and (retrospectively) tying their tradition to respected authorities of earlier periods. These might be the almost infinitely pliable examples of the tradition's formative heroes (such as Moses, Muhammad, 'Ali, or Abu Bakr), or figures of only local prominence; mooring spiritual filiation in this way became a common feature in the institutionalization of the mystical orders, which appeared only later.[81] Saints' Lives, strikingly absent in the early

---

[77] Thus, *La passion d'al-Hosayn-ibn-Mansour al-Hallaj*, ed. L. Massignon (2nd edn., Paris, 1975); tr. H. Mason, *The Passion of al-Hallaj*, 4 vols. (Princeton, 1980), i, 291. The definitive work on saints' miracles is now R. Gramlich, *Die Wunder der Freunde Gottes* (Wiesbaden, 1987).

[78] Cf. Goldziher, 'Veneration of Saints', 259: 'It became possible to ascribe to men supernatural attributes which participated in the divine powers only after the complete transformation of the Islamic doctrine of prophecy.' As should be clear by now, the transformation was less than complete. For a very useful survey of the Qur'anic evidence, see P. Antes, *Prophetenwunder in der Aš'ariya bis al-Gazali (Algazel)* (Freiburg, 1970), 23 ff.; for a survey of miracles in the *sira*, see J. Horovitz, 'Zur Muhammadlegende', *Der Islam*, 5 (1914), 41–53; and, for an exemplary discussion of how Muhammad changed in the eyes of the exegetes, see H. Birkeland, *The Lord Guideth: Studies on Primitive Islam* (Oslo, 1956).

[79] For a relatively late source, see Ibn Sayyid al-Nas, *'Uyun al-athar fi funun al-maghazi wa'l-shama'il wa'l-siyar* (Cairo, 1356 A.H.), ii, 286 ff. For a translated survey in a relatively late source, see al-Qadi 'Iyad, *Muhammad Messenger of God: Ash-Shifa of Qadi 'Iyad*, tr. A. A. Bewley (Granada, 1991), ch. 4.

[80] I borrow the account from C. E. Ernst, *Ruzbihan Baqli: Mysticism and the Rhetoric of Sainthood in Persian Sufism* (Richmond, 1996), 61.

[81] For one example, see W. Madelung, 'Yusuf al-Hamadani and the Naqšbandiyya', in F. de Jong (ed.), *Atti del XIII Congresso dell'Union Européenne d'Arabisants et d'Islamisants (Venezia 29 settembre—4 ottobre 1986)*, = *Quaderni di Studi Arabi*, 5–6 (1987–8), 499–509; for a broader discussion of later

Islamic canon to those with late antique expectations, thus emerged; but it should come as no surprise that their authors ignored late antique precedents, adopting instead the biographical and historical genres already worked out by their more respectable Muslim contemporaries.[82]

developments, see J. Paul, 'Hagiographische Texte als historische Quelle', *Saeculum*, 41 (1990), 17–43.

[82] I. Hafsi, 'Recherches sur le genre *Tabaqat* dans la littérature arabe II', *Arabica*, 24 (1977), 1–41, at 27 ff.; Melchert, 'Transition', 53 f., and for one example of what a local tradition could produce, see B. Radtke, 'Theologen und Mystiker in Hurasan und Transoxanien', *Zeitschrift der Deutschen Morgenländischen Gesellschaft*, 136 (1986), 536–69.

12

The etiquette of devotion in the Islamic cult of saints

JOSEF W. MERI

THE Qur'an embodies the pure monotheistic message revealed by God to the Prophet Muhammad, asserting the unity of God with verses such as 'Say He God is One, the Everlasting, He did not beget nor was He begotten'.[1] The veneration of saints and prophets and making pilgrimage to tombs and shrines posed a threat to the Unity of God and Islamic orthodoxy.[2] However, from the conquests of the seventh and eighth centuries down to the present the veneration of saints and pilgrimage to their shrines has been an integral part of religious life for most Muslims as for most Christians in late antiquity and in medieval Europe. The absence of an ecclesiastical hierarchy in Islam did not in any way marginalize or preclude the proliferation of dynamic forms of saint veneration which were widespread not only in North Africa and Egypt but in most parts of the Islamic world, not least in Palestine, Syria, Iraq, and Persia. This essay focuses on the development and practice of the cult of saints in medieval Islam from the ninth through to the sixteenth centuries with particular reference to ritual practice within the *ziyara* or pilgrimage to saints' tombs and to attempts of Islamic theologians to define a proper etiquette for those who visited tombs.

Just as Christians sought intercession from saints, so too did Jews and Muslims. Yet turning to intermediaries for intercession was perceived as contrary to the monotheistic message of Islam. Indeed, it is condemned in Scripture when God proclaims, 'To God belongs exclusively the right to grant intercession: to Him belongs the dominion of the heavens and the earth: In the End, it is to Him that

The author is grateful to Professor Wilferd Madelung and the editors of the present volume for their comments and suggestions.

[1] Qur'an 112.

[2] The confession of faith (*shahada*)—affirming the Unity of God and that the Prophet Muhammad is the Messenger of God—is one of the five pillars of Islam.

ye shall be brought back.'[3] The Qur'an warns against seeking intercession from those other than God on the Day of Judgement,[4] and
against the practices of Jews and Christians who venerate their
sages and monks: 'They take their priests and their anchorites to be
their lords in derogation of God, and they take as their Lord Christ
the son of Mary; yet they were commanded to worship but One
God: there is no god but He. Praise and glory to Him: Far is He from
having the partners they associate with Him.'[5] Although the early
sources are silent about the issue of seeking intercession from saints,
the Prophet encouraged Muslims to offer supplication (*du'a'*) on
behalf of the dead, in order that they might attain paradise at the
Day of Judgement:[6] 'The Messenger of God, may peace be upon
him, said, "If a company of Muslims numbering one hundred prays
over a dead person, all of them interceding for him, their intercession on his behalf will be accepted".'[7]

The Hungarian Orientalist Ignaz Goldziher, among others, has
argued that in seeking intermediaries Muslims adapted and assimilated earlier pagan practices: 'the believers sought to create,
through the concept of saints, mediators between themselves and
an omnipotent Godhead in order to satisfy the need which was
served by the gods and masters of their old traditions now defeated
by Islam.'[8] This view misrepresents the place of the *ziyara* within
Islam. The process by which those who embraced Islam throughout
the Middle Ages incorporated practices from earlier faiths by
redefining them in Islamic terms is difficult to reconstruct, but it is
inaccurate to see the basic forms of ritual such as making votive
offerings, lighting candles, prostrating before or kissing a shrine as
intrinsically pagan, Jewish, Christian, or Muslim. Within the multi-
faith environment which existed in the medieval Near East similarities in ritual practice were only natural—they were common to all
and were arguably intrinsic to 'religion' itself in this part of the

---

[3] Qur'an 39: 44.
[4] Other Qur'anic verses pertaining to the intercession of God include, 20: 109,
34: 23, and 39: 44. They generally refer to seeking the intercession of God for believers on the Day of Judgement or polytheistic practices, as in Qur'an 34: 22.
[5] Qur'an 9: 31.
[6] For a discussion of 'shafa'a', see A. J. Wensinck and D. Gimaret, 'Shafa'a', in
*EI*², ix, 177–9.
[7] Muslim b. al-Hajjaj, *Sahih Muslim*, 8 pts. (Istanbul, 1911–15), iii, 52–3.
[8] 'Veneration of Saints in Islam', in idem, *Muslim Studies*, tr. S. M. Stern and
C. R. Barber, 2 vols. (London, 1967–71), ii, 255–341, at 259.

world. The universality of the 'prophet' as a figure of holiness is suggested, indeed, by those occasions on which Muslims, Jews, and Christians venerated together at common shrines, such as the Cave of the Patriarchs in Hebron. The concepts of the internalization, accommodation, or assimilation of non-Islamic practices and notions of centre versus periphery and heterodoxy versus orthodoxy are not sufficient to explain the place of the cult of saints within the Islamic world. Such categories simply fail to recognize the ubiquity of these ritual forms and activities. Moreover, the boundaries between heterodoxy and orthodoxy were never clearly defined with regard to the cult of saints, because the majority of devotees were not, on the one hand, deeply concerned with such matters, and because much local practice never caught the eye of those legal thinkers who were interested in such matters, on the other. The matter was, moreover, open to diverse responses, since the canonical *hadith* (that is, the corpus of the sayings, deeds, and silent affirmations of the Prophet, his Companions, and their Followers) offered few explicit precedents either affirming or denying the veneration of saints and the making of pilgrimage to tombs.

HAJJ AND ZIYARA

The phenomenon of pilgrimage occurs in many world religions, but falls into two distinct categories within Islam: the *Hajj* and the *ziyara*. The *Hajj* or canonical pilgrimage to Mecca, which takes place over a six-day period during the twelfth Islamic month of *Dhu al-Hijja*, is one of the five pillars of Islam and is, as prescribed in the Qur'an,[9] incumbent upon Muslims at least once during their lifetimes. Before the rise of Islam, pagan Arabs venerated idols in the sacred precinct of the Ka'ba, which is believed to have been built by the Prophet Abraham and which contains the Black Stone. Muhammad destroyed the idols and reconsecrated the sacred precinct to God. In performing the *Hajj*, Sunni and Shi'ite Muslims—men, women, and children from all over the world—put on white garments as they converge upon the sacred precinct to perform the rites. Pilgrims follow legally prescribed etiquette with respect to dress, comportment, supplication, and prayer. They

[9] Qur'an 3: 97.

retrace the footsteps of the Prophet and his Companions in the rite, which includes circumambulating the Black Stone seven times. After the last day, many pilgrims also make the recommended visit to the mosque of the Prophet in Medina where he is buried and where they supplicate God on his behalf. While the *Hajj* is a rite incumbent upon everyone once in their lifetime by the command of the Prophet, the *ziyara* (which means literally 'a visiting' or 'a visit')[10] comprises pilgrimage to local tombs and is widespread, even though it lacks the authority of Scripture and the Traditions of the Prophet Muhammad.

The emergence of the *ziyara* may be seen as a reflection of three factors. Devotion to the Family of the Prophet and the veneration, by Shiʿa especially, of the descendants of his cousin ʿAli and the latter's son Husayn, created a first category of distinctly Islamic saints in early Islam. Not only did the martyrdom of the Prophet's grandson Husayn at Karbala, Iraq, in 680 lead decisively to the Shiʿite–Sunni schism, it contributed to the formation of a cult around him and his descendants and institutionalized pilgrimage to their shrines throughout the Islamic world in Egypt, Syria, Lebanon, Palestine, Medina, Iraq, and Iran by all Muslims, not just Shiʿa. However, the Shiʿa frequented shrines at which they alone venerated. Husayn's body was believed to have been buried at Karbala, while shrines believed to contain his head were to be found in Cairo, Najaf, Karbala, and with his body in Medina, Damascus, Raqqa, and Ascalon.

The rise of the Sufi holy man in the eastern Islamic world in the cities of Iran and Iraq, particularly in Khurasan, gave impetus, secondly, to the veneration of living saints and scholars. As Chase Robinson has shown in greater detail elsewhere in this volume, Sufism or Islamic mysticism with its recognition of living saints along with the *ziyara* developed in ninth- and tenth-century Iraq, Khurasan, and Isfahan among other urban centres, and not merely at the periphery of the Islamic world. The emergence of the holy man posed a formidable problem for theologians who attempted to reconcile the existence of this highly variegated class of men (and sometimes women) who were not specifically mentioned in the Qurʾan or in the Traditions of the Prophet with the popularity which they enjoyed with their followers and devotees before and

---

10 Other expressions include, *safar* 'journeying' and *safar ila-ziyarat al-qubur* 'journeying to visit graves'.

after death. Muslims in Iraq, Syria, Egypt, and Palestine were aware
that Jews and Christians were venerating sages and theologians.[11]
It can be argued that the Christian holy man in his various manifestations contributed to the veneration of saints, living and dead,
in Islam, but it should not be assumed that this was a conscious,
direct, or deliberately conceived process of appropriation. Muslims,
including the Prophet himself, frequently travelled to Syria where
they encountered such men. A famous case in point is the Syrian
monk Bahira who predicted that Muhammad would become a
prophet. Syria and Iraq remained significantly Christian throughout
the Middle Ages, but it does not follow that the veneration of saints
by Muslims developed in imitation of Christian practice or that the
ascetic saint within Islam was modelled on his Christian counterpart. An interest in asceticism was common to both religions. It was
only natural that the ordinary Muslims, theologians, scholars,
rulers, and mystics from whose ranks saints emerged should have
striven to attain ascetic ideals within their lifetimes.[12] Faced with
the rationalist threat posed by the Mu'tazilites (who denied, among
other things, the ability of saintly individuals to perform miracles),
theologians of the Hanafite school of jurisprudence[13] affirmed the
existence of saints and their miracles in a number of creeds (or
statements of theological orthodoxy) drawn up during the ninth
century. Though not negating the existence of saints and miracles,
the theologians of the Hanbalite school[14] denied that the living
gained any benefit from the dead and impugned those who made
pilgrimage to particular tombs for the purpose of supplication. Thus,
one of the most controversial of the Hanbalite theologians, Ibn
Taymiyya (1263–1328), granted that

> belief in the miracles of the saints (*karamat al-awliya'*) and in the supernat-
> ural acts which God achieves through them in all varieties of knowledge,
> inspirations (*mukashafat*), power, and impressions (as it is handed down
> about the ancient nations in Surat al-Kahf [that is, in Qur'an 18] and in
> other Qur'anic chapters and as it is known of the early men of this
> Community of Believers among the Companions and Followers and of
> the rest of the generations of this Community of Believers) is among the

---

[11] Qur'an 9: 31.
[12] For an important study of Muslim asceticism and its relationship to Christian
monasticism in the early Islamic context, see further O. Livne-Kafri, 'Early Muslim
Ascetics and the World of Christian Monasticism', *JSAI* 20 (1996), 105–29.
[13] W. Heffening and J. Schacht, 'Hanafiyya', *EI²*, iii, 162–4.
[14] H. Laoust, 'Hanabila', *EI²*, iii, 158–62.

fundamentals of the people of the Sunna. It will be with them to the Day of Resurrection.[15]

Finally, the prophets and patriarchs played a central role in the development of the *ziyara*. There was a natural tendency to venerate the great leaders of the monotheistic tradition, such as Abraham, Moses, Elijah, and Ezekiel. It was common for Muslims, Jews, and Christians to venerate these figures at the same shrines and to participate in their festivals together. One of the examples best-known to this day is the Cave of Elijah on Mount Carmel where Jews, Muslims, and Christians venerate the prophet. Jews and Muslims venerated Ezekiel and Ezra at shrines in Iraq until the twentieth century. Syrian Muslims and Christians used to visit the monastery in a village outside of Damascus, which contained the famed icon of the Virgin Mary.

PILGRIMAGE GUIDES

It is appropriate to indicate a number of the most important sources for the *ziyara*. With the Islamic territorial expansion of the seventh to ninth centuries, Muslim scholars took an interest in recording traditions concerning the burial sites of the Companions of the Prophet who settled in the garrison towns and those early Muslims who were martyred in battle. Other types of traditions found in many of these guides concern the sanctity of cities and pilgrimage sites. The systematic compilation of these traditions in the ninth to twelfth centuries contributed to the emergence of regional histories for such cities as Cairo, Damascus, Aleppo, and Baghdad and other genres which mention pilgrimage, most notably the pilgrimage guides for Egypt and Syria. There never existed a universal tradition of pilgrimage guides in Islam, but rather many traditions reflecting local and regional practices. The *Kitab al-Isharat ila Ma'rifat al-Ziyarat* (*Guide to Knowledge of Pilgrimage Sites*) by the Syrian scholar and ascetic 'Ali ibn Abi Bakr al-Harawi (d. 1215) is the earliest and only known specimen of pilgrimage literature to cover the entire Islamic world as well as parts of the Christian Mediterranean and Byzantium from the late twelfth and early thirteenth centuries. He

[15] Ahmad ibn Taymiyya, *al-'Aqida al-Wasitiyya*, ed. J. Sourdel-Thomine (Paris, 1986), 25. The translation is my own.

did not visit all the pilgrimage sites he covers, relying in many cases upon the testimony of others. The work was an important source for later medieval pilgrimage guides and regional histories. Unlike other pilgrimage guides, there is no evidence to suggest that it was used during *ziyara*. In fact, the author dedicated the work to the Abbasid Caliph who was the spiritual and political head of the Islamic community in Baghdad.

Whereas al-Harawi's guide was written in the form of a travel itinerary, the typical Egyptian pilgrimage guide was written for devotees making pilgrimage to the Qarafa cemeteries of Cairo on Jabal al-Muqattam—the primary Muslim pilgrimage sites in Cairo from at least the tenth century. The earliest of these guides is *Murshid al-Zuwwar ila Qubur al-Abrar* (*Pilgrimage Guide to the Tombs of the Righteous*) of the jurisconsult and Hadith scholar 'Abd al-Rahman ibn 'Uthman (d. 1218). A later guide from the fifteenth century, Ibn al-Zayyat's *Kawakib al-Sayyara fi Tartib al-Ziyara* (*The Planets in the Organization of the Ziyara*), discusses the sacred topography of Cairo and the famous cemeteries of Jabal al-Muqattam outside Cairo. Aside from enumerating the burial places of saints, the authors of these Egyptian and the authors of Syrian pilgrimage guides devote much attention to the matter of pilgrimage etiquette. The earliest extant pilgrimage guide for Syria is from the early sixteenth century—Ibn al-Hawrani's (d. 1556) *Kitab al-Isharat ila Amakin al-Ziyarat* (*Guide to Pilgrimage Sites*). It covers Damascus and the outlying villages, as well as a number of northern Syrian localities like Aleppo and its surrounding villages, and includes an important appendix on pilgrimage etiquette.[16] Although these pilgrimage guides for Cairo and Damascus tend to be concerned with urban shrines, it should not be assumed that the cult of saints was stronger in the city than in the countryside. What emerges from these guides is a sense of the all-pervasiveness of the saints in Muslim life and thought.

These guides show that there were variations in the types of saints venerated within Islam. The prophets and other figures from monotheistic tradition such as Abraham, Elijah, and Ezekiel were venerated everywhere. Veneration of the Prophet Muhammad's Family and his descendants through his cousin and son-in-law 'Ali

---

[16] Iraq is a region for which no Sunni guides are known for the medieval period, though traditions certainly appear to have existed concerning the burial sites of prominent Muslims.

and daughter Fatima, the Companions of the Prophet and the Followers, and the martyrs of the early battles and conquests of Islam (which category also includes the four Rightly-guided Caliphs who were among the Companions of the Prophet and his successors as head of the Muslim community)[17] was not universal, however. Their veneration divided along historical and doctrinal lines. The Shiʿa did not venerate all the Companions of the Prophet or the first three caliphs (whom, they believed, had usurped the caliphate from ʿAli). Similarly, Sunnis did not normally venerate Shiʿa imams. Yet more localized was the veneration of mystics, rulers, scholars, and theologians—learned individuals who were venerated by their associates and disciples and by the rulers and common people. Local history largely dictated the patterns of their veneration. For instance, in the predominantly Shiʿite Aleppo of the twelfth century one finds the proliferation of tombs of the prophets and the descendants of ʿAli, including ʿAli himself, or in Cairo of the tenth and eleventh centuries the institutionalized veneration by the Shiʿite Fatimid dynasty of the descendants of Husayn and his descendants the Shiʿite Imams. In Damascus from the twelfth century one finds in addition to the veneration of the Family of the Prophet, the veneration of theologians, mystics, and scholars, particularly among their disciples. Medieval pilgrimage guides for Cairo and Damascus enumerate various categories of saints. However, the Egyptian guides do not refer to the prophets as a distinct category. For instance, Ibn al-Zayyat in *The Planets* lists ten different categories of scholars and other varieties of saints including the Companions and Household of the Prophet and the Followers, judges, rulers, martyrs, and various categories of mystics and scholars. Late medieval guides for Syria do not adhere to as elaborate a structure, but often include the prophets, the Companions, and numerous local scholars, theologians, and mystics, not to mention the occasional local ruler.

The emergence of a tradition of living saints was deeply rooted in a culture of religious learning. Indeed, sainthood was dependent upon the attainment of an exemplary level of learning and pious devotion. The process of recognizing a living saint was both personal and informal. Among the ranks of living saints one finds mystics, theologians, and other men of learning and great piety who

---

[17] That is, Abu Bakr, ʿUmar, ʿUthman, and ʿAli.

were renowned for their *baraka* (that is, variously, for their blessings and their holiness). Scholars and their disciples, rulers and common people routinely visited living saints in order to be in their presence, to partake in their *baraka* and to benefit from their knowledge. In eleventh-century Syria, rulers, scholars, and theologians visited these men who were often mystics, and writers enumerated their countless miracles (*karamat*). Among the more colourful varieties of saints were the 'majdhub' who lacked the faculty of reasoning and the charismatic 'muwallah' or 'the one madly enamoured with God'. Such individuals went against the orthodox pattern of learning and piety, sometimes departing from the Sunna of the Prophet and sometimes adopting a state of uncleanliness and ritual impurity. Unorthodox behaviour was also a common trait of some Sufi saints. Nonetheless, theologians and historians frequently mention in biographical works that Muslims routinely sought *baraka* from them as they did from other saints.

SHRINES

Shrines to saints were ubiquitous, notwithstanding the Prophet's stricture against building over tombs. Though located mainly in cemeteries, especially in three of the most important Sunnite pilgrimage centres in the medieval Islamic world—Cairo, Damascus, and Jerusalem as well as the Shi'ite cities of Kufa, Karbala, Najaf, and Mashhad—holy tombs and shrines were to be found everywhere in the Near East from city gates, mosques, and tomb complexes, to citadels, caves, mountains, and even around holy rocks where saints were believed once to have passed or sat. Just as the cities, towns, and villages of medieval and Renaissance Europe had their patron saints, so too did their Islamic counterparts. Similarly, local, regional, and even competing cults existed within cities and outlying villages.

The veneration of the same saint at many different centres was a common phenomenon. The Prophet's grandson Husayn's body was believed to have been buried in Iraq at Karbala where he was martyred in 680, while shrines believed to contain his head were to be found in Najaf, Kufa, Medina, Damascus, Raqqa, Cairo, and Ascalon. Both head and body were also to be found in Kufa. In the case of the Qarafa cemeteries in Cairo and the Small Gate Cemetery in Damascus, many of the Household and descendants of the Prophet were believed to have been buried there, when other sources state that the tombs of many were either unknown or that they lay in the Arabian peninsula or in the eastern Islamic world. Although, for example, it was commonly believed that Bilal, the first muezzin of Islam, was buried in Medina along with the many other Companions of Muhammad, two additional tombs were ascribed to him: one in Cairo and another in the Small Gate Cemetery in Damascus which remains an important pilgrimage site for Sunnis and Shi'a to this day.

In a well-known tradition, the Prophet urged Muslims to level tombs and not to use gypsum in their construction lest they should become places of idolatry. Nonetheless, shrines of many types were constructed in due course, ranging from cairns, sacred rocks, and stone pillars to tombs, vision mausolea, and elaborate tomb complexes such as the *turba* or the *jawsaq* or rest houses of Cairo and Damascus. The word *mazar* is used for such pilgrimage places in the broadest sense, but two types were distinguished: the tomb or *qabr*, the monument most often mentioned in the sources, and the vision-mausoleum or *mashhad* (literally 'a place of witnessing' or 'martyrdom'). The latter type was often connected with the appearance of the Prophet Muhammad, his Family, and Companions in dreams and visions, and such shrines served as surrogates for the actual tombs of the saints in question. One example, a tomb of a descendant of the Prophet in Damascus, bears an inscription attesting its authenticity, naming four prominent theologians and supplying the words of the Prophet who had appeared in a vision to one of Damascus' inhabitants. Although little if any description of the numerous tombs and shrines is provided in the medieval sources, a significant number from the tenth century onwards remain remarkably well preserved. (This distinction, between a *qabr* and a *mashhad*, is not, it should be noted, absolute. For many *mashhads* are popularly believed to contain the remains of saints and were often founded as a result of a vision of the saint.) A third important category, the *maqam* or 'station', was the supposed product of a saint's physical contact with a location—that is, a place through which he was said to have passed, sat, or prayed. Such sites often contained an *athar*—that is, a sacred trace, footprint, or imprint left by a saint or his mount—and did not necessarily have memorials constructed over them.

The veneration of saints at these shrines was far from 'peripheral' in the Islamic world. Peter Brown, echoing the anthropologists Gellner and Geertz, offers a provocative contrast between the situation of tomb-centred saints' cults in the medieval Christian and Islamic worlds:

The holy tomb, though of inestimable importance throughout all regions of the Islamic world, existed always a little to one side of Muslim orthodoxy. Vivid ethnographic material on the function of modern Muslim shrines, which seems to carry us back directly in time into the western Europe of the early middle ages, comes not from the dry centre of the Islamic tradition, but from its ever-fertile peripheries—from the mountains of Morocco and from Sufi lodges scattered between Indonesia and the Atlas. . . . Public and private, traditional religious leadership and the power of the holy dead never coincided to the degree to which they did in western Europe.[18]

Local shrines did indeed exist in an uneasy relationship to Muslim 'orthodoxy', but they were also ubiquitous. Ironically, this tension projected the cult of saints into the centre of controversy. In Islam, it was not the leadership, but rather the absence of centralization, which permitted the cult to become thoroughly interwoven into the fabric of the faith and to sustain itself throughout the centuries. In such a situation, the saints ultimately exercised control over the living through dreams and visions and the tomb became in Brown's words, 'a place where the normal laws of the grave were held to be suspended',[19] a public space where Muslims spiritually, physically, and ritually interacted with saints.

LEGALITY OF *ZIYARA* DEBATED

It is clear that the *ziyara* or pilgrimage to tombs was widespread in Islam by the high medieval period. It was an anomaly, however, for which no legal precedent existed, but its practitioners did not regard it as contradictory to their belief, nor did theologians consider that it was unorthodox to visit tombs for the purpose of remembering the

---

[18] Brown, *CS*, 10, citing I. Goldziher, 'Veneration of Saints', E. Gellner, *Saints of the Atlas* (London, 1969), and M. Gilsenan *Saint and Sufi in Modern Egypt* (Oxford, 1973), among other works. Brown's contrast between the 'fertile peripheries' and 'Muslim orthodoxy' seems to rest on a misinterpretation of Gellner, *Saints of the Atlas*. Gellner's 'fertility' of the periphery lies in a more robust adherence to a kind of 'orthodoxy'.

[19] *CS*, 10–11.

dead, reciting the Qur'an, or remembering God, the Prophet Muhammad, or the Day of Judgement. For the Prophet had been accustomed to visiting his dead companions and to seeking intercession from God for them. He once said, 'I previously prohibited you from visiting tombs, now visit them . . . '[20] This was sometimes taken as proof of the permissibility of visiting saints' tombs: various traditions maintain that the dead are aware of their visitors on a specific day of the week—Friday, Monday, or Wednesday. The *ziyara* was, in this sense, defensible, but many of its rituals were not. Popular beliefs and practices associated with the *ziyara* often generated tension, such that a wide variety of positions evolved among the theologians ranging from outright condemnation to more subtle attempts to define a proper etiquette for making *ziyara*. The fact that the Prophet never explicitly mentioned these rituals made it necessary for theologians to interpret Scripture and Tradition through individual reasoning (*ijtihad*) and systematic reasoning or analogy (*qiyas*). The theologians saw no less than nine problems in the ritual aspects of the *ziyara*: the validity (1) of praying for the dead; (2) of addressing the dead while regarding them as aware of visitors; (3) of praying directly to the dead; (4) of supplicating and seeking intercession for oneself and for others; (5) of glorifying and venerating the dead either through ritual acts or erecting commemorative structures; (6) of making physical contact with the tomb; (7) of asking the dead directly to answer prayers and (8) to fulfil requests and to work miracles; and (9) of participating in pilgrimage festivals.

Concerted opposition to the *ziyara* first surfaced during the ninth century in Iraq, where saint veneration was deep-rooted among Christians and Jews. It was only at a later stage, namely in the eleventh century, that opposition to *ziyara* practices took root in Syria, but it never reached the same scale there as in Iraq, which was a bastion of Hanbalite jurisprudence until the Mongol conquest of Baghdad in 1256. The issue of how one should conduct oneself when visiting all tombs (not just those of the saints) was posed as early as the seventh and eighth centuries by the Iraqi preacher al-Hasan al-Basri (d. 728), who severely criticized people for forgetting the solemn purpose of visiting tombs and for engaging in unacceptable behaviour such as eating at tombs. However, it was not

---

[20] *Sahih Muslim*, iii, 65.

until after the ninth century, with the growth of the Hanbalite school of jurisprudence, that serious opposition to the *ziyara* crystallized here. The school's founder, Ibn Hanbal (d. 855), had at first forbade reciting the Qur'an at funerals but later changed his mind.[21] Subsequent disciples went much further, however, in identifying practices that went against the Qur'an and the Sunna. They argued that the performance of *ziyara* was to be considered a heretical innovation (*bid'a*) and venerating saints as polytheism (*shirk*) in so far as there was no explicit authorization in the Qur'an or Sunna for making *ziyara* to the tombs of the saints. They also rejected the *ziyara* on the grounds that it encouraged immoral practices, such as the intermingling of the sexes, especially at festivals and on saints' days or *mawsims*. One of the earliest Hanbalite condemnations of the *ziyara* comes from the eleventh-century Baghdadi jurisconsult and resident of Damascus Ibn 'Aqil (1040–1119), who castigates the 'ignorant and wretched' for practices 'which they have created for themselves', namely the glorifying of tombs and the touching of them.

However, the Syrian Ibn Taymiyya, the foremost antagonist of the cult of saints and the author of several extensive works on the *ziyara*, distinguished between the heretical *ziyara* (*al-ziyara al-bid'iyya*) which he associates with pagans, Jews, and Christians, and the legal *ziyara* (*al-ziyara al-shar'iyya*), which is enjoined by the Prophet. This position caused such controversy that he was put in prison and died there. He mentions the tomb of Ubayy ibn Ka'b (d. 650), an early Jewish convert to Islam and Follower of the Prophet, who was alleged to have been buried in Damascus but who was actually believed to have been buried in Medina:

Some of the people used to say that it is the tomb of a Christian. This is not unlikely. The Jews and Christians are the ones who established a precedent in the veneration of tombs and shrines. It is for this reason that the Prophet, may peace be upon him, said in a [sound] tradition: 'May God curse the Jews and Christians: They have taken the tombs of their prophets as places of prayer' [literally, 'prostration']. Such behaviour is to be warned against.[22]

---

[21] Ghazali, *Ihya' 'Ulum al-Din*, 5 vols. (Cairo, 1955), iv, 492.
[22] Ahmad ibn Taymiyya, *Majmu' Fatawa Shaykh al-Islam Ahmad ibn Taymiyya*, ed. 'Abd al-Rahman b. Muhammad b. Qasim al- 'Asimi al-Najdi al-Hanbali, 37 vols. (Riyad, 1991), xxvii, 460.

He defines the heretical *ziyara* as when 'the visitor intends that his supplication be fulfilled at the tomb or that he would supplicate the deceased, supplicate for rain through him, and make a request of him or take an oath (*abjure*) by God in requesting a need'.[23] Ibn Taymiyya does not deny, however, the possibility that a request might be fulfilled, going so far as to say that 'if anything is granted, it should be attributed to the personal merit of the tomb's patron'.[24] While some theologians, as is shown below, acknowledged the symbiotic nature of the relationship between the living and the dead, Ibn Taymiyya argues that 'In the legally permissible *ziyara*, the living does not have need for the dead by making a request of him (*mas'ala*) or seeking his intercession (*tawassul*). But rather, the dead derives benefit from the living. God the Exalted has mercy upon the living who supplicates for the dead.'[25]

In two further examples, he comments on Christian practices and suggests that they have exercised some influence upon Muslim devotees to the cult of saints:

The Christians are more fanatic in this than the Jews according to what is said in the two major authoritative collections of canonical Hadith: on the authority of 'A'isha (the Prophet's favourite wife) that the Prophet, may peace be upon him, Umm Habiba and Umm Salama (two of his wives) . . . mentioned to him a church in Abyssinia. They mentioned its beauty and the murals contained within it. The Prophet said that when a righteous man (*rajul salih*) died among them those people constructed a place of worship [literally, 'a place of prostration'] over his tomb and painted on it those icons. These creations will be the most evil to God on the Day of Resurrection.[26]

Elsewhere, he turns his attention to the veneration of saint relics and Muslim-Christian ritual practices:

Christians mainly venerate the relics (*athar*) of their saints (*qiddisun*). It is not improbable that they passed this [practice] on to some ignorant Muslims, namely that this is the tomb of one whom the Muslims extol so that they would agree to venerate him with them. How is it not so seeing that they have misguided many ignorant Muslims such that they even

---

[23] Ahmad ibn Taymiyya, *Majmuʿ Fatawa Shaykh al-Islam Ahmad ibn Taymiyya*, ed. ʿAbd al-Rahman b. Muhammad b. Qasim al- ʿAsimi al-Najdi al-Hanbali, 37 vols. (al-Riyad, 1991), 31–2.

[24] Ibn Taymiyya, *Iqtidaʾ al-Sirat al-Mustaqim Mukhalafat Ahl al-Jahim*, ed. Muhammad al-Fiqi (Cairo, 1950), 374.

[25] Ibn Taymiyya, *Majmuʿ Fatawa*, xxvii, 71.   [26] Ibid., 420.

began to baptise their children by alleging that it insures longevity for the infant. The Christians even got them to visit the cathedrals and churches they glorify. Many ignorant Muslims even made votive offerings to places which the Christians venerate. By the same measure, many visit churches and receive blessings (*yaltamisuna al-baraka*) from their priests, monks and the like . . .[27]

The polemical tone of these arguments, which were characteristic of the Hanbalites, is obvious. Ibn Taymiyya views the cult of saints as one of several popular religious phenomena brought about by Christian contamination. It is an extreme view, which may have some basis in reality given the strength of Christianity in Iraq, Syria, and Egypt. But much more work is needed to clarify the actual relations of Muslims with Christian shrines and vice versa. Ibn Taymiyya also condemns prayer for rain at tombs of the prophets and reputed saints, although there was an authoritative precedent for such practices: the second Caliph 'Umar had once requested that the Prophet's paternal uncle 'Abbas lead the supplication prayer for rain at the Prophet's grave. Ibn Taymiyya reasons that this was an exception to the rule, permissible only because of the latter's relationship to the Prophet. In addition to the Qur'an and the traditions of the Prophet, Ibn Taymiyya turns to the founders of the four schools of jurisprudence to argue against the legality of making *ziyara* to tombs of prophets:

As for journeying for the sole purpose of making *ziyara* to Abraham's tomb in [Hebron] or other tombs of prophets and righteous men, their shrines (*mashahid*), and their relics (*athar*), not one of the imams of the Muslims recommended it, none of the four [that is, the founders of the four schools of jurisprudence], nor have others.[28]

The Hanbalites were in fact going much further than the other schools in rejecting the *ziyara* and in insisting that tombs and saints should not be singled out for prayer and supplication, as well as denying the performance at them of miracles in response to such activities.

Ibn Taymiyya's disciple, Ibn Qayyim al-Jawziyya (1292–1350), continued his master's crusade against practices which threatened Islamic orthodoxy. In a scathing indictment he argues that Syrians were observing rites (*manasik*) similar to those of the pilgrimage to

---

[27] Ibid., 460–1.   [28] Ibid., 20.

Mecca, warranting the concern of theologians.[29] He refers to a pilgrimage guide, possibly of Shi'ite origin, entitled *Rules for Making Pilgrimage to Shrines*:[30]

Should you see the fanatics of those who take [tombs] as places of frequenting, they dismount from their saddles and mounts when they behold them from afar. They place their faces upon the tomb, kiss the ground, bare their heads and their voices become raised in a clamour. They cry almost weeping. They see themselves having received greater benefit than the pilgrims to Mecca. They seek the aid of one who does not grant it the first time or the second. They call out but from a distant place. In approaching it, they pray two *rak'as*[31] near the tomb and believe that they have obtained recompense—not the recompense of the one who prays toward the two *qiblas* [that is, towards Mecca and Jerusalem]. You see them prostrating, bending themselves, and seeking favour and satisfaction from the dead [only to fill their hands] with disappointment and loss: To other than God, rather to Satan—their tears flow there, their voices rise. The deceased is called upon to fulfil needs, to dispel sorrows, make the indigent free of want, to relieve the diseased and afflicted. After that they turn to circumambulating around the grave in imitation of the Bayt al-Haram [that is, the Ka'ba] which God had made holy and guidance unto the inhabitants of the world. Then they begin to kiss [it] and touch it [*istilam*].[32] Did you not see the Black Stone and what those visiting the Bayt al-Haram do with it? Then they soil their foreheads and cheeks near it [that is, near the grave] which God knows are not soiled thus before it in prostration. Then they conclude the rites [*manasik*] of the pilgrimage to the grave with shortening and shaving their hair there.[33] They take pleasure in their share from that idol since they do not have a share with God. They offer up sacrifices to that idol. Their prayers, ceremonies and sacrifices were to other than God, the Lord of the inhabitants of the world. If you beheld them, they would congratulate one another saying, 'May God lavish you with abundant recompense and good fortune.' When they return, the fanatics of those who remained behind ask of them for one of them to sell the recompense of the pilgrimage to the grave [*hijja*] for the Pilgrimage of the one setting out on the

---

[29] Ibn Qayyim al-Jawziyya, *Ighathat al-Lahfan min Masayid al-Shaytan*, ed. Muhammad al-Fiqi (Beirut, 1986), i, 220.

[30] The evidence that this is a Shi'ite guide is not conclusive, but it includes such things as references to the practice of circumambulating a tomb or shrine. This common Shi'ite practice is attested in modern and pre-modern Shi'ite pilgrimage guides but not in Sunni guides.

[31] *Rak'a* refers to the three primary movements of the body in Islamic prayer.

[32] Ibn Qayyim al-Jawziyya is referring to the practice of kissing and touching the Black Stone.

[33] Men shave their heads during the *Hajj*.

Pilgrimage to the Bayt al-Haram. He would say, 'No, [not] even with your making Pilgrimage every year'.

The similarities between these rituals and those of the *Hajj* are readily apparent. Ibn Qayyim was personally aware of people imitating the rites of the *Hajj* in their performance of the *ziyara*. This had, as he saw it, dangerous implications for Islamic orthodoxy. Indeed, the author of a *History of Irbil*, Ibn al-Mustawfi (d. 1239), specifically mentions that *hajj* was being made to the tomb of a Sufi saint of the twelfth century, especially at the time of the *Hajj* to Mecca![34] Muslim theologians were in general agreement that such practices were heretical. Some Sunnis as well as Shiʿites engaged in these practices, but there is insufficient evidence to conclude that many Muslims were guilty of the deviations condemned by Ibn Qayyim. It is possible to argue that these examples were isolated phenomena, only occurring during his lifetime.

AFFIRMING THE *ZIYARA*

Writing in defence of the *ziyara* in his *Revivification of the Religious Sciences*, the eleventh-century Khurasanian-born theologian and resident of Baghdad Abu Hamid al-Ghazali (1058–1111) took the opponents of *ziyara* to task, affirming the existence of saints and the permissibility of making *ziyara* to all tombs. But he too qualified the meaning of *ziyara*, which he did not merely confine to the special dead. It was the presence of holiness as manifest in the deceased and the presence of God and His holiness, which made a given place significant. This is a more universal sense of holiness which Muslims shared with Christians.[35] Al-Ghazali observes,

What is intended from visiting tombs [*ziyarat al-qubur*] is for the visitor to reflect on the *ziyara* and for the visited to benefit from his supplication. The visitor ought not to be heedless of supplicating for himself and for the deceased or on reflecting on him. He is in a state of reflection when he pictures in his heart the dead how his members have separated and how he will be resurrected from his grave.[36]

[34] Al-Mubarak Ibn al-Mustawfi, *Taʾrikh Irbil*, ed. Sami Saqqar (Baghdad, 1980), i, 54.
[35] See Brown, *CS*, 10–11, on the encounter of the living with the holy dead and the presence of holiness.
[36] Ghazali, *Ihyaʾ ʿUlum al-Din*, iv, 492.

The visitation should be conducted in accordance with the Tradition of the Prophet. For al-Ghazali, the goals of the *ziyara* were contemplation, remembering death, and obtaining blessings, concepts with which even Ibn Taymiyya would agree in principle. He cites two traditions, one of which affirms that the Prophet serves as an intercessor on the Day of Judgement for those who visit him: 'Visiting tombs is altogether recommended for remembrance and contemplation. Visiting the tombs of the righteous is recommended for the purpose of seeking blessings [and] contemplation. The Messenger of God . . . forbade visiting tombs and then permitted that afterwards.'[37] Al-Ghazali then quotes a canonical Tradition related by the Prophet's son-in-law 'Ali in which the former changed his mind about permitting Muslims to visit the dead:

'Ali, may God be pleased with him, related from the Messenger of God . . . that he said, 'I forbade you to visit graves. Visit them, they make you remember the Hereafter for do not say foul words'. The Messenger of God . . . visited his mother's tomb . . . He was never seen crying as much as on that day. He said, 'He permitted me to visit her without seeking mercy'.[38]

Al-Ghazali did not distinguish between *ziyara* to the tombs of loved ones and those of saints. The goals were one and the same: supplicating God on behalf of the dead. Since the Prophet visited his mother's grave, it was permissible for Muslims to visit all graves and to remember the dead at them. However, the Prophet never kissed, rested upon, or rubbed against tombs.

Precisely because the veneration of saints could be challenged in Islam, Muslims who were ready to countenance it had to define in detail what constituted legitimate ritual practice. Thus, many texts were composed on *ziyara* etiquette. They have no counterpart in medieval Christian literature and point to the existence of considerable variation in the way in which ritual evolved from one region to another. Al-Ghazali provides one of the earliest examples. He did not merely condone visiting saints' tombs. In fact, he advocated visiting such places so long as one did not engage in practices which the theologians had forbidden (such as using the canonical form of prayer to God, which involved facing the *qibla*—that is, facing the direction of Mecca) or which they had identified as being pagan, Christian, or Jewish or as being contrary to the nature of Islam, such as kissing or lying upon tombs:

[37] Ghazali, *Ihya' 'Ulum al-Din*, iv, 490.   [38] Ibid.

It is recommended in visiting graves that one should stand with one's back to the *qibla*, facing the deceased in order to greet him, and that one should not wipe, touch, or kiss the tomb. Those are among the Christian practices. Nafi' said, 'I saw Ibn 'Umar[39] a hundred times or more come to the Prophet's tomb and say, "Peace be upon the Prophet. Peace be upon Abu Bakr,[40] Peace be upon my father", and he would leave.' From Abu Umama who said, 'I saw Anas Ibn Malik visiting the tomb of the Prophet . . . He stood there, raised his hands, such that I thought he was beginning to pray, greeted the Prophet . . . and then left.'[41]

Al-Ghazali goes on to relate the true story of a man who tells of seeing in his sleep a deceased acquaintance speaking to him from Paradise, whereupon the latter tells him that the dead are aware of those who make *ziyara* to their graves on Fridays, the day of Communal prayer. One tradition even indicates the particular merit or *fadl* of Friday. Al-Ghazali associates the *ziyara* with the Friday prayer and in so doing legitimizes it. According to a Companion of the Prophet, 'Whoever visits a tomb before sunrise on Saturday, the dead is aware of his visit.' It was asked: how is that? He said, 'Because of the importance of Friday'.[42] Other such traditions mention Wednesday and Saturday at dawn. The fourteenth-century Egyptian historian al-Maqrizi likewise mentions Fridays and Saturdays, with Wednesdays being the customary day.[43]

Similarly, the Egyptian theologian and author of *The Pilgrims' Guide to the Tombs of the Righteous* (*Murshid al-Zuwwar ila Qubur al-Abrar*), Ibn 'Uthman (d. 1218), does not distinguish between visiting the tombs of saints and family members. Defending the existence of saints was not the most crucial issue for Muslim theologians, but rather explaining how one should go about performing the *ziyara* and properly venerating the dead. The fact that Ibn 'Uthman and other theologians do not mention such fundamental ritual forms as obtaining *baraka* (blessings) from saints, lighting candles, and making votive offerings suggests that they did not regard them as problematic. Ibn 'Uthman's conception of the *ziyara* did not simply include the veneration of saints. In his twenty guidelines for visiting tombs, he stresses the merits of making *ziyara* to the tombs of

---

[39] The son of the second Caliph 'Umar ibn al-Khattab (r. 634–44).
[40] The first Caliph (r. 632–4).
[41] Ghazali, *Ihya' 'Ulum al-Din*, iv, 491.
[42] Ibid.
[43] Ahmad ibn 'Ali al-Maqrizi, *al-Mawa'iz wa-al-I'tibar bi-Dhikr al-Khitat wa-al-Athar* 2 vols. (Bulaq, 1853–4), ii, 461.

prophets, and the Family and Companions of the Prophet Muhammad. Like al-Ghazali, Ibn ʿUthman affirms the tradition of performing the *ziyara* on Fridays, Thursdays, or Saturdays and that Wednesday is the accepted custom in Egypt. He condemns walking among and sitting on graves, laughing, kissing tombs and rubbing soil from them on oneself, striking cheeks, and rending clothes. Instead, devotees should treat the dead as the living, recite the Qurʾan, offer prayer on behalf of the dead, pray and supplicate for the Prophet Muhammad, make supplication for themselves, recollect the best qualities of the dead, and so on.

In Ibn al-Zayyat's *al-Kawakib al-Sayyara fi Tartib al-Ziyara* (*The Planets in the Organization of the Ziyara*), one hears of learned guides leading devotees in circuits around the tombs and shrines of the Qarafa cemeteries recounting the saints' miracles and praiseworthy qualities during their lifetimes, but also the efficaciousness of the tombs and shrines. Each shrine possessed a unique history, which normally included a Life of a saint, which learned pilgrims and pilgrimage guides transmitted to devotees taking part in the *ziyara*. Ibn al-Zayyat and other pilgrimage guide writers also record and discuss conflicting traditions regarding particular tombs, not merely accepting them at face value, as well as accepted *ziyara* customs, practices which were generally observed by all segments of society who visited shrines. Like other writers of pilgrimage guides, Ibn al-Zayyat was particularly concerned with pilgrimage etiquette. His defence of the importance of visiting shrines is followed by a detailed and systematic description of the proper way to conduct *ziyara*:

As for the greatest of the most honourable prophets and messengers [that is, the prophets to whom Scripture was revealed], the visitor comes to them—seeking these far-away places is incumbent upon them. If he should come to them, then let him possess humility, dejection, utter humility, poverty, need, dire need, great necessity, humility and submission and let him betake his heart and mind toward them and toward viewing them with his heart [literally, his heart's eye] and not with his eyesight since they never decompose nor change. Then the visitor praises God the Most High with what is worthy of him. Then he prays over them, seeks that God be pleased with their companions and seeks the mercy of God for their followers with unwavering sincerity in faith down to the Day of Judgement. Then he turns in intercession through them to God the Most High in fulfilling his wishes and seeking forgiveness for his sins. Next, he seeks their aid, requests from them fulfilment of his needs, and positively resolves himself to their *baraka* . . . for they are God's open gate. The *Sunna* of the Most

Sublime and Most Exalted is applicable to fulfilling needs through and on account of them. He, who is unable to travel to them, let him then bid them peace and mention what it is he requires of his needs, forgiveness for his sins, and guarding his foibles. They are the noblest masters. The Noble never reject him who makes a request of them, or seeks their intercession or who journeys to them, nor he who has recourse in them. These [were] words pertaining to making *ziyara* to the prophets and the elect.[44]

During the fourteenth century another North African Shafi'ite theologian, Ibn al-Hajj, commented on proper *ziyara* etiquette in his *Madkhal*. He begins by defending the practice of seeking intercession from saints and prophets, including the Prophet Muhammad. In direct contrast to Ibn Taymiyya, he argued that it was permissible to seek rain through any tomb, because the Companion and later caliph 'Umar did so through the Prophet and his uncle Abbas:

If the dead to whom *ziyara* is made are among those whose *baraka* is sought, then the intercession of God the Exalted is sought through him. Likewise, the visitor seeks the intercession of him whom he sees as dead from those whose *baraka* is sought through the Prophet. . . . Rather, the visitor begins by seeking the intercession of God the Exalted through the Prophet . . . since He is the Support in intercession and the ultimate source and enabler of all of this. He would seek his intercession . . . and those who follow him with unwavering sincerity in faith down to the Day of Judgement. Al-Bukhari reports on the authority of Anas, may God be pleased with him: 'Umar ibn al-Khattab,[45] whenever they would experience drought, would pray for rain through [the Prophet] saying, 'Oh Lord we were seeking the intercession of your Prophet . . . for grant us rain. And we seek your intercession through Abbas, the paternal uncle of your Prophet . . .' Then he would seek the intercession of the inhabitants of those graves, that is, the righteous [*salihun*].[46]

After quoting Tradition, Ibn al-Hajj proceeds to outline a proper etiquette which includes sitting on tombs facing the deceased whilst one engages in prayer and supplication:

Peace be upon you all the dead, and so on. Oh God forgive us and them [our sins]. Do not add nor subtract from these words . . . exert great effort in supplication on their behalf. They are the people most deserving of that because of the cessation of their good works. Then the visitor should sit at the *qibla* of the [grave] of the deceased [that is, facing Mecca] and greet him

[44] Ibn al-Zayyat, *al-Kawakib al-Sayyara fi Tartib al-Ziyara* (Cairo, 1907), 257-8.
[45] The second Caliph (r. 634-44).
[46] Ibn al-Hajj, *al-Madkhal* (Cairo, 1929), i, 254-5.

face-to-face, he being free to sit in the vicinity of his feet toward his head or opposite his face. Then the visitor should praise God the Most High with whatever comes to mind. Then he should pray a lawful prayer for the Prophet, may peace be upon him. Then he should supplicate for the deceased with what he can and likewise he should supplicate near these graves [remembering] an incident which happened to him or to the Muslims and entreat God the Most High to dispel it and reveal it [that is, its true nature] to him and them. This is a description of *ziyarat al-qubur*.[47]

For Ibn al-Hajj, the *ziyara* consists of a series of ritual acts beginning with the salutation to the dead and ending with supplication. Ibn al-Hajj and Ibn al-Zayyat were proponents of the *ziyara*, but even they take care to distance themselves from various practices such as kissing, rubbing, and lying on tombs and making votive offerings. Both explicitly state that tombs are sources of *baraka*, which is trans- ferred to the devotee—a view that the Hanbalites rejected. Only Ibn al-Hajj permits sitting on tombs, something which al-Ghazali and Ibn 'Uthman prohibit on the authority of the Prophet.[48]

Although their pilgrimage guides belong to a later period and to a milieu where the *ziyara* was less hotly contested, there is evidence that its Syrian defenders were also concerned to define its etiquette. Ibn al-Hawrani argues that it begins with the remembrance of God and the intent to perform pilgrimage:[49]

It is necessary for one who desires to undertake visiting the tomb of a Companion, *wali*, or scholar that he intends with his visit first: Getting nearer to God the Exalted through visiting His beloved and the special dead from among His servants, supplicating for the tomb's patron and receiving his blessing, and bringing mercy upon the visitor. . . . It is customary prac- tice to position oneself facing the face of the tomb's inhabitant, to approach, and greet him. The pilgrim stands near the tomb comporting himself, hum- bling himself, surrendering himself, bowing his head to the ground with dignity, God-inspired peace of mind, and awe, casting aside power and chieftainship. He should imagine himself as if he were looking at the tomb's inhabitant and he looking at him. Then he should look with introspection to what God had granted to the one visited of loftiness, dignity and divine

---

[47] Ibn al-Hajj, *al-Madkhal* (Cairo, 1929), i, 254.

[48] See *Sahih Muslim*, iii, 62: 'Do not sit on the graves and do not pray facing towards them. In another tradition, he states, "It is better that one of you should sit on live coals which would burn his clothing and come in contact with his skin than that he should sit on a grave." '

[49] Ibn al-Hawrani, *Kitab al-Isharat ila Amakin al-Ziyarat*, ed. Bassam al-Jabi (Damascus, 1981), 155–61.

secrets and how God has made him a locus of sainthood, for secrets, closeness, obedience [or, 'submission'], and divine gnostic truths.

Al-Hawrani then indicates that the devotee reflects upon himself
and his sins which prevent him from nearing God:

He looks with . . . steadfastness to his self how God prevented it from competing with the saints because of that and prevented it from imbuing himself with the moral virtues of His pious servants and His beloved and
attaching himself to the trail of their way and their paths to their Lord and
realising their high and precious truths. Then he conceives in his mind of
the Day of Judgement, the Resurrection, the arising of the [saints] from
their tombs happy with God's pleasure with them, delighted, riding on the
loftiness of mercy. The angels surround them and upon their heads are
crowns of their pious devotions, interceding on behalf of sinners.

According to Ibn al-Hawrani, the devotee then enters a cathartic
state in which he rebukes and scolds himself and then weeps. Then
he supplicates God and reads from the Qur'an. The devotee must be
sincere in reaching his goal and not speak foul words and recall the
Hadith of the Prophet:

'Whoever desires to visit a grave, then let him do so; but say not foul
words'.[50] . . . For that brings down its doer from the eye of God the Exalted,
invoking His ire, and it is feared that he would regress, be defiant, [suc-
cumb to] ignominy, his state fading to perdition, all the while he is not per-
ceiving this. Caution and again caution. . . . Let his sole concern be in the
state of his *ziyara* with all of his senses focused on remembrance of God the
Exalted, prayer and reading the Qur'an. That is great proof of the sound-
ness of the *ziyara* and its acceptance, descent of mercy, fulfilment of supplication and attaining the desired object.

For Ibn al-Hawrani, the *ziyara* was not only a means of fulfilling
personal supplications, it was also an act of supplication before God,
contingent upon bringing Him and the afterlife to mind, upon praying and reading the Qur'an. This act of recalling the central aspects
of Islam was, for Ibn al-Hawrani, the ultimate purpose of *ziyara*.
This, in the end, is what all of the *ziyara*'s defenders considered most
important. All define the remembrance of God, the Prophet, the
hereafter, and the deeds of the dead as the underlying purpose of
ziyara, all authorize the making of requests and the supplication
of God on behalf of the dead, all prohibit facing the tomb when

[50] A *hadith* of the Prophet.

praying, with al-Ghazali going as far as to prohibit 'canonical prayer' altogether, all, finally, encourage the recitation of the Qur'an at tombs.

CONCLUSION

The links between Sufi mysticism and the veneration of saints, the relationship between the veneration of saints in medieval Islam and its counterparts in Eastern Christianity and Judaism, may be far from being fully understood; but it is clear that the *ziyara* meant much more to medieval Muslims than just 'pilgrimage'. For most it was a way of honouring the holy dead through experiencing spiritual closeness to God at their tombs. It was ubiquitous and the focus of much contemporary debate, so much so that it cannot be regarded as the product of the periphery. The multiplicity of practices associated with it underscores its centrality and vitality in medieval Islam. Tombs and shrines were integrated into every aspect of daily life. Pilgrimage to them was cut across the boundaries between public and private, between the city and the countryside, between rich and poor, and between learned and illiterate—however much the manner in which rituals were conducted may have differed from place to place and from class to class. Even today, the practice of *ziyara* in modern Syria and Egypt testifies to its variety and to its central role in the life of large sections of the population. In Damascus, one can still see Damascene, Iranian, and Central Asian pilgrims performing *ziyara* to the many shrines of the Family of the Prophet. I have myself seen veiled women sitting at the shrine of one of Husayn's descendants weeping together, while men and women circumambulate the shrine touching and kissing its grill in order to receive *baraka*. The spontaneity of the cult of saints remains very much alive in the hearts and minds of Muslims today as it did in the Middle Ages.

THE CONTRIBUTORS

AVERIL CAMERON

Warden of Keble College, Oxford, Averil Cameron is the editor of volume 13 of *The Cambridge Ancient History: The Late Empire, AD 337-425*, and her many distinguished publications include *Procopius and the Sixth Century* (London, 1985) and *Christianity and the Rhetoric of Empire* (Berkeley and Los Angeles, 1991).

PAUL FOURACRE

Paul Fouracre is Lecturer in Early Medieval History at Goldsmith's College, London. He is the author of 'Merovingian History and Merovingian Hagiography', *Past and Present*, 127 (1990), 3-38, and, with Richard Gerberding, of *Late Merovingian France: History and Hagiography, 640-720*, Manchester Medieval Sources Series (Manchester and New York, 1996), and the editor of volume one of *The New Cambridge Medieval History: c. 500-700*.

PAUL ANTONY HAYWARD

Formerly Junior Research Fellow in Modern History at Jesus College, Oxford, Paul Hayward works on the cult of saints in Anglo-Saxon and Anglo-Norman England. His monograph *Kingship, Childhood and Martyrdom in Anglo-Saxon England* is to be published by Cambridge University Press.

PAUL A. HOLLINGSWORTH

Paul Hollingsworth is a specialist in Byzantine and medieval Slavic history, and the author of *The Hagiography of Kievan Rus'*, HLEUL 2 (Cambridge, Mass., 1992). He is currently engaged by the State Department of the United States of America to work on Russian issues.

JAMES HOWARD-JOHNSTON

University Lecturer in Byzantine Studies at Oxford and Fellow of Corpus Christi College, James Howard-Johnston's principal current concern is with the history of the Near East in the seventh century. He edited *Byzantium and the West, c. 800-c. 1200* (Amsterdam,

1988) and wrote, jointly with Nigel Ryan, *The Scholar and the Gypsy: Two Journeys to Turkey, Past and Present* (London, 1992).

PAUL MAGDALINO

Lecturer in Byzantine History in the Department of Mediaeval History at the University of St Andrews, Paul Magdalino is the author of *The Empire of Manuel I Komnenos, 1143–1180* (Cambridge, 1993), and the editor of *The Perception of the Past in Twelfth-Century Europe* (London, 1992).

JOSEF W. MERI

Currently Research Fellow at the Department of Near Eastern Studies, Berkeley, Josef Meri is revising, for publication, his Oxford doctoral thesis entitled 'Sacred Journeys to Sacred Precincts: The Cult of Saints Among Muslims and Jews in Medieval Syria'.

RICHARD M. PRICE

Richard Price is Lecturer in Church History at Heythrop College of the University of London. He has translated Theodoret's *Historia Religiosa* (*Theodoret of Cyrrhus: A History of the Monks of Syria*, CStud. 88 (1985)), and is the author of 'Boris and Gleb: Princely Martyrs and Martyrology in Kievan Russia', in *The Church and Childhood*, ed. D. Wood, SCH 31 (Oxford, 1993), 105–15.

CLAUDIA RAPP

Assistant Professor in the History Department of the University of California at Los Angeles, Claudia Rapp's Oxford doctoral thesis was an edition and study of the Life of Epiphanius of Salamis. She is the author of numerous articles on late antique and early Byzantine hagiography.

CHASE ROBINSON

Chase Robinson is University Lecturer in Islamic History and Fellow of Wolfson College, Oxford. He is presently writing *Islamic Historiography* for Cambridge University Press.

PHILIP ROUSSEAU

Associate Professor at the University of Auckland, Philip Rousseau is presently Visiting Distinguished Professor of Early Christian Studies at the Catholic University of America, Washington, DC.

Among his more recent works are *Basil of Caesarea* (Berkeley, 1994) and *Pachomius: The Making of a Community in Fourth-Century Egypt* (Berkeley, 1985).

IAN N. WOOD

Author of *The Merovingian Kingdoms, 450–751* (London, 1993) and of numerous articles on the Franks, their kingdoms and their historiography, from the fifth to the tenth centuries, Ian Wood is presently Professor of Early Medieval History and Deputy Director of the Centre for Medieval Studies at the University of Leeds.

INDEX